MW00892278

U.S. Patent Prosecution for Support Staff

A Desk Reference

Rosaleen A. Walsh

Copyright © 2013 Rosaleen A. Walsh
All rights reserved.

ISBN: 1492921629
ISBN 13: 9781492921622
Library of Congress Control Number: 2013919139
CreateSpace Independent Publishing Platform
North Charleston, South Carolina

Table of Contents

Preface

Who Is This Book For?

This book is intended to be a desk reference for paralegals, secretaries, and other support staff working with registered patent practitioners. This book is written to address the perspective of support staff professionals and it is designed to build knowledge progressively by tracking the chronological steps of U.S. patent prosecution. This desk reference covers the filing requirements, deadlines, forms, and related prosecution considerations. It includes invaluable practical tips and suggestions to help make patent prosecution support staff more efficient and effective. This book details the complex rules and regulations that govern patent prosecution in the United States, and translates them into easy-to-understand step-wise procedural filing requirements. The content includes the most recent provisions of the America Invents Act, the America Invents Act Technical Corrections Bill, and the Patent Law Treaty.

Whether you are a novice to the field of patent prosecution or a veteran support staff professional, this guidebook will help you learn what you need to know to contribute at the highest possible level in supporting patent practitioners.

Definition of Support Staff

Throughout this book, the term "support staff" is used as a generic label for individuals who provide support to patent practitioners on completing patent filings in a deadline-driven practice. Patent prosecution support staff can be found within practice groups of law firms of various sizes or in-house in companies that need help in administering patent portfolios. Irrespective of their work environment, patent prosecution support staff are tasked with providing a cross-section of support that can range from completing compliant filings to monitoring and coordinating a patent portfolio to ensure all filing deadlines are accounted for. All such positions require that patent prosecution support staff possess a solid and current understanding of U.S. patent prosecution filing rules and regulations.

How to Use this Book

This guidebook can be used as an at-a-glance quick reference, or as a guide to augment hands-on training. Information is presented in a progressive, layered manner that starts with more basic concepts and builds up to more complex filing situations that support staff may encounter. Designed to assist patent prosecution support staff at all levels of employment and learning, this book takes a progressive and layered approach that encourages comprehensive learning, while also serving as a stand-alone desk reference to which support staff can quickly refer when reviewing specific filing requirements without having to command knowledge of the entire book. As the patent laws continue to evolve, support staff need to be able to complete compliant patent filings that range from simple to more complex in a deadline-driven environment. This book details filing requirements in a clear and concise manner to help support staff provide dynamic support to patent practitioners.

The information in the first eleven chapters is a high-level presentation of the intricacies of patent prosecution practice and serves as a thorough introduction to new or aspiring support staff, as well as a rigorous brush-up for support staff veterans. More challenging learning is presented in chapters twelve through nineteen, to assist support staff in developing or updating the breadth and depth of their knowledge. The final two chapters of the book are focused on new contested proceedings and related provisions of the America Invents Act. To support new learning related to the America Invents Act, "AIA Impact" headings have been distributed throughout the book to help support staff professionals digest the most significant changes to the patent rules in several decades.

About the Author

Rosaleen (Rose) A. Walsh is a registered patent agent with the United States Patent and Trademark Office. Rose has over fifteen years of patent filing and patent support staff management experience. She has held positions ranging from a patent secretary at an IP boutique firm to an IP paralegal manager across offices for an international law firm.

Through her years of professional experience and her engagement in continued learning in the patent prosecution arena, Rose has accumulated extensive experience in the hands-on completion of compliant patent filings and in overseeing the work of highly specialized patent filing paralegals. Rose has an appreciation for, and mastery of, the extent of specialized knowledge required from patent prosecution support staff professionals.

Rose has a Bachelor of Science in Biochemistry, a Master of Science in Occupational Health & Ergonomics, and a Diploma in High School Teacher Certification, all attained at the National University of Ireland (Galway).

Disclaimer

This book has been prepared as an educational guide for support staff professionals and is not intended to be used as substantive legal advice. It is based upon sources believed to be accurate and reliable and is intended to be current as of the time it was written. However, patent rules and regulations are subject to change and no rule or statement in this book should be relied upon without confirming that the information has not been affected or changed by recent developments. This book is sold with the understanding that neither the author nor the publisher are engaged in the rendering of legal advice. If legal advice is sought, the reader should consult with the appropriate registered patent practitioner with respect to the intricacies of patent filings rules and regulations. The statements expressed herein are those of the author and not those of the author's employer. The author shall not be liable for any consequential exemplary damages resulting, in whole or in part, from the reader's use of or reliance upon the content of this book.

Acknowledgments

I would like to thank my family and friends for their unwavering support for this book. In particular, I would like to thank Brian for his help and advice on the design and layout of this book. Thank you, Brian, for enduring all the weekends I spent writing this book and for helping me move past my writing frustrations by helping me focus on the finish line.

I would like to thank attorney Holliday C. Heine, who took the time to explain the "what" and the "why" of U.S. patent prosecution to me when I was her secretary. Her patience and commitment to my formative learning laid the foundation for this book. Thank you, Holly, for your continued support and willingness to proofread initial drafts of this book.

Thank you to Doris Graney and all those who helped by proofreading parts of this book. Each of you offered helpful suggestions and comments that made this book better.

Finally, I want to acknowledge that the content of this book is heavily reliant on the content from the USPTO website and on subject-matter-related public presentations given by the employees of the Office. My objective in writing this book is to support the dissemination of information related to the U.S. patent filing rules and regulations across groupings of support staff professionals to strengthen their ability to provide informed assistance to registered patent practitioners.

List of Figures

List of Tables

List of Abbreviations

ADS	Application Data Sheet
ABBS	Automated Biotechnology Sequence Search
AE	Accelerated Examination
AESD	Accelerated Examination Support Document
AFCP	After Final Consideration Pilot
AIA	America Invents Act
AIPA	American Inventors Protection Act
AOTH-P	Assignment on the Web for Patents
ASCII	American Standard Code for Information Interchange
ASD	Assignment Services Division
BPAI	Board of Patent Appeals and Interferences
CBM	Covered Business Method
C.F.R.	Code of Federal Register
CIP	Continuation-in-Part Application
CN	Customer Number
CON	Continuation Application
CPA	Continued Prosecution Application
CRF	Computer Readable Format
CRU	Central Reexamination Unit
DAS	Digital Access Service
DIV	Divisional Application
DO	Designated Office
DNC	Do Not Cite
EBC	Electronic Business Center
EESR	Extended European Search Report
EFS	Electronic Filing System
EFT	Electronic Fund Transfer
EMP	Extended Missing Parts Pilot Program
EO	Elected Office
EPAS	Electronic Patent Assignment System
EST	Eastern Standard Time
FAI	First Action Interview

FDA	Food and Drug Administration
FIU	File Information Unit
GATT	General Agreement on Tariffs and Trade
GUI	Graphical User Interface
IB	International Bureau
IDS	Information Disclosure Statement
IFW	Image File Wrapper
IPEA	International Preliminary Examining Authority
IPR	*Inter Partes* Review
IPRP	International Preliminary Report on Patentability
ISA	International Searching Authority
ISR	International Search Report
ITC	International Trade Commission
MDC	Multiple Dependent Claim
MPEG	Motion Picture Experts Group
MPEP	Manual for Patent Examining Procedures
NAFTA	North American Free Trade
NARA	National Archives and Records Administration
NIRC	Notice of Intent to Issue an *Ex Parte* Reexamination Certificate
OCR	Optical Character Recognition
OED	Office of Enrolment and Discipline
OFF	Office of First Filing
OPAP	Office of Patent Application Processing
OSF	Office of Second Filing
PAIR	Patent Application Information Retrieval
PALM	Patent Application Location Monitoring
PASS	Patent Application Services and Security
PCT	Patent Corporation Treaty
PDE	Priority Document Exchange
PDF	Portable Document Format
PDX	Priority Document Exchange
PE	Prioritized Examination
PESD	Pre-Examination Search Document
PGR	Post Grant Review

PKI	Public Key Infrastructure
PLT	Patent Law Treaty
PPH	Patent Prosecution Highway
PRPS	Patent Review Processing System
PSIPS	Publication Site for Issued and Published Sequences
PTA	Patent Term Adjustment
PTAB	Patent Trial and Appeal Board
PTE	Patent Term Extension
QPIDS	Quick Path Information Disclosure Statement
RAM	Revenue and Accounting Management
RCE	Request for Continued Examination
SCORE	Supplemental Complex Repository for Examiners
SE	Supplemental Examination
SIR	Statutory Invention Registeration
SNQ	Substantial New Question of Patentability
TD	Terminal Disclaimer
TIFF	Tagged Image File Format
U.S.C.	United States Code
URAA	Uruguay Round Agreement Act
USDA	United States Department of Agriculture
USPS	United States Postal Service
USPTO	United States Patent and Trademark Office, also referred to as "the Office"
USRO	United States Receiving Office
WO	Written Opinion
WIPO	World Intellectual Property Organization
WTO	World Trade Organization

Chapter 1
Functions and Core Concepts of the Patent System

What is a Patent?

A patent is a government-administered contract between inventors and society that grants the owner rights to exclude others from making, selling, using, or importing the invention for a limited period of time. Patent rights do not give the owner affirmative exclusive rights to make and use the invention; they confer exclusionary rights to prevent others from making, selling, using, or importing the invention for the duration of the patent term. The patent owner must affirmatively assert the rights attached to patents—rights do not automatically confer—and the patent owner must be an active participant in enforcing established patent rights. An inventor who is also an owner of a patent can prevent competitors from profiting from the invention as defined in the claims for the duration of the patent's enforceable term.

Functions of the Patent System

The patent system is designed to promote progress and innovation in science and technology by granting an inventor exclusive rights to his or her invention for a limited period of time. A patent is a government-issued contract that incentivizes the development of new technology by providing government-enforced remedies and means to protect inventors' rights. In return, the inventor agrees to make public the best mode of how to make and use the invention, thereby adding to society's collective public knowledge base.

In contrast, in the absence of a patent system, inventors would not be afforded any legal property rights for their inventions. Without an orderly administrated protection system, the inventors who expend time and creative effort would be marginalized by commercial entities or organizations that have the technology and financial resources to commercialize inventions to reap profits and to add value to their bottom lines. In a society where "might would become right," individual inventors would be more likely to conceal their inventions rather than allow organizations to benefit at their cost.

Even though it is clear that a rational patent system for protection of inventions is vital to induce inventions among the economically weaker members of our industrial society, it would be a serious mistake to think that the more powerful large corporations do not also need such a system. Even though a rational patent system may not be essential for the more powerful in our society, no private organization of any substantial size can function efficiently without reasonable rules of relationships with its competitors. An intellectual property system in technological innovation enables organizations to plan rationally and effectively. It enables organizations, either through exercising exclusionary rights or by effective licensing, to form arrangements to carry out business activities relative to new technology in an orderly way. A developed patent granting system provides predictability to inventive organizations. It permits such organizations to treat the expenses of invention, innovation, and patenting as a cost of doing business, which is transferable directly to the product and services costs paid by consumers (Patent Resources Institute, Inc., 2004).

Patents as Property

Patents are legal instruments with attributes similar to those of personal property; patents are intangible assets whose property-related benefits are only practically understood through enforcement of rights. Similar to property rights, patent rights define a geographic location and property boundary of what is owned. Patent rights can be recorded as title ownership, which can be transferred from one owner to another through assignment or licensed agreement. The equivalent property-related attributes of patents are shown in Table 1.

Table 1: Property Attributes of Patents

Property Attribute	Equivalent Patent Attribute
Geographical Location	Patent rights are limited geographically; a U.S. patent cannot be enforced outside of the United States.
Documented Ownership	Patent rights infer ownership through a legal instrument; ownership is by title and recordable in public databases. Recorded title acts as a public notice of ownership of patent rights.
Defined Property Boundary Lines	The claims of an issued patent determine the boundaries of what is covered by the invention. The claims are used to define what is owned, and the inventor's exclusive rights are conferred constitutionally; injunctive relief afforded by the federal courts is designed to *warn infringers to stay off the property* in the future. If infringement of patent rights is established, the courts will require the infringer to pay damages for loss of royalty rights during the period of enforceability. The *exclusionary rights* do not attach until the patent issues unless publication of the application can be established as notice right and infringement is deemed to have been willful.
Ownership is Transferable	Patent rights are transferable to others during the exploitation period in the life of the patent through assignment or license agreements, or both.

Source: Patent Resources Group, Inc. (2004)—Patent Practice

Why Obtain Patent Protection?

There are many reasons why an inventor or company would pursue patent protection. While initial considerations may be profit, many companies build their intellectual property assets to establish their expertise in a defined technology field. The reasons for obtaining patent protection are informed by complex considerations, which include the following (Jester, 1964):

- Financial Benefit: As patent rights can be sold or licensed, they ensure that the inventors are monetary benefactors of their own inventive effort. Patents provide a means to generate revenue to offset the costs of securing the patent.
- Effect on Competitors: A patent enables inventors to stop competitors from making or using their inventions by providing enforceable exclusionary rights. Market competitors cannot copy an invention and profit from it while escaping the associated research and development costs. Competitors cannot mass produce the invention and sell it in the market for a lower per unit price until the exclusive term of the patent has expired.
- Competitive Advantage: For a company that wants to protect its core technology, patents are intangible assets that add to the value and market recognition of the company as an established owner of patented technology. The ability to assert enforceable patents on core technology is desirable from the perspective of existing and prospective investors. Maintaining exclusivity to patented technology affords a competitive advantage. Successful commercialization of an invention helps build the value of the company and make it more palatable for any future venture capital investments, bank financing, and public sales of stock.
- Defensive Blocking: Companies can use patents to protect against competitors asserting patents against them by establishing their shielding rights. In such cases, the company has secured a patent of broad scope that claims basic enabling technologies. Competitors or potential infringers would have to design around the broad-scope patent by developing an alternative product or process not covered in the claims. Defensive blocking with broad-scope claims allows negotiation of more favorable license terms.
- Recognition of Technical Excellence: Patents increase the prestige of a company and its employees, allowing them to gain notoriety for being innovative and on the cutting edge of technology advancements. Patents put competitors on notice of established expertise in a given technical area. Patents can be used to measure the

intellectual potential of research and development teams that distinguish a company and its employees from its market competitors.

Patent Term

The term of a patent is the maximum number of years that the exclusive rights of the patent remain in force. The patent term starts from the filing date of the patent application or from the date the patent is granted. A patent may be enforced starting on the date it is issued and will run the length of the patent term unless it expires earlier due to failure to pay maintenance fees. To keep a patent in force, maintenance fees have to be paid on regular intervals during the term of enforceability. Failure to pay such maintenance fees will result in lapsing of the patent before its term. Currently, the term of a U.S. patent is the longer of the two possible patent terms (seventeen years from the issue date, or twenty years from the earliest filing date). When the patent expires, the invention is dedicated to the public.

Patent Filing Strategies

While the decisions informing patent filing strategies are deliberated between clients and attorneys, it is useful that patent support staff have at least a rudimentary knowledge of the thought processes involved. Companies must develop a sophisticated patent filing strategy beyond filing patent applications early and often. A patent filing strategy must be based on a company's business model and its business plan. It must also take into account the larger picture of the company's business environment and its endgame. Patents provide potential leverage for obtaining cash, technology, and desired collaborations through licensing. They are also attractive assets to potential investors, collaborators, and acquiring companies (Karny, 2005). With the emergence of global markets, companies need to perform due diligence research to identify their core technology competitors and implement a patent strategy that provides geographical protection in key technology or distribution countries. Applicants must also consider any constraints of their technology base that can impact their filing decisions. Pharmaceutical inventions tend to have a longer development or regulatory phase, which means that costly global filing decisions usually need to be made at early stages in the product life cycle, when return on investment from any potential commercialization is rather uncertain (Silverman, 2005). The complexity of the patent filing decisions are shown in Figure A. Patent filing decision makers must weigh the costs associated with the protection required against the potential revenue streams from commercialization of the invention. The filing strategy decision must balance portfolio management against competitive advantage in a market-driven economy.

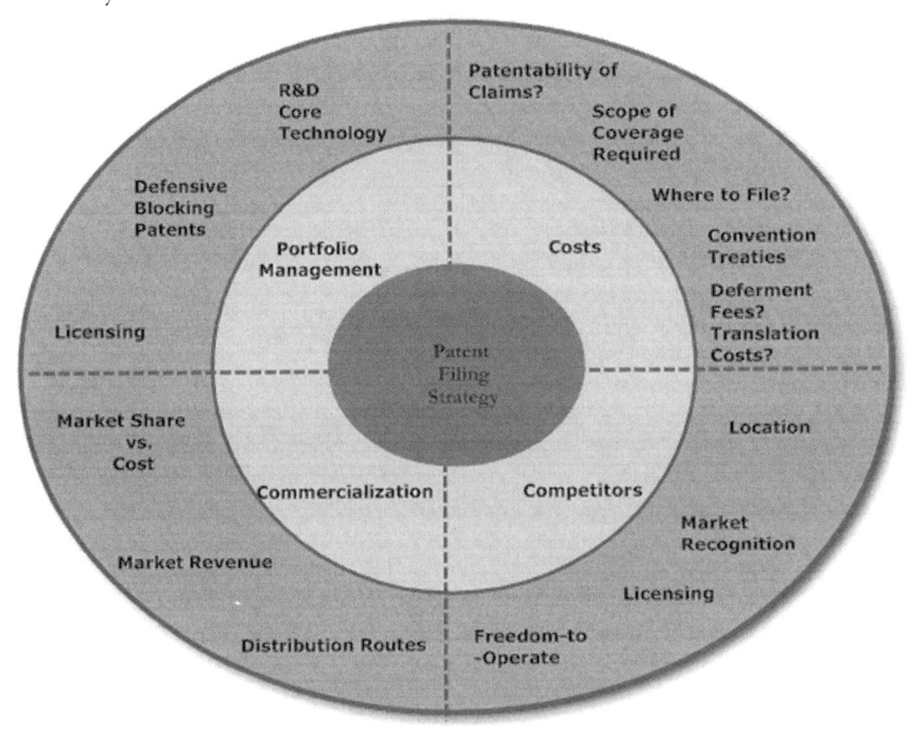

Figure A: Patent Filing Strategy Considerations

Source: Adapted from Silverman, (2005)

The ultimate objective of all patent applicants is to maximize the value of monies invested in seeking patent protection by establishing a greater market presence for their invention or product. All patent applicants seek revenue from commercial sales to offset patent procurement costs and to allow them to exploit the value of their technology during the period of exclusivity. Pursuing a patent filing strategy often involves the investment of significant up-front monies when any potential income from licensing or commercialization can be distant and uncertain. It is imperative that a company complete its due diligence work and define a patent strategy to ensure core technology is protected. Patents are intangible assets that require an asset management approach, including investment of time, monies, marketing, and commercialization. If the portfolio management strategies are successful, they have the potential to provide a profitable return on investment over time.

Chapter 2
U.S. Patent Laws, Rules, and Regulations

Historical Development of United States Patent Law

Support staff should have an awareness of the milestones that informed the development of the existing United States' patent laws. The current criteria for patentability evolved from a series of patent rule changes that were primarily informed by Supreme Court rulings and the need to define a patent system that supports the mission of the United States Patent and Trademark Office.

The United States Constitution empowered Congress to establish a national patent system to "promote the progress of science and useful arts by securing for limited time to authors and inventors the exclusive right to their respective writings and discoveries." In 1790, Congress enacted the first patent statute and provided a designated group of executive officers to determine if an invention was "sufficiently useful and important." Three years later, Congress further defined the 1790 act to include the importance of determination and authorized patents for "any useful art, machine, manufacture, or composition of matter, or any new and useful improvement thereon, not known or used before the application." The 1790 and 1793 patent statutes, and court decisions interpreting them, introduced fundamental concepts that remain features of current United States' patent law. The statutes authorized a patent owner to sue for infringement but allowed the accused infringer to defend by alleging and proving the patent invention lacked novelty or was insufficiently disclosed in the inventor's specification.

Amendments in 1800s

In 1836, Congress enacted a major revision of the patent laws by creating a Patent Office and a system of examination of patent applications for compliance with the requirements of "novelty over the prior art." It introduced a statutory requirement of clear claiming and codified that the inventor's discovery be "not in public use or on sale with the applicant's consent or allowance at the time of filing of the application for patent." In 1839, the patent law was amended to provide a two-year grace period for publication or use of the invention by the applicant before the applicant filed a patent application. In 1897, Congress made two changes in the statutory bar provisions, adding patent and "description in a printed publication" to the public use and on sale bar (an offer to sell more than one year before the effective filing date of the U.S. application) as loss of rights events, and it further specified that "public use or on sale activity must be in this country" to be a bar to patentability. The 1790 and 1793 statutes did not explicitly establish a first-to-invent priority rule but did require a patentee to be "the first and true inventor." The 1836 Act established procedures for resolving the question of priority right to the invention and introduced the concept of reasonable diligence in conceiving and "reducing to practice" the concepts of the invention. The 1870 act created within the Patent Office a means and system of determining the first to invent a concept, thereby creating the basis for current interference proceedings.

Amendments in the 1900s

In 1925, responsibility for the Patent Office was transferred to the Department of Commerce and Labor. In 1929, appellate review of decisions of the Patent Office was transferred from the Court of Appeals for the District of Colombia to the newly created Court of Customs and Patent Appeals. In 1930, the Plant Patent Act provided for the possibility of patent protection for asexually reproduced plants. In 1941, the Supreme Court suggested that to be patentable, an invention must "reveal the flash of creative genius not merely the skill of the calling." In 1939, the two-year grace period that had existed since 1839 with respect to some statutory bars was reduced to one year on the ground that "under present conditions two years appears unduly long and operates as a handicap to industry." In 1940, the duration of the grace period relating to acts of prior use or prior publication by the inventor, which were to be excused as novelty-destroying acts, was reduced from two years to one.

Title 35 of the United States Code

In 1952, Congress passed a new patent act, United States Code Title 35, which is still in effect today. To a large extent, the 1952 Act rearranged existing statutory provisions and stated in statutory form matters previously recognized only in court decision and Patent Office practice but did make several specific changes and additions. The main provisions of the 1952 Act were:

- confirmed use of means-plus-function claim limitations;
- clarified that patentability cannot bc negated by the manner in which the invention was made, thereby introducing the concept of "flash of genius"; and
- provided a definition of contributory infringement.

Most significantly, Congress for the first time included a statutory provision on non-obviousness, Section 103, which was further defined in 1966 by the establishment of Graham tests for non-obviousness (Chisum, 1993).

Amendments in 1980s

In the 1980s, the patent statute was further amended to include the following primary provisions (Ladas & Parry LLP, 2009):

- requirement to pay maintenance fees to keep patent in force;
- special provisions made for inventions made with Federal assistance;
- provision made for third parties to cite prior art to USPTO;
- possibility of requesting reexamination created;
- United States rebuffs attempts by developing countries to amend Paris Convention to permit exclusive compulsory licensing;
- Supreme Court upholds the patentability of a genetically modified bacterium, quoting the Congressional report leading up to the 1952 Act that "anything made by man under the sun" should be patentable;
- applications permitted to be filed without signature by the inventor as long as the inventor had authorized the application to be filed;
- term of all design patents fixed at fourteen years from grant;
- possibility of extending patent term to compensate for delay in securing marketing authority from FDA to sell new drugs for humans;
- protection from finding of obviousness over work of co-employees;
- clarification that to be a joint inventor the inventors did not have to work together or each be an inventor of subject matter of every claim;
- introduced defensive publications under the Statutory Invention Registration (SIR) system;
- succeeded in causing inclusion of intellectual property issues in Uruguay Round of GATT negotiations; and
- provided for the possibility of extending patent term to compensate for delay in securing marketing authority from FDA to sell new drugs for animals.

The American Inventors Protection Act

In 1999, the United States patent laws were significantly revised on the passage of the American Inventors Protection Act (AIPA). The full provisions of the AIPA apply to all applications filed on or after November 29, 2000. The primary AIPA provisions can be summarized as follows:

- Domestic Publication: Established pre-grant publication at eighteen months from the earliest claimed filing date unless applicant certifies that no subsequent foreign filing is intended. Applies to applications filed on or after November 29, 2000.
- Request for Continued Examination: Provided an option to continue examination activity in an application already on file after the prosecution was deemed closed without having to file a new continuation application. Applies to application filed on or after May 29, 2000; does not apply to design applications.
- Patent Term Guarantee: Designed to ensure that, except where the patent is subject to a terminal disclaimer, the term of a patent is extended for one day for each day that prosecution has been delayed as a result of delays caused by the USPTO. Removed the caps on the terms of possible extensions as a result of secrecy orders, interferences, and appeals that were introduced when the term of a patent was changed from seventeen years from grant to twenty years from filing, and adds to the situations in which extensions may be granted. Applies to utility or plant applications filed on or after May 29, 2000.
- Optional *Inter Partes* Reexaminations: To encourage third parties to use reexamination procedures for determination of patent validity issues and so reduce the volume of patent litigation in the district courts. Applies only to patents issued on applications filed on or after November 29, 2000.

Pre-Grant Publication and Provisional Rights

Under the AIPA, a non-provisional application filed on or after November 29, 2000, would be published approximately eighteen months from the earliest claimed filing date. All domestic and foreign priority benefit claims must be made within the later of four months from the filing date of an application, or sixteen months from the filing date of the priority application. The pre-grant publication required that all drawing and sequence listing requirements be completed for inclusion in publication. Publication at eighteen months would allow third parties to submit patents and printed publications to the USPTO for consideration during examination of an application. Pre-grant publication could be avoided by filing a certification that the application has not been, and will not be, filed in any country that requires publication. A published application would qualify as prior art as of its filing date. The publication of the application at eighteen months also establishes provisional rights to the inventor/applicant to pursue a reasonable royalty for the period between the date of publication and the issue date of the patent. To be entitled to the reasonable royalty, the patentee must provide proper notice to the alleged infringer, and the claims as published must be substantially identical to the claims in the issued patent (Covington & Burling, 2001). The procedures and practice related to pre-grant publication are discussed in more detail in Chapter 9.

Patent Term Adjustment

The term of a non-provisional application filed on or after May 29, 2000, extends twenty years from the effective U.S. filing date, together with any patent term adjustment caused by USPTO delays during examination. The AIPA established a patent term adjustment that can be accrued by the applicant when the Office fails to take certain actions within prescribed time limits. Patent term adjustments can also be accrued for delays caused by secrecy orders, interference proceedings, and appeals. Patent term adjustment is offset by any delays caused by the applicant in concluding examination of the application (Covington & Burling, 2001). The procedures and practices related to patent term adjustment are discussed in more detail in Chapter 17.

Request for Continued Examination

The request for continued examination (RCE) procedure was intended to replace the continued prosecution application (CPA) procedure. For all applications filed after May 29, 2000, only a RCE can be filed; CPA practice is only available to utility applications filed before May 29, 2000. A RCE is not considered a new application; it is considered a request to continue the examination of an existing application by paying the basic filing fee. The procedures and practices related to filing of a RCE are discussed in more detail in Chapter 14.

Inter Partes Reexamination

The AIPA included provisions for an optional *inter partes* reexamination procedure that allowed third-party requesters to participate throughout the reexamination proceeding. *Inter partes* reexamination will not be covered in this book as it was phased out on September 16, 2012, under the America Invents Act.

The America Invents Act

On September 16, 2011, the President signed into law the America Invents Act (AIA), which includes the most sweeping changes to U.S. patent law since the 1952 Patent Act. An overview of the prosecution-based provisions of the AIA is provided below (Ramage et al, 2011):

- **First-Inventor-To-File**: The AIA changed the U.S. patent system from a first-to-invent to a first-to-file system, thereby aligning the U.S. patent system with international patent systems.
- **Expanded Inventive Entities:** The AIA permitted owners or individuals with proprietary interest in an invention to file a patent application, although an oath or declaration from the inventors will still be required before the patent is granted.
- **E-Filing Incentive Fee:** The AIA imposed an additional non-electronic filing fee under 37 C.F.R §1.16(t) for applications filed in paper (excluding provisional applications). This surcharge fee is designed to incentivize applicants to e-filing to improve the compatibility of filings with the USPTO e-commerce systems.
- **Establishment of Micro Entities:** The AIA established a micro entities category that includes applicants primarily employed by, or who assign their application to, an institute of higher education. Such micro entities will be entitled to a 75 percent reduction in patent filing fees.
- **Prioritized Examination:** The AIA created a new method to have an application examined on a fast-track schedule without a prior art search burden on payment of a substantial prioritized examination filing fee. Initially, the USPTO will only accept ten thousand applications per fiscal year for prioritized examination based on filing date order. Priority examination was also established for technologies important to the national economy or national competitiveness.
- **Pre-Issuance Submission of Prior Art by Third Parties:** The AIA established a mechanism for third parties to submit prior art references to an examiner while the application is still pending.
- **Post-Grant Review Proceedings:** The AIA provided for three new procedures for reviewing a patent after it issues, namely:
    - *Inter Partes* Review: Replaces the *inter partes* reexamination process; however, it includes changes to the standard for granting review and the reviewing entity.

- Post Grant Review: Allows a third party to challenge the validity of a patent on any statutory grounds within nine months of issuance.
- Supplemental Examination: Allows the patent owner or assignee the chance to open the issued patent for additional examination to address issues that raise a substantial new question of patentability.

- Derivation Proceedings: The AIA replaced interference proceedings with a new derivation proceeding used to determine if the concepts of the invention were communicated to another who later filed an application for a patent without the inventor's authorization.

Support staff will need to develop functional knowledge and practical application of the provisions of AIA to allow them to provide a full range of support to registered practitioners. The following progressive introduction to the new features of the AIA can be supplemented by more details on filing requirements and associated deadlines in subsequent referenced chapters of this book.

First-Inventor-To-File System

Migration to a first-inventor-to-file system is intended to bring greater transparency, objectivity, predictability, and simplicity to patentability determinations. It is also another step towards harmonizing U.S. patent law with that of other industrialized countries.

Effective March 16, 2013, section 3 of the AIA changed the U.S. patent system from a first-to-invent system to a first-to-file system. This patent reform measure aligned the U.S. patent system with worldwide patent systems that award a patent to the first inventor/applicant to file rather than the first inventor/applicant to invent. Prior to AIA, the United States awarded a patent based on the first-to-invent system, which allowed for interference proceedings before the Board of Patent Appeals and Interferences (BPAI) to determine which applicant is not entitled to the patent if both parties claim the same invention. The U.S. first-to-invent system allowed a party that had failed to file a patent application on time to challenge the inventorship of another pending application if certain requirements were met. The transition to a first-to-file system would eliminate the need for interference proceedings and reduce the time-consuming and expensive litigation associated with these proceedings.

Under a first-to-file system, each patent application will be given an effective filing date, and patentability will be judged on whether any prior art was available before the effective filing date. The one-year grace period will remain in effect, but only for inventors' own disclosures and not those derived from the inventor. Obviousness will also be judged as of the effective filing date, and inventors will no longer be able to swear behind prior art references based on claiming an earlier date of invention. The transition from a first-to-invent to a first-to-file patent system instantly added almost every application filed prior to the applicant's invention to prior art. This instant addition to prior art applies for obviousness as well as anticipation and is a more stringent rule than that applied by the European patent office, where an application not published as of an applicant's filing date can be used to defeat only novelty. The one exception to this rule is that an applicant's publication or a publication under common ownership would only be prior art as of its publication date. In addition, the applicant has the additional benefit of a one-year grace period to file. The one-year grace period applies only to a disclosure made by or through the inventor. The one-year grace period is measured backward from the filing date and offers no protection against third-party disclosure (Sunstein, 2011). Additional analysis of the effects of the AIA on redefining prior art is provided in Chapter 13.

Expanded Inventive Entities

Effective September 16, 2012, section 4 of the AIA permitted the filing of an application by an entity other than the inventor. Such non-inventive entities can include an assignee where the inventor has assigned, or is under an obligation to assign, the invention. In more obscure situations, non-inventive entities can include a person who otherwise shows sufficient proprietary interest on behalf of and as agent for the inventor. Any patent granted on an application filed by a person other than the inventor will be granted to the real party in interest. Authority is given in 35 U.S.C. §115 to an individual who is under an obligation of assignment to include certain required statements in an executed assignment in lieu of filing these statements in a separate oath or declaration. Identification of each applicant's citizenship is no longer required by statute. Additional information or other inventor statements are not required if they are equivalent to those provided in a combined assignment-declaration document. The impact of expanded inventive entities with respect to declarations, assignments, and application data sheets are discussed in more detail in Chapter 6 and Chapter 11.

E-Filing Incentive Fee

Effective November 15, 2011, section 10 of the AIA imposed a surcharge filing fee under 37 C.F.R §1.16(t) for an original patent application (except for a design, plant, or provisional application) that is not filed electronically. The e-filing incentive fee is subject to small entity discount. The e-filing incentive fee applies to a patent application filed by mail, rather than via the USPTO electronic filing system (EFS-Web). This includes PCT international applications filed with the USPTO as the receiving office as well as national stage applications under 35 U.S.C. §371. All applications filed by mail or hand delivery on or after November 15, 2011, must include the additional non-electronic filing fee under 37 C.F.R §1.16(t), which is subject to a small entity discount if applicable. If the e-filing incentive fee applies and is not paid or authorized, the USPTO will treat the submission as having an insufficient fees. To avoid this detrimental effect, applicants are encouraged to provide a general fee authorization in the physical application filing papers to cover all applicable fees. The e-filing incentive fee is discussed in more detail in Chapter 3.

Establishment of Micro Entities

Effective September 16, 2012, section 10 of the AIA established a micro entity status as a subset of small entity status. The AIA defines a micro entity as an applicant who:

- qualifies as a small entity;
- has not been named as an inventor on more than four previously filed patent applications;
- did not, in the calendar year preceding the calendar year in which the applicable fee is paid, have a gross income exceeding three times the median household income; and
- has not assigned, granted, or conveyed (and is not under obligation to do so) a license or other ownership interest in the application concerned to an entity that, in the calendar year preceding the calendar year in which the applicable fee is paid, had a gross income exceeding three times the median household income.

Micro entity status and related entitlements and the related impact on filing fees are discussed in more detail in Chapter 3.

Prioritized Examination

Effective September 26, 2011, the AIA established a mechanism for applicants to request expedited review and examination of a patent application on payment of additional fees. Prioritized examination is available for all non-provisional utility and plant applications with no more than four independent claims, thirty total claims, and no multiple dependent claims. Requests for prioritized examination of non-provisional utility applications must be filed using EFS-Web, and the request for prioritized examination must be present on filing of the application. Under the prioritized examination process, the USPTO must provide a final disposition within twelve months of prioritized status having been granted. All of the filing fees required must be paid on filing of the request for prioritized examination; the small entity discount applies to fees, but the micro entity discount does not apply. The specific filing requirements, processing, and advantages of the prioritized examination program are discussed in more detail in Chapter 12.

Pre-Issuance Submission of Prior Art by Third Parties

Effective September 16, 2012, section 8 of the AIA provided a mechanism for third parties to submit patents, published patent applications, or other printed publications of potential relevance to the examination of a pending patent application with a concise explanation of the asserted relevance of each document submitted. Third parties can file pre-issuance submissions of prior art within six months of publication or before the first rejection of the claims (or before the date of a notice of allowance), whichever is later. There is no limit to the number of documents that can be submitted. Third parties cannot submit prior art after the application has been allowed. The third-party submitter can remain anonymous and is not required to meet any threshold for the significance of the documents submitted. The third-party submitter is not precluded from later challenging the patent if it is allowed.

Renaming of the Board

The AIA renamed the Board of Patent Appeal and Interference (BPAI) to the Patent Trial and Appeal Board (PTAB). The PTAB members are the Director, the Deputy Director, the Commissioner for Patents, the Commissioner for Trademarks, and administrative patent judges. The PTAB will be the chief forum for the two new post-grant review proceedings: post grant review and *inter partes* review. Under the AIA, three-member panels of administrative patent judges conduct all post grant review and *inter partes* review proceedings. The duties of the PTAB will also cover all appeals of adverse decisions by examiners on applications in regular prosecution and on proceedings in *ex parte* reexamination (and existing *inter partes* reexamination until replaced by *inter partes* review). The PTAB provides the highest level of decision-making authority at the PTO, and appeals from the PTAB in applications and reexamination proceedings may be made directly to the U.S. Court of Appeals for the Federal Circuit. There are no provisions for district court review of post grant review and *inter partes* review final decisions. The changes with respect to the PTAB have an effective date of one year from enactment of the AIA. However, some provisions took effect immediately with respect to certain ongoing reexaminations proceedings. The threshold for initiating an *inter partes* reexamination will immediately change from whether the request sets forth a "substantial new question of patentability" to whether "the information presented in the request shows that there is a reasonable likelihood that the requester would prevail with respect to at least one of the claims challenged in the request."

The rules of practice will likely vary depending upon the particular proceeding pending before the PTAB. While the AIA establishes proceedings before the PTAB as an alternative to District Court litigation on validity, Congress charges the Director with developing the specific rules of conduct and evidence for the proceeding. It is clear from the legislation, though, that the new post grant review and *inter partes* review proceedings are likely to have strict time deadlines and many characteristics of a litigation directed to fact-finding and case presentation. With respect to timing, both the post grant review and *inter partes* review processes must yield a final determination within one year, absent good cause. Where good cause is shown, the proceeding may only be extended an additional six months (Messinger et al, 2011).

Post-Grant Review Proceedings

One major aim of the reform legislation is to establish the Patent and Trademark Office as an alternative forum to U.S. district courts for vetting the validity of issued U.S. patents. The related legislation modifies existing practice and provide entirely new structures and legal bases for deciding patentability questions at the PTO (Messinger et al, 2011). Under the AIA, there are three distinct ways to challenge the patentability of an issued patent, namely:

- Post Grant Review (PGR): A third-party petitioner (not the patent owner) may request to cancel one or more claims on any ground that could have been raised under utility, novelty, obviousness, and supportive specification (except best mode). PGR is limited to patents issuing from an application filed under the first-inventor-to-file system. The PGR must be requested within nine months of broadening reissue or patent issuance;

- *Inter Partes* Review (IPR): A third-party petitioner (not the patent owner) may request to cancel as unpatentable one or more claims of a patent based on novelty or obviousness using patents or printed publications. The petition must be filed before the later of nine months after the grant of a patent or issuance of a reissue patent or before the termination date of any post-grant review proceeding; and
- Supplemental Examination (SE): Gives patent owners a chance to clear up problems with their patents before launching infringement litigation.

The above post-grant review proceedings and their respective filing requirements are discussed in more detail in Chapter 21.

Derivation Proceeding

Effective March 16, 2013, section 3 of the AIA established derivation proceedings to replace interference proceedings. A derivation proceeding allows a person to correct the named inventors on an application or patent. In a derivation proceeding, an inventor can correct the named inventor of an application if the inventor can establish that an inventor named in an earlier-filed application derived the claimed invention from an inventor. The petitioning inventor would also have to establish that the earlier application was filed without authorization from the inventor in the later-filed application. A petitioner must institute a derivation proceeding within the one-year period beginning on the date of first publication of a claim to an invention that is the same or substantially the same as the earlier applicant's claimed invention (Pelletier, 2011). Any application or resulting patent that contains or at any time contained a claimed invention with an effective filing date on or after March 16, 2013, or a corresponding priority reference, is subject to a possible derivation proceeding. Derivation proceedings are discussed in more detail in Chapter 21.

AIA Technical Corrections Bill

On January 5, 2011, an AIA Technical Corrections Bill (H.R. 6621) was enacted, making the following technical changes to the AIA (Sterne, Kessler, Goldstein & Fox PLLC, 2013):

- eliminated a nine-month "dead zone" for *inter partes* review of patents granted for applications having an effective filing date before March 16, 2013;
- eliminated a prohibition on post-grant review for reissue patents with narrowing amendments;

- extended the time for filing the signed inventor's oath or declaration until the payment of the issue fee;
- clarified the calculation for patent term adjustment;
- clarified the standards for initiating derivation proceedings; and
- repealed 35 U.S.C. § 373, which restricted the types of inventors or applicants that could file PCT applications at the U.S. Patent Office.

Eliminating Inter Partes Review Dead Zone

The AIA Technical Correction Bill amended 35 U.S.C. §311(c) to remove the so-called "dead zones" in which no review of first-to-invent patents and reissue patents was available under the AIA. Now, petitioners need not wait to file *inter partes* review of those first-to-invent patents issuing within nine months of, or after, September 16, 2012, as the technical correction makes Section 311(c) inapplicable to first-to-invent patents. Similarly, the technical correction made the nine-month tolling provision inapplicable to reissue patents (Sterne, Kessler, Goldstein & Fox PLLC, 2013).

In addition, the AIA Technical Corrections Bill revised the filing deadline for *inter partes* review to be after the later of either (Crouch, AIA Technical Amendment Becomes Law, 2013):

- nine months after the grant of a patent; or
- the termination date of any post grant review.

Time for Filing a Signed Inventor Oath or Declaration

The AIA Technical Corrections Bill amends 35 U.S.C. §115(f) and changed the deadline for filing a signed inventor's oath or declaration (or substitute statement or recorded assignment) to "no later than the date on which the issue fee for the patent is paid." However, patent applicants should file a signed inventor oath or declaration (or substitute statement or recorded combination declaration-assignment) as early as possible to avoid possible abandonment of an application if an oath or declaration, or substitute statement, cannot be executed by the issue fee deadline.

Calculation of Patent Term Adjustment

The AIA Technical Corrections Bill amended the patent term adjustment (PTA) provisions of 35 U.S.C. §154(b) in two ways. First, 35 U.S.C. §154(b) was amended to clarify that tolling of the fourteen-month period for the Office to issue the first office action will begin to accrue upon commencement of the U.S. national stage under §371 (when applicant pays the basic filing fee and submits a copy of the international application, thirty months from the earliest claimed priority date). Previously, the tolling of the fourteen-month period to issue the first office action began when applicant completed the filing requirements under §371 (when applicant pays of all fees, submits a copy of the international application, and submits a signed inventor declaration). This change permits U.S. national stage applicants to delay submission of an executed inventor oath or declaration without risking a loss of potential PTA. To maximize the benefit of this amendment, applicants can maximize PTA by filing a U.S. national stage application and pay only the required basic filing fee, thereby activating the fourteen-month calculation period. In addition, applicants can respond to a Notification of Missing Requirements at the three-month period, by paying for a one-month extension, as this further consumes the fourteen-month PTA period, while allowing the applicant the maximum response period without incurring applicant delay (Tietz, 2013).

Secondly, 35 U.S.C. §154(b) was amended to specify that a civil action filed in the U.S. District Court for the Eastern District of Virginia is the exclusive remedy for challenging a USPTO decision on a request for reconsideration of a PTA determination. Previously, the applicant was given 180 days after the grant of the patent to file a civil action. This amendment tolled the 180-day period until after the Director's decision on an applicant's request for reconsideration of PTA determination. As a result, applicants can file a request for reconsideration of PTA within two months of issuance of the patent and then await the decision of the Director before proceeding with filing a civil action (Tietz, 2013).

Derivation Provisions Clarified

The AIA Technical Corrections Bill provided two clarifications to the derivations provisions under 35 U.S.C. §135(a). First, the corrections bill divided section 135(a) into subsections to improve readability. Second, the corrections bill clarified that a petition to institute a derivation proceeding must be filed on the earlier of:

- within one year after grant of the derived claim; or
- within one year after publication of the earlier application containing such claim.

The Corrections Bill modified requirements for applicants filing petitions to institute derivation proceedings and delineates the criteria applied to deem an application as an earlier-filed application with respect to an invention relative to another application.

Applicants for International Application

The AIA Technical Corrections Bill repealed a provision prohibiting the USPTO from accepting certain international applications designating the United States from anyone not qualified under specified application requirements.

Patent Law Treaty

The Patent Law Treaty (PLT) seeks to harmonize and streamline requirements associated with filing and processing patent applications in patent offices of its contracting parties. While the PLT applies only to applications permitted for filing as an international PCT application (i.e., non-provisional applications, including procedures for reexamination and supplemental examination), the new rules also will affect some provisional, reissue, plant and design application procedures. The new rules are generally more lenient on application filing requirements, deadlines and other procedures. The provisions of the PLT became effective on December 18, 2013, and include the following significant revisions (Johnson et al, 2013):

- more permissive requirements for receiving a filing date;
- acceptance of late claims for benefit of priority; and
- late issue fee and maintenance fee payments, and revival of abandoned applications.

The impact of the main revisions of the PLT are discussed in more detail in the following section.

Non-Provisional Application Filing Date Requirements and Filing by Reference

Non-provisional applications (including the U.S. national phase entry of a PCT application) filed on or after December 18, 2013 do not need claims to receive a filing date under 35 U.S.C. §111(a). For applications filed without claims, applicants will be required to submit claims (and pay any excess claims fees) in a manner like current procedures for late payment of filing, search, and examination fees. The applicants entitlement to a filing date despite the late filing of the claims, however, does not mean that the application meets the requirements of Section 112 for those late-filed claims. The specification must comply with the written description and enablement requirements for the claimed invention. Given that claims originally filed with an application may themselves provide sufficient written description support, applicants are encouraged to continue including claims with the initial filing. Failure to include claims leaves the applicant at risk of filing an application that lacks support for the claimed invention.

Under section 111(c) of the PLT, patent applicants will have the option of filing an application by reference to a previously-filed application, including a foreign application, by identifying the prior application in an application data sheet (ADS). The specification and drawings of that prior application then constitute the new application and must be filed within the prescribed time period identified in a Notice issued by the Office. Applicant should be careful in ensuring that the previously-filed application is correctly identified by application number and filing date. Applicants should recognize that filing "by reference" may not guarantee a timely or proper priority claim, and that additional requirements such as providing a certified copy of a priority foreign application may apply. This mechanism may be useful when a convention date deadline is fast-approaching and a copy of the priority application is not immediately available.

Delayed Priority Claim

Applicants will be able to file an application and claim priority to an earlier-filed provisional or foreign application up to two months after the priority deadline (i.e., up to fourteen months from the filing date of a utility application, eight months for a design application) if the delay in claiming priority was unintentional. The priority claim must be filed within four months of the application's filing date or within sixteen months of the priority application's filing date, whichever is later, along with payment of a petition fee and a statement that the delay was unintentional. The PLT states that the two-month timeframe is not an extension of time, and the delay must be unintentional. There is no equivalent two-month window of time with respect to the copendency requirement for claiming priority to a non-provisional or PCT application

Late Issue Fee and Maintenance Fee Payment and Revival of Abandoned Applications

Under section 27(11) of the PLT, the USPTO can accept late payment of issue and/or publication fees. As with a late priority claim, an applicant must show that the delay in payment was unintentional and pay a petition fee and the balance due for issuance. Section 27 will also allow the Office to accept late maintenance fee payments at any time, revive abandoned applications, and accept late responses by a patent owner in a re-examination proceeding under the same "unintentional" standard. The new rules eliminate the "unavoidable" standard currently applicable to missed maintenance fee payments, giving patentees wider leeway to reinstate expired patents. These provisions apply to any application filed before, on, or after December 18, 2013, and any patent issuing from such an application.

The PLT provides applicants and patent owners with additional options, such options cannot be used to accumulate patent term adjustment (PTA) by slowing prosecution through late submission of claims or delayed filing of a copy of the prior application when filing by reference. The PLT also permits applicants and assignees to sign certain USPTO filings of a procedural nature, including fee transmittal letters, requests for corrected filing receipts, and submission of a copy of an earlier-filed application under the new filing by reference provision.

The PLT introduced safeguards against irrevocable loss of patent rights, and provided greater flexibility in filing requirements and patent procedures. These safeguards should be considered exceptional rather than routine. The USPTO warns that the protracted timeframes and filing options should not be considered to prescribe best practices, but rather protection against loss in rights due to a technicality.

The PLT also provides applicants with additional time of two months (instead of one month) to reply to the following requirements or notices (Nutter McClennen & Fish LLP, 2014):

- Restriction Requirements;
- Notices of Informal or Non-Responsive Amendments;
- Notices of Informal or Non-Responsive RCE Amendment;
- Notices of Required Fees Due; and
- Letters Requiring Computer Readable Format because it was unreadable, non-compliant, or not submitted.

Previously, applicants had one month to respond to the USPTO for these matters before extension fees began to accrue, but now applicants have two months to respond without paying a fee. This additional amount of allotted time harmonizes the United States laws with the Patent Law Treaty adopted in Geneva. Under international standards applicants must have a time period of at least two months to reply.

Administration of Patent Rules and Regulations

The United States Patent and Trademark Office (USPTO) is the federal agency tasked with granting U.S. patents and trademarks. In doing so, the USPTO fulfills the constitutional mandate to:

> Promote the progress of science and the useful arts by securing for limited times to inventors the exclusive right to their respective discoveries.

The strength and vitality of the U.S. economy depends directly on effective mechanisms that protect new ideas and investments in innovation and creativity. The continued demand for patents and trademarks underscores the ingenuity of American inventors and entrepreneurs. The USPTO is the reservoir for establishing rights to innovative technology, progress, and achievement.

The USPTO advises the President of the United States, the Secretary of Commerce, and U.S. Government agencies on intellectual property policy, protection, and enforcement, and it promotes the stronger and more effective protection of IP around the world. The USPTO furthers effective IP protection for U.S. innovators and entrepreneurs worldwide by working with other agencies to secure strong IP provisions in free trade and other international agreements. It also provides training, education, and capacity-building programs designed to foster respect for IP and to encourage the development of strong IP enforcement regimes by U.S. trading partners. According to the USPTO website, the mission of the office is:

> To foster innovation and competitiveness by providing high quality and timely examination of patent and trademark applications, guiding domestic and international intellectual property policy, and delivering intellectual property information and education worldwide.

The USPTO examines applications and grants patents on inventions when applicants are entitled to them, it publishes and disseminates patent information, records assignments of patents, maintains search files of U.S. and foreign patents, and maintains a search room for public use in examining issued patents and records.

The USPTO website provides links to the entire texts of consolidated patent rules (Title 37–Code of Federal Regulations) and the patent laws (United States Code Title 35–Patents). In addition, links are provided to the Manual for Patent Examining Procedures

(MPEP), the American Inventors Protection Act (AIPA), the America Invents Act (AIA) microsite, the AIA Technical Corrections Bill, and the Patent Law Treaty. The USPTO established an AIA Microsite that contains valuable reference information on the provisions of the most extensive changes to U.S. patent law since the 1950s.

For ease of reference, the remaining chapters of this book will conclude with an identification of the respective U.S. patent rules and regulations that are pertinent to the content of the chapter. The content of this book relies heavily on the MPEP, and support staff should be able to dynamically search for detailed filing requirements within the manual. Where possible, specific reference to the relevant sections of the MPEP are provided to support informed searching or to identify and validate detailed filing requirements, or both. Support staff should be able to independently research filing requirements and extract key procedural concepts from dense patent USPTO rules, regulations, and manuals. As the patent laws continue to evolve, support staff need to ensure that their knowledge development resources remain current and comprehensive to enable them to provide a full complement of support services to registered practitioners.

CHAPTER-SPECIFIC REFERENCE MATERIAL

Reference Source	*U.S. Patent Laws, Rules, and Regulations*
Title 35 of the U.S. Code	*http://www.uspto.gov/web/offices/pac/mpep/consolidated_laws.pdf*
Title 37 of the Code of Federal Regulations	http://www.uspto.gov/web/offices/pac/mpep/consolidated_laws.pdf
Manual of Patent Examination Procedures (MPEP, 8th Edition)	http://www.uspto.gov/web/offices/pac/mpep/index.htm
American Inventors Protection Act (AIPLA)	http://www.uspto.gov/patents/law/aipa/index.jsp
America Invents Act (AIA)	http://www.uspto.gov/aia_implementation/patents.jsp

Chapter 3

Filing Methods and Handling of Papers by the USPTO

Correspondence Identification Requirements

Irrespective of the filing method used, all correspondence related to an application already filed with the USPTO must be identified with the assigned application number and the assigned filing date. The USPTO uses such information to match incoming papers with the application file to which they belong. The USPTO recommends that all incoming papers pertaining to a filed application include the following application-specific caption:

- application number;
- filing date;
- title of invention;
- confirmation number (unique identifier for the application in USPTO file system);
- art unit (confirm from Patent Application Information Retrieval system or most recently USPTO correspondence); and
- name of examiner who prepared the most recently issued correspondence.

The application-specific caption should also be included on the front within the top margin of each drawing sheet filed. In situations where the application number or filing date has not yet been assigned, the attorney docket number should be provided.

Correspondence Signature Requirements

Every paper filed by a practitioner must be personally signed by the practitioner. When signing papers filed with the USPTO, the practitioner is certifying that statements made are subject to the declaration that all statements made are based on information believed to be true and under the premise that knowingly making false statements will be subject to disciplinary actions against the practitioner and could jeopardize the validity of the application or document and the enforceability of any resulting patent. The USPTO permits two types of signatures:

- a handwritten pen signature; and
- a digital S-signature that is electronically created.

For digital signatures, the person signing must insert his or her own signature between forward slash marks. A secretary or paralegal is not permitted to sign or insert a practitioner's signature, and a practitioner is not permitted to insert an inventor's signature on a document. The name of the person signing must be printed or typed immediately adjacent to (above, below, or beside) the S-signature. The name of the person signing may be inserted by someone other than the person signing, but the person signing must personally insert the S-signature. A registered practitioner may S-sign, but his or her registration number is required either as part of the s-signature or immediately below or adjacent to the signature, as shown below.

S-Signature Examples

Signature: /John T. Smith/ <u>or</u> /John T. Smith Reg. No. XX,XXX/
John T. Smith John T. Smith
USPTO Registration Number XX,XXX

A person's handwritten signature may be an original blue pen signature or copy of same. Where copies of correspondence are acceptable, photocopies or facsimile transmissions may be filed. The original signed document should be retained as evidence of proper execution in the event that questions arise as to the authenticity of the signature reproduced on the photocopy or facsimile-transmitted correspondence. If a question of authenticity arises, the USPTO may require submission of the original signed document.

AIA Impact—Signature of Papers

Effective September 16, 2012, under the AIA, amendments and other papers, except for written assertions, filed in an application must be signed by:

- a patent practitioner of record;
- a patent practitioner not of record who acts in a representative capacity; or
- an assignee (juristic entity—owner of the entire interest.

Unless otherwise specified, all papers submitted on behalf of a juristic entity (organizational assignee) must be signed by a patent practitioner. A juristic entity may only prosecute a patent application through a patent practitioner.

Correspondence Certification Requirements

The USPTO's mailing or transmission certification procedures allow applicants to sign and date a statement of verified mailing or fax transmission on the indicated date. This provision allows the USPTO to deem the papers as timely filed if the indicated mailing or fax transmission certification date is on or before the filing deadline. The USPTO will honor such certifications and will deem the papers to be timely filed even if the papers do not actually reach the USPTO until after the end of the period of reply. The certificate of mailing procedure does not apply to papers mailed in a foreign country. Certificate of transmission procedures do apply to both facsimile and EFS-Web submissions even if the papers are filed from a foreign country.

The certification of mailing or transmission requires a signature. Where possible, the certification statement and signature block should be placed on the front of each distinct document. A certification statement may be included on a separate sheet with an itemized list of the filing component documents, which must be securely attached to the papers filed and should include the application number and filing date for identification purposes. If the certification appears on a document that also requires a substantive content signature by a registered practitioner, then two signatures may be required, one for the certification of mailing or transmission and one for the substantive filing paper. The person indicated on the certification and the substantive signature does not have to be the same individual. An unsigned certification will not be considered acceptable.

Electronic Filing Support Services

The USPTO has invested significant time and monies to ensure that it utilizes technology to improve the efficiencies of the patent-filing process. The USPTO has an online services hub that allows applicants to search existing patents and applications, file new patent applications and related submissions, pay fees, and obtain status information on existing patents or applications. The Office offers digital access and electronic filing support systems through its Electronic Business Center (EBC) interface. The patent e-commerce services consist of a digital access system and an electronic filing system that are both supplemented by online help tutorials and system documentation. The online help and tutorials allow customers to become knowledgeable and proficient in using the latest USPTO electronic business products, including the tools, techniques, and practices used to successfully submit an electronically filed patent application.

The EBC assists patent customers with electronic patent application submissions via the Electronic Filing System (EFS-Web) and with the review of patent applications in Public and private PAIR. The EBC offers online electronic filing information, instructional material, PatentIn and Checker support and is available to assist users through one-on-one support during its normal business hours. More specifically, the following tools and related resource websites are available through the EBC:

- Electronic Filing System (EFS-Web);
- Patent Application Information Retrieval (PAIR) System;
- Priority Document Exchange (PDX);
- Publication Site for Issued and Published Sequences (PSIPS);
- Electronic Patent Assignment System (EPAS);
- Assignment on the Web for Patents (AOTH-P);
- Official Gazette Online;
- Patent Attorney/Agent Search; and
- Quick Links and Downloads.

The EBC is the single point of customer contact for all electronic products and is a portal frequently used by patent prosecution support staff. The EBC customer service representatives can help to answer inquires and ensure value-added support for the EBC products, tools, and services.

Customer Number Program

A customer number (CN) is uniquely assigned by the USPTO and associates a single correspondence address, a group of patent practitioners, and a fee address with submitted patents and applications. Customer numbers are also required for on-line customer access to pre-publication application status information using private PAIR. When a customer receives a customer number, the customer should request bulk association of all applications and patents with this number by completing and filing a Customer Number Upload Spreadsheet with the EBC. Customer numbers provide the following functionalities:

- links a correspondence address with patent applications;
- links a group of patent practitioners with patents and patent applications;
- links a maintenance fee address to issued patents;
- permits access to private PAIR (along with a PKI digital certificate); and
- permits access to EFS-Web for retrieving applications in progress and for submitting follow-on submissions (along with a PKI digital certificate).

Advantages of Using a Customer Number

The primary advantages of using the customer number program are as follows:

- allows the correspondence information of associated applications to be easily updated without having to file application-specific requests for updates; and
- allows registered practitioners, persons granted limited recognition, and independent inventors to be associated with as many customer numbers as needed. This controls access to pending application information for organizations with multiple client groups.

Customer Number Practice

With customer number practice, a patentee is also able to designate a fee address for the receipt of maintenance fee correspondence and a different address for the receipt of all other prosecution correspondence. The USPTO will also accept requests submitted electronically via a computer-readable medium to change the correspondence address of a list of applications or patents or the fee address of a list of patents to the address associated with a customer number. Customer number practice does not affect the prohibition against appointment of a specified law firm, as the USPTO has no independent means of verifying if a practitioner submitting documents is associated with a given law firm. The USPTO will permit an appointment of all practitioners associated with a CN because the USPTO can ascertain from its records for the specified CN whether a particular practitioner is associated with a customer number.

In most situations, law firms or companies assign one individual as the administrator of their customer numbers. The administrator must be a registered practitioner associated with the customer numbers, which allows him or her to use their PKI certificate to view and electronically change the details of associated customer numbers, including the associated address and mode of correspondence (via mail or e-mail). The administrator can also control access to the customer numbers by adding or deleting practitioners associated with the customer numbers. In addition, generally the customer number administrator would also control the individuals authorized to make charges to firm or company deposit accounts and would add or remove authorized individuals in sync with changes made to the customer number practitioner listings.

Public Key Infrastructure

The Public Key Infrastructure (PKI) is used by the USPTO to permit e-commerce customer transactions using a digital certificate that assures secure user identity. PKI technology supports e-commerce interactions that maintain confidentiality, strong authentication, and integrity. High-level certification using PKI certificates can be obtained by independent inventors and registered practitioners and is required to use private PAIR and EFS-Web.

Advantages of Using PKI Certificates

The USPTO identifies the following advantages associated with use of PKI certificates:

- ensures strong e-commerce security in conducting electronic business transactions with the USPTO;
- establishes a unique customer profile that authorizes users to conduct e-commerce business with the USPTO;
- permits secure access to private PAIR for status updates on submitted patent applications and patents; and
- allows secure submission of follow-on papers to existing patent applications via EFS-Web.

Digital Certificate Management

Digital certificate management allows users to easily self-enroll, maintain, and recover their digital certificates all from the USPTO web-based portal. The systems will allow users to:

- create new user digital certificates;
- recover corrupted user certificates;
- register for USPTO self-recovery codes; and
- assign and manage a registered e-mail address.

Patent Application Information Retrieval

The Patent Application Information Retrieval (PAIR) system allows users to view the status of their own pending application and any patented or published applications. There are two access interfaces to PAIR, public PAIR and private PAIR. Public PAIR provides access to all issued patents and published patent applications. Private PAIR allows registered users to access pending application information in addition to what is also available in Public PAIR. PAIR provides web-based access to public and pending patent information and eases the process of tracking patents, patent applications, and follow-on documents through the USPTO approval process. The access requirements, information provided, and respective advantages of public and private PAIR are compared and contrasted in Table 2.

Table 2: Patent Application Information Retrieval—Public vs. Private PAIR

	Public PAIR	Private PAIR
Software	Requires no PKI software to access.	Requires high-level PKI Certificate and association of applications with CN to access.
Users	Provides status and history information for granted patents to the general public with unrestricted access to issued patent and published applications. Also provides access to the PTO file Image File Wrapper (IFW) for online viewing and downloading of documents.	Provides independent inventors, registered practitioners, and persons granted limited recognition the ability to access real-time status of their pending applications. Also provides access to PTO file document images. Users can also view and download cited U.S. patents and U.S. publication references in PDF format.
Information Provided	▪ Prosecution history. ▪ Status of a published application or patent. ▪ Physical location of file within the USPTO. ▪ Image File Wrapper (IFW) contents. ▪ Supplemental content.	▪ Prosecution history. ▪ Status of pre-publication application or patent. ▪ Limited bibliographic data. ▪ Current CN details including attorney or agent of record, or both, and correspondence address. ▪ Ongoing correspondence notification. ▪ Image File Wrapper (IFW) contents. ▪ Supplemental Content. ▪ First-Action Prediction and Status Letter.

Advantages	▪ Allows access to published application IFW content via the Internet. ▪ Allows customers to search and select published applications to download and print and conveniently order certified copies online.	▪ Permits secure online searching by application, patent, publication, attorney docket, and CN to retrieve information on prosecution history, status, and location. ▪ Allows users to join the e-office action program to retrieve, on the same day, new PTO mailings on applications or patents associated with the CN.

Private PAIR Access

Private PAIR allows independent inventors, registered patent attorneys, and patent agents the ability to access all of the content of Public PAIR, as well as real-time status information, application documents, and transaction histories for their pending patent applications using a secure Internet connection. Private PAIR is only available to customers who have pre-registered with USPTO as trusted e-filers. For registered e-filers with applications associated with a CN, all of the application information and IFW are available via the web. The USPTO identifies the following requirements to access private PAIR:

- a registered patent attorney/agent or an independent inventor;
- a CN; and
- a digital PKI certificate to obtain secure transmission of the application to the USPTO.

Private PAIR Tab System

Each application or patent accessed through private PAIR contains a series of tab-based displays that provide additional information to the related application or patent. Support staff should validate patent application information, data, and documents with respect to the USPTO record file through private PAIR.

Application Data Tab

This tab contains the bibliographic data related to the application or patent, which includes the following information:

Application Number	Customer Number
Filing or 371(c) Data	Status
Application Type	Status Date

Examiner Name
Group Art Unit
Confirmation Number
Attorney Docket Number
Class/Subclass
First Named Inventor
Title of Invention
Location
Location Date
Earliest Publication Date
Patent Number
Issue Date

Transaction History Tab

This tab contains a transaction history by date in chronological order, including a brief description of the transaction.

Image Filing Wrapper Tab

This tab contains the electronic documents contained in the image file wrapper, sorted in chronological order. The contents are displayed by mailroom date and include the document description code, a short descriptive name of the document, and an indication of page count of each document. Users can reorder the list by any of the criteria and can download some or all of the document from the image file wrapper by selecting the document under the PDF column.

Continuity Data Tab

This tab contains the parent and child continuity data. The continuity date includes the type of priority claimed, the parent application number, filing date, status, and patent number if applicable. Users can access the details of any application claimed in priority from this tab.

Foreign Priority Tab

This tab contains the details of any foreign patent application claimed in priority, including the name of the foreign country, the priority application number, and the priority application filing date.

Fees Tab

This tab contains a history of all prosecution phase fees paid, in chronological order, including the fee code, the fee amount, the mailroom date, and the payment method used. This fee tab also includes any maintenance fee history for issued patents.

Published Documents Tab

This tab identifies any pre-grant publications associated with the application, including the publication number, publication date, and full-text image. Users can access the published application using this tab.

Address & Attorney/Agent Tab

This tab identifies the correspondence address of record for the application or patent. The address includes the name of the addressee, the address, and if the address is associated with a customer number. This tab also includes a list of attorneys or agents of record in the application or patent. Users can confirm if an attorney or agent has power of attorney and is of record by verifying that his or her PTO registration number and name are included in this list. Only the attorneys or agents listed are considered of record in the application or patent.

Assignment Tab

This tab contains the patent assignment abstract of title associated with the application or patent. The patent assignment abstract identifies assignment information recorded against the assignment database, including the associated reel and frame, the date received, the date recorded, the date mailed, the number of pages, the conveyance, the assignors, the date executed, the assignee name and address, and the correspondent of record. This tab may include multiple assignments recorded against the matter in chronological order.

Display References Tab

This tab contains any information disclosure statements (IDS) filed, including the mailing date of the IDS and an indication of the page count. Users can view and download e-patent references from this tab and save them to a local desktop folder. The e-patent references system will retrieve a list of cited U.S. references available for download if this functionality is available for the application or patent. The downloaded cited references will be in bookmarked PDF format. Java and Adobe reader software are required to download e-patent references.

First-Action Predictor Tab

This tab indicates the number of projected months from the filing date for the USPTO to issue the first office action. Users can convert the information in this tab to a letter for their record retention purposes by using the "print letter" option.

Publication Review Tab

This tab displays the publication date for the application, including the projected publication date, the filing date, the application data details, the correspondence name and address, the assignee name and address, the applicant-selected figure for publication, any other publication of the application, the parent continuity data, and any foreign priority data. Users can request data changes to the publication data by submitting an on-screen correction request form.

Electronic Filing System

EFS-Web is the USPTO's easy-to-use web-based patent application and document submission electronic filing system. EFS-Web utilizes standard web-based screens and prompts to enable submission of portable document format (PDF) documents directly to the USPTO within minutes. EFS-Web allows users to choose the tool, process, and workflow to convert and submit PDF files to the USPTO's secure hosted servers. EFS-Web complements the electronic patent application management process used by patent examiners.

Advantages of EFS-Web

The USPTO has identified the following benefits of electronically filing through EFS-Web:

- Safe: Filing completed through EFS-Web provides the same legal protection as paper-based filings. EFS-Web produces an electronic acknowledgment receipt and confirmation, and it includes the ability to print and save the receipt for record retention.
- Simple: The filing interface supports the most complex patent application filings through submission PDF files or the completion of simple web screens.
- Secure: EFS-Web submissions are protected through state-of-the-art security methods using digital certificates for registered filers.
- Fast: EFS-Web allows the efficient submission of a patent application, including payment of fees, in a few minutes.
- Flexible: EFS-Web does not require filers to learn how to use new authoring tools for patent application and documents.
- Forgiving: EFS-Web validates PDF files to ensure that they meet the formatting requirements for submission. If a PDF file has formatting issues, EFS-Web provides an on-screen explanation of the file defect to allow the filer to make corrections.

AIA Impact—E-Filing Incentive Fee

In the AIA, the USPTO took the opportunity to implement an e-filing incentive fee. The objective of imposing an e-filing incentive fee was to encourage applicants to file in a mode that is more compatible with USPTO systems and processes. The AIA imposed the e-filing incentive fee under 37 C.F.R §1.16(t) on any application filed by paper on or after November 15, 2011; the fee is subject to a small entity discount and is intended to encourage applicants to use EFS-Web for all permitted submissions to the USPTO. The non-electronic filing fee under 37 C.F.R §1.16(t) does not apply to provisional application filings.

Submissions Permitted via EFS-Web

EFS-Web supports a broad range of new application filings and follow-on documents for previously filed applications. A registered e-filer may file the following types of new applications:

- Accelerated Exam
- Prioritized Examination
- Design
- Design Reissue
- International Application for filing in the U.S. receiving office
- Provisional
- Reexam
- Utility
- Utility Reissue
- U.S. National Stage under 35 U.S.C. §371.

In addition, EFS-Web permits the filing of the following follow-on documents:

- Petition to Accept Unintentionally Delayed Payment of Maintenance Fee in an Expired Patent under 37 C.F.R. §1.378(c);
- Petition to Make Special based on Age under 37 C.F.R. §1.378(c); and
- Pre-Grant Publication under 37 C.F.R. §1.211 to §1.221.

Submissions Not Permitted via EFS-Web

The following filings cannot be completed using EFS-Web:

- plant patent applications and associated documents;
- requests for reexamination for plant patents and associated documents;

- color drawings and color photographs for international applications that have not entered the national stage;
- initial submission for patent term extension;
- documents that require certification by statute;
- correspondence in an application subject to secrecy order;
- documents filed in contested cases before the Board of Appeals and Interferences;
- maintenance fee payments;
- assignment documents (must be filed using Electronic Assignment System); and
- documents related to registration practice or any disciplinary proceeding.

Working with the EFS-Web Interface

Registered e-filers have both an assigned CN and a digital certificate. When support staff are working with the EFS-Web interface, they are considered users authorized by the digital certificate owner. EFS-Web requires an initial user authentication step, which can only be successfully completed if both the encrypted digital certificate (.epf file) and the password are valid. Support staff working under the authority of the digital certificate owner must provide their names and e-mail addresses. When the user authentication step is completed, the user must specify if this is a new application submission or a follow-on document submission for a previously filed application.

The EFS-Web interface provides the user with screen prompts that guide him or her through the e-filing process in addition to providing a tab-based view of the user's progression through the process. The status tabs allow forward or backward movement within the EFS-Web pages. However, forward movement is only permitted if the user has been on that tab page. If the user uses tabs to go back and make changes, the user must click "Continue" to save those changes. If tab forward is used, the changes made will be lost. Users must specify the title of the invention, the first named inventor, and the correspondence address. On the next screen, the bibliographic data entered by the user is displayed for review and validation. If any errors are found, the user can go back and correct them by selecting "Application Data."

The filing component documents being submitted can be uploaded if the user browses to the location they are saved. The filing component documents should be in PDF format; EFS-Web can accommodate a PDF file that has multiple documents. PDF files that contain multiple documents must be separately indexed to be labeled properly in the IFW. For example, a patent application PDF file may contain a specification, claims, abstract, and drawings that should be listed as separate documents in the IFW. Users should enter the page ranges for each section so that the documents are properly displayed in the IFW. The user must select a filing category and document description from the drop-down menus provided. This step must be performed for each document uploaded. Users can attach additional documents by selecting "Add File" and repeating the steps. If any uploaded documents need to be deleted, select "Delete" corresponding to the document file row. EFS-Web imposes a 25-MB size limit per file uploaded.

The user then selects "Upload and Validate" to automatically check the documents for compliance with formatting requirements. EFS-Web can validate a maximum of twenty files uploaded at one time. A maximum of sixty documents can be uploaded per e-filing submission. EFS-Web can upload one sequence listing (.txt) file up to 100 MB per submission. The sequence listing file must be uploaded separately from other types of files. If the sequence listing does not conform to the ST.24 or ST.25 format, a warning will display. The interface will give the user an on-screen warning of errors in the documents before submission. If a document could not be validated, an error message will appear informing the user of the reason for the validation failure. Attaching a document that is not a PDF, TXT, or PCT ZIP will cause a failure to validate, as will not choosing a document description. Errors found on validation can be corrected by selecting "Attach Files."

Any fees due can be paid through the interface using an interface-generated transmittal. The fees due are calculated based on values entered by the user. The user must indicate any entitlement to reduced fees. New application filings can be submitted without paying fees at the time of filing; in such situations, users would skip the fee calculation step.

EFS-Web provides interim sandbox storage capacity for uploaded validated documents prior to final submission. Users can save the uploaded documents for submission later pending a final quality review by the signing attorney or agent. The final step in the e-filing process is when users confirm and submit. This is the final opportunity to review and confirm or edit application data, edit fees, or remove or edit filing component documents. When the application is successfully submitted, an on-screen summary of the submission and application number and confirmation number with a corresponding EFS ID will be displayed. EFS-Web uses the confirmation number and application number to decrease the potential of mismatching submissions with existing applications. The electronic acknowledgment receipt indicates the time and date of the submission, the application identifying information, and a listing of filing component documents.

Most documents submitted via EFS-Web will be viewable via the Patent Application Information Retrieval (PAIR) system within an hour after the USPTO receives the documents if the user has associated the applications with a CN.

EFS-Web Interface—Practical Tips

The USPTO offers the following practical tips on resolving technical issues with the EFS-Web interface:

- To ensure that all fonts are embedded when creating a PDF file, utilize the Adobe Job Options file, which contains configuration settings that, when selected, will produce a document consistent with the USPTO PDF submission requirements profile. If it is not possible to embed fonts, create an image PDF using the advanced print settings on the PDF printer driver, and select "print as image" and "300 dpi."
- To correct file-naming errors, start the file name with any combination of characters selected from uppercase alphabet, lowercase alphabet, and digits zero through nine. Do not include unauthorized characters (brackets, commas, spaces, or symbols), according to file-naming standards. Do not start a file name with an underscore or hyphen; if used, underscores and hyphens must be within the file name. The last four characters of the file name must be lowercase .pdf. The length of file name is limited to a maximum of one hundred characters, including the required four-character .pdf file extension.
- When indexing a document through EFS-Web, the category is the overall grouping of document descriptions that identify the nature of the attached file, and the document description is the description of the file being attached. Use of the EFS-Web category is optional and is intended to help users locate the appropriate document description quicker by filtering the list to those descriptions that are pertinent to the category name.
- If an acknowledgment receipt is not received when filing an application through EFS-Web, access "My Workplace" within EFS-Web and access the documents that you have just submitted. It may take up to three hours for the acknowledgment receipt to generate. If the receipt is still not available after that time frame, the user should contact the EBC to confirm that the documents were received. The application should not be resubmitted until is it confirmed with the EBC that it was not received.

E-Filing an Initial Application

The e-filing processing steps related to an initial application filing are shown in Figure B. EFS-Web users must pay particular attention to indexing of documents and ensure that all uploaded documents pass the interface validation tests. Support staff should complete a comprehensive post-filing review by carefully reviewing the electronic acknowledgment receipt to ensure that all documents filed are indicated, if the receipt is to be relied upon later as a proof of submission. If documents required to complete the filing are inadvertently omitted, EFS-Web users can submit such documents or pay fees by completing an additional same-day filing, which the USPTO will consider part of the original filing submission. To ensure the documents filed are all accounted for and have not been distorted through file conversions completed by the USPTO, a post-filing review of the PAIR IFW is an important quality assurance step.

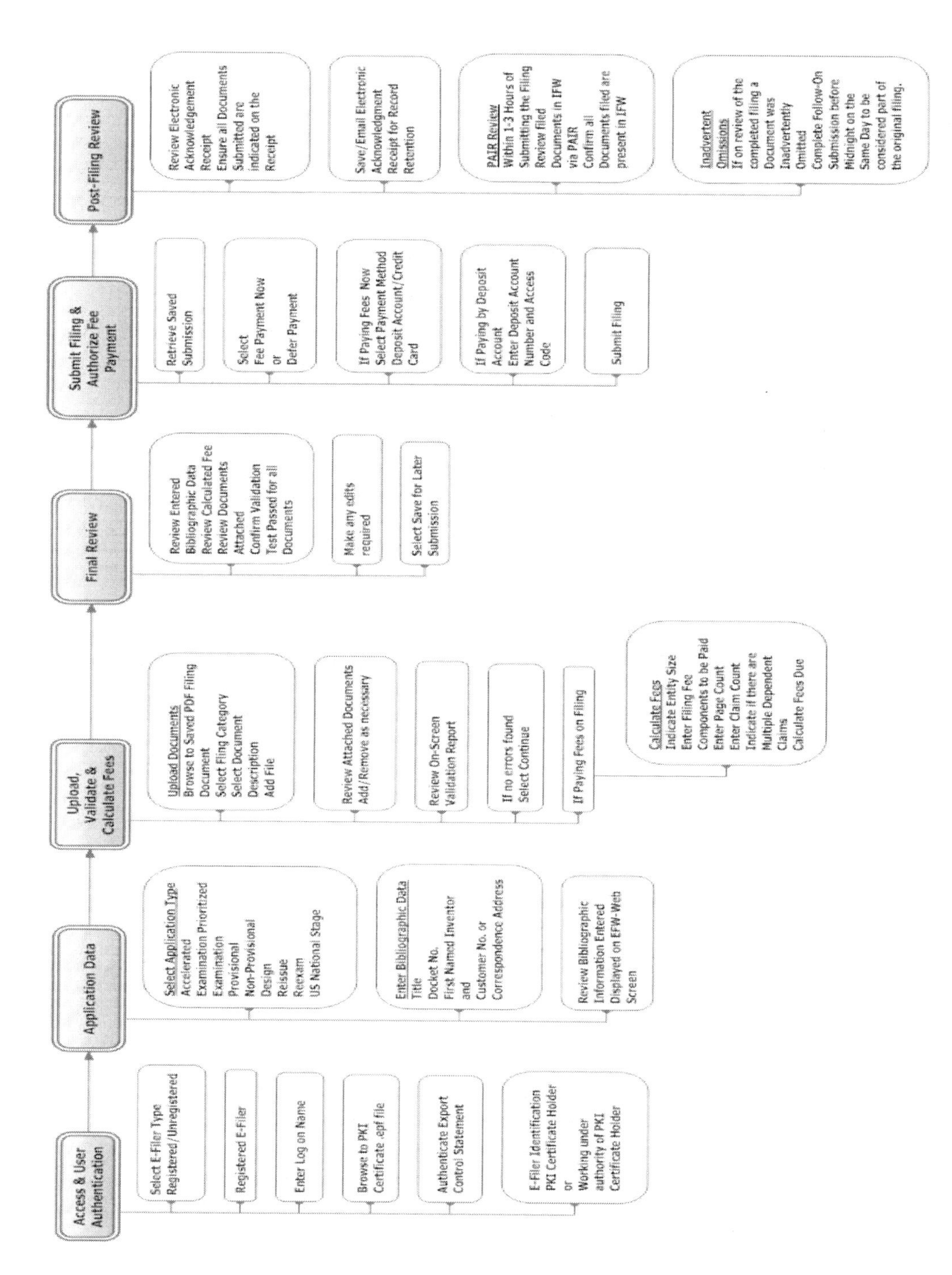

Figure B: E-Filing Processing Steps—Initial Application Filing

Document Indexing

Document indexing is applying a document description to a PDF, TXT, or ZIP file. All files or the documents in a multi-document PDF file must be indexed. There are nearly two hundred document descriptions offered in EFS-Web. However, the document description lists are presented based on the filing type chosen. The e-filer still has the ability to choose a category to condense the document description list even more. Indexing has no legal relationship to the patent application; indexing is a function for processing the submission. Document indexing allows for quicker and more accurate downstream processing of e-filed submissions by ensuring that documents are instantly routed to the IFW. The document indexing process also generates workflow and assigns the submission to the appropriate USPTO personnel for further processing. The USPTO provides the following general rules for document indexing:

- Applications must be broken out into separate sections (specification, claims, abstract, and drawings).
- Paper associated with amendments must be separated out to different document descriptions. Typical amendments will include:
    - Amendment transmittal document. This is the first document discussing the type of amendment being filed (amendment after non-final, amendment after notice of allowance, preliminary amendment, amendment after final);
    - Application parts that are applicable (specification, claims, abstract, drawings); and
    - Remarks (applicant arguments or remarks made in an amendment) document description.
- Foreign references and non-patent literature references must be separated out as separate documents.
- Appeal briefs do not have to have the claims section separated out.
- Petitions that are accompanied with amendments must have separate application parts and documents descriptions as mentioned above, but if the petition cites the application part, that part should not be separated out.

Saved Submission Sheet

The EFS-Web interface produces a saved submission sheet that displays the attorney docket number and title of the invention to which the documents have been uploaded. Support staff should carefully review the saved submission sheet to ensure that the intended filing documents were uploaded to the correct application number. The saved submission sheet should also be used to validate that all filing component documents required are account for, and that the correct documents have been uploaded to the correct document descriptions. Support staff should cross-check that the attorney docket number or application number used in the name of each filing component document matches the application to which the documents have been uploaded as indicated on the top of the saved submission sheet. A careful and thorough review of the interface generated saved submission sheet is imperative in identifying and preventing pre-filing errors.

E-Filing Follow-On Submissions

Registered EFS-Web users are permitted to file follow-on documents in patent applications and reexamination proceedings. Follow-on documents are defined as documents filed after the initial submission of the application or request for reexamination, which include, but are not limited to, the following: amendments, information disclosure statements, pre-grant publication-related requests, replies to office actions, and formality notices and petitions. Follow-on documents also include any documents submitted on the same day as the application but after the initial application submission. Non-registered EFS-Web users are not permitted to file follow-on documents and must file subsequent documents by first-class mail, Express Mail, or hand delivery.

Format Requirements for EFS-Web Submissions

Submissions filed using EFS-Web must comply with guidelines and instructions provided by the USPTO on use of the interface. EFS-Web users should ensure that all submissions comply with the following requirements:

- PDF File Format: EFS-Web accepts standard PDF documents up to 25 megabytes per file and sixty electronic files per submission. PDF files created from scanned documents and submitted via EFS-Web must be created using scanning resolutions no lower than 300 dpi. PDF files with multiple layers must be flattened prior to submission to ensure the entire document is received and readable to an examiner.
- Data Entry: EFS-Web collects information from on-screen entries made by the user through graphical user interface (GUI) data collection-screens that identify the type of application being filed or the application number if a follow-on submission is

being made. For a new application filing, the USPTO uses the information entered to assign the application number, create the application, and process the application. For follow-on submissions, the USPTO uses the information to upload the documents into the application files specified by the user. The USPTO also uses the document description selected by the user to route the submission to the required official. As a result, EFS-Web users should ensure that the information entered on the data collection and that the correct document description used are accurate to ensure the USPTO processes the submission most efficiently and correctly.

- Application Type: When a user is submitting a new patent application via EFS-Web, the user is initially required to select the application type (e.g., design, provisional, or non-provisional). When this initial selection is made, only document descriptions and fee codes to the application type selected will be available. The USPTO system will automatically generate an application number based on the application type selected. Further routing of the application will also be based on the application type selected by the user and will be indicated on the electronic acknowledgment receipt generated after the submission is completed.
- Document Indexing: EFS-Web users must select from an interface-generated list of document descriptions to specify and index the documents being submitted. The USPTO converts the document description selected by the user to create document codes that dictate how the document submitted will be forwarded to the appropriate organization or official for processing or consideration. The IFW and PAIR systems use the document code for identifying the document maintained in the application file. Therefore, accurate document indexing is important to facilitate efficient processing and proper consideration by the USPTO.

Submission of Photographs and Color Drawings

When applicants are required to submit drawings to aid the understanding of the invention, the USPTO prefers black-and-white drawings be filed. The USPTO will accept photographs and color drawings in utility and design applications if they are the only practical medium for illustrating the claimed subject matter. Any photographs or color drawings submitted must be of sufficient resolution quality that allows them to be reproduced in black-and-white for inclusion in the printed patent. The following procedures should be followed when submitting photographs or drawings:

- Black-and-White Line Drawings: Can be filed via EFS-Web in patent applications and reexamination proceedings. EFS-Web users must use the document code DRW for document description of black-and-white line drawings filed in provisional, non-provisional, U.S. national phase, reissue applications, and reexamination proceedings. Black-and-white line drawings will be converted to TIFF images and stored in the IFW.
- Non-Black-and-White Drawings: Photographs, color drawings, and grayscale drawings can only be submitted via EFS-Web in provisional applications, non-provisional utility, design applications, reissue utility applications, and reexamination utility and design applications. EFS-Web users should use the document code DRW. NONBW should be used for the document description for photographs, color drawings, grayscale drawings, and any other drawings that are not black-and-white line drawings filed in provisional, non-provisional, U.S. national phase–and reissue applications, in addition to reexamination proceedings. Non-black-and-white drawings will be stored in the supplemental complex repository for examiners (SCORE) tab, and a black-and-white copy will be stored in the IFW with a SCORE placeholder sheet. When filing color drawings, they must be accompanied by a petition and fee under 37 C.F.R. §1.84(a), and an explanation why color drawings are necessary. It is not necessary to file color drawings in triplicate; one set of the color drawings is sufficient.

The USPTO's PAIR system can only display drawings in portrait orientation; as a result, EFS users should not submit landscape-oriented drawings, as PAIR will automatically convert the image to portrait, which may result in image distortion or loss of resolution.

Submission of Text Files

All sequence listings, large tables, or computer program listing appendices must be submitted as ASCII text files (.txt file extension) for national applications and reexamination proceedings. Submission of ASCII text files on compact disc is also a filing option. When ASCII text files are submitted via EFS-Web, the specification must contain a statement in a separate paragraph that incorporates by reference the material in the ASCII text file identifying the name of the ASCII text file, the date of creation, and the size of the file in bytes.

The USPTO recommends that sequence listings be submitted as ASCII text files via EFS-Web rather than as a PDF document. If the ASCII text file sequence listing complies with sequence listing submission requirements, the text file will serve as both the required paper copy and the required computer readable form (CRF). It is not necessary to file a separate PDF copy of the sequence. If an applicant submits a sequence listing as an ASCII text file via EFS-Web in response to a requirement notice, the sequence listing text file must be accompanied by a statement that the submission does not contain any new matter that goes beyond the disclosure of the application as filed. There is a file size limit of 100 megabytes on sequence listing text files that cannot be separated into multiple files.

PDF Fillable Forms

When used in conjunction with EFS–Web, PDF fillable forms improve the filing and submission process and accelerate the processing of patent applications and documents. Fillable PDF forms are interactive forms with various file types and formatting options that auto-load field information directly into the USPTO Patent Application Locating and Monitoring (PALM) system. By extracting data directly out of fillable PDF forms, EFS-Web users can minimize rework and improve data accuracy for all types of filings. PDF fillable forms improve the accuracy of data entered into the corresponding patent file by reducing the errors associated with manual data entry. PDF fillable forms also support the real-time processing of petition requests. Fillable PDF forms do not required specific PDF creation software; the forms can be created by using the free version of Adobe Reader 7.0.8, 7.0.9, 8.1.1, or 8.1.2. The following PDF fillable forms are available on the USPTO website:

- SB08a Information Disclosure Statement (IDS)
- SB14 Application Data Sheet (ADS)
- SB16 Provisional Application for Patent Cover Sheet
- SB28 Petition to Make Special Under Accelerated Examination Program
- SB30 Request for Continued Examination (RCE) Transmittal
- SB66 Petition to Accept Unintentionally Delayed Payment of Maintenance Fee in an Expired Patent
- SB130 Petition to Make Special Based on Age

Advantages of Using PDF Fillable Forms

The USPTO identifies the following function-related advantages associated with using PDF fillable forms:

- users can print and save forms with data embedded;

- users can modify the data entered after saving the form;
- users can circulate the form for multipoint access and updating;
- users can import data in SML format from document management systems and other databases; and
- users have the ability to export data in XML format to document management systems and other databases.

E-Petitions Program

The e-Petitions program allows registered e-filers to file a limited number of electronic petitions via EFS-Web. When using e-Petitions, the submitter is able to directly input the requisite information into a secure web interface and immediately receive an e-Petition decision. E-Petitions can be accessed through the registered e-filer page under existing application/patent by selecting the radio button "e-Petitions (for automatic processing and immediate grant, if all petition requirements are met)." When the e-Petitions option is selected, the screen will display all available e-Petitions types. There are two distinct types of e-Petitions, namely:

- PDF-based e-Petitions that require the download and completion of the respective EFS-Web Fillable PDF Form; and
- Web-based e-Petitions that allow information to be entered directly into EFS-Web screens eliminating the need to submit a separate PDF document.

PDF-Based E-Petitions

The PDF-based e-Petitions require the use of an EFS-Web e-Form. Such e-Forms are completed by positioning the cursor on a fillable area or element, then left-clicking to type the required text or to check a box or radio button. The tab key can be used to move from one field to the next. Some fields limit the maximum number of characters that can be entered, and when the limit is reached, the form will automatically advance the user to the next field. A copy of the completed e-Form should be saved to update the related matter-specific file. The following PDF-based e-Petitions are available and can be filed at any time during prosecution of the application.

- Petition to Make Special Based on Age under 37 C.F.R. §1.102; the related PDF fillable e-Form can be found at http://www.uspto.gov/ebc/portal/efs/petitionagesb130.pdf
- Petition to Accept Unintentional Delayed Payment of the Maintenance Fee under 37 C.F.R. §1.378(c); the related PDF fillable e-Form can be found at

EFS-Web-Based e-Petitions

The EFS-Web-based e-Petitions can be filled out completely online through Web-based screens. The submitter will be prompted to enter application or patent identifying information. The EFS-Web system will display a screen with the selections made to allow the user to confirm the details, choices, and necessary options. The petition-request PDF document is generated by EFS-Web to show the information entered. The document can be reviewed by clicking on the hyperlink petition-request PDF. When the confirmation of details on the document is completed, the submit button should be used to file the e-Petition. The document will be loaded into the IFW if the e-Petition is granted. The following EFS-Web-based e-Petitions are available:

- Request for Withdrawal as Attorney or Agent of Record under 37 C.F.R. §1.36.
- Petitions to Withdraw from Issue after Payment of the Issue Fee.
    - Petition to Withdraw from Issue after Payment of the Issue Fee under 37 C.F.R. §1.313(c)(1) or (2).
    - Petition to Withdraw from Issue after Payment of the Issue Fee under 37 C.F.R. §1.313(c)(3).
    - Petition to Withdraw from Issue after Payment of the Issue Fee under 37 C.F.R. §1.313(c)(1) or (2) with Assigned Patent Number.
    - Petition to Withdraw from Issue after Payment of the Issue Fee under 37 C.F.R. §1.313(c)(3) with Assigned Patent Number.
- Petitions for Revival
    - Petition to Accept Late Payment of Issue Fee—Unintentional Late Payment under 37 C.F.R. §1.137(b).
    - Petition for Revival of an Application based on Failure to Notify the Office of a Foreign or International Filing under 37 C.F.R. §1.137(f).
    - Petition for Revival of an Application for Continuity Purposes Only under 37 C.F.R. §1.137(b).
    - Petition for Revival of an Abandoned Patent Application Abandoned Unintentionally under 37 C.F.R. §1.137(b) (For Cases Abandoned After 1st Action and Prior to Notice of Allowance).
- Petition to Correct Assignee After Payment of Issue Fee under 37 C.F.R. §3.81(b).

The submitted e-Petitions can be saved on EFS-Web for up to seven days. Saved submissions can be retrieved under "My Workplace" for EFS-Web registered e-filers.

The e-Petition to request immediate withdrawal of attorney or agent of record can only be used for a non-provisional utility patent application (including reissue utility applications and national stage applications under 35 U.S.C. §371) and design application (including reissue design applications). The e-Petition option to request withdrawal of attorney or agent of record should not be used in a reexamination proceeding. To file an e-Petition to request withdrawal of attorney or agent of record, EFS-Web will verify the attorney's registration number with the power of attorney on record in the application. If the submitter does not have power of attorney, a validation error will be displayed on-screen. If power of attorney is assigned to a CN, the submitter will be required to change the correspondence address. If the power of attorney is assigned to individual attorney registration numbers, the user will not be required to change the correspondence address unless all attorneys of record are being withdrawn.

Advantages of E-Petitions

Electronic petitions are automatically processed and granted immediately upon submission if the petition meets all of the requirements. The time saved using e-Petitions can be advantageous for critical petitions where an automatic petition grant would reduce delays in restoration of patent rights, expedite withdrawal from representation and redirect Office correspondence to the new correspondence address, and initiate the revival of an abandoned application to save patent term adjustment time. Petition decisions are uploaded to the IFW and are not be mailed. For web-based e-Petitions, the systems has a built-in validation step that will display an error message on the screen near the data field that contains the error.

E-Terminal Disclaimer

The USPTO has released an e-Terminal Disclaimer via EFS-Web for non-provisional utility and design applications (including reissue). The web-based e-terminal disclaimer can be filled out completely online through web-screens, and no EFS-Web fillable forms are required. E-terminal disclaimers are auto-processed and approved immediately upon submission if the request meets all of the requirements. Each e-terminal disclaimer filed requires a single terminal disclaimer fee but can include up to fifty reference applications and fifty prior patents.

Payment of Fees via EFS-Web

Non-registered and registered users may submit the filing fees using the online fee payment transmittal generated by the EFS-Web interface. Application filing fees include distinct component fees, namely, a basis filing fee, search and examination fee, and excess claims fees, which may be paid in part or in full on filing of a patent application or request for reexamination. Only registered users may submit payment of fees in a previously filed patent application or request for reexamination. EFS-Web allows payment of fees by credit card, deposit account, or electronic fund transfer.

Users may also authorize charge of fees to a deposit account by including a separate fee transmittal form or letter as a filing component document. A transmittal authorizing a credit card payment should not be submitted via EFS-Web because the information regarding the credit card number, signature, and expiration dates would be made of public record when such a document is loaded into the IFW. When the online fee payment through EFS-Web is unavailable, a deposit account authorization transmittal may be included as a separate filing component document.

When the USPTO notifies the applicant that fees are due and specifies the amounts owed, the applicant must timely pay the indicated fees. If the applicant timely submits the specified fee, compliance with requirements are met, and the application should not be abandoned. If the fees paid are insufficient because of an error in the notice or because of a subsequent change in the fee since the fee notice was issued, the applicant will be notified of a need to pay additional fees and given a shortened period to reply. When fees are authorized or paid, they should be itemized according to how fees are applied by the USPTO. Fee authorization to a deposit account must be itemized, clear, and unambiguous; otherwise, the USPTO may interpret the authorization in a manner other than intended. Prior to authorizing deposit account charges, the applicant should ensure that sufficient funds to cover the fees authorized are available in the deposit account.

Many filings contain default language authorizing the debit of any additional fees due or the credit of any fee overages to an indicated deposit account. If applicant wishes to defer payment of fees, this intention needs to clearly indicated, and no contradictory default fee authorization statement should be in any of the documents filed.

Application Size Fee for Applications Submitted via EFS-Web

For provisional, non-provisional, design, and reissue applications filed via EFS-Web, an application size fee is required under 37 C.F.R. §1.16(s). The paper size equivalent of the specification, including claims and drawings, will be considered 75 percent of the number of sheets of paper present in the application as e-filed when entered in the IFW for purposes of determining the application size fee required. The paper size equivalency for EFS-Web filings does not apply to national stage submissions. Any sequence listing or computer program listing filed in ASCII text format through EFS-Web will be excluded when determining the application size fee required. If sequence listings or computer program listings are submitted as PDF files, they will be included in the application size fee required.

Small Entity Status

The USPTO affords a 50 percent discount on designated fees to any small business concern, independent inventor, and some nonprofit organizations. The USPTO's requirements for designation for entitlement to claim small entity status are based on the defined criteria established by the Small Business Administration as follows:

- A Person: Any inventor or other individual who has not assigned, granted, conveyed, or licensed, and is under no obligation under contact or law to assign, grant, convey, or license, any rights in the invention. An inventor or other individual who has transferred some rights in the invention to one or more parties, or is under an obligation to transfer some rights in the invention to one or more parties, can also qualify for small entity status if all the parties who have had rights in the invention transferred to them also qualify for small entity status either as a person, small business concern, or nonprofit organization under this section.
- Small Business Concern: Any business concern that has not assigned, granted, conveyed, or licensed, and is under no obligation under contract or law to assign, grant, convey, or license, any rights in the invention to any person, concern, or organization that would not quality for small entity status as a person, small business concern, or nonprofit organization and meets the size standards, namely whose number of employees, including affiliates, does not exceed five hundred persons.
- Non-Profit Organization: Any nonprofit organization that has not assigned, conveyed, or licensed, and is under no obligation under contract or law to assign, grant, convey, or license, any rights to any person, concern, or organization, and is either:

- a university or other institution of higher education located in any country;
- tax-exempt under the U.S. Internal Revenue Service Code or would qualify as tax-exempt under statute of state if located in the United States of America;
- a non-profit scientific or educational entity under statute of the state of the United States of America or would qualify as non-profit scientific or educational entity under statute of state if located in the United States of America.

Small entity status must be established for each patent application to permit the applicant to pay reduced fees to the USPTO. In order to establish small entity status for the purpose of paying fees, the applicant must make an honor-based assertion of entitlement to small entity status. For applications where the ownership rights may be divided between an independent inventor, small business concern, or non-profit organization, or any combination of such parties, all are required to meet the definition of small entity status. If any party to the matter does not meet the requirements for designation as a small entity, the status cannot be claimed.

Any inventor, assignee, and attorney/agent of record can assert entitlement to small entity status. The USPTO holds that the person making the assertion to entitlement to small entity status is a person in a position to know the facts about whether or not status as a small entity can be properly established. The assertion can also be made by paying the small entity basic filing fee upon filing the application. If the initial filing fee is not paid as a small entity, payment of any subsequent fees at that level must be accompanied by a written assertion of entitlement to small entity status. Table 3 summarizes the filing activities to which a claim to small entity status would discount the associated filing fees, in addition to some filing activities where small entity discounting does not apply.

When the claim to small entity status is made, the applicant can continue to pay fees as a small entity even if the status changes and until payments of the issue fee or maintenance fees are due. If there is a change in small entity entitlement, a notification of loss of small entity status must be filed in the application on payment of the earliest of the issue fee or maintenance fees due after the date of loss of small entity status. Small entity status must be asserted in each separate application filed; it does not transfer from a parent to a subsequently filed child application.

Table 3: Small Entity Status—Impact on PTO Filing Fees	
Small Entity Discount Applies	Small Entity Discount Does Not Apply
Patent application filing fees, including the basic filing fee, the search and examination fees, the application size fee, and excess claims fees.	Petition and processing fee (other than revival).
Extensions of time fee.	Document supply fee.
Revival and appeal fee.	Certificate of correction fee.
Issue and maintenance fees.	Request for reexamination fee.
Statutory disclaimer fee.	International application fee.

If an application is filed as a large entity and filing fees are paid, the applicant has three months from the date such fees were authorized to request a refund of the filing fees based on later-established entitlement to small entity status.

AIA Impact—Assertion of Small Entity Status

Effective September 16, 2012, under the AIA, a written assertion of small entity status can be signed by:

- the applicant;
- a patent practitioner of record or a practitioner acting in a representative capacity;
- the inventor or joint inventor, if the inventor is the applicant; or
- the assignee.

Correcting Errors in Small Entity Status

If small entity status is established in good faith and reduced fees were paid to the USPTO and it is later established that small entity status does not apply, deficiency payments must be made to the USPTO. The deficiency amount is calculated using the date on which the deficiency was paid in full. More specifically, the deficiency owed is the difference between the current fee amount for a large entity and the small entity fee amount previously paid. The deficiencies owed must be itemized, and any subsequent decrease to the small entity amount paid should not be used in the calculations. The paper field to correct the entity status from small to large should identify the following:

- the small entity fees previously paid;
- the deficiency amount owed for each fee paid in error (including distinguishing fees for extensions of time); and
- the total deficiency (sum of individual deficiencies) owed.

If the change in entity status affects multiple applications, a separate paper must be filed in each application to correct the error. The USPTO treats the papers submitted as a notification of loss of small entity status. For maintenance fees, payments paid as a small entity amount when it is later established that that small entity status does not apply must be corrected by filing deficiency maintenance fee payments with a statement regarding change in entity status.

AIA Impact—Micro Entity Status

The AIA established a new entity status—micro entities, which are entitled to a 75 percent discount on USPTO filing fees. Micro entity status can be based on income status or on institute-of-higher-education status. To claim micro entity status based on gross income, the following certifications must be made using form SB/15A:

- applicant qualifies as a small entity;
- applicant has not been named as an inventor on more than four previously filed patent applications;
- applicant did not, in the calendar year preceding the calendar year in which the applicable fee is paid, have a gross income exceeding three times the median household income; and
- applicant has not assigned, granted, or conveyed (and is not under obligation to do so) a license or other ownership interest in the application concerned to an entity that, in the calendar year preceding the calendar year in which the applicable fee is paid, had a gross income exceeding three times the median household income.

When applying the micro-entity definition, applicants are not considered to be named on a previously filed application if the individual has assigned, or is obligated to assign, ownership rights as a result of previous employment. The definition includes applicants who are employed by an institute of higher education and have assigned, or are obligated to assign, ownership to that institute of higher education. Such applicants must also qualify as a small entity.

The applicant must also not be under an obligation to assign rights in the application to another party that exceeds the maximum income requirement. If an application is submitted by multiple applicants, each must qualify as a micro entity to be eligible for the 75 percent discount. If a micro entity applicant's income level changes so as to no longer qualify, the applicant does not retain the status as it would apply to discounts on future fee payments (Durta, 2012).

Institutes of higher education designated for learning only, can qualify for micro entity status. Such institutes of higher education learning cannot include non-profit research foundations, technology transfer organizations, and federal government research laboratories legally separate from a university. If a university is claiming micro entity status, it should not be named as the applicant (the inventor should be named as the applicant and should assign his or her rights in the invention to the university). The university must be the assignee of 100 percent interest in the title of the invention. There is no limit to the number of applications that the university has filed to qualify for micro entity status. To claim micro entity status based on institution-of-higher-education basis, the following certifications must be made, using form SB/15B:

- the applicant qualifies as a small entity; and
- the applicant has assigned, granted, conveyed, or is under an obligation by contract or law to assign, grant, or convey a license or other ownership interest in the particular application to an institution of higher education as defined in section 101(a) of the Higher Education Act of 1965 (20 U.S.C. §1001(a)).

To claim micro entity status, a certification statement must be made and validated with the client each time a payment is made for which the micro entity status is claimed. Claiming micro entity status does place a significant ongoing burden on the applicant to review and recertify entitlement to the status on payment of any fee subject to micro entity discounting. Micro entity status does not carry over to related continuing and reissue applications and the entitlement to status must be re-certified for each new filing.

Signature of Micro Entity Certification Statements

The certification of micro entity status forms (forms SB/15A and SB/15B) may only be signed by an authorized party, as identified in 37 C.F.R. §1.33(b). This means that the only parties who may sign a certification of micro entity status form are:

- a registered patent practitioner, meaning a registered attorney or agent who is either of record or acting in a representative capacity under 37 C.F.R. §1.34;
- an inventor who is named as the sole inventor and identified as the applicant; or
- all of the joint inventors who are identified as the applicant. If qualified for micro entity status, joint inventor applicants should sign separate copies of the relevant micro entity certification forms.

An officer of an assignee corporation or organization is not authorized to sign a certification of micro entity status form.

Post-Filing Quality Assurance

When documents are filed electronically through EFS-Web, users can take a few precautionary post-filing steps to ensure that the filing is complete and accurate.

Review of the Electronic Acknowledgment Receipt

The EFS-Web interface generates an electronic acknowledgment receipt, which identifies the date and time the USPTO received the submitted documents. The electronic acknowledgment receipt itemizes the documents submitted, identifying them by the document description selected by the user on filing and accounting for page count and byte size for each document. For new application filings, the filing date, which will be subsequently indicated on the filing receipt, is based on the date indicated on the electronic acknowledgment receipt, assuming that, after review, the documents submitted, were compliant with the requirements for assignment of an actual filing date. If the official version of any document received by the USPTO via EFS-Web is lost, damaged, or rendered unreadable or unrecoverable from the IFW, the USPTO will immediately notify the user. In such circumstances, the electronic acknowledgment receipt will serve as proof that the USPTO received the submitted documents, and the situation will be remedied by providing a copy of the documents, with a copy of the electronic acknowledgment receipt, showing the itemized submissions indicated as received by the USPTO. If the electronic acknowledgment receipt is to be relied upon as proof of a filing, it must include the correct description and indexing of the documents filed. Support staff should carefully review the electronic acknowledgment receipt when the filing is completed to ensure that all documents are accounted for.

For follow-on documents filed in a patent application or reexamination proceeding after an initial filing, the documents are accorded a receipt date as of the date a compliant filing is completed. If a follow-on document is filed within the set period for response as indicated by the USPTO, it will be considered timely filed if submitted via EFS-Web before expiration of the set period. EFS-Web records the date of receipt of documents according to Eastern Standard Time irrespective of where the EFS-Web submitter is located.

Private PAIR Review

When the USPTO receives documents that are submitted in compliance with EFS-Web filing requirements, the PDF documents are converted into tagged image file format (TIFF) images and made of official record in the IFW. If color or gray-scale drawings are filed, they are stored in the supplemental complex repository for examiners (SCORE). Sequence listings or computer programs that are submitted as ASCII text files are also stored in the SCORE system. Fee transmittal and electronic acknowledgment receipts, which are EFS-Web interface-generated documents, are also stored as TIFF images.

In addition to the careful review of the post-filing electronic acknowledgment receipt, EFS-Web users should review the document posted in the IFW, accessible through private PAIR. EFS-Web users should confirm that all documents filed are accounted for, complete, and posted to the correct application number. If drawings were filed, the resolution of the PDF document in the IFW should be reviewed to ensure all content is captured and no technical distortion has occurred on file conversion.

Inadvertent Omissions

One of the primary advantages of electronically filing an application via EFS-Web as a registered user is the ability to view the submission in private PAIR relatively soon after completing a filing. In situations when, on review of the completed submission in the IFW, an applicant notes the inadvertent omission of a filing document, a corrective filing can be submitted up to midnight (EST) on the same day, and the USPTO will consider it part of the original filing. The following examples provide insight on the potential implications and corrective actions available for inadvertently omitted documents:

- Inventor Oath or Declaration: Applicant may file an executed oath or declaration as a follow-on submission on the same day as the application filing date, and the oath or declaration will be considered timely filed and not subject to late-filing surcharge fees.
- Filing Fees: Applicant may file the filing fees (e.g., the basic filing fee, search and examination fees, application size fee, or excess claim fee) as a follow-on submission document on the same day as the application filing date, and the fees will be considered timely filed and not subject to late-payment surcharge fees.
- Non-Publication Request: Applicant must file any intended non-publication request with the application; inadvertent omission of this document from the original application filing cannot be corrected by a follow-on submission via EFS on the same day. If applicant does not wish to have the original application published, the following actions must be taken:
    - file a new application with a non-publication request;
    - and immediately file a petition for express abandonment to avoid its publication under 37 C.F.R. §1.138 (c), including the associated fee in the initial application filed. The petition must be reviewed in sufficient time to allow it to be recognized and acted on by removing the application from the eighteen-month publication queue.
- Drawings: Applicant may file the missing drawings as a preliminary amendment follow-on submission on the same day as the application filing. The drawings will be considered part of the original disclosure of the application. This procedure can also be used to correct a situation where the wrong drawings were filed with the original application filing. An amendment adding new drawings and deleting the wrong drawings filed after the filing date of the application may raise new matter issues.
- Claims: Applicant may file claims as a preliminary amendment as a follow-on submission on the same day as the application filing. Such claims will be considered as part of the original disclosure of the application. To be accorded a filing date, nonprovisional applications filed must contain at least one claim.
- Parts of the Specification: Applicant may file the missing part of the written description as a preliminary amendment as a follow-on submission on the same day as the application filing. Amendments adding content to the written description section of the specification will be considered part of the original disclosure.

Legal Consequences of Twenty-Four-Hour Availability of EFS-Web

Given that EFS-Web is available twenty-four hours a day, an applicant can technically file applications seven days per week, including weekends and federal holidays, within the District of Columbia. When the last day for filing a response or paying a fee falls on a Saturday, Sunday or federal holiday within the District of Columbia, the next-business-day rule applies. The response or fee payment will be considered timely filed on the next succeeding business day.

If the twelve-month convention filing date of a provisional application falls on a Saturday, Sunday, or federal holiday within the District of Columbia, the period of pendency of the provisional application will be considered extended to the next business day. However, applicants should be aware of Article 4 of the Paris Convention, which controls priority filing dates for foreign jurisdictions and stipulates the following:

> If the last day of the period is an official holiday or a day when the Patent Office is not open to accept filings in the country where protection is claimed, the period shall be extended until the first following working day.

As EFS-Web system is available twenty-four hours a day, seven days per week, technically the first following working day for electronic filings would be the next business day even if it fell on a Saturday, Sunday, or federal holiday in the District of Columbia. As a result of this interpretation of the Paris Convention priority period definition, an applicant could potentially face adverse consequences regarding the determination of priority periods when filing international applications with the United States Receiving Office (USRO) under the Paris Convention. Specifically, the implication that EFS-Web is available for filings twenty-four hours a day, seven days a week, may result in loss of priority rights in foreign jurisdictions designating an international application filed with the USRO. A foreign patent office may deny the priority claim on the basis that the international application was not timely filed with the USRO. For this reason, it is prudent that applicants do not rely on the next-business-day rule when filing an international application with the USRO. Such international applications should be filed with the USRO before expiration of the twelve-month Paris Convention date.

EFS-Web Availability

The hours of operation of EFS-Web are clearly indicated when users log on to the system. The USPTO will post advance notifications of any scheduled EFS-Web downtime required for system maintenance. EFS-Web users may file patent documents electronically during the hours of operation of EFS-Web every day of the week, including weekends. If a submission is attempted during EFS-Web downtime, the interface should notify the user that electronic filings cannot be completed at this time and advise the user to consider other filing methods.

If EFS-Web is unavailable during an unscheduled outage, the USPTO will post a notification of the primary portal and provide a link to an EFS-Web contingency option on the EFS-Web Internet page. The EFS-Web contingency option will only permit users to electronically file new applications, national stage submissions, and requests for reexamination accompanied by only the basic filing fee. In addition, a limited number of petitions (petition to make special based on age, petition to accept an unintentional delay in payment of a maintenance fee, petition to make special under the accelerated examination program) can be filed via the EFS-Web contingency option. Other follow-on documents and fee payments cannot be filed via the EFS-Web contingency option. Submissions made via the EFS-Web contingency option must meet the same file format requirement as EFS-Web and will be subject to the same interface file validation process. If the EFS-Web contingency option is used, the documents filed should not be resubmitted via EFS-Web when its availability is restored. When the primary EFS-Web portal is unavailable, applicants may also file initial applications or reexamination requests via Express Mail or hand-delivery services.

Official Record of E-Filed Submissions

When the USPTO successfully receives PDF documents filed via EFS-Web, they are converted into TIFF image files and stored in the IFW as part of the official record. Color and grayscale drawings are stored in SCORE as part of the official record. Any sequence submissions or computer programs filed as ASCII text files are also stored in SCORE. As a result, the official record for the patent applications and reexamination proceedings may include documents stored in the IFW and SCORE storage locations. The original PDF documents are stored exactly as filed in a separate location.

Paper Based Filing Methods

To accommodate a broad spectrum of individuals who file patent applications and related correspondence, the USPTO offers electronic and paper based filing options. For applicants who have not yet adapted to advances in technology, the USPTO permits filing of papers via facsimile, first-class mail, Express Mail, and hand delivery. In addition, the USPTO permits correspondence requiring expedited processing to be hand-delivered to a customer service window at the USPTO. The submission requirements, advantages, and limitations of paper based filing methods are discussed in more detail in the remainder of this chapter.

Filing by Facsimile

The USPTO has established a centralized facsimile number for receipt of official patent application-related correspondence.

USPTO Central Facsimile Number: (571) 273-8300

Replies to office actions, including after final amendments, that are transmitted by facsimile must be directed to the central facsimile number. Correspondence directed to the examiner's attention, such as drafts of proposed amendments for interviews, should be transmitted by facsimile to the Technology Centers and should be made of record as part of the interview summary record. To improve the processing time for correspondence, the USPTO has established some service-dedicated facsimile numbers, as identified in Table 4.

Table 4: USPTO Dedicated Facsimile Numbers

USPTO Office	Fax Number	Use for
Office of Data Management	(571) 273-2885	Payment of an issue fee and any required publication fee by authorization to charge a deposit account. Can include drawings but may reduce the quality and resolution of the reprinted drawings.
Assignment Branch	(571) 273-0140	Assignments or other documents affecting title.
Office of Petitions	(571) 273-0025	Petitions to withdraw from issue (only).
Office of Finance	(571) 273-6500	Request for refund, deposit account inquiries, and maintenance fee payments.
Electronic Business Center (EBC)	(571) 273-0177	Application for CN and Requests for CN Data Change.

Submissions filed by facsimile provide instantaneous proof of transmission and receipt by the USPTO. The date of receipt accorded to any correspondence filed by facsimile is the date the complete transmission is received by an USPTO facsimile unit unless the transmission is completed on a Saturday, Sunday, or federal holiday within the District of Columbia. Facsimile correspondence received on a Saturday, Sunday, or federal holiday in the District of Columbia will be accorded a receipt date of the next business day. In the event that the USPTO contends that it did not receive the facsimile transmission or challenges if it was timely filed, a record of the successful transmission from the sender's facsimile machine will be required as a proof of timely submission. As a result, it is recommended that transmission reports from the sender's facsimile machine be retained in addition to any PTO-generated auto-reply transmission.

The USPTO recommends that patent-related correspondence that requires immediate attention be sent by facsimile to the Office of Data Management or hand-carried to the appropriate office for processing. Examples of such correspondence are:

- petitions for express abandonment to avoid publication under 37 C.F.R. §1.138(c);
- petitions to withdraw an application from issue under 37 C.F.R. §1.313(c); and
- request for expedited examination of a design application (rocket docket).

Submissions Prohibited by Facsimile

The following papers cannot be filed by facsimile:

- documents that are required by statute to be certified;
- provisional or non-provisional initial application filing or other correspondence filed to obtain an application filing date;
- color drawings;
- correspondence in interference proceedings, including agreement between parties and correspondence before the Board;
- correspondence to be filed in a patent application subject to a secrecy order;
- U.S. National (371) application filing with accompanying payment of basis filing fee; and
- request for reexamination.

Filing by First-Class Mail

The USPTO has the following general mailing address for correspondence in patent-related matters:

Commissioner for Patents
P. O. Box 1450
Alexandria, Virginia 22313-1450

Mail Stop Addresses

USPTO has established special Mail Stop addresses to expedite the routing and forwarding of particular types of mail to the appropriate personnel. A list of approved mail stops is published weekly in the Official Gazette. Only the correspondence to be directed to a given Mail Stop address should be included in the addressed envelope; including documents not specified will significantly delay their processing. Where a Mail Stop address is applicable, it should be used in combination with the main Director address indicated below. The most commonly used USPTO Mail Stop addresses are as follows:

- Mail Stop Assignment Recordation Services: for documents sent to the Assignment Division for recordation;
- Mail Stop Document Services: for request for certified or uncertified copies of patent documents; and
- Mail Stop Issue Fee: for post allowance correspondence (except petitions to withdraw from issue).

The USPTO has expressed a preference that applicants include the applicable Mail Stop address in correspondence filed electronically to enable Office staff to quickly determine where the correspondence should be sent for further processing. For most correspondence (e.g., new patent applications), no mail stop is required because the processing of the correspondence is routine. Some noteworthy fee-based addresses include the following:

A payment to replenish a Deposit Account must be mailed to:

Director of United States Patent and Trademark Office
Attn: Deposit Accounts
2051 Jamieson Avenue
Suite 300
Alexandria, VA 22314

Maintenance fee payments must be mailed to:

Director of United States Patent and Trademark Office
Attn: Maintenance Fees
2051 Jamieson Avenue
Suite 300
Alexandria, VA 22314

For any correspondence for which there is no specified address, the following USPTO Director based mailing address should be used:

Director of United States Patent and Trademark Office
P. O. Box 1450
Alexandria, VA 22313-1450

Return Receipt Postcard

All correspondence filed by mail should be accompanied by a self-addressed, postage-affixed, return receipt postcard itemizing documents submitted. If a postage meter is used on the postcard, the meter postmark should not show the date. The United States Postal Service (USPS) will not deliver a return receipt postcard containing a dated meter postmark. The USPTO will stamp the receipt date on the postcard and place it in the outgoing mail. A postcard receipt that itemized and properly identifies the items filed can serve as evidence of receipt in the USPTO of all the items listed thereon. Identifying information on the postcard should include the applicant's name, applicant number (if known), filing date, title of the invention, and the types of papers submitted, including the number of pages per document. For an initial application filing, pages of the specification, number of claims, and number of sheets of drawings should be indicated. In addition, the number of pages of any declaration included should be indicated. The stamped post card receipt will not serve of evidence of receipt of any item that is not adequately itemized on the postcard.

The USPTO employee receiving the filed papers will check the listing on the postcard against the paper documents filed to ensure they are properly identified and that all items listed on the postcard are present. If any of the items listed on the postcard were not received, those items will be crossed off and the postcard will be initialed by the employee receiving the papers. Upon receipt of the return postcard from the USPTO, support staff should promptly review the stamped postcard to ensure that every item specifically denoted as filed was received by the USPTO. If a postcard is annotated by a USPTO employee to indicate that an item was not received, the postcard will not serve as evidence of receipt of that item by the USPTO. For initial application filings, an employee of the Office of Patent Application Processing Unit will assign an application number and filing date sticker to the return receipt postcard prior to placing it in the outgoing mail.

Filing by Express Mail

Correspondence filed by Express Mail must be under the USPS post office. This service requires the use of a mailing label (with a unique number) that clearly indicates the date on which the particular Express Mail package was deposited with the USPS Express Mail packages should be addressed to:

U.S. Patent and Trademark Office
P. O. Box 1453
Alexandria, VA 223136-01450

Express Mail Label

Correspondence filed by Express Mail should be handed over the counter to a USPS employee, who should complete the Express Mail label by clearly indicating the "date-in." If an applicant has to later file a petition to correct an assigned filing, a copy of the Express Mail label clearly indicating the "date-in" and stamped by the USPS will be required as evidentiary proof of the filing date. The USPTO discourages the use of the Express Mail drop box, where the Express Mail label cannot be completed by a USPS employee in possession of the Express Mail package deposit. To be effective as a reliable proof of the date of filing, the Express Mail label number should be placed on each separate paper and each fee transmittal; it should be either directly adhered to the first page of each document or included as a separate paper securely attached to the documents filed, with an itemized list of contents. Placing the Express Mail label on the front sheet of each separate document filed will be considered sufficient proof that such documents were all part of the original application filing.

Petitions Related to Express Mail Filing Date

Where there is a discrepancy between the filing date accorded by the USPTO and the "date-in" entered by the USPS on the Express Mail label, the applicant can petition to have the filing date corrected. Table 5 summarizes the distinct situations that may occur with respect to Express Mail related filing dates, including the petition and showings required to resolve any discrepancies. In general, a showing must be corroborated by evidence from the USPS or evidence that came into being after deposit and within one business day of the deposit of the correspondence as Express Mail. Evidence from the USPS may be in the form of a statement from the Express Mail corporate account showing a charge for an Express Mail deposit on the date of interest. Evidence that came into being one day after the deposit of the correspondence as Express Mail may be in the form of an Express Mail log book that is used to record daily Express Mail filings and tracks the Express Mail label number, the attorney docket number, the place, time, and initials of the individual who deposited the Express Mail with the USPS, and the date, time, and initials of the individual completing the entry into the log. Such petitions cannot be used if Express Mail correspondence was returned by the USPS due to an incorrect address or insufficient payment of the fee for Express Mail service.

Table 5: Petitions Related to Express Mail Filing Date

Petition	Filed Under	Filing Requirements
Petition to Correct Filing Date and Date-In Discrepancy	37 C.F.R. §1.10(c)	Petition must be promptly filed as soon as applicant becomes aware of the discrepancy; ▪ include a showing that the Express Mail label number was placed on each piece of correspondence prior to the original mailing; and ▪ include a true copy of the Express Mail mailing label showing the "date-in" or other official notation of the USPS.
Petition to Correct Incorrectly Entered Date-In	37 C.F.R. §1.10(d)	Petition must be promptly filed as soon as applicant becomes aware that the USPTO has accorded, or will accord, a filing date based on the incorrect entry by the USPS; ▪ include a showing that the Express Mail label number was placed on each piece of correspondence prior to the original mailing; and ▪ include a showing that the correspondence was deposited as Express Mail on the requested filing deadline.

Petition for Correspondence Never Received	37 C.F.R. §1.10(e)	Petition must be promptly filed after the applicant becomes aware that the USPTO has no evidence of receipt of the correspondence; ▪ include a showing that the Express Mail label number was placed on each piece of correspondence prior to the original mailing; ▪ include a true copy of the originally deposited correspondence showing the Express Mail label number thereon, a copy of any returned postcard receipt, and a copy of the Express Mail mailing label showing the "date-in" or other official notification of the USPS; and ▪ include a statement signed by the person who deposited the documents as Express Mail with the USPS indicating the date and time of the deposit and declaring that the copies of the correspondence, Express Mail label, and return receipt postcard accompanying the petition are true copies.
Petition for Correspondence *Returned* Due to Postal Interruptions or Emergency	37 C.F.R. §1.10(g)	Petition must be promptly filed after applicant becomes aware of the return of the correspondence; ▪ include a showing that the Express Mail label number was placed on each piece of correspondence prior to the original filing; ▪ include a copy of the original correspondence showing the Express Mail mailing label number and a copy of the Express Mail mailing label showing the "date-in"; and ▪ include a statement that establishes that the copy of the original correspondence is a true copy of the correspondence deposited with the USPS on the requested filing date. The USPTO may require a letter from the USPS confirming that the return was due to an interruption or emergency in the Express Mail service.

Petition for Correspondence *Refused* Due to Postal Interruption or Emergency	37 C.F.R. §1.10(h)	Petition must be promptly filed after applicant becomes aware of the refusal of the correspondence; ▪ include a showing that the Express Mail mailing label number was placed on each piece of correspondence prior to the original mailing; ▪ include a copy of the original correspondence showing the Express Mail label number thereon; and ▪ include a statement by the person who originally attempted to deposit the correspondence with the USPS that establishes that the copy of the correspondence provided is a true copy of the correspondence deposited with the USPS on the requested filing date. The USPTO may require a letter from the USPS confirming that the refusal was due to an interruption or emergency in the Express Mail service.
Petition for Correspondence Unable to be Deposited due to Director-Designated Postal Interruption or Emergency	37 C.F.R. §1.10(i)	Petition must be promptly filed after the applicant becomes aware of the notice of a Director-designated interruption or emergency in the Express Mail service; ▪ include a copy of the original correspondence; ▪ include a statement that the correspondence would have been deposited with the USPTO but for the designated interruption or emergency in the Express Mail service and that the copy of the correspondence provided is a true copy of the original correspondence attempted to be deposited with the USPS on the requested filing date.

Official Stamp Date of USPTO

The USPTO stamps papers and fees filed by first-class mail with an official date stamp, which is the date of receipt of the papers by the USPTO. New patent applications filed in accordance with Express Mail submission requirements will be stamped by the USPTO with the date of deposit with the United States postal service Express Mail system as evidenced by the "date-in" stamp, as completed by a member of the USPS counter staff. For correspondence submitted via EFS-Web, the USPTO provides an electronic acknowledgment receipt date as the date and time the submission was electronically filed. For documents hand delivered to the USPTO Customer Service

Window, the official stamp date will be the date the application papers were accepted at the Customer Service Window.

Postal Service Interruptions and Emergencies

In the event of a postal interruption or emergency, an announcement will be placed on the USPTO's website, and a notice will be published in the Official Gazette providing instructions about the filing of patent applications and other related correspondence. Such provisions permit an applicant to petition the Director to have correspondence, which was unable to be deposited by mail or Express Mail with the USPS, as having been filed on a particular date in the USPTO. For petition provisions to apply, the Director must declare a status of postal interruptions and emergencies. Petitions related to postal interruptions and emergencies must include proof that the correspondence was ready to be deposited or filed as of the deadline date and would have been timely filed but for the impact of the declared postal interruption of emergency. In such situations, where use of first-class or Express Mail may be unavailable, applicants should resort to facsimile or electronic filing with signed and dated certification of facsimile or electronic filing. If facsimile filing is the only option available, and the intended submission cannot be filed by facsimile or facsimile certification is not acceptable as proof of timely submission, the applicant may file a precautionary request for continued examination in a pending application. New application filings should be filed by Express Mail to be accorded the filing date of the date of deposit with the U.S. Postal Service as evidenced by the "date-in" notations on the Express Mail label. New application filings cannot benefit from first-class mailing certifications and should not be filed by first-class mail.

Filing by Hand Delivery

Office papers related to any pending application cannot be personally delivered to the assigned Technology Center unless subject to a secrecy order or national security classified. Patent-related papers may be hand carried to the USPTO, such papers must be delivered to:

Customer Service Window
Randolph Building
401 Dulany Street
Alexandria, VA 22314

The USPTO has established locations for hand delivering specific types of correspondence. All hand deliveries should be preceded by a call to the respective office confirming its hand delivery requirements, including any building security registration requirements. The USPTO provides specific hand delivery instructions as follows:

- Requests for access to published patent application files may be hand-carried to the File Information Unit (FIU), Randolph Square, 3rd Floor, 2800 South Randolph Street, Arlington VA 22206.
- Requests for access to unpublished IFWs, including a power to inspect and copy, may be hand carried to Public Search Facility, 1st Floor, Madison East Building, 600 Dulany Street, Alexandria, VA 22314.
- Requests for Patent Term Extensions under 35 U.S.C. §156 may be hand carried to the Office of Patent Legal Administration (OPLA), Room 07D85, Madison West Building, 600 Dulany Street, Alexandria, VA 22314.
- Requests for recordation of assignments may be hand carried to the Office of Public Records Customer Service Window, Randolph Square, 3rd Floor, 2800 South Randolph Street, Arlington VA 22206.
- Correspondence related to applications subject to Secrecy Order under 35 U.S.C. 181 or national security classified may be hand carried to Licensing and Review, Room 4B31, Knox Building, 501 Dulany Street, Alexandria, VA, 22314.
- Petitions for Expedited Foreign Filing License under 37 C.F.R. §5.12(b), including petitions for retroactive license 37 C.F.R. §5.25, may be hand carried to a drop box located in the Knox Building, 501 Dulany Street, Alexandria, VA, 22314.
- Petitions to Withdraw from Issue may be hand carried to the Office of Petitions, 7th Floor, Madison West Building, 600 Dulany Street, Alexandria, VA, 22314.

Handling of Papers by the USPTO

When a patent application is received at the USPTO, the office conducts an administrative review to determine compliance with requirements for form, content, adequacy, and payment of appropriate fees. If the application was filed by a paper-based method, the USPTO must convert the paper documents into electronic images for loading into its electronic system. When initial data capture is complete, the application is managed electronically, including assignment of the official filing date and application serial number, and inputting the patent bibliographic data (e.g., filling date, priority date, abstract) in PALM system. A summary of the pre-examination to post-examination handling of papers by the USPTO is shown in Figure C.

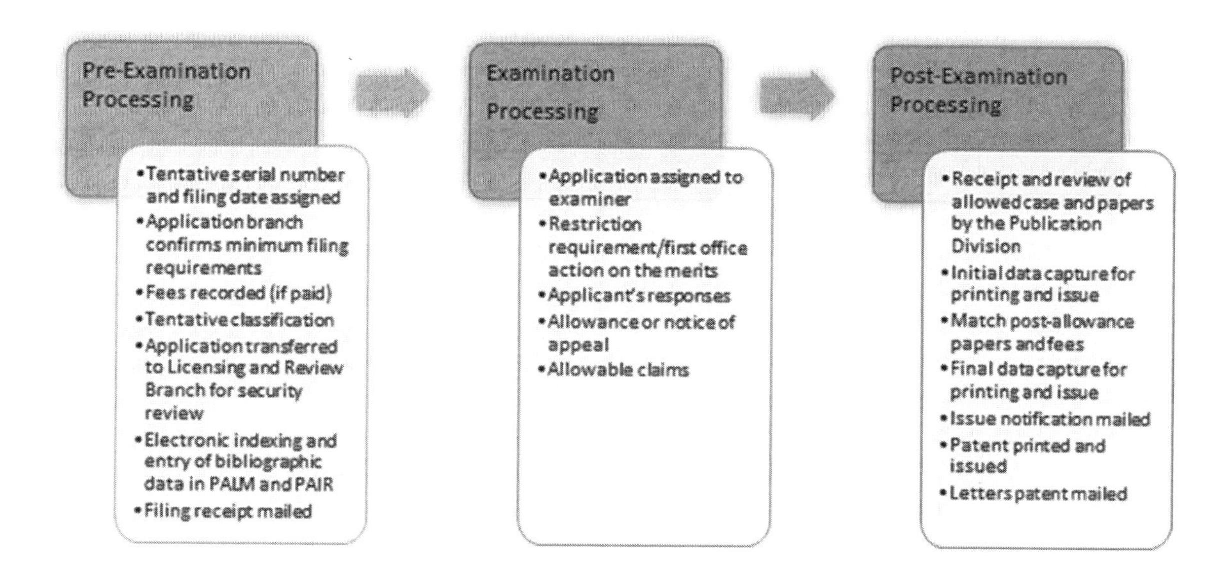

Figure C: Handling of Papers by the USPTO

Electronic Correspondence from USPTO

The electronic patent filing systems of the USPTO are designed to increase the efficiency of processing a high volume of communication. To maintain consistency with the e-filing submission system used by applicants, the USPTO has a system for sending electronic communications to applicants. The e-Office Action program is designed to be compatible with the existing electronic formatting requirements for documents submitted to the USPTO and gives registered e-filers a greater sense of control over how they receive communications from the USPTO.

E-Office Action Program

The e-Office action program is designed to notify applicants, via e-mail, that a new Office communication is available for viewing and downloading in private PAIR. Applicants who opt in to the program will receive a daily e-mail notification that will replace the postal mailing of an Office communication. Program participation is optional and is based on patent applications that are associated to a CN.

The e-Office action program provides efficiency benefits to applicants; new communications from the USPTO can be received several days faster than by postal mail, and any risks associated with delayed or lost postal mail are eliminated. The ability to download the correspondence from PAIR expedites the availability of documents for capture in a central docketing system and for subsequent reporting to a client.

The e-Office action program accommodates up to three e-mail addresses to receive e-mail notifications to ensure that recipients at difference locations can receive simultaneous notifications. E-mail notifications are sent daily, including weekends, and the system includes the ability to receive a reminder postcard when none of the new Office correspondence has been viewed within seven calendar days after receipt of the initial e-mail notification, and at least one of the communications requires an applicant's reply.

Applicants can enroll in the e-Office action program by viewing the details of the CN, and under the "request an update screen," selecting the option to "Receive Correspondence Notifications via e-Mail" in the customer details section of the CN screen. At least one e-mail address must be entered, and a test e-mail will be sent to each e-mail address entered. Documents issued through the e-Office action program have document codes found in the IFW. The Office provides a table listing of the document description for each IFW document code on the website http://www.uspto.gov/patents/process/status/e-Office_Action.jsp). Documents can be downloaded in PDF or XML format. All recipients of the e-mail notifications should add the "USPTO.gov" domain to the white list in their e-mail filtering program to allow e-Office action notification messages to be received.

When applicants have opted into the e-Office action program, they can choose to opt out at any time and revert to receiving Office communications via postal mail. If opting out of the program, it is important that at least one e-mail address is left in private PAIR for at least fifteen days to ensure documents in process get to the correct destination.

Paper Based Correspondence from the USPTO

The USPTO sends communication to the correspondence address of record in the application or patent. Applicants who have a CN can select how they wish to receive correspondence from the USPTO. All CNs default to receiving correspondence by mail to the associated correspondence address. When an applicant has a CN associated with an application, it is used to populate an associated mailing address for the applicant.

CHAPTER-SPECIFIC REFERENCE MATERIAL

Reference Source	Filing Methods and Handling of Papers by the USPTO Applicable Rules, Regulations, and Procedures
USPTO Website Guides	Electronic Business Center http://www.uspto.gov/patents/ebc/about.jsp Private PAIR Quick Start Guide Customer Number Details http://www.uspto.gov/patents/process/status/private_pair/customerdetails-v2_09_07_07.pdf E-Office Action Program Quick Start Guide http://www.uspto.gov/patents/process/status/private_pair/e-oa_quick_start_guide.pdf About EFS-Web http://www.uspto.gov/patents/process/file/efs/index.jsp EFS-Web Guidance and Resources http://www.uspto.gov/patents/process/file/efs/guidance/index.jsp PDF Fillable Forms http://www.uspto.gov/patents/process/file/efs/guidance/Form_fillable_pdfs_available.jsp Document Indexing http://www.uspto.gov/ebc/portal/efs/rules_doc_codes.htm
	E-Petitions http://www.uspto.gov/patents/process/file/efs/guidance/epetition-quickstart.pdf
AIA Frequently Asked Questions	Electronic Filing Incentive Micro Entities http://www.uspto.gov/aia/implementation/faq.jsp

Title 37 of the Code of Federal Regulations	37 C.F.R. §1.4 Nature of correspondence and signature requirements. §1.5 Identification of patent, patent application, or patent-related proceeding. §1.6 Receipt of correspondence. §1.7 Times for taking action; Expiration on Saturday, Sunday, or Federal holiday. §1.8 Certificate of mailing or transmission. §1.9 Definitions. *§1.10 Filing of papers and fees by Express Mail.*
Manual of Patent Examination Procedures (MPEP, 8th Edition)	Chapter 500 Receipt and Handling of Mail and Papers

Chapter 4

Representative Capacity and Power of Attorney

Representation Before the USPTO

An applicant for a patent may file and prosecute his or her own application acting on his or her own behalf before the USPTO. If patentable subject matter is disclosed in a pro se (filed by the inventor on his or her own behalf) application, and it is apparent that the applicant is unfamiliar with the application preparation and prosecution procedures, the USPTO may suggest to the applicant to employ a registered patent agent or attorney. However, the USPTO cannot aid in the selection of a patent agent or attorney. An applicant may give power of attorney to one or more patent practitioners or joint inventors to act in a representative capacity on his or her behalf before the USPTO.

Acting in a Representative Capacity

A registered patent attorney or agent who is not of record with direct power of attorney in an application can sign applicant replies in a representative capacity. When acting in a representative capacity, the registered patent attorney or agent must include his or her name and registration number with his or her signature. The ability of a registered patent attorney or patent agent to act in a representative capacity obviates the need for filing a power of attorney in each individual application or patent when there are changes in the composition of law firms or corporate patent department legal staff. Examiner interviews with a registered attorney or agent not of record will be conducted only on the basis of information and files supplied by the attorney or agent. A person acting in a representative capacity cannot sign the following documents:

- a power of attorney;
- a document granting access to an application (except where an executed oath or declaration has not been filed, and the patent practitioner was named in the papers accompanying the application filing);
- a terminal disclaimer; or
- a request for an express abandonment without filing a continuing application.

There is no limit to the number of practitioners who may be given an authorization to act in a representative capacity. Practitioners who are authorized to act in a representative capacity are not entered into the Office's computer system and are not considered an attorney or agent of record.

Power of Attorney

A power of attorney is a written document by which a principal authorizes one or more patent practitioners or joint inventors to act on his or her behalf. A principal may be either an applicant for patent or an assignee of entire interest of the applicant for patent or, in a reexamination proceeding, the assignee of the entirety of ownership of a patent. The principal executes a power of attorney designating one or more patent practitioners or joint inventors to act on his or her behalf.

Pre-AIAContent Requirements

Pre-AIA power of attorney practice under 37 C.F.R. §1.32, requires that a power of attorney naming firms of attorneys or agents filed in patent applications will not be recognized. A power of attorney that names more than ten patent practitioners will only be entered if CN practice is used or if such power of attorney is accompanied by a separate paper indicating which ten patent practitioners named in the power of attorney are to be recognized by the Office as being of record in the application or patent. If a power of attorney is not entered because more than ten patent practitioners were named, a copy of the power of attorney should be refiled. Where a power of attorney is given to ten or fewer patent practitioners, the name and registration number of each patent practitioner must be stated in the power of attorney. If the name submitted on the power of attorney does not match the name associated with the registration number from the USPTO roster of registered practitioners, the person that the Office will recognize as being of record will be the person associated with the registration number provided, because the Office enters the registration number, not the name, when making the practitioner of record. Accordingly, if the wrong registration number is provided, a new power of attorney will be required to correct the error. For a power of attorney to be valid, the attorney or agent appointed must be registered to practice before the USPTO. Any power of attorney given to a practitioner who has been suspended or disbarred by the Office is ineffective and does not authorize the person to practice before the Office or to represent applicants or patentees in patent matters.

AIA Content Requirements

Under the AIA, an applicant for patent may file and prosecute the applicant's own case, or the applicant may give power of attorney to be represented by one or more practitioners or joint inventors, except that a juristic entity (organizational assignee) must be represented by a patent practitioner. An applicant can be the principal that signs a power of attorney for an application or patent, including a patent is a supplemental examination or reexamination proceeding. An applicant can also sign a revocation of power of attorney. AIA amended §1.32(b) to provide that a power of attorney

- must: be in writing;
- name one or more representatives;
- give the representative power to act on behalf of the principal; and
- be signed by the applicant for patent or the patent owner.

This provision applies to reissue applications, supplemental examination proceedings, and reexamination proceedings. A patent owner who is not the applicant must appoint a power of attorney that applies to reissue applications, supplemental examination proceedings, and reexamination proceedings.

The AIA permits the carryover of a power of attorney in continuing applications where no inventors are being added in the continuing application. A copy of the power of attorney from the prior application must be filed in the continuing application unless:

- the power of attorney was granted by the inventor; and
- the continuing application names an inventor who was not named as an inventor in the prior application.

If the power of attorney was granted by the originally named inventive entity and an added inventor does not provide a power of attorney consistent with the one granted, the addition of the inventor results in the loss of power of attorney.

A copy of the power of attorney must be filed in the continuing application, as doing so will force a review with respect to any change in power of attorney in the prior application, and will make the record clear with respect to who has power of attorney. The assignee may become the applicant and revoke any previous power of attorney granted.

Power of Attorney and Correspondence Address

Under the AIA, if an applicant provided more than one correspondence address (in a single paper or different papers in the same submission), the Office will select one of the specified addresses to use as the correspondence and will select the correspondence address associated with a customer number (CN) over a typed correspondence address. This change forces an applicant to review his or her submission carefully to ensure that the USPTO receives clear instructions regarding the correspondence address.

The correspondence address may be changed by the practitioner of record or the applicant. Prior to the appointment of any power of attorney, the correspondence address may be changed by any practitioner named in the application transmittal papers who acts in a representative capacity.

For applications filed on or before September 16, 2012, where a copy of an inventor's oath or declaration from a prior application is filed with a continuing application and the correspondence address was changed during prosecution of the prior application, an ADS or separate paper identifying the correspondence address to be used for the continuing application must be submitted.

A practitioner acting in a representative capacity may change the correspondence address after a patent has issued, provided that the change of correspondence address is accompanied by a statement that notice has been given to the patentee or owner.

Power of Attorney Forms

The USPTO has multiple forms related to revocation and appointment of power of attorney, some of which include a change of correspondence address.

Pre-AIA Forms

For applications filed before September 16, 2012, pre-AIA power of attorney requirements under 37 C.F.R. §1.32 apply. The power of attorney must be in writing and be signed by the applicant or the assignee of the entire interest of the applicant. The power of attorney may appoint one or more joint inventors, up to ten registered practitioners, or practitioners associated with a CN. The CN is used to propagate the correspondence address of record. The pre-AIA power of attorney and correspondence address-related forms and their respective uses are summarized in Table 6.

Table 6: Pre-AIA Power of Attorney and Correspondence Address-Related Forms (For aplications filed before September 16, 2012)		
Form No.	Form Description	Use Guidelines
SB/80	Power of Attorney to Prosecute Applications before the USPTO	Use when the assignee is giving power of attorney to registered practitioners (either by individual names or to all registered practitioners associated with a CN) for all applications assigned to the assignee and when individual patent application numbers are not indicated. Master power of attorney can be signed by the assignee of record of the entire interest when accompanied by a Statement under 37 C.F.R. §3.73(b). After execution of a single SB/80 form by the assignee, a copy of the executed SB/80 form, together with a Statement under 37 C.F.R. 3.73(b) (form SB/96 form), which identifies one specific patent application (which may be executed by a practitioner if the practitioner is authorized to act on behalf of the assignee), may be filed in the one specific application to establish a power of attorney for the registered practitioners in that specific application.
SB/81	Power of Attorney or Revocation of Power of Attorney with a New Power of Attorney and Change of Correspondence Address for a Pending Application	Use to revoke existing power of attorney and appoint new power of attorney or to appoint a list of practitioners or all practitioners associated with a CN, including a change of correspondence address to the address associated with a CN or a firm or individual. SB/81 can be signed by the applicant/inventor or the assignee of record of the entire interest when accompanied by a Statement under 37 C.F.R. §3.73(b).

SB/81A	Power of Attorney or Revocation of Power of Attorney with a New Power of Attorney and Change of Correspondence Address for an Issued Patent	Use to revoke existing power of attorney and appoint new power of attorney or to appoint a list of practitioners or all practitioners associated with a CN, including a change of correspondence address to the address associated with a CN or a firm or individual. SB/81A can be signed by the patentee or the assignee of record of the entire interest when accompanied by a Statement under 37 C.F.R. §3.73(b). This form will not affect any maintenance fee address of record for the patent.
SB/82	Revocation of Power of Attorney with New Power of Attorney and Change of Correspondence Address	Use to revoke existing power of attorney and appoint new power of attorney and change correspondence address. Available in Chinese, German, Spanish, French, Italian, Japanese, Korean, Dutch, Russian, and Swedish language. SB/82 can be signed by the applicant/inventor or the assignee of record of the entire interest when accompanied by a Statement under 37 C.F.R. §3.73(b).
SB/83	Request for Withdrawal as Attorney or Agent and Change of Correspondence Address	Use to withdraw individual attorney or agent of record or all practitioners of record or practitioners listed on form or practitioners associated with a CN. Must provide a reason for withdrawal and a certification that the attorney or agent of record has given reasonable notice to the client prior to expiration of the response deadline of intention to withdraw or that all related papers and funds have been delivered to the client or the authorized representative, including identifying any responses that may be due and the time period for response. Must provide a correspondence address associated with a CN or mailing address for the client or the authorized representative. SB/83 can be signed by an attorney or agent of record.

SB/122	Change of Correspondence Address for a Pending Application	Use to change the correspondence of an individual application to the address associated with the CN. SB/122 can be signed by the applicant/inventor, the assignee of record of the entire interest when accompanied by a Statement under 37 C.F.R. §3.73(b), attorney or agent of record, or registered practitioner named on application transmittal where a signed oath or declaration has not yet been filed.
SB/123	Change of Correspondence Address for an Issued Patent	Use to change the correspondence of a patent to the address associated with the CN. SB/123 can be signed by the patentee, assignee of record of the entire interest when accompanied by a Statement under 37 C.F.R. §3.73(b), or the attorney or agent of record.

For a pre-AIA application filed before September 16, 2012, where there are one or more inventors, where there is no assignment, form SB/81A should be signed by the inventors. Form SB/80 can be used for an application. If the pre-AIA application contains one or more inventors, with an assignment, but the assignee does not want to be listed as the applicant, form SB/81A and a Statement under §3.73(b) signed by the assignee should be used. Form SB/80 can be used for an application.

If a U.S. national phase application is filed off a PCT application having an international filing date before September 16, 2012, then the power of attorney for the U.S. national phase application should be treated as though the application were filed before September 16, 2012, and pre-AIA forms apply.

AIA Forms

For applications filed on or after September 16, 2012, the power of attorney filed must be signed by the applicant for patent or the patent owner. The AIA power of attorney forms account for the expanded category of entities that may file a patent application, including inventors, non-inventor owners (assignees), or an individual or juristic organization that shows sufficient proprietary interest. When an assignee is named as the applicant in the patent application as indicated on a signed application data sheet (ADS) accompanying the initial filing papers, then the assignee-applicant can give power of attorney using the form AIA/82. The AIA power of attorney and correspondence address-related forms and their respective uses are summarized in Table 7.

Table 7: AIA Power of Attorney and Correspondence Address-Related Forms (For applications filed on or after September 16, 2012)

Form No.	Form Description	Use Guidelines
AIA/80	Power of Attorney to Prosecute Applications Before the USPTO	For use by assignees who want to become the applicant and appoint a power of attorney. This form may also be used by assignee-applicants who were named as the applicant when the application was filed. Form AIA/80 must be accompanied by a Statement under 37 C.F.R. §3.73(c). The form is styled like a general power of attorney and does not identify a specific patent application. An assignee who is not the applicant may sign a power of attorney only if the assignee becomes the applicant per C.F.R. §1.46(c), as the power of attorney must be signed by the applicant for patent. The power of attorney must be signed by someone who is authorized to act on behalf of the assignee-applicant (i.e., a person with a title that carries apparent authority or a person who includes a statement of authorization to act). A patent practitioner is not authorized to act on behalf of an assignee simply by existence of authority to prosecute an application. However, where an assignee gives the practitioner specific authority to act on behalf of the assignee (e.g., authority given by organizational resolution), a practitioner may sign the AIA/80 on behalf of the assignee.

AIA/81	Power of Attorney to One or More of the Joint Inventors and Change of Correspondence Address	For use by *pro se* inventors who are the applicants for patent to appoint one or more of the joint inventors as having power of attorney in the application file. *Pro se* means prosecuting the application without a patent practitioner. This power of attorney permits the appointed inventors to sign all correspondence on behalf of all of the inventors. If no power of attorney is given to one or more of the joint inventors, then all of the joint inventors who are the applicant for patent must sign all patent application correspondence filed.
AIA/82 (Part A and B)	Transmittal for Power of Attorney to Prosecute Applications Before the USPTO	For use by the applicant for patent to appoint one or more registered practitioners as having power of attorney in the application file. This form is a two-page form, Part A and B. Part A of this form is used to identify the application to which the power of attorney is directed and must be signed in accordance with 37 C.F.R. §1.33(b) (e.g., a patent practitioner). For example, an inventor who is named as the applicant could sign both pages of the form, or the inventor could sign only Part B of the form and the patent practitioner could complete and sign Part A of the form. Part B of this form is the power of attorney. The correspondence address may also be specified on this form. Where there are multiple applicant parties, a power of attorney signed by each party must be submitted. Power of attorney may only be given by the applicant for patent (e.g., if the applicant for patent is the assignee, the inventors may not give power of attorney). If desired, Part B may be executed once by the applicant, and copies could be used for submission to the Office. Then, Part A of the form could be completed and signed by a patent practitioner and filed with a copy of Part B into each respective application for which power is being given.

		Part B of this form must be filed together with Part A or an equivalent (e.g., signed transmittal letter) to identify the application to which the power is directed.
PTO AIA/122	Change of Correspondence Address for Pending Application	Can be used to change the correspondence address in a pending application. The correspondence address can be changed to an address associated with a CN or to a firm or individual address. The form can be assigned by the applicant, attorney or agent of record, or a registered practitioner named in the application papers who acts in a representative capacity under C.F.R. §1.34.
PTO AIA/123	Change of Correspondence Address for Issued Patent	Can be used to change the correspondence address in an issued patent. The correspondence address can be changed to an address associated with a CN or to a firm or individual address. The form can be signed by the patentee, the attorney or agent of record, or a patent practitioner acting in a representative capacity whose correspondence address is the correspondence address of record, stating that notice has been given to the patentee or owner. This form will not affect any maintenance fee address of record for the patent.

For AIA applications filed on or after September 16, 2013, where there are one or more inventors, and no assignment, the inventors should sign form AIA/82. For AIA applications where there are one or more inventors, but the assignee does not want to be listed as the applicant, the inventors should sign form AIA/82. It should be noted that an assignee that is not an applicant in an AIA application must become the applicant under 37 C.F.R. §1.46(c) in order to revoke or appoint power of attorney. For AIA applications where there are one or more inventors, with an assignment, and the assignee is listed as the applicant at the time of filing, the assignee should sign form AIA/82 (no Statement under 37 C.F.R. §3.73(c) is required). Applicant may also use AIA/82B for multiple applications by the same applicant with a different

AIA/82A form subject to the client's consent. If the power of attorney is being filed after the initial application filing, form AIA/80 and a Statement under 37 C.F.R. §3.73(c) signed by the assignee should be filed.

If a U.S. national phase application is filed off a PCT application having an international filing date on or after September 16, 2012, then the power of attorney for the U.S. national phase application should be treated as though the application were filed on or after September 16, 2012, and AIA forms apply.

Power of Attorney under the AIA – Practice Tips

Applicants should adhere to the following best practices when using filing the power of attorney in applications filed on or after September 16, 2012.

- Ensure the power of attorney contains the assignee name if the assignee is the applicant.
- Ensure that Statement under 37 C.F.R. §3.73 contains the assignee name and reel and frame number.
- The power of attorney must be signed by the applicant (if one exists), if the original ADS does not establish an applicant then the power of attorney must be signed by all of the inventors.
- The applicant of record must be added or changed before a power of attorney by applicant will be accepted and made of record.
- If applicant was not originally named on ADS, a corrected ADS should be filed adding the applicant before filing the executed power of attorney signed by the applicant.

Changing Power of Attorney

If a power of attorney is filed in an application giving power of attorney to a list of patent practitioners and the applicant wishes to appoint practitioners associated with a CN, the applicant or assignee must sign a new power of attorney. If the power of attorney is to be changed to a CN, which may include practitioners in addition to those with an existing power of attorney, or exclude other practitioners who currently have power of attorney, a new power of attorney document must be executed to effect the change.

If an application is filed with a power of attorney naming more than ten practitioners and a separate list naming a subset of ten practitioners to be made of record and applicant wishes to change the subset of practitioners of record, there are two ways to achieve the change. First, the subset of practitioners of record can be changed by filing a new power of attorney naming ten or fewer practitioners or a CN. Any new power of attorney filed will be treated as a revocation of the earlier power of attorney. Second, the applicant can file a copy of the originally filed power of attorney with a new separate paper listing the different subset of practitioners to be made of record. A signature for the correspondence will be required and can be completed by any of the following individuals:

- a practitioner of record (identified in the originally filed power of attorney);
- one of the practitioners named in the new separate paper listing the new practitioners of record;
- a practitioner not of record but acting in a representative capacity;
- the assignee of the entire interest; or
- all of the applicants.

When filing a continuation application, applicant can use a copy of the oath or declaration from the prior application. If the oath or declaration from the parent application names more than ten practitioners or appoints a firm and was executed before the changes to the power of attorney rules then a separate paper listing the ten practitioners to be made of record should be filed. If the separate paper is not filed, no power of attorney will be entered, and the patent practitioners listed on the power of attorney will not be entered.

Revocation of Power of Attorney

Revocation means the cancellation by the principal of the authority previously given to a patent practitioner or joint inventor to act on his or her behalf. An assignee of record of the entire interest can revoke the power of attorney of applicant and can appoint a new power of attorney. A power of attorney by the assignee of the entire interest revokes all powers given by the applicant and prior assignees if the assignees establish their right to take action as provided for in a consent of assignee Statement under 37 C.F.R. §3.73(b). A power of attorney given by the inventors who have signed the declaration may be revoked by an assignee of the entire interest of the available inventors (i.e., the applicant). The assignee of the applicant would sign the power of attorney, and a newly appointed practitioner, having authority to take action on behalf of the assignees, would sign a Statement under 37 C.F.R. §3.73(b), for the application in which the general power of attorney is to be used. Revocation of power of the principal revokes any associated powers granted by him or her to other attorneys. Revocation of power of attorney becomes effective on the date that the revocation is received in the USPTO, not on the date it is accepted.

Appointment by Less than All Applicants or Owners

Papers giving or revoking a power of attorney in an application generally require signatures by all the applicants or owners of the application. Papers revoking or giving a power of attorney in an application will not be accepted by the USPTO when signed by all the applicants or owners unless they are accompanied by a petition under 37 C.F.R. §1.36(a) and a fee under 37 C.F.R. §1.17(f) with a sufficient showing of cause requesting waiver of the requirement. The acceptance of such papers will result in more than one attorney, agent, applicant, or owner prosecuting the application at the same time. Each of the parties must sign all subsequent replies submitted to the USPTO. When an assignee's rights are given by a declaration signed by fewer than all the inventors and a previous non-signing inventor has now joined the application, petition to waive the power of attorney requirement is not required.

When the USPTO accepts papers appointing or revoking a power of attorney that are signed by fewer than all of the applicants or owners, the USPTO will indicate to applicants who must sign subsequent replies. The USPTO will not conduct dual correspondence, and the acceptance of such papers results in one or more applicants or owners prosecuting the application. Correspondence will be mailed to the first named attorney or agent unless all parties agree to a different correspondence address.

Withdrawal from Representation

The USPTO no longer requires at least thirty days between approval of the withdrawal and the next applicant response period to approve the request for withdrawal from the practitioners. The USPTO will not approve a request to withdraw from practitioners who acted in a representative capacity. The USPTO requires that the practitioners certify that they have given reasonable notice to the client, prior to the expiration of the response period, of the intention to withdraw from the representation on the record. All papers and property, including funds to which the client is entitled, must be delivered to the client or a duly authorized representative. The client must be notified of any responses that may be due and the time frame within which the client must respond to avoid abandonment of the application.

The withdrawal is effective when approved by the USPTO rather than when received. The USPTO will no longer accept address changes to a new practitioner, absent a new power of attorney, when processing a request to withdraw. The USPTO will change the correspondence address of record to the assignee of the entire interest who has properly become of record or the first named inventor.

For applications filed on or after September 16, 2012, form AIA/83 can be used to request withdrawal as attorney or agent and change of correspondence address. The form may also be filed as a web-based e-Petition.

Power of Attorney—Practice Tips

The USPTO provides the following practice tips related to power of attorney (USPTO, Patent Practice Tips, 2010):

- Must be in writing; gives the representative power to act on behalf of the principal.
- Must be signed by the applicant for patent or the assignee of the entire interest in the applicant.
- Must name one or more representatives, namely one or more joint inventors, up to ten registered patent attorneys or registered patent agents, or those registered patent practitioners associated with a CN.
- If the power of attorney names more than ten patent practitioners, it must be accompanied by a separate paper indicating which patent practitioners named in power of attorney, up to ten, are to be recognized by the Office as being of record in the application or patent to which power of attorney is directed. If no separate paper is included, no power of attorney will be entered. The separate paper can be signed by one of the attorneys or agents of record, by an attorney or agent acting in a representative capacity, by the assignee, or by all the applicants.
- A filing receipt will only list up to ten patent attorneys or agents regardless of the number of record.
- If multiple powers of attorney are filed, the last-filed power of attorney will be treated as revoking the first-filed.

Death of Practitioner

The power of a principal patent practitioner will be revoked or terminated by his or her death. Such revocation would also extend to any powers of those appointed by the deceased practitioner. If the applicant or assignee notifies the USPTO of the death of the principal practitioner, and the application is up for action by an examiner, correspondence will be sent to the applicant or assignee who appointed the deceased practitioner.

Death of Inventor

If the inventor dies, the death of the inventor terminates the power of attorney given by the deceased inventor. A new power of attorney from the deceased inventor's heirs, administrators, executors, or assignees is necessary if the deceased inventor is the sole inventor or if all powers of attorney in the application have been terminated. Administrators or executors of the deceased inventor must provide proof of their authority to act as legal representatives. When an inventor who has prosecuted an application after assignment dies, the administrator of the deceased applicant's estate may carry on the prosecution on filing letters of administration and until the assignee intervenes.

When an inventor dies after filing an application and executing an oath or declaration, the executor or administrator should intervene, but allowance of the application will not be withheld if the executor or administrator does not intervene. Where joint inventors remain after the death of one inventor, they must submit proof of the death of the inventor. The USPTO will then only require signatures of the living joint inventors if the legal representative of the deceased inventor does not intervene. If the legal representative of the deceased inventor wishes to intervene, they must submit an oath or declaration stating his or her authority and the residential address of the deceased inventor. When the legal representative of a deceased inventor intervenes in the application, the signature of the living joint inventors and the legal representative are required on all papers filed with the USPTO.

Legal Incapacity of Inventor

When an inventor becomes legally incapacitated prior to the filing of an application and prior to execution of the oath or declaration and no legal representative has been appointed, one must be appointed by the court of a competent jurisdiction for the purpose of execution of the oath or declaration of the application.

Inventor Unavailable

An application filed without a signed oath or declaration from all identified inventors is deemed an incomplete application by the USPTO. As a result, an examiner will not mail an official action in an application without a fully executed oath or declaration unless the application has been granted a petition regarding a non-signing inventor. Proof of a bona fide attempt to contact the inventor must be provided to the Office to support acceptance of a non-signing inventor. Granting of a petition recognizing a non-signing inventor will not alter the ownership interest or title of the application. If the non-signing inventor has not signed a recorded assignment document then the assignee is not the owner of the entire interest of the application.

Proof of Unavailability

A statement of facts and steps taken to reach a non-signing inventor must be made and will be relied upon by the USPTO to establish that a diligent effort was made. The fact that a non-signing inventor is on vacation, out of town, or in the hospital will be dismissed as inappropriate grounds for petitioning for recognition of a non-signing inventor. The statement must be signed by a person having first-hand knowledge of the contents. Copies of documentary evidence such as Internet searches and certified mail return receipts of cover letter and application execution instructions should be provided in support of the statement. The steps taken to locate the inventor should also be included.

Pre-AIA Requirements for Unavailable Inventor

For applications filed before September 16, 2012, if at least one joint inventor remains available to file an application, they will file on behalf of a joint inventor who cannot be found or reached after a diligent effort or who refused to join in an application. In such situations, the following filing documents must accompany the application filing:

- an oath or declaration signed by all available joint inventors with the signature block of the non-signing inventor left blank;
- proof that the non-signing inventor cannot be found or reached after a diligent effort or that he or she refuses to execute the application; and
- a statement of last known address of the non-signing inventor.

If no inventor is available, a corporation with demonstrated proprietary interest can make an application on behalf of an inventor who cannot be found or reached or who refuses to sign the application. In such situations, the following filing documents are required:

- an oath signed by an officer (President, Vice-President, Secretary, Treasurer, or Chief Executive) of the Corporation stating relationship to the inventor;
- proof that the inventor cannot be found or reached after a diligent effort or refuses to execute the application papers;
- a statement of last known address of the non-signing inventor;
- a showing that the invention has been assigned to the Corporation or that the inventor has agreed in writing to assign the invention or otherwise demonstrate a proprietary interest in the subject matter of the application; and
- applicant must prove that the filing of the application is necessary to preserve the rights of the parties or to prevent irreparable damage.

AIA Requirement for Unavailable Inventor

For applications filed on or after September 16, 2012, the AIA greatly simplifies the requirements with respect to inventors who are unavailable. If an inventor is unavailable, an assignee, obligated assignee, or other party that shows sufficient proprietary interest can sign a substitute statement in lieu of an inventor oath or declaration to preserve patent rights. The substitute statement is a simple form that is easy to file where there is an assignee of the entire interest or an obligated assignee. The provisions of the AIA no longer require filing of documentary evidence of the inventor's refusal to sign, although that does not eliminate the need for factual inquiry and preservation of evidence of the diligent effort to obtain the inventor's signature, as detailed under 37 C.F.R. §1.47. The substitute statement practice merely postpones review of such facts and evidence until any subsequently filed litigation.

Inventor Refuses to Sign

When an inventor is under obligation to assign their rights in any inventions discovered during their term of employment to their employer, they are considered under obligation of assignment. Such obligation is established by a signed employment agreement that details the obligation to assign and the related inventor royalties. In a situation where an inventor refuses to sign an inventor oath or declaration, it is most often because his or her relationship with a former employer has deteriorated and the inventor is now being uncooperative.

Proof of Refusal to Sign

To prove the refusal of an inventor to join in execution of the application, a copy of the application papers sent to the inventor at his or her last known address, including execution instructions, should be provided. It must be clearly established that the inventor understands exactly what he or she is being asked to sign and refuses to execute the application papers.

Where a refusal of the inventor to sign the application is alleged, proof of presentation of the application papers and of the refusal must be provided in a statement of facts by the person who mailed the application papers for signature. If the inventor refused to accept delivery of the papers or expressly stated that the application papers should not be sent, such situations should be reduced to a statement of actions taken and responses or lack thereof received. If the inventor verbally refuses to sign the papers, that fact, along with the time and place of the refusal, must be included in the statement of facts. Whenever a non-signing inventor gives a reason for refusing to sign the application, oath or declaration, that response should be noted in the petition to accept a non-signing inventor.

Pre-AIA Requirements for Non-Signing Inventor

The oath or declaration signed by the available inventors and including an identified non-signing inventor must be filed with a petition under 37 C.F.R. §1.47 requesting the acceptance of a non-signing inventor. The petition for acceptance of a non-signing inventor must include the following:

- proof of the pertinent facts and a showing that such action is necessary to preserve the rights of the parties or to prevent irreparable damage;
- the petition fee under 37 C.F.R. §1.17(g); and
- the last known address of all of the inventors.

The USPTO will send notice of the filing of the application to all inventors who have not joined in the application at the addresses provided and publish notice of the filing of the application in the Official Gazette, including the name of the non-signing inventor. The USPTO will also notify the non-signing inventor by sending a letter to the last known address of the non-signing inventor or his or her legal representative.

AIA Requirements for Non-Signing Inventor

For applications filed on or after September 16, 2012, the requirements with respect to inventors who refuse to sign application papers are more streamlined. If an inventor refuses to sign, an assignee, obligated assignee, or other party that shows sufficient proprietary interest can sign a substitute statement in lieu of an inventor oath or declaration to preserve patent rights. The substitute statement is a simple form that is easy to file where there is an assignee of the entire interest or an obligated assignee. The provisions of the AIA no longer require filing of documentary evidence of the inventor's refusal to sign, although that does not eliminate the need for factual inquiry and preservation of evidence of the diligent effort to obtain the inventor's signature, as detailed under 37 C.F.R. §1.47. The substitute statement practice merely postpones review of such facts and evidence until any subsequently filed litigation.

Rights of Non-Signing Inventor

The non-signing inventor is entitled to inspect any paper in the application, order copies of prosecution documents, and make his or her position of record in the USPTO file of the application. A non-signing inventor is not entitled to a hearing, and is not entitled to prosecute the application if the USPTO has accorded the status of the non-signing inventor or if proprietary interest in the applicant has been shown to the satisfaction of the Office.

A non-signing inventor may join in an application by filing an appropriate oath or declaration under 37 C.F.R §1.63. Even if the non-signing inventor joins the application, he or she cannot revoke or give power of attorney without agreement of the signing inventors and/or applicants. The rights of a non-signing inventor are protected by the fact that the patent resulting from an application with a granted non-signing inventor petition is the same as the rights if the non-signing inventor had joined in the application. If a non-signing inventor holds that he or she is the sole inventor of an invention naming him or her as a joint inventor, the non-signing inventor may file his or her own application and request that the application be placed in interference/derivation proceeding. If the claims in both the non-signing inventor's application and the signing joint inventors' application are otherwise found allowable, an interference/derivation proceeding may be declared. When an application is accepted by the USPTO with a non-signing inventor status, papers filed by the signing and non-signing inventors, who may join the application, are placed in the file wrapper.

CHAPTER-SPECIFIC REFERENCE MATERIAL

Reference Source	Representative Capacity and Power of Attorney Applicable Rules, Regulations, and Procedures
USPTO Website Guide	Power of Attorney Frequently Asked Questions http://www.uspto.gov/patents/law/poafaqs.jsp
Title 37 of the Code of Federal Regulations	37 C.F.R. §1.31 Applicant may be represented by one or more patent practitioners or joint inventors. §1.32 Power of attorney. §1.33 Correspondence respecting patent applications, reexamination proceedings, and other proceedings. §1.34 Acting in a representative capacity. *§1.36 Revocation of power of attorney; withdrawal of patent attorney or agent.* §1.41 Applicant for patent. §1.42 When the inventor is dead. §1.43 When the inventor is insane or legally incapacitated. §1.45 Joint inventors. §1.46 Assigned inventions and patents. §1.47 Filing when an inventor refuses to sign or cannot be reached. §1.48 Correction of inventorship in a patent application, other than a reissue application.
Manual of Patent Examination Procedures (MPEP, 8th Edition)	Chapter 400 http://www.uspto.gov/web/offices/pac/mpep/mpep_e8r5_0400.pdf

Chapter 5

Types of Patent Applications

Overview

The U.S. Patent and Trademark Office (USPTO) issues several different types of patent documents offering different kinds of protection and covering different types of subject matter. The subject matter specific types of patent applications are as follows:

- Utility Patent: Issued for the invention of a new and useful process, machine, manufacture, or composition of matter, or a new and useful improvement thereof, it generally permits the owner to exclude others from making, using, or selling the invention for a period of up to twenty years from the date of patent application filing. Includes provisional applications and continuing applications of non-provisional applications. Approximately 90 percent of the patents issued by the USPTO in recent years have been utility patents.
- Design Patent: Issued for a new, original, and ornamental design for an article of manufacture. Permits the owner to exclude others from making, using, or selling the design for a period of fourteen years from the date of patent grant.
- Plant Patent: Issued for a new and distinct, invented or discovered asexually reproduced plant including cultivated sports, mutants, hybrids, and newly found seedlings, other than a tuber-propagated plant or a plant found in an uncultivated state. Permits the owner to exclude others from making, using, or selling the plant for a period of up to twenty years from the date of patent application filing.

While the remaining chapters of this book relate to utility-type applications, including reissue and reexamination of any related patents, patent prosecution support staff should have knowledge of filing requirements for design and plant applications. The remainder of this chapter will focus on the attributes and filing requirements for design and plant applications, including how each differ from utility-type applications.

Design Applications

The general purpose served by granting patents on designs is to encourage the decorative arts in improving the appearance of articles of manufacture or portions of articles of manufacture in order to increase their salability and satisfy the aesthetic sense of the purchaser. Among such articles that are commonly the subject of design patent applications are both two- and three-dimensional objects such as apparel, household articles, furnishings, weavings, lamps, automobiles, packages and containers, games, toys, and jewelry. Graphical user interface icons and type fonts for computer displays are now important commercial subjects. Many design patents have issued for software-generated icons and other graphical elements used in computer video displays. The USPTO considers designs for computer-generated icons (design) shown on a computer screen, monitor, or other display panel (article of manufacture) to be statutory subject matter eligible for design patent protection (Patent Resources Institute, Inc., 2004).

Design patents may be granted to anyone who invents a new, original, and ornamental design for an article of manufacture. The subject matter of a design patent application may relate to the configuration or shape of an article, to the surface ornamentation applied to an article, or to the combination of configuration and surface ornamentation. A design consists of the visual ornamental characteristics embodied in, or applied to, an article of manufacture. A design for surface ornamentation is inseparable from the article to which it is applied and cannot exist alone. It must be a definite pattern of surface ornamentation, applied to an article of manufacture. A design patent protects only the appearance of the article and not structural or utilitarian features.

Attributes of Design Applications

Design patents are processed through the same system as utility patents with the same laws and rules applying. Design patent applications are much simpler in content and include only a single, formal, non-descriptive claim. The boundaries of the exclusionary right of a design patent are defined solely with reference to the drawings. Design patents protect against infringing appearance rather than function. The USPTO deems a design to be a statutory subject matter when it is "a definite preconceived thing, capable of reproduction and not merely the change result of a method." The attributes of design application are identified in Table 8; any intended foreign filing must be completed within six months of the U.S. filing date to be entitled to claim priority benefit.

Table 8: Attributes of Design Patent Applications

Subject Matter	Covers the ornamental (aesthetic) external (non-functional) appearance of an article. Relates to the configuration or shape of an article, to the surface ornamentation applied to an article, or to the combination of configuration and surface ornamentation. Design cannot only be in the abstract; it must be attached to an article that can be manufactured.
Preparation and Filing	The preferred order or arrangement of the elements of a design application are as follows: ▪ Design application transmittal form ▪ Fee transmittal form ▪ Application data sheet ▪ Specification ▪ Drawings or photographs ▪ Executed oath or declaration
Arrangement of the Specification	The design application specification should include the following sections in the order shown below: ▪ Preamble, stating the name of the applicant, title of the design, and a brief description of the nature and intended use of the article in which the design is embodied ▪ Cross-references to related applications (if applicable) ▪ Statement regarding federally sponsored research or development (if applicable) ▪ Description of the figures or the drawings ▪ Feature description ▪ A single claim No abstract required Best mode requirements not applicable to design applications

Drawings or Photographs	Design patent drawings are the crux of the design patent protection. Black-and-white and color drawings and photographs are permitted. Photography and drawing may not be combined in a single application. ▪ For color drawings and photographs, use must be accompanied by a petition and fee explaining why the variant from black and white is necessary. Triplicate copies must be submitted. If color drawings or photographs are filed with the original application, color will be considered as an *integral part* of the claimed design. ▪ For black-and-white photographs, no petition is required and only one copy of the photograph needs to be submitted. As drawings constitute the entire disclosure, the USPTO strictly enforces drawing rules in design applications. The object of the drawing is to illustrate the configuration and surface ornamentation of the design as applied to the article. An insufficient drawing may be fatal under the description requirement. More than one view is ordinarily necessary to show the appearance of a design unless it is on a design for a flat article. Perspective views are favored; sectional views can be used to facilitate design drawing comparison but should not show internal structural or mechanical features. Figures should be appropriately shaded to show clearly the character and contour of all surfaces represented. The description of figures should account for perspective views and delineate planes and surfaces. Informal drawings are acceptable to obtain a filing date and may even be used for examination. Every part of the design that is being claimed should be shown in solid lines in the drawing; other environmental structures that form no part of the design should be illustrated using dotted or broken lines.

Claims	Only single claim permitted. The claim defines the design that the applicant wishes to patent, in terms of the article in which it is embodied or applied. The claim must be in formal terms as follows: "The ornamental design for (the article which embodies the design or to which it is applied) as shown." The description of the article in the claim should be consistent in terminology with the title of the invention.
Fees	As specified under 37 C.F.R. §1.16 (f) Small entity discount applies.
Form	For design applications filed on or after September 16, 2012, form AIA/18 can be used as a design application transmittal.
Application Number	Assigned sequential numbers beginning with "D" e.g., DXXX,XXX
Patentability Criteria	Must be "new," parallel requirments for novelty as in utility patents Must be "original," meaning that the inventor made the new design independently without copying or derivation.
Patent Term	Fourteen years from issue, no maitenance fees apply.

Differences Between Design and Utility Applications

In general, a utility patent protects the way an article is used and works, while a design patent protects the way an article looks. Both design and utility patents may be obtained on an article if invention resides both in its utility and ornamental appearance. While utility and design patents afford legally separate protection, the utility and ornamentation of an article are not easily separable. Articles of manufacture may possess both functional and ornamental characteristics. Table 9 compares and contrasts design and utility patent applications.

Table 9: Differences Between Design and Utility Patent Applications		
Criteria	Design Applications	Utility Applications
Subject Matter	Protects ornamental appearance, limited to visual characteristics	Protects any new invention or functional improvements on existing inventions
Criteria for Patentability	Must be an article of manufacture Must be new Must be original Must be ornamental	Must be new Must be useful Must not be obvious
Disclosure Requirements	Sufficient written description and visual representation	Written description, enablement, and best mode
Expedited Examination Available	Yes	Yes
Drawings	Drawings required	Drawings optional, only if aid understanding of the claimed invention
Claims	Single claim	One or more claims
Priority Claim	No	Yes, domestic or foreign
Pre-Grant Publication	No	Yes, at eighteen months from filing date
Foreign Filing	Six months from filing date	Twelve months from filing date

Features of Examination	Search of prior art for novelty and nonobviousness Office actions Replies requesting reconsideration Final rejection Appeals	Search of prior art for novelty and nonobviousness Office actions Replies requesting reconsideration Final rejection Appeals
Amendments	Rarely filed	Frequently filed
Restriction Practice	Yes, mandatory	Yes, discretionary
Double Patenting Rejections	Yes	Yes
Continuing Application Options	Continued Prosecution Application (CPA) and Divisional (DIV) No Request for Continued Examination (RCE), no Continuation-in-Part (CIP)	Request for Continued Examination (RCE), Continuation (CON), Divisional (DIV) and Continuation-in-Part (CIP) No CPA
Patent Term	14 years from issue date, no maintenance fees	17 years from issue date/20 years from filing date, maintenance fees apply

Source: Adapted from Patent Resources Group, Inc. (2004)

Plant Applications

The plant patent act is an incentive for discovery and reproduction of mutations, hybrids, and sports of plants and thus encourages the proliferation of new, often superior, varieties of plant life incapable of reproduction by seed, at least some of which could otherwise vanish from the face of the earth, never to recur (Patent Resources Institute, Inc., 2004).

A plant patent is granted to an inventor who has invented or discovered and asexually reproduced a distinct and new variety of plant, other than a tuber-propagated plant or a plant found in an uncultivated state. The grant, which lasts for twenty years from the date of filing the application, protects the inventor's right to exclude others from asexually reproducing, selling, or using the plant so reproduced. This protection is limited to a plant as defined by the following terms:

- A living plant organism that expresses a set of characteristics determined by its single, genetic makeup or genotype, which can be duplicated through asexual reproduction, but which cannot otherwise be "made" or "manufactured."
- Sports, mutants, hybrids, and transformed plants are comprehended; sports or mutants may be spontaneous or induced. Hybrids may be natural, from a planned breeding program, or somatic in source. While natural plant mutants might have naturally occurred, they must have been discovered in a cultivated area.
- Algae and macro fungi are regarded as plants, but bacteria are not.

Attributes of Plant Applications

Asexual reproduction is a prerequisite requirement for a plant patent, and inventors should ensure that they can asexually reproduce the variety of plant before applying for a patent. Plant patents substitute the requirement of "distinctiveness" in place of "usefulness" associated with utility patents. The distinctiveness requirement is very concrete and should not be interpreted to mean superior to other plant varieties. The attributes of plant patent applications are identified in Table 10.

Table 10: Attributes of Plant Patent Applications

Subject Matter	The subject matter of the application would be a plant that was developed or discovered by the applicant and which has been found stable by asexual reproduction. Not a potato or other edible, tuber-reproduced plant.
Priority Claim	Can claim the benefit of a provisional application. For continuing applications (continuation and divisional) can claim benefit to parent applications.

Arrangement of the Specification	Must contain a technical disclosure of the botanical aspect of the new plant and must identify the genus and species, as well as the variety denomination of the plant. The plant application specification should include the following sections in the order shown below: ▪ Title of the Invention. The title of the invention may include an introductory portion stating the name, citizenship, and residence of the applicant. ▪ Cross-Reference to Related Applications (if any) ▪ Statement regarding Federally sponsored research and development (if any) ▪ Latin name of the genus and species of the plant claimed ▪ Variety denomination ▪ Background of the invention includes Field of the Invention and Description of relevant prior art ▪ Summary of the Invention ▪ Brief Description of the Drawing ▪ Detailed Botanical Description of the Plant ▪ Abstract of the Disclosure
Drawings or Photographs	Normally photographic but may be presented in other mediums, such as in permanent watercolor renderings, which faithfully present the appearance of the plant. Such drawings are not mechanical drawings and should be artistic and competent in their execution. Figure numbers and reference characters need not be used unless specifically required by the examiner. The drawing must disclose all of the distinctive characteristics of the plant that are capable of visual representation. ▪ Drawings may be in color. Where color is a distinguishing characteristic of the new plant, the drawing must be in color. The colors depicted must correspond with their respective color designations as identified in the specifications or defined in a recognized color dictionary, which is identified in the specification. ▪ Two copies of color drawings must be submitted. ▪ Color drawings may be made either in permanent watercolor or oil. Photographs or permanently mounted color photographs are acceptable.

	▪ The paper used in mounting plant drawings must correspond in sizes, weight, and quality to the paper required for other drawings in a utility-type application. ▪ The margin requirements of drawings are also the same as with other patent drawings. Filing requirements for drawing must be strictly adhered to because the claim incorporates the drawing by reference.
Claims	Only single claim permitted.
Fees	As specified under 37 C.F.R. §1.16(g) Include the appropriate filing fee, search fee, and examination fee with the application to avoid processing delays.
Forms	For plant applications filed on or after September 16, 2012, form AIA/19 can be used as a design application transmittal form.
Declaration	Must be signed by applicants who invented or discovered and asexually reproduced the new and distinct variety of plant for which the patent is sought. Must also state that applicants have asexually reproduced the plant. If the plant is a newly found plant, the oath or declaration must also state that the plant was found in a cultivated area.
Term	Twenty years from filing date; no maintenance fees apply.
Other Filing Options	Reissue and reexamination applications apply.

By far the most patented plant category has been roses of the species hybrid tea and grandiflora. The next most patented plant category is fruit trees, including peaches, nectarines, and apples.

CHAPTER-SPECIFIC REFERENCE MATERIAL

Reference Source	Design Applications Applicable Rules, Regulations, and Procedures
USPTO Website Guide	http://www.uspto.gov/patents/resources/types/
Title 35 of the U.S. Code	35 U.S.C. §171 Patents for designs. §172 Right of priority. §173 Term of design patent.
Title 37 of the Code of Federal Regulations	37 C.F.R. §1.151 Rules applicable. §1.152 Design drawings. §1.153 Title, description, and claim, oath or declaration. §1.154 Arrangement of application elements in a design application. *§1.155 Expedited examination of design applications,* number, filing date, and completion of application.
Manual of Patent Examination Procedures (MPEP, 8th Edition)	Chapter 1500 Design Patents

Reference Source	Plant Applications Applicable Rules, Regulations, and Procedures
USPTO Website Guide	http://www.uspto.gov/web/offices/pac/plant/
Title 35 of the U.S. Code	35 U.S.C. §1.161 Rules applicable. §1.162 Applicant, oath or declaration. §1.163 Specification and arrangement of application elements in a plant application. §1.164 Claim. §1.165 Plant Drawings. §1.166 Specimens. §1.167 Examination.

Title 37 of the Code of Federal Regulations	37 C.F.R. §1.161 Rules applicable. §1.162 Applicant, oath or declaration. §1.163 Specification and arrangement of application elements in a plant application. §1.164 Claim. §1.165 Plant drawings. §1.166 Specimens. §1.167 Examination.
Manual of Patent Examination Procedures (MPEP, 8th Edition)	Chapter 1600 Plant Patents

Chapter 6
Inventorship, Non-Inventor Applicants, Ownership, and Assignment

Inventorship

Inventorship is a question of who actually invented the subject matter claimed in a patent. The right to obtain a patent on an invention belongs to the inventors. When an application is filed or a patent issues in the name of only one inventor and he or she has not subsequently assigned the patent rights to another entity, the sole inventor is also the individual owner of the patent rights.

Pre-AIA, the statutory laws of U.S.C §116 required that the true inventors of the patent application be identified in an oath or declaration signed by each inventor. Under §116, when an invention is made by two or more persons jointly, they should apply for the patent jointly and each sign the required oath or declaration. Inventors may apply for a patent jointly even though:

- they did not physically work together or at the same time;
- each did not make the same type or amount of contribution; or
- each did not contribute to the subject matter of every claim of the patent.

Pre-AIA, only inventors could be the applicants on a U.S. patent application. A patent can be held invalid if any individual identified as an inventor is not an inventor. The inventorship can be corrected by adding, removing, or substituting the proper inventors for the erroneously designated inventors. However, the invalidity of fewer than all claims of a patent for improper inventorship cannot invalidate the remaining claims unless there has been deceptive intention (Patent Resources Institute, Inc., 2004).

Definition of Inventor

An inventor is a person who, alone or in combination with others, conceives a complete and operative manner of performing a process, or making a machine, manufacture, or composition of matter, or improvement thereof, which process constitutes an embodiment falling within the scope of, and which support, the claims in the application for patent. The making of an invention involves three stages:

- conception (complete performance of the mental part of the inventive act, including all the limitation of the claims);
- reduction to practice (converting the mental plan of the invention into tangible operative form); and
- interim activity directed toward accomplishing the reduction to practice.

Reduction to practice and the steps toward its accomplishment can be done by anyone under the inventor's direction. Conception is done solely by the inventors. The determination of inventorship always requires a determination of conception. If more than one person has independently conceived the invention, all three stages may be pertinent in determining who is the first inventor, but all those who independently conceived the invention are inventors. Unless a person contributes to the conception of the invention, he or she is not an inventor (Patent Resources Institute, Inc., 2004).

Sole and Joint Inventorship

An invention may be made by one or more persons jointly. To be a sole inventor requires that a single person was responsible for formulation of a definite and permanent idea of the complete and operative invention. Joint inventorship requires that two or more persons jointly contributed to the conception. To be a joint inventor, an individual must make a contribution to the conception of the claimed invention that is not insignificant in quality when the contribution is measured against the dimension of the full invention. In addition, there must be communication, direct or indirect, between joint inventors. The contribution of joint inventors need not be of equal importance; their contribution can be partial (Patent Resources Institute, Inc., 2004).

Determination of Inventorship

When the claims of an application are directed to a combination of elements separately conceived by different individuals, determination of inventorship is more complicated. For joint inventorship, it is not necessary that exactly the same idea should occur to each at the same time or that the inventors must work out together the embodiment of the invention. If one individual conceives the main parts of the invention but another individual makes suggestions of practical value, which makes the invention operative, he or she is considered an inventor even though the contribution was comparatively minor. If multiple inventors are named in a non-provisional application, each inventor must have made a contribution, individually or jointly, to the subject of at least one claim of the application.

Pre-AIA, an applicant for a patent was required to assert by oath or declaration that he or she believes himself to be the original and first inventor. A first inventor is an original inventor who:

- first conceived the invention; and
- was diligent in reducing the invention to practice from a time prior to the conception of the invention by another who was the first to reduce the invention to practice.

If a person is found to have derived the conception of the invention from another, the issue must be resolved in an interference or derivation proceeding. Interference or derivation proceedings are used to resolve competing claims of originality and priority.

Inventorship in Provisional Applications

Provisional applications are not required to include claims and do not require the filing of an inventor oath or declaration; however, one or more inventors must be named when filing the application. At the time of filing the non-provisional application, claiming benefit to an earlier-filed provisional application, the correct and true inventors must be named. To be entitled to claim the benefit of the earlier-filed provisional application, the non-provisional application must include at least one correct inventor who was also named in the provisional application.

Pre-AIA Correction of Inventorship Under 37 C.F.R. §1.48

If the inventive entity is erroneously named in a patent application or an issued patent filed before September 16, 2012, the error may be corrected while the application is pending or after the patent has issued. The error in identification of inventorship must have been made without deceptive intent.

Correction of Inventorship During the Application Stage

The inventive entity can be corrected during the application stage by one of the following procedures:

- amending the application to name the true inventors; or
- filing an continuing application that names the true inventors.

Correction of Inventorship by Amendment

35 U.S.C. §116 allows correction of inventorship by amendment in pending applications. The correction to inventorship is implemented by 37 C.F.R. §1.48, which implies that the naming of an incorrect inventive entity in an application may be the result of one of the following five circumstances—three in a non-provisional application and two in a provisional application:

- in a non-provisional application, an incorrect inventive entity was mistakenly named in the oath or declaration;
- in a non-provisional application, amendment to or cancellation of claims during prosecution changed the correct inventive entity such that not all of those who executed the oath or declaration were the inventors of the subject matter of those amended claims;
- in a non-provisional application, amendment to the claims during prosecution changed the correct inventive entity such that one or more persons who did not sign the oath or declaration were inventors of the subject matter of those amended claims;
- in a provisional application, the name of one or more of the inventors was omitted from the application papers as filed; or
- in a provisional application, one or more persons were incorrectly named as inventors.

The requirements for correction of an error in an inventive entity depends on circumstances such as whether the application is a non-provisional or provisional application, whether the incorrect identification of the inventive entity is the result of error or changes to or cancellation of claims during prosecution, and whether correction involves addition of inventors or removal of non-inventors (Patent Resources Institute, Inc., 2004).

Correction of Inventorship in Non-Provisional Applications

Under 37 C.F.R. §1.48(a), correction of an unintentional error in the inventive entity named in an executed oath or declaration in a non-provisional application requires the following submissions:

- a request to correct the inventorship that identified the desired change;
- a statement from each person being added as an inventor and from each person being deleted as an non-inventor that the error in inventorship occurred without deceptive intent on his or her part;
- an oath or declaration by the actual inventors;
- the processing fee under 37 C.F.R. §1.17(i); and

- if an assignment has been executed by any of the original named inventors, the written consent of the assignee in a statement under 37 C.F.R. §3.73(b).

It is not necessary to submit an explanation of when the error in inventorship was discovered or how it occurred. A simple statement of lack of deceptive intent suffices. There is no requirement that an amendment correcting inventorship be diligently made. While written consent of the assignee named in an executed assignment is recommended, it is not a prerequisite to correction of inventorship, as inventors have a legally recognized right to be identified on a patent claiming their invention, even if the patent has been assigned (Patent Resources Institute, Inc., 2004).

Removing Inventors

If the correct inventors were named in the oath or declaration of an application, but claim amendments or cancellation during prosecution result in fewer inventors than those originally named, 37 C.F.R. §1.48(b) permits deletion of the non-inventors by submission of the following:

- a request, signed by an attorney or registered agent, to correct the inventorship that identified the named inventors being deleted and acknowledges that the inventor's invention is no longer being claimed in the non-provisional application; and
- the processing fee under 37 C.F.R. §1.17(i).

As the inventorship was proper at all stages of prosecution, there is no need for any inventor's statement regarding lack of deceptive intent. A simple, straightforward statement identifying each deleted inventor and acknowledging that his or her invention is no longer being claimed suffices.

Adding Inventors

If the correct inventors were named in the oath or declaration of an application, but claim amendments during prosecution claim subject matter disclosed but not claimed, resulting in more inventors than originally named, 37 C.F.R. §1.48(c) permits addition of inventors by submission of the following:

- a request to correct the inventorship that identified the desired changes;
- a statement from each person being added as an inventor that the addition is necessitated by amendment of the claims and that the inventorship error occurred without deceptive intention on his or her part;

- an oath or declaration by the actual inventors;
- the processing fee under 37 C.F.R. §1.17(i); and
- if an assignment has been executed by any of the original named inventors, the written consent of the assignee in a Statement under 37 C.F.R. §3.73(b).

If no oath or declaration is submitted with a non-provisional application as filed and the inventive entity named in the application is incorrect, the later submission of an oath or declaration executed by the correct inventors acts to automatically correct the earlier identification of inventorship. This provision, however, does not apply for U.S. national phase (371) applications as the inventive entity is transferred from the international (PCT) application.

Correction of Inventorship in Provisional Applications

The naming of the inventor in a provisional application can be more complicated because claims are not required in provisional applications. Given that claims are used to determine inventorship, it is prudent to at least draft claims in a provisional application (even if not filed) to allow an initial determination of inventorship (Patent Resources Institute, Inc., 2004).

Removing Inventors

37 C.F.R. §1.48(e) permits the deletion of one or more persons erroneously named as inventors in a pending provisional application by the submission of:

- a request to correction the inventorship that identifies the inventors being deleted;
- a statement by the persons whose names are being deleted that the inventorship error occurred without deceptive intention on the part of the deleted inventor;
- the processing fee under 37 C.F.R. §1.17(q); and
- if an assignment has been executed by any of the original named inventors, the written consent of the assignee in a statement under 37 C.F.R. §3.73(b).

Adding Inventors

37 C.F.R. §1.48(d) permits the addition of one or more true inventors in a pending provisional application by the submission of:

- a request signed by an attorney or registered agent to correct the inventorship that identifies the inventors being added and states that the inventorship error occurred without deceptive intention on the part of the omitted inventors; and
- the processing fee under 37 C.F.R. §1.17(q).

If no cover sheet is submitted with a provisional application as filed and the inventive entity is not correctly named in the application, the later submission of a cover sheet naming the correct inventors will automatically correct the earlier defect.

Correcting Inventorship by Filing a Continuing Application

The inventive entity named in a patent application can also be changed by filing a continuing application without the need for a petition and other submissions if the continuing application includes at least one inventor named in the parent application. If an inventor is being added, a newly executed oath or declaration by the new inventive entity must be filed with a request for priority benefit under 35 U.S.C. §120 and a request for abandonment of the parent application.

Correcting Inventorship in an Issued Patent

35 U.S.C. §256 authorizes correction of inventorship in an issued patent when an inventor was named in error or not named in error and there was no deceptive intention. Under such circumstances, the Director may issue a certificate correcting the error on the application by all the parties and assignees including a proof of the facts under which the error occurred. The procedural aspect of §256 require the following submissions:

- a statement from each person being added as an inventor that the error in inventorship occurred without deceptive intention on his or her part;
- a statement from any named inventor who is not being deleted, either agreeing to the change of inventorship or stating that he or she has not disagreed with the requested change;
- a statement from all assignees of the inventors being added or remaining as named inventors agreeing to the change; and
- the fee under 37 C.F.R. §1.20(b).

Incorrect inventorship in an issued patent may also be corrected by filing a reissue application under 35 U.S.C. §251, but the process is more complicated, more expensive, and more time-consuming and can expose the patentee to another complete substantive examination.

AIA Impact—Expanded Inventive Entities

The AIA separates the owner of the application from the person who must execute the oath or declaration, which is the inventor if no assignee has been made of record. Support staff will need to understand a broader range of terminology with respect to patent applicants. The AIA statutorily changes patent practice from an inventor-applicant system to an assignee-applicant system. The definitions of the differentiated AIA terms are as follows:

- Inventor-Applicant: means the inventors who conceived the invention are the applicants if there is no assignee, or if the assignee has opted not to file the application for patent and does not take over the prosecution of the application to the exclusion of the inventors.
- Applicant: means the assignee or obligated assignee or person who otherwise shows sufficient proprietary interest in the application. Applies when the assignee (or obligated assignee or person who otherwise shows sufficient proprietary interest in the matter) has filed the application for patent, or if the assignee has taken over the prosecution of the application to the exclusion of the inventor.
- Assignee: means the assignee of the entire right, title, and interest in the application regardless of whether the assignee filed the application for patent or has taken over prosecution of the application to the exclusion of the inventor.
- Non-Inventor Applicant: means a juristic entity (owner), an assignee, or an obligated assignee or party that shows sufficient proprietary interest that can sign a substitute statement in lieu of an inventor declaration or become a non-inventor applicant.

Non-Inventor Applicants

The AIA provided new prosecution rights to owners, rather than individual inventors. For applications filed on or after September 16, 2012, an assignee, or an obligated assignee, or a party that shows sufficient proprietary interest can sign a substitute statement in lieu of an inventor oath or declaration when an inventor cannot be found after a diligent effort or refuses to sign but is under an obligation to assign. Under the AIA, non-inventor owners can be applicants, and such juristic entities must ensure that each inventor has assigned or is under obligation to assign to the juristic entity. An obligation to assign is most often accounted for in an employment agreement that states that the inventor agrees to assign (or hereby assigns) all inventions discovered during his or her term of employment to his or her employer, who becomes the owner of the patent title rights. Juristic entities should carefully retain signed employment agreements that contain an obligation to assign and may want to consider recording such documents with the Assignment Division for continuity of the record.

The AIA does not even require permission or knowledge by the inventor in advance of the filing by the owner. Applications filed pre-AIA required an oath or declaration by the inventor claiming to be the original inventor. Applications filed under AIA can accommodate non-inventor juristic entities as applicants. Under AIA, non-inventor applicants can take the following actions (Oppedahl, 2012):

- sign a terminal disclaimer;
- sign a substitute statement in lieu of an inventor oath or declaration;
- sign an ADS;
- grant access to an assignment record;
- grant access to a non-published application;
- sign a small entity statement;
- grant or revoke a power of attorney;
- sign a 37 C.F.R. §3.73(b) statement; and
- change the correspondence address on an issued patent.

The provisions of the AIA shifts prosecution toward corporations and away from individual inventors. Prior to AIA, corporations were never considered patent applicants; inventors were the applicants, even when the ultimate rights were owned by a corporate entity. Under AIA, a patent applicant will no longer be tagged to inventorship but will instead be associated with ownership. Under the AIA, all juristic entities must prosecute the application via a registered patent practitioner. All papers submitted on behalf of a juristic entity must be signed by a patent practitioner (Crouch, AIA Shifts USPTO Focus from Inventors to Patent Owners, 2012).

Inventor Oath or Declaration Under AIA

An inventor oath or declaration filed in an application with a filing date on or after September 16, 2012, must contain new AIA language. AIA inventor oath or declaration forms remove language related to being the "first" inventor to align with the first-inventor-to-file system as opposed to the first-to-invent system. To accommodate non-inventor applicants, the post-AIA oath or declaration forms do not require the inventor to have "reviewed and understood" the application or acknowledge the inventor's duty to disclose material information. In addition, the AIA oath or declaration forms do not include sections for claiming domestic or foreign priority, as such claims must be made in an AD under the provisions of the AIA. The specific requirement for AIA oaths and declarations are discussed in more detail in Chapter 8.

Assignee as Applicant under the AIA

Under AIA, an assignee of the entire interest can choose to become the applicant or not. If the assignee chooses not to become the applicant, then the applicant by default is all of the inventors. If the assignee chooses to become the applicant, the assignees is acting as a non-human juristic entity and must be represented by a registered practitioner. The assignee may sign a power of attorney in such situations, and a statement under 37 C.F.R §3.73(b) is not required. If the assignee does not want to retain a registered practitioner, then the assignee should not become the applicant, and the inventors should remain the applicant.

Correction of Inventorship under the AIA

The AIA streamlines the procedures for correction of inventorship, correction of inventor's name, and changes in the order of the names of the joint inventors. Applicants may name the inventorship of a non-provisional application under 35 U.S.C. §111(a), in an ADS filed with the initial application filing. If inventorship is not final, the filing practitioner should not sign the ADS. If the inventorship is final, the ADS must be signed to enter the inventive entities in the record. If applicants wish to take advantage of the ability to name the inventors in an ADS, the ADS must be signed and present on filing or be filed prior to the filing of any inventor's oath or declaration. If an inventor's oath or declaration is filed prior to a signed ADS, the inventorship named in the inventor's oath or declaration controls.

If an inventor's name is misspelled or needs to be updated due to marriage, the provisions of the AIA make the process of updating the inventor record much easier. Any request to correct or update the name of the inventor or a joint inventor or the order of the names of joint inventors in a non-provisional application must include:

- an ADS that identifies each inventor by his or her legal name in the desired order; and
- the processing fee under 37 C.F.R. §1.17(i).

If an ADS is not filed before or concurrently with the inventor's oath or declaration, the inventorship is the inventor or joint inventors identified in the oath or declaration. When a signed ADS or inventor's oath or declaration is filed in a non-provisional application, any correction of inventorship must be made under §1.14. If an ADS or a inventor's oath or declaration is not filed during the pendency of the non-provisional application, the inventorship is the inventor or joint inventors identified in the application papers.

The inventorship of a provisional application is the inventor or joint inventors identified in the provisional application cover sheet. Any correction or change to inventorship in a provisional application after filing of the provisional application must include:

- a request, signed by a party to the matter, to correct the inventorship that identifies each inventor by his or her legal name; and
- the processing fee under 37 C.F.R. 1.17(q).

The inventorship of an international application entering the national stage under 35 U.S.C. §371 is the inventor or joint inventors identified in a signed ADS filed with the initial submission under 35 U.S.C. §371. The applicant in an international application may change inventorship at to the U.S. at the time of national stage entry by simply filing a signed ADS with the initial submission naming the inventor or joint inventors. Unless the submission under 35 U.S.C. §371 is accompanied by a signed ADS identifying the inventor or joint inventors, the inventorship is the inventor or joint inventors identified in the international application, which includes any changes effected under the international phase.

Ownership

Ownership is a question of who owns legal title to the subject matter claimed in a patent. Ownership of a patent gives the patent owner the right to exclude others from making, using, offering for sale, selling, or importing into the United States the invention claimed in the issued patent. Patent ownership does not infer on the owner a right to make, use, offer for sale, sell, or import the claimed invention because there may be other legal considerations that preclude the production right. On filing of a patent application, the ownership initially vests with the named inventors. The ownership interest and rights to a patent or patent application can be transferred through a written legal instrument that identifies the invention. The initial owner, who is transferring the interest, is the assignor, and the party that is receiving the interest is the assignee.

Joint Ownership

Joint inventors of an invention claimed in an application or patent are joint owners of the patent or application. Each owns an equal, undivided interest in the application or patent regardless of the amount of his or her inventive contribution. Each joint inventor is entitled to practice the invention of any of the claims without the consent of, and without accounting to, the other inventors. Each joint inventor may transfer to another by assignment or license his or her equal, undivided interest in the application or patent, including the right to practice the invention of any and all claims without the consent of and without accounting to the others. The right of joint patent applicants or owners to operate independently of one another does not apply to prosecution of applications. All replies to office actions must be signed by all inventors, by an appointed practitioner, or by a joint applicant (Patent Resources Institute, Inc., 2004). Joint ownership occurs when there are multiple partial assignees or multiple inventors who have not assigned their rights, or a combination of both situations. Each individual inventor may only assign the interest he or she holds; therefore, assignment by one joint inventor renders the assignee a partial assignee. All parties having a portion of the ownership in the patent property may act together as a composite before the USPTO.

Attributable Owner

Under proposed rulemaking dated January 24, 2014, the USPTO would require more transparency from applicants and patentees in recording attributable owners (also referred to as the real party in interest). Under the proposed attributable owner rules, the USPTO would require patent applicants and owners to regularly update ownership information when they are involved in proceedings before the Office. The USPTO defines attributable owner as:

- a titleholder that has been assigned title to the patent or application; or
- an enforcement entity necessary to be joined in a lawsuit in order to have standing to enforce the patent or any patent resulting from the application.

It is intended that attributable owner information would be made available to the public. Under the proposed attributable owner rules, a patentee would likely have to identify an exclusive licensee with respect to enforcement entity. Applicants would have to specifically identify the ultimate patent entity in control of the patent or application. In the proposed rulemaking the USPTO identified the following dates for which recordation of the attributable owner (title holder or enforcement entity) would be required (Durta, PTO Publishes Proposed Rules for Periodic Reporting of Application and Patent Ownership, 2014):

- upon or shortly after filing a patent application;
- within three months of any change in attributable ownership while the application is pending;
- upon payment of a patent issuance fee;
- upon payment of any patent maintenance fee; and
- whenever the patent becomes involved in a post-issuance proceeding, which includes post-grant review, *inter partes* review, covered business method review, supplemental examination, and *ex parte* reexamination.

Assignments

Assignments transfer ownership of the patent from the assignor (inventor) to the assignee (company). A patent and its invention are owned by the inventors unless the inventors assign their rights to another person or entity (the assignee) by contract. Inventors can also be obligated to assign their inventions to their employers as agreed in their employment terms.

Assignment is the act of transferring to another party all or part of the right, title, and interest in a patent or patent application. An assignment of a patent or patent application is the transfer from an owner to another party the entire or percentage ownership interest in the invention. The transfer must include the entirety of the rights associated with the right, title, and interest in the patent or patent application.

Benefits of Recording Assignments

The Assignment Recordation Branch in the Public Records Division processes and records assignment documents for both patent and trademark properties. Recordation of assignment does not convey title; the contract or employment agreement conveys the title. Recorded assignments provide a rebuttable presumption of valid title over a subsequent purchaser of the patent. An assignment can be made of record in the USPTO in two different ways. First, an assignment can be made of record in the Assignment division of the USPTO to provide legal notice to the public of the assignment and to establish the assignee's title to the patent rights. Recording of an assignment is a ministerial act; it does not constitute a determination by the USPTO of the validity of the assignment document or the effect of the assignment on the ownership of the patent property. When an assignment is recorded within three months from the date of assignment, it provides constructive notice of the assignee's ownership of the patent or application to any subsequent would-be buyer. Second, an assignment can be made of record in the file of a patent application, patent, or reexamination proceeding to permit the assignee to take action as a party to the matter. An assignee of a patent application has a right to file an application on behalf of the inventor under certain circumstances, the right to prosecute the application, and the right to file a reissue application. Assignments can also be used to eliminate prior art references applied against the claims if common ownership can be established at the time of filing.

Recordation of assignment in the assignment records of the USPTO does not by itself permit the assignee to take action in the patent application, patent, or reexamination proceeding. If a patent is to issue in the name of the assignee, an assignment must have been recorded with the USPTO and the applicant must indicate the assignee name and address on the Issue Fee Transmittal Form; otherwise, the patent will issue in the name of the inventors.

Requirements for Recording Assignments

While no specified assignment form is required, the assignment document specifies that the assignment runs not only to the assignee named but also extends to its successors. The assignment should convey title to the invention and should specifically refer to all previously filed domestic or foreign applications and any further intended domestic or foreign applications if the assignee is to claim domestic or foreign priority benefit, or both. The assignment should also convey rights in any subsequently filed continuation or divisional applications to permit transferring of the assignee's rights to such applications. Any subsequently filed continuation-in-part applications will required preparation and recordation of a new assignment form to cover newly added matter. The USPTO will record an assignment if it meets the following criteria:

- it is in writing in the English language (or accompanied by an English translation if in a foreign language);
- it identifies the name of the inventors and the title of the invention;
- it is accompanied by assignment cover sheet identifying the name of the assignor, the name and address of the assignee, the applications or patents, or both, assigned, and the date of the execution of assignment; and
- it includes a recording fee for each application and patent assigned by the document.

Assignment Recordation Cover Sheet

All the searchable information used to create the public searchable record of ownership is transcribed directly from the recordation cover sheet. The Assignment Division does not compare the contents of the cover sheet to the underlying document to determine what data should be entered or to attempt to identify and resolve discrepancies. Recordation of assignment is a ministerial function; the USPTO does not make a determination of the legality of the transaction or the right of the submitting party to convey the title. The assignment recordation cover sheet must include the following information:

- the name of the party conveying the interest (the assignor);
- the name and address of the party receiving the interest (the assignee);
- a description of the interest conveyed or transaction to be recorded (assignment, security agreement, joint research agreement, government interest agreement, confirmatory license, merger, or change of name);
- an identification of each patent application number or patent number against which the document is to be recorded, or an indication that the document is filed together with a patent application;
- payment method for recordation fee (deposit account authorization, electronic fund transfer, or credit card payment, or no fee required for recordation of government interest not affecting title);
- the name and address of the party to whom correspondence concerning the request to record the document should be mailed;
- the date the document was executed; and
- the signature of the party submitting the document.

Methods of Filing Assignments

Assignments can be submitted to the Assignment Division for recordation by first-class mail, by facsimile, or they can be electronically filed directly with the assignment division.

If the request for recordation of assignment is filed with the initial application filing, the recordation documents should be addressed to:

Commissioner for Patents
P.O. Box 1450
Alexandria, VA 22313-1450

If the request for recordation is filed after the initial application filing, the recordation documents should be addressed to:

Mail Stop Assignment Recordation Services
Director of the U.S. Patent and Trademark Office
P.O. Box 1450
Alexandria, VA 22313-1450

If the request for recordation is filed by facsimile, the recordation documents can be submitted directly into the automated patent and trademark assignment system, and the resulting Notice of Recordation of Assignment will be sent via e-mail (if an e-mail address is provided) or via return fax to a fax number provided. If the USPTO is unable to complete transmission of the recordation notice to the return facsimile number, the notice will be printed and mailed to the applicant.

Electronic Patent Assignment System

The Assignment Services Division (ASD) of the Office of Public Records has a dedicated portal that allows applicants to electronically file through the Electronic Patent Assignment System (EPAS). EPAS allows the user to create and submit a recordation cover sheet by completing on-line web forms and attaching the supporting legal documentation as TIFF or PDF files. The discrete steps in the process related to the web forms are summarized in Figure D. The assignment information provided by the user will be recorded as provided and will not be verified or modified by the USPTO. When all required forms are completed and the appropriate supporting legal documentation files are attached, a validation screen will appear displaying the information provided. The current submission can be temporarily saved to the USPTO server. A URL link will be provided on-screen and by e-mail, which allows access to and retrieval of the saved submission. If the information displayed is correct, the user can proceed with payment of the recordation fees using a credit card, electronic fund transfer (EFT), or an existing USPTO deposit account. If the information is incorrect, the user can return to the appropriate screen by using the on-screen navigation controls and make the required corrections.

A confirmation of receipt (an html attachment) with the EPAS tracking identification number acknowledging receipt for the submission will be displayed on the screen and transmitted via e-mail upon completion of the payment process. Users must mark the appropriate check box if they do not wish to receive the e-mail with the attached html receipt. Users may also print a copy of this receipt screen for their records. When submitted, the request for recordation cannot be canceled unless the request fails to satisfy the minimum filing requirements. All forms filed via EPAS will be marked with an U.S. Eastern Standard Time stamp when received on the USPTO server. Upon completion of the fee payment process, a confirmation of receipt will be displayed, and the EST time stamp will then be applied to the submission. Effective January 1, 2014, any entity size applicant can electronically file an assignment for free. The time stamp applied by the EPAS server is the time of official USPTO receipt. The notice of recordation will be sent via e-mail to the address provided within hours of the submission. If the recordation notice is undeliverable to the e-mail address provided, the notice will be sent to the submitter via postal mail.

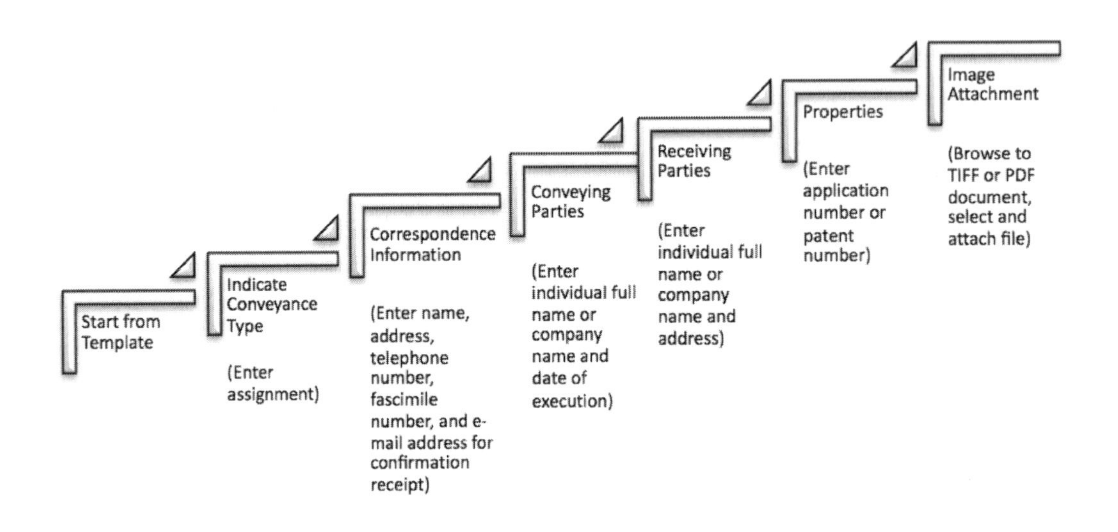

Figure D: Submitting Assignments via EPAS

Electronic Filing of Assignments—Practice Tips

The assignment division offers the following practical advice on using the EPAS interface:

- Do not use your browser's "back" and "forward" buttons to navigate. Use only the navigation controls on the EPAS screens.
- Legal supporting documentation may be either a TIFF or a PDF file. Documents must be black and white. Users may attach more than one file in more than one format.
- A thumbnail image of the attached document will appear on the screen for validation.
- To save a submission, use the "Advanced" button on the validation screen, and choose the "Save Submission" button on the following screen. The URL link is valid for four days.
- Data from a submission, namely: correspondence information, conveying parties, receiving parties, and properties can be downloaded to your workstation as a template to reuse in future submissions. To download a template, use the "Advanced" button on the validation screen, and choose the "Customize Template" button on the following screen.

Procedures for Correcting Errors in Recorded Assignments

Assignment documents and cover sheets that are returned to the submitter are stamped with the original date of receipt by the USPTO. The returned assignment will be accompanied by a letter that will indicate that if the returned papers are corrected and resubmitted within the time specified in the letter, the USPTO will consider the original date of receipt of the papers as the date of recording of the document. If the returned papers are not corrected and resubmitted within the specified period, the date of receipt of the corrected papers will be considered the date of recording of the document. The specified period to resubmit returned papers is not extendable.

Assignment documents are usually returned to the submitter as non-recordable for one of three reasons:

- a critical piece of bibliographic information was omitted from the cover sheet;
- the document itself is illegible or of such poor quality that it cannot be scanned electronically; or
- the correct fee was not paid.

An error in a recorded assignment document will be corrected by the Assignment Division provided a corrective document is submitted. The corrective submission must include:

- a copy of the original assignment document including the cover sheet marked up with the corrections required, and the corrections must be initialed and dated by the party conveying the interest;
- a new recordation cover sheet indicating the submission is a corrective document under the other category and indicating the reel and frame number where the incorrectly recorded document appears; and
- the recordation fee for each patent application or patent against which the corrective document must be recorded.

Correcting Errors in the Recordation Cover Sheet

An error in the recordation cover sheet will only be corrected if the error is apparent from a comparison with the recorded assignment document. During the recording process, the Assignment Division will check to see that a cover sheet is complete and record the data exactly as it appears on the cover sheet. The Assignment Division does not compare the cover sheet with the assignment document and when recordation is complete, a notice of recordation will be sent to the submitter. The submitter should carefully review the notice of recordation against the assignment cover sheet submitted. If typographical errors were made by the Assignment Division when entering information from the assignment cover sheet, the errors will be corrected promptly and without charge upon written request to the Assignment Division. If the error on the notice of recordation was as a result of a typographical error on the submitted assignment cover sheet, then the submitter will have to request correction and pay the recordation fees necessary to correct the error. A request to correct a typographical error in a recorded cover sheet should include:

- a copy of the originally recorded assignment document including the cover sheet
- a corrected cover sheet;
- under nature of conveyance other section, an indication of type of correction (e.g., correction to spelling of assignor's name, correction of application number) and identify the reel and frame numbers where the incorrectly recorded document appears; and
- the required fee for each application or patent to be correct if the submitter was responsible for the error.

The Assignment Division will then compare the corrected cover sheet with the original cover sheet and the originally recorded assignment document to determine whether the correction is typographical in nature. If the error is typographical in nature, the Assignment Division will record the corrected cover sheet, update the assignment database, assign a new reel and frame to the corrective document and send a corrected notice of recordation to the submitter.

If the typographical error does not affect title to the application or patent against which the original assignment or name change is recorded, the Assignment Division will correct the assignment database and permit the recording party to keep the original date of the recordation. If the typographical error affects title to the application or patent, the recording party will not be entitled to keep the original recordation date. In such circumstances, the Assignment Division will correct the assignment database and change the date of recordation to the date the corrected cover sheet was received.

Correcting Errors in the Recorded Assignment Document

If there is an error in the recorded assignment document, rather than on the recordation cover sheet, a new assignment must be created and recorded or corrections can be made by marking up to the original assignment document and re-recording it. All corrections must be initialed and dated by the assignor. If the original assignor is unavailable to correct an original assignment, or execute a new one, the assignee may submit an affidavit or declaration identifying the errors and requesting correction. The affidavit or declaration must be accompanied by a copy of the originally recorded papers, a cover sheet and the required fee for each application or patent to be corrected.

Correcting Improper Recordation by Third Party

If the owner of an application or patent discovers that due to a typographical error a third party has improperly recorded an assignment or name change against the owner's application or patent, the owner must correct the error by having a corrected cover sheet filed with the Assignment Division. The owner should contact the party who recorded the papers with the erroneous information and request that they record corrective papers.

If the third party cannot be located, or is unwilling to file corrective papers, then the true owner must record the necessary papers with the Assignment Division to correct the error. The owner should submit the following documents:

- a completed cover sheet identify the application or patent against which the assignment was improperly recorded;
- under nature of conveyance other section on the cover sheet indicate that the submission is to correct an error made in a previously recorded document that erroneously affects the identified application(s) or patent(s);
- the name of the correct owner should be entered in both the conveying party and receiving party to indicate that there is no change in ownership;
- an affidavit or declaration identifying the true owner by true chain of title, stating that the previously recorded document was submitted with erroneous information and providing the reel and frame number of the previously recorded document; and
- the required fee for each application or patent to be corrected.

Recording an assignment is not a determination of the validity of the underlying document, and does not involve an assessment of the rights of such parties to claim ownership to the title of the invention. If an assignment is executed based on a conditional event or action, it is treated as an absolute assignment. The USPTO will not determine whether the condition has been fulfilled. The USPTO treats the submission of such an assignment for recordation as signifying that the act or event has occurred. The USPTO policy regarding recordation of assignment documents is directed toward maintaining a complete history of the claimed interests in the title and, therefore, recorded assignment documents cannot be expunged even if they are subsequently found to be invalid.

Assignments and Priority Applications

If a non-provisional application claims benefit to an earlier-filed provisional application and it includes only subject matter disclosed in the provisional application, an assignment recorded against the provisional application will be effective against later-filed non-provisional application. If the non-provisional application contains subject matter in addition to that disclosed in the provisional application, new assignment papers must be recorded in the non-provisional application.

For continuation or divisional applications, a prior assignment recorded against the parent application is effective for the divisional or continuation application, because the assignment recorded against the parent application gives the assignee rights to the subject matter common to both applications. Although the assignment recorded against a parent application, is applied to the divisional or continuation application, it does not eliminate the requirement to actually record an assignment document against the divisional or continuation application for purposed of public notice of ownership.

For a continuation-in-part application, where there is new matter added, when compared to the parent application, a new assignment is required. A prior assignment from the parent application cannot be applied to the continuation-in-part application because the recorded assignment in the parent application only gives the assignee rights to the subject matter that is common in both applications. For all continuation-in-part applications, new assignment documents should be prepared, executed and recorded.

Support staff should be aware that the chain of title should be continuous through the priority family and any breaks in the recorded ownership in the priority chain can compromise the recorded ownership rights. Support staff should review the chain of title of a family of applications to ensure that there are no breaks in the title. If a there is a name change that effects title it is very important that the correct sequence of conveyance be recorded to ensure that the public record of ownership is continuous and correct.

Assignment and Issuance

For a patent to issue to an assignee, a request for issuance of the application in the name of the assignee must be included on the issue fee transmittal, otherwise the application will issue in the name of the inventor(s). The request to issue in the name of the assignee must indicate that an assignment document to this effect has been previously recorded with the Assignment Division. If the assignment has not been previously recorded, the request must state that the assignment document has been submitted for recordation concurrently. If a request for issuance to an assignee is submitted after payment of the issue fee, it must be in the form of a certificate of correction. The certificate of correction must state that the assignment was submitted for recordation before issuance of the patent. The USPTO will issue a certificate of correction to reflect that the patent issued to the assignee provided the all requirements are met.

Where multiple assignees are of record and indicated on the issue fee transmittal, only the name of the first assignee will be printed on the patent. This printing practice will not however affect the existing practice of recording assignments for multiple entities against the same patent or application. The assignee data printed on the patent is based solely on the information provided on the issue fee transmittal. Assignment information printed on the cover page of the patent is not updated after the patent issues and is not reflective of any assignment recorded subsequent to issuance of the patent. The most current assignment information on issued patent can be found by performing a search for the patent number in the assignment database.

Rights of the Assignee

The owner or assignee of the entire right to a patent property can take action in a patent application or patent proceeding under numerous instances. More specifically, the owner or assignee can take the following actions:

- Appoint its own registered patent practitioner to prosecute an application.
- File an application on behalf of an inventor when the inventor is unavailable or refuses to sign.

- Sign a reply to an office action.
- File a continuing application (continuation or divisional)
- File a request for continued examination.
- File a continued prosecution application.
- Sign a terminal disclaimer.
- Sign fee transmittals.
- Sign a request for a status update.
- Grant a power to inspect an application.
- Acquiesce to express abandonment of an application.
- Consent to the filing of a reissue application.
- Consent to the filing of a petition to correct inventorship.

Establishing Ownership

When an assignee first seeks to take action in a matter before the USPTO with respect to a patent application, patent, or reexamination proceeding, the assignee must establish its ownership of the property to the satisfaction of the Director. The assignee must provide documentary evidence of a chain of title from the original inventor(s) to the assignee by referring to a reel and frame number where such evidence is recorded. Documents submitted to establish ownership must be recorded, or submitted for recordation, as a condition to permit the assignee to take action in a pending matter. The establishment of ownership by the assignee must be submitted prior to, or at the same time as, the paper requesting or taking action is submitted. If the documents establishing ownership are not present, the assignee's action will not be entered.

Statement Under 37 C.F.R. §3.73(b)

The submission establishing ownership by the assignee is a Statement under 37 C.F.R. §3.73(b) (Form SB/96). The submission establishing ownership by the assignee must be signed by a party who is authorized to act on behalf of the assignee. When ownership is established, the assignee can continue to take action in the application, patent or reexamination proceeding without filing proof of ownership each time as long as that ownership has not changed.

The Statement under 37 C.F.R. §3.73(b) must be signed by a party authorized to act on behalf of the assignee. If the assignee is an organization (e.g., corporation, partnership, university, or government agency) the statement may be signed by an authorized officer (e.g., (chief executive officer, president, vice president, secretary or treasurer) for the organization. The officer is presumed to have been appointed to sign on behalf of the organization. For corporations, the signature of the chairman of the Board of Directors is acceptable, but the signature of an individual Director is not acceptable. If the statement is signed by any person other than the above, evidence of the person's authority to sign on behalf of the organization will be required.

AIA Impact - Statement Under 37 C.F.R. §3.73(c)

The provision of the AIA streamlined the requirements for an assignee to become the applicant. The Statement under 37 C.F.R. §3.73(c) is a complement to the Power of Attorney to Prosecute Applications before the USPTO (Form AIA/80) which is the power of attorney used by assignees who want to become the applicant. The Statement under 37 C.F.R. §3.73(c) should be used when the inventors are listed as the applicant in the ADS that accompanied the initial application filing, but the assignee would later like to become the applicant. The Statement under 37 C.F.R. §3.73(c) can also be used when an assignee revokes a previous power of attorney.

Employment Agreements

While title to the invention originates in the inventor, the title is subject to vesting in another entity under a variety of circumstances. The most common expressed agreement to vesting of title is a contractual employment agreement. In contractual employment agreements the inventor (employee) agrees to assign the title of any inventions conceived their term of employment to the company (employer). The employer acquires title to the invention often in exchange for covering the prosecution costs associated with securing a patent, while the inventor is paid a royalty rate that is detailed in the employment agreement (Patent Resources Institute, Inc., 2004).

Under a contractual employment agreement, an inventor (employee) is under the obligation to assign his/her inventions to their employer. If in the future the employee-employer relationship becomes uncooperative, the employer can assume the role of applicant with the support of an obligation to assignee employment agreement.

Multiple Assignees

When an assignee wants to take action in an application, patent or reexamination proceeding and the right, title and interest is held by more than one assignee, each partial assignee must submit a Statement under 37 C.F.R. §3.73(b). The multiple statements must each indicate the percentage of each assignees interest to allow the USPTO to determine if all right, title and interest holders have joined in action. If the extent of the partial assignee's ownership interest is not indicated, the USPTO will refuse to accept the submission as an establishment of ownership interest.

Searching Assignment Records

The USPTO assignments on the web system provides all publicly available information recorded at the assignment division. If multiple properties (patent or trademark) are associated with a particular assignment recordation, the system displays all data within that assignment document provided the information is open to public inspection. In addition, if a patent property has been recorded in the USPTO more than once, all recorded assignment data will be retrieved and displayed. Cross-references to additional details associated with the assignor or assignee names will also be available.

The USPTO assignments on the web system offers searching by indexed search fields related to recorded assignment documents. Searchable patent assignment fields are patent number, publication number, assignor name, assignee name, and reel/frame number. The search results will display the reel/frame number, application or patent numbers, conveyance data, assignor name, assignee name, correspondence address, and recordation and execution dates. The search results also include the issue or publication date and the named inventors.

Access to Assignment Records

The assignment records, relating to original or reissue patents and published patent applications, are open to public inspection at the USPTO. Members of the public can obtain copies of patent assignment records upon request and payment of a fee to the Certification Division. All records of patent assignments recorded before May 1, 1957, are maintained by the National Archives and Records Administration (NARA). The records are open to public inspection. Certified and uncertified copies of those assignment records are provided by NARA upon request and payment of the required fees. If the application on which a patent was granted was based on a priority claim to an earlier-filed application, the assignment records of the earlier-filed application are also open to public inspection. Assignment records for reissue applications are also open to public inspection.

Copies of any assignment records that are not available to the public can only be obtained upon written authority of the applicant or assignee (or their appointed patent attorney or patent agent) upon a showing that the person seeking such information is a bona fide prospective or actual purchaser, mortgagee, or licensee of the application. A request for a copy of an assignment record of an unpublished pending or abandoned application must include:

- a petition, including the fee under 37 C.F.R. §1.17(g); or
- written authority granting access to the member of the public to the particular assignment records from the applicant or assignee (or their appointed patent attorney or agent of record).

An order for a copy of an assignment or other document should identify the reel and frame number where the assignment or document is recorded.

Recordation of Documents Other Than Assignments

The Assignment Services Division will also record some documents that relate to patents or applications that do not constitute a transfer or change of title. The most common non-assignment documents submitted for recordation are security agreements, merger agreements, change of name, license, lien, contract, and joint research agreements. Such documents are recorded in the public interest in order to give third parties notification of equitable interest or other matters relevant to the ownership of a patent or application. The recordation of a document is not a determination of the effect of the document on chain of title. The determination of the effect a document has on title will only be made by the USPTO when ownership must be established to take certain actions that require consent or authorization of all parties to a matter.

Certificates of change of business name or merger or business issued by appropriate federal or state authorities are recordable. Although a mere change of name does not constitute a change in legal entity, it is properly a link in the chain of title. Such documents may also represent a change of entity as well as a change of name.

Licensing

Licensing is a means to transfer less than the entire ownership rights of an application or patent. The rights licensed may be limited by time, geographical area, or field of use. A patent license is a contractual agreement that the patent owner will not sue the licensee for patent infringement if the licensee makes, uses, offers for sale, sells, or imports the claimed invention, as long as the licensee fulfills its obligations and operates within the bounds defined in the license agreement. An exclusive license may be granted by the patent owner to a licensee. Such an exclusive license would prevent the patent owner from selling a further license to another party that would compete with the exclusive licensee as to the geographic region, the length of time, or the field of use as defined in the exclusive licensee agreement. A license is the transfer of a bundle of rights that is less than the entire ownership interest; even if the license is exclusive, it is not the equivalent of an assignment of patent rights in the patent or application. The USPTO will record a license agreement, but its recordation does not provide the same constructive knowledge as recordation of assignment. However, recordation of a license agreement may be beneficial as a public notice of the existence of a license to a prospective buyer.

Recordation Across Multiple Properties

A document recorded in the Assignment Division in connection with a patent or application is only effective against the identified patent or application. If recordation of the document against additional patents or applications, or both, is desired, the following should be submitted to the Assignment Division:

- a copy of the original document (which may consist of the previously recorded papers on which the Assignment Division has stamped the reel and frame numbers where they were recorded or a copy of such papers);
- a completed cover sheet identifying the additional properties that the document should be recorded against; and
- the appropriate recording fee per property identified.

The Assignment Division will assign a new recording date to that submission, update the assignment database, and microfilm the cover sheet and document as part of the official record.

CHAPTER-SPECIFIC REFERENCE MATERIAL

Reference Source	Inventorship, Non-Inventor Applicants, Ownership, and Assignment Applicable Rules, Regulations, and Procedures
Title 35 of the U.S. Code	35 U.S.C. §261 Ownership; assignment. §262 Joint owners.
Title 37 of the Code of Federal Regulations	37 C.F.R. §1.12 Assignment records open to public inspection. §1.41 Applicant for patent. §1.42 When the inventor is dead. §1.43 When the inventor is insane or legally incapacitated. §1.45 Joint inventors. §1.46 Assigned inventions and patents. §1.47 Filing when an inventor refuses to sign or cannot be reached. §1.48 Correction of inventorship in a patent application, other than a reissue application.
Manual of Patent Examination Procedures (MPEP, 8th Edition)	Chapter 300 Ownership and Assignment
Assignment Division Guide	Frequently Asked Questions http://www.uspto.gov/faq/assignments.jsp

Chapter 7

Provisional Patent Applications

Introduction

On June 8, 1995, the adoption of the provisions of the Uruguay Round Agreements Act (URAA) enabled the USPTO to permit U.S. and foreign inventors to file an informal provisional patent application, thereby establishing a domestic priority system. The Act provides a mechanism to enable domestic applicants to quickly and inexpensively file provisional applications. Under the provisions, applicants are entitled to claim the benefit of priority in a given application in the United States. The domestic priority period will not count in the measurement of the twenty-year patent term. Thus, domestic applicants are placed on equal footing with foreign applicants with respect to the patent term.

Attributes of Provisional Applications

A provisional application is a regular national filing that starts the one-year grace period for any subsequent Paris Convention foreign filings. Any intended foreign filing must be made within twelve months of the filing date of the provisional application, if the applicant wishes to make a priority benefit claim in the foreign-filed applications. The option for provisional patent filing was implemented in conjunction with the changes from a seventeen-year patent term from the date of grant to a twenty-year patent term from the date of filing. The primary purpose of implementing the provisional application filing option was to give U.S. inventors the opportunity to obtain an initial filing date that does not serve as the basis from which the twenty-year term of patent protection is measured. The intent was to put U.S. inventors on the same playing field as foreign inventors who file in the United States claiming priority under the Paris Convention to an earlier-filed foreign national application (Migliorini, 2007). For these foreign patent applicants, the U.S. patent term is measured from the date of U.S. filing, not the date the foreign priority application was filed. The attributes of provisional applications are summarized in Table 11. A provisional application must be filed not more than one year from the first sale, offer for sale, public use in the United States, or date of first publication anywhere in the world. To preserve foreign patent rights, the provisional application needs to be filed before first sale, offer for sale, public use, or publication in absolute-novelty foreign countries.

Table 11: Attributes of Provisional Patent Applications	
Type of Application	Provisional applications can only be filed for utility and plant type applications. Not applicable for design applications.
Exceptions	No claims required; if claims are filed, no additional fees apply. No inventor declaration required.
Claiming Priority	Considered domestic priority. Cannot claim priority to a previously filed application, either foreign or domestic.
USPTO Application Number	Assigned sequential numbers beginning with "6" e.g., 60/XXX,XXX or 61/XXX,XXX
Publication	Not published; remains confidential.
Examination	No examination on the merits. No prior art search. No Information Disclosure Statement (IDS) filed by applicant.
Amendments	No amendments permitted after filing, other than those to make the provisional application comply with filing requirements.
Inventorship	If there are multiple inventors, each inventor must be named in the application. If multiple inventors are named, each inventor named must have contributed individually or jointly to the subject matter disclosed in the application.
Assignment	Can be recorded at any time and may be necessary when certified copies of the provisional application are provided to a foreign patent office to validate priority-benefit claim.
Duration	Automatically abandoned twelve months after its filing date (or next business day). No revival or restoration options. Does not start patent term.

Access to Provisional Application	Access to a provisional application is restricted to the inventors, assignee, or attorney or agent of record. Only one of these parties can obtain access and order certified copies of the provisional application if required for subsequent foreign filing. The provisional application remains confidential unless it is identified in a U.S. patent.
Effect/Result	A provisional application cannot result in a U.S. patent unless one of the following two events occur within twelve months of the provisional application filing date: ▪ a corresponding non-provisional application for patent entitled to a filing date is filed that claims the benefit of the earlier-filed provisional application (claiming the benefit approach); or ▪ a grantable petition to convert the provisional application into a non-provisional application is filed (conversion approach).

Source: Adapted from Migliorini, (2007)

Filing Requirements

To secure a filing date, a provisional application must contain:

- a written description of the invention, complying with all requirements of the first paragraph of ; and
- any drawings necessary to understand the invention.

To complete a provisional application, the following items can be filed at a later date on payment of a surcharge for late submission:

- a cover sheet identifying the application as a provisional application for patent;
- the names of all inventors;
- inventor residences;
- title of the invention;
- name and registration number of attorney or agent and docket number (if applicable);
- correspondence address; and
- any U.S. Government agency that has a property interest in the application.

The filing date of a provisional application is the date on which a specification and any drawing required to aid the understanding of the invention are filed. No amendment, other than to make the provisional application comply with the patent statute and all applicable regulations, may be made to the provisional application after the filing date of the provisional application.

Provisional Application Cover Sheet

Provisional applications filed under 37 C.F.R. §1.53(c)(1) must be filed with a cover sheet, which may be an application data sheet (ADS) or a cover letter identifying the application as a provisional application. The provisional application cover sheet (Form SB/16) or ADS must include the following information:

- the full name of the inventors and their cities and states of residence;
- the full title of the invention;
- the correspondence address to be used (either by CN or firm/individual name and address);
- identify all enclosed parts of the application (ADS, number of sheets of drawings, number of pages of specification, and any other enclosure);
- indicate the method of payment (check, money order, credit card, or deposit account) of applicable fees, and include any entity status claim to reduced fees;
- identify if any U.S. Government funding was used to make the invention, and provide the detail of any such funding by contract number and funding agency; and
- be signed and dated by a registered practitioner including his or her PTO registration number.

If a provisional application is filed without a complete cover sheet, the applicant will be notified and given a time period of two months to provide the necessary cover sheet and fees in order to avoid abandonment of the provisional application. This time period may be extended on payment of monthly extension of time fees; a surcharge will also apply to the provision of any required filing components that did not accompany the initial provisional application filing.

Substantive Requirements

The provisional application must include a description of the invention. While this description does not need to conclude with claims, the description must still meet the best mode and enablement requirements. If the provisional application does not meet these requirements, it cannot be relied upon for a priority benefit claim to a later-filed non-provisional application. A provisional application is not limited to a single invention; it may contain a large number of disclosures to either related or unrelated inventions. Provisional applications will never turn into actual granted patents. In order to obtain patent protection, a formal non-provisional application must be filed within one year of the filing date of the provisional application. If a non-provisional patent application is not filed by the end of this year, the provisional application will expire.

Filing Fees

The basic filing fee must be paid in a provisional application on filing or within the time period identified in a post-filing notice requesting payment of the filing fee. The filing fee must be paid in the provisional application if any claim for benefit under 35 U.S.C. §119(e), is to be claimed in a subsequently filed non-provisional application. In addition to payment of the basic filing fee, an additional filing fee applies for each additional fifty sheets exceeding one hundred. A small entity discount applies on claim of entitlement to such status. A surcharge applies for filing the basic filing fee or the cover sheet on a date later than the original application filing date.

Processing by the USPTO

When the USPTO receives a provisional application, it is reviewed for four requirements, namely, designated as a provisional application, a specification, drawing, and at least one named inventor. If one or more of these filing requirements are missing, the USPTO will mail a notice of incomplete application to the applicants, and a filing date will not be assigned. The USPTO also reviews the content of the specification for national-security-sensitive material as an assessment for granting a foreign filing license. The USPTO does not examine a provisional application or assess the completeness of the disclosure relative to the written description, enablement, and best mode requirements, either prior to or after the filing of an associated non-provisional application. The adequacy of a provisional disclosure may never be reviewed unless the USPTO identifies prior art with an effective date between the provisional and associated non-provisional filing dates, or the patent granted from the non-provisional application is litigated. The provisional application is maintained in confidence by the USPTO until a patent grants claiming priority to it or if it is referenced in a U.S. patent (Migliorini, 2007).

Cost-Benefit Analysis

Provisional applications provide a number of advantages for domestic and foreign applicants. A comprehensive filing strategy requires that applicants weigh the potential costs against the potential benefits to ensure their filing decisions are comprehensive. A cost-benefit analysis of provisional application is shown in Figure E.

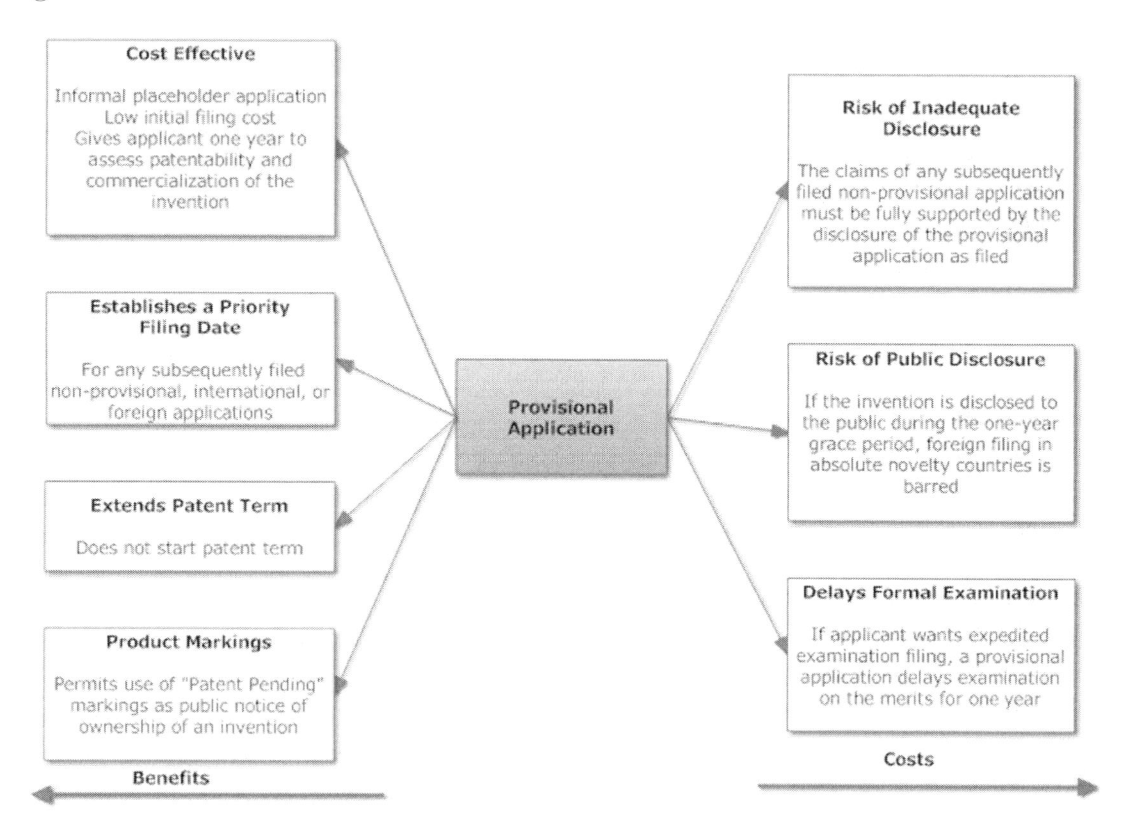

Figure E: Provisional Applications—Cost-Benefit Analysis

Source: Adapted from Migliorini, (2007)

Patent applicants have increasingly utilized provisional filings as a strategic tool since their introduction in 1995. Provisional filings will continue to be used as a placeholder application that allows applicants and their respective attorneys/agents to define a patent filing strategy, assess the patentability of the invention, and identify licensing or commercialization opportunities that can be used to offset the costs of further domestic or foreign patent filing.

AIA Impact—Provisional Applications under First-To-File System

As of March 16, 2013, the AIA changed the U.S. patent system from a first-to-invent to a first-to-file patent system. Under the new system, whoever files a patent application on a claimed subject matter first will be entitled to a patent over another inventor who later files an application on the same claimed subject matter, regardless of who first invented the claimed subject matter. Under the first-inventor-to-file system, applicants will no longer be able to rely on proving an earlier date of invention that was before their filing date to swear behind references that may have an assertable prior art date that is before applicant's earliest filing date.

The first-to-file rule changes will put pressure on applicants to file early and often. Disclosure documents will have to be reviewed and filed quickly to secure the benefits of the first-to-file date. It is likely that the AIA will increase the volume of provisional application filings and will put increased pressure on ensuring the specification is supportive of all claims to be filed in a non-provisional application. If the provisional application as filed is not fully supportive of all the claims in the subsequently filed non-provisional application, the benefit of the provisional filing date in a first-to-file system is negated. A hastily drafted provisional application, filed to secure the first-to-file date, could potentially be used against the inventor as evidence that he or she was not in full possession of all the embodiments of the invention on the date of the first-filed application.

Convention Date Filing Decision

A provisional application becomes abandoned one year from the filing date, thereby ending the one-year grace period and establishing a convention filing date by which further domestic and foreign filing decisions must be made. As shown in Figure F, where a provisional application is the first-filed U.S. application, the applicant must now decide if he or she is going to refile the provisional application after the year date has expired or file a non-provisional application that will be subject to the full rigor of patent examination. The end of the one-year grace period also requires a simultaneous decision on foreign filing with the requirement to either file an international application under the Patent Corporation Treaty (PCT) or direct foreign national applications in PCT or non-PCT member countries, or both.

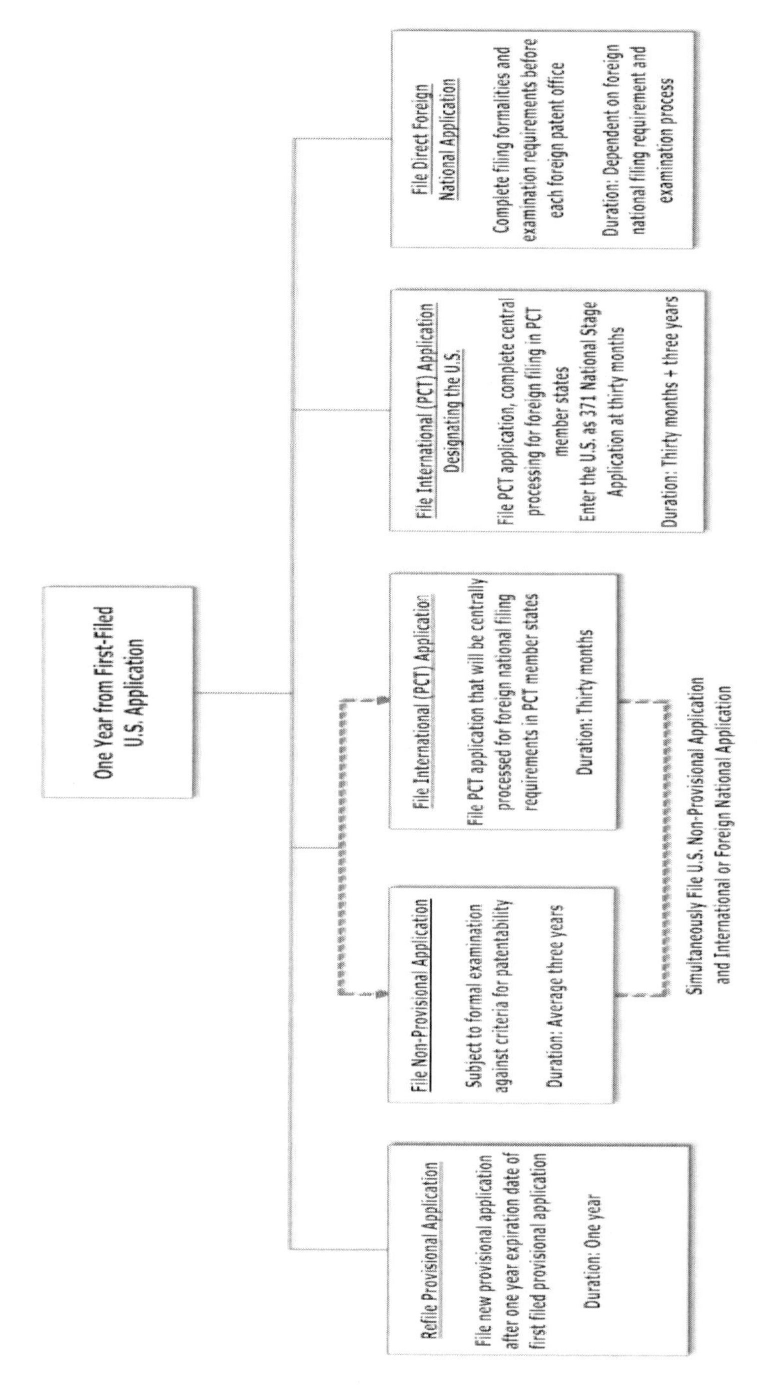

Figure F: Convention Date Filing Options

A further option to filing a formal U.S. non-provisional application on the one-year date would be to file an international application designating the United States for national phase entry on completion of the thirty-month international phase. Perhaps one of the most common convention deadline filing decisions is to file a U.S. non-provisional application and an international (PCT) or foreign national application simultaneously one year from the filing date of the first-filed U.S. application. This simultaneous filing decision establishes a U.S. patent filing and foreign-filing track. It allows applicants to gain some insight from the examination of the non-provisional application while allowing the international application to proceed through formality processing requirements. The international processing through the PCT will provide applicants with a preliminary search of the prior art and an assessment of the patentability of the claims in a written opinion. As a result, before the thirty-month expiration of the international processing, the applicant has an initial assessment of the likelihood of attaining foreign patent protection for the invention.

CHAPTER-SPECIFIC REFERENCE MATERIAL

Reference Source	Provisional Patent Applications Applicable Rules, Regulations, and Procedures
USPTO Website Guide	*Provisional Application* http://www.uspto.gov/patents/resources/types/provapp.jsp
Title 35 of the U.S. Code	35 U.S.C. §111 Application. §112 Specification. *§113 Drawings.*
Title 37 of the Code of Federal Regulations	37 C.F.R. § 1.9 Definitions. §1.51 General requisites of an application. §1.53 Application number, filing date, and completion of application.
Manual of Patent Examination Procedures (MPEP, 8th Edition)	*Chapter 200* *Types, Cross-Noting, and Status of Application* Chapter 600 Parts, Form, and Content of Applications

Chapter 8
Non-Provisional Patent Applications

Introduction

A non-provisional patent application is a formal application for patent that is subject to the full rigors of examination. A non-provisional application that meets the criteria for patentability can mature into a patent with an associated term. Applicants can file an application as their first-filed U.S. application or claim priority benefit of an earlier-filed domestic or foreign application.

Phases of Patent Prosecution

U.S. patent prosecution progresses through distinct phases, from the initial application filing to completion of pre-examination filing formalities to the rigors of formal examination with the applicant's expectation that the process will lead to allowance of at least some of the filed claims. If the applicant secures an issued patent, post-allowance maintenance fees must be paid throughout the term of the patent. When the applicant has an issued patent, an array of post-issuance filing options become available from reissue and reexamination to the new post-grant proceeding of the AIA. An overview of the distinct phases of patent prosecution and the associated time lines are shown in Figure G. It is important that support staff are able to identify where in the process an application lies to be able to understand what options there are for proceeding from that point. The remaining chapters of this book will provide more detailed views of each distinct phase of patent prosecution by identifying the associated filing requirements, filing deadlines, and filing options.

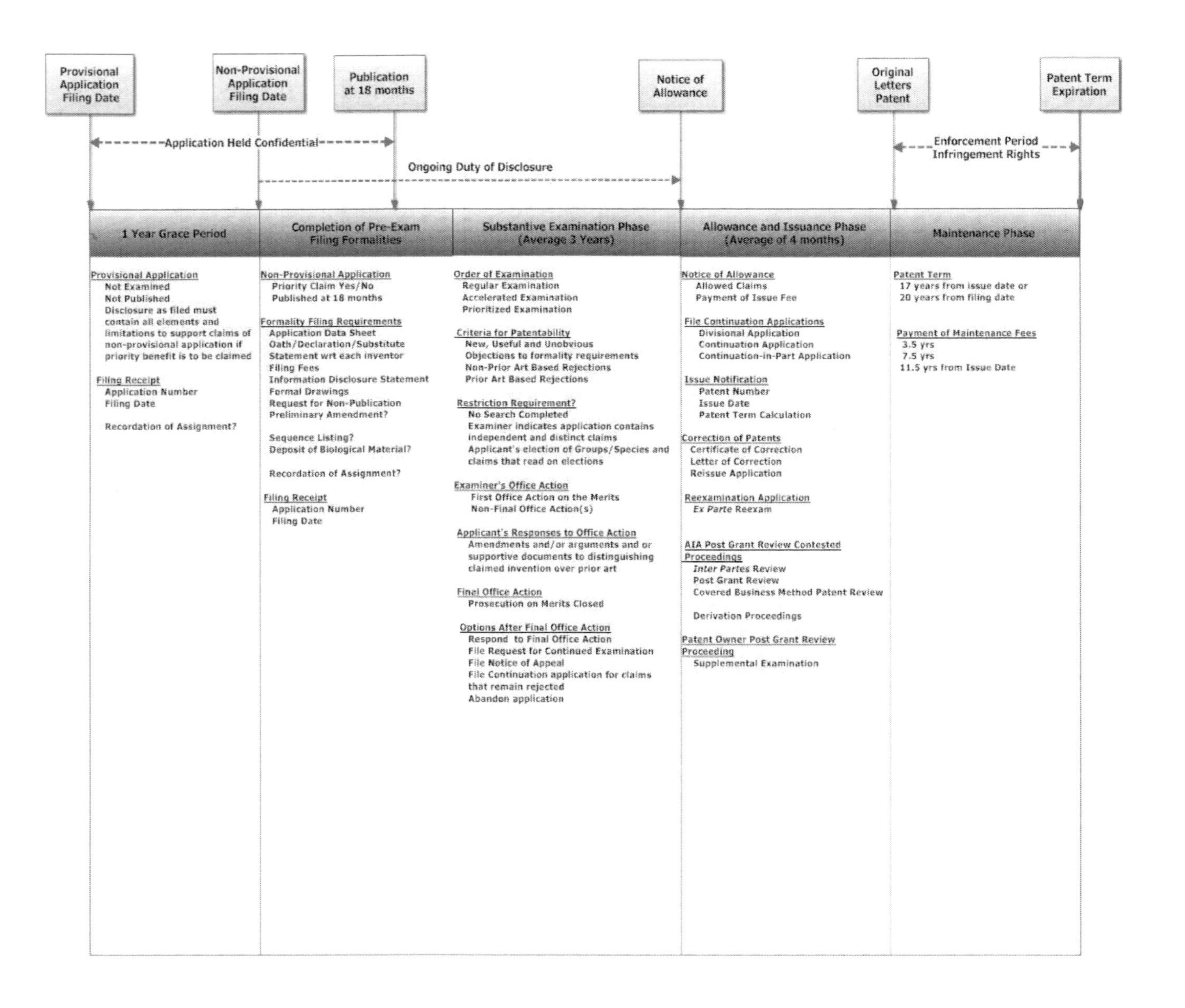

Figure G: Phases of Prosecution, including the Provisions of the America Invents Act

Attributes of Non-Provisional Applications

A non-provisional application is a detailed descriptive document that identifies the claimed invention and must contain all elements and limitations that may be relied upon during prosecution to define the claims over the existing prior art. A non-provisional patent application is a narrative document that must satisfy very stringent standards with respect to form and content. The manner in which it is originally written and later amended during the course of negotiations with the patent examiner is crucial to obtaining the maximum exclusive rights to which the invention is legally entitled (Jester, 1964). The established attributes of non-provisional applications are identified in Table 12.

Table 12: Attributes of Non-Provisional Applications

Type of Application	Utility type of application consisting of specifications, claims, abstract, and drawings (if necessary to understand the invention). Formal written narrative document that details all elements and limitations of the claimed invention. Must adhere to strigent requirements with respect to form, content, and parts.
Can be Filed By	The inventors, assignee, or obligated assignee or person who otherwise shows proprietary interest. Inventive entity must be identified in a signed ADS prior to examination.
Priority Claim	A non-provisional application can claim priority to an earlier-filed domestic provisional application under 35 U.S.C. §119(e) or to an earlier-filed foreign application under 35 U.S.C. §119(a)-(d).
Publication	Published at eighteen months from earliest claimed filing date.
Examination	Full formal examination; examiner carries out prior art search and evaluates the claims of the applications against relevant prior art and criteria for patentability. Examiner issues office action containing objections or rejection of the specification or claims, or both. Applicant submits responses or amendments, or both, to overcome examiner's rejections over prior art and cirteria for patentablity.

Duty of Disclosure	Ongoing duty of disclosure implied on all parties to bring information material regarding patentability to the examiner's attention during prosecution of the application. Such prior art references should be cited in an Information Disclosure Statement. Can be subject to third-party pre-issuance submissions under the AIA.
Inventorship	If there are multiple inventors, each inventor must be named in the application. If multiple inventors are named, each inventor must have contributed individually or jointly to the subject matter disclosed in the application.
Assignment	Can be recorded at any time during prosecution or patented term.
Patent Term	If issued as a patent, the non-provisional application filing date starts twenty-year patent term.

Filing Requirements

A filing date will be accorded to a non-provisional application only when it contains:

- a specification, including one or more claims;
- a drawing, if a drawing is necessary to understand the subject matter of the invention; and
- a non-provisional application transmittal form.

To complete the filing requirements for a non-provisional application the following items can be submitted at a later date on payment of a surcharge:

- a brief abstract of the technical disclosure in the specification;
- an oath or declaration signed by the inventors. Submission of the signed inventor oath or declaration can be postponed until the application is otherwise in condition for allowance as long as the inventor's legal name, residence, and mailing address are provided in a signed ADS;
- the filing fee under 37 C.F.R. §1.16; and
- an application data sheet (ADS).

The use of a utility application transmittal form is optional. For applications filed on or after September 16, 2012, form AIA/15 should be used if an application transmittal form is being filed with the application.

Filing Date Requirements Under the Patent Law Treaty

Effective December 18, 2013 under the Patent Law Treaty non-provisional applications (including U.S. national phase applications) do not need claims to receive a filing date under 35 U.S.C. §111(a). For applications filed without claims, applicants will be required to submit claims (and pay any excess claim fees) in a manner similar to current procedures for late payment of filing, search, and examination fees. However, the later-filed claims must meet the requirements of §112 and the specification filed must comply with the written description and enablement requirements for the claimed invention. Applicants are encouraged to continue to include claims with the originally filed application to avoid any issues under §112 (Johnson et al, 2013).

Filing Fees

For non-provisional applications filed under 35 U.S.C. §111(a), the following fees must be paid:

- basic filing fee under 37 C.F.R. §1.16(a)(1), (b)(1), (c)(1) or (e)(1);
- search fee under 37 C.F.R. §1.16(k), (l), (m), or (n);
- examination fee under 37 C.F.R. §1.16(o), (p), (q), or (r);
- application size fee under 37 C.F.R. §1.16(s), (if applicable); and
- excess claims fees under 37 C.F.R. §1.16(h) and (i), (if applicable).

The basic filing, search, and examination fees are due on filing of the non-provisional application. These fees may be paid on a date later than the filing date of the application, provided they are paid within the time period identified in a notice requesting payment of outstanding fees. Late payment of filing fees will incur a surcharge under 37 C.F.R. §1.16(f).

If the specification, including claims and drawings (excluding a sequence listing or computer program listing filed in an electronic medium), exceeds one hundred sheets of paper, an application size fee applies. The application size fee applies for each additional fifty sheets or fraction thereof over one hundred sheets of paper. For purposes of determining the application size fee required under 37 C.F.R. §1.16(s), if the specification is submitted in whole or in part on an electronic medium other than through EFS-Web, each three kilobytes of content submitted on an electronic medium will be counted as a sheet of paper. The paper-size equivalent of the specification submitted via EFS-Web will be considered to be 75 percent of the number of sheets of paper present in the specification (including claims and drawings) when entered into the image file wrapper.

Excess claims fees are also due for each independent claim in excess of three and for each total claim in excess of twenty. Fees for a proper multiple dependent claim are calculated based on the number of claims to which the multiple dependent claim refers, and a separate surcharge fee under 37 C.F.R. §1.16(j) is due on the first presentation of multiple dependent claims. For an improper multiple dependent claim, the fee charged is that charged for a single dependent claim. The filing fees are subject to entity size discounting where entitlement to claim such a status exists and is requested.

Formatting Requirements

The specification must have a left and top margin of at least 2.5 centimeters (1 inch) and all other margins of at least 2.0 centimeters (3/4 inch). The paper size can be A4 (21 centimeters X 29.7 centimeters) or letter size (8.5 X 11 inches), with 1.5 or 2.0 line spacing. The specification should be written on flexible, strong, smooth, non-shiny, durable white paper.

The specification should be on one-sided paper in portrait orientation. The specification should be presented in a form having sufficient clarity and contrast between the paper and the writing to permit the direct reproduction of readily legible copies in any number by use of photographic, electrostatic, photo-offset, and microfilming processes. The specification must also be amenable to electronic capture by use of digital imaging and optical character recognition.

Arrangement of the Application

The specification is a written description of the invention and of the manner and process of making and using the invention. The specification must be in such full, clear, concise, and exact terms as to enable a person of ordinary skilled in the art or science to which the invention pertains to make and use the invention. The specification should include the following sections in the indicated order:

- Title of the Invention
- Cross-reference to related applications
- Statement regarding Federally sponsored research and development
- Reference to Sequence Listing (if applicable)

- Background of the Invention
- Brief Summary of the Invention
- Brief Description of the Drawings
- Detailed Description of the Invention
- A claim or claims
- Sequence Listing (if applicable)
- Abstract

Title of Invention

The title of the invention should not exceed five hundred characters in length and must be as short and specific as possible. The title of the invention should appear as a heading on the first page of the specification. The title should be brief, technically accurate, and descriptive. If a satisfactory title is not supplied by the applicant, the patent examiner may change the title by examiner's amendment upon allowance of the application.

Cross-Reference to Related Applications

If the applicant is claiming the benefit of one or more prior-filed copending non-provisional or provisional applications, the claim to domestic priority must be made in an ADS. In addition, the first sentence of the specification following the title, under the subheading "Cross-Reference to Related Application(s)," should contain a reference to any earlier-filed application for which priority benefit is claimed. The priority applications should be identified by application number and filing date, including an indication of the relationships of such earlier-filed applications to the current filed application. An example of such a such a priority benefit claim to an earlier-filed provisional application is as follows:

> This non-provisional application claims the benefit under 35 U.S.C. 119(e) of U.S. Provisional Application No. 60/123,456, filed March 1, 2008, the whole disclosure of which is incorporated by reference herein.

Incorporation by Reference

Use of "incorporation by reference" is an efficient time- and space-saving technique for making lengthy text in one document part of a document under preparation without repeating the text per se. Incorporation by reference enables reliance on the disclosure of the priority application to support the claims of the later-filed application.

Filing by Reference Under the Patent Law Treaty

Effective December 18, 2013 under the Patent Law Treaty, patent applicants will have the option of filing an application by reference to a previously-filed application, including a foreign application, by identifying the prior application in an application data sheet (ADS). The specification and drawings of that prior application then constitute the new application and must be filed within the prescribed time period identified in a Notice issued by the USPTO. This method can be useful when a priority deadline is fast-approaching and a copy of the priority application is not immediately available. Applicant must also comply with any additional requirements to perfect the priority claims (Johnson et al, 2013).

Claiming Priority

The statute and rules governing provisional application priority were promulgated for the purpose of offering U.S. citizens priority rights equitable to the foreign priority rights that benefit primarily foreign citizens. An application for patent for an invention disclosed in compliance with the requirements of the first paragraph of U.S.C. §112 in an application previously filed in the United States by an inventor named in the previously filed application will have the same effect as though filed on the date of the prior application. The later-filed application must be filed before the patenting, abandonment of, or termination of proceedings on the earlier-filed application and must be amended to contain a specific reference to the earlier-filed application. The claims to the priority benefit of an earlier-filed application must be made within a specified time limit, and failure to do so will be considered a waiver of any such priority benefit.

Requirements for Claiming Priority

When certain conditions are satisfied, a patent application is entitled to the benefit of the filing date of an earlier-filed domestic or foreign application. The following general rules apply to the claiming of priority benefit to an earlier-filed domestic or foreign application:

- any claim to domestic or foreign priority must be made in an ADS;
- the specification of the application being filed should include a reference to such an earlier-filed domestic or foreign application by identifying the type of priority

claim being made, the application number and filing date of the earlier-filed application, and the relationship between the earlier-filed application and the current application

- when there is a priority claim to a chain of earlier-filed applications, the relationship must be stated for each application to establish the required co-pendency throughout the chain.
- the claim to the benefit of an earlier-filed application must be made before the later of four months from the actual filing date of the current application or sixteen months from the filing date of the earlier-filed application; this time period is not extendable.

A claim to domestic priority can be made to one or more earlier-filed provisional applications under 35 U.S.C. §119(e) or to an earlier-filed parent non-provisional application under 35 U.S.C. §120 in continuing applications.

- A claim to foreign priority can be made to one or more earlier-filed foreign applications under. The foreign priority claim must satisfy a few more requirements than a claim for domestic priority. In particular, the claim must identify the foreign application for which priority is claimed by specifying:
- the application number of the priority document;
- the country (or intellectual property authority) with which the priority document was filed;
- the day, month, and year the priority document was filed.

The AIA amended the patent rules of practice to mandate that any claim to domestic or foreign priority be made in an ADS. It will no longer be sufficient to include the priority benefit claim in the "cross-reference to related application" section of the specification or in the inventor declaration. Any updates or corrections to the domestic or foreign priority claim should be completed by filing a new ADS, marked-up to show the changes. The claiming conditions and submission requirements for claiming benefit to a provisional application, compared to a foreign application, are summarized in Figure H.

Provisional Priority Claim under U.S.C. §119(e)

Claiming Conditions

The claimed subject matter in the non-provisional application is adequately supported by the disclosure in the provisional application.
There is at least one inventor in common to the inventive entity named in the non-provisional application and the provisional application.
Non-provisional application is filed not later than 12 months after the provisional application is filed.
The non-provisional application contains, or is amended to contain, a specific reference to the provisional application.
The requsite filing fee is paid.

Submission Requirements and Time Limits

Claim must be made in an ADS.
A claim for priority identifying the provisional application number and filing date must be filed during the pendency of the non-provisional application.
The benefit claim must be submitted within the non extendable period of either:
4 months from the actual filling date of the application itself; or
16 months from the filing date of the prior filed provisional application,
whichever is later.

Foreign Priority Claim under U.S.C. §119 (a)-(d)

Claiming Conditions

Foreign appliction must be filed in recognized World Trade Organization country.
The claimed subject matter of the U.S. application must be adequately supported by the disclosure in the foreign application.
The inventors of the U.S application must be the same as the inventors/applicant in the foreign application.
U.S. application must be timely filed, with 12 months of the foreign application filing date.
Claim for priority and the required submissions must be timely filed.

Submission Requirements and Time Limits

Claim must be made in an ADS.
A claim for priority identifying by application number, country and filing date of the foreign application on which the claim is based must be filed during the pendency of the application.
The beneift claim must be submitted within the non-extendable period of either:
4 months from the actual filing date of the U.S. application; or
16 months from the filing date of the prior filed foreign application,
whichever is later.

A certified copy of the foreign application sepcification and drawings on which priority is based mustbe filed before the U.S. patent is granted; but if filed after the issue fee is paid, the certified copy must be acompanied by a processing fee and the patent as issued will not include the priority claim.

Translations of the certificed copy may be reuqired if there is intervening prior art.

Figure H: Provisional vs. Foreign Priority

Benefits of Claiming Priority

A priority claim to an earlier-filed domestic application gives the applicant the benefit of an earlier effective filing date. This earlier effective filing date can shield the applicant against intervening prior art events with an effective reference date within the applicant's priority year. A priority claim to a provisional application does not start the patent term clock and does not negatively impact any resulting patent term. The applicant's application has an effective date as a prior art reference date as of the provisional application filing date. A priority claim to an earlier-filed foreign application date can be used to overcome rejections based on patents or printed publication, public knowledge or used by others that occurred prior to the U.S. application filing date, but subsequent to the effective foreign priority date.

Delayed Priority Claim Under the Patent Law Treaty

Effective December 18, 2013 under the Patent Law Treaty, applicants will be able to file an application and claim priority to an earlier-filed provisional or foreign application up to two months after the (i.e., up to fourteen months from the filing date of a non-provisional application, eight months for a design application) if the delay in claiming priority was unintentional. The priority claim in a non-provisional application must be filed within four months of the application's filing date or within sixteen months of the priority application's filing date, whichever is later, along with payment of a petition fee and a statement that the delay was unintentional. The two month period is not an extension of time and the delay must be unintentional. The delayed priority claim two month provision does not apply to the copendency requirement for claiming priority to a non-provisional or international PCT application (Johnson et al, 2013).

Statement Regarding Federally Sponsored Research

If the invention was conceived or developed using Federal funds under a grant or contract with the government, the applicant is required to insert a statement identifying the extent of government rights in the invention. An example of such a statement regarding federally sponsored research is as follows:

> This invention was researched and developed using Federally sponsored funding. The U.S. Government has rights to this invention as provided for by the terms of [Contract No. or Grant No.] awarded by [Government Agency].

Reference to Content on Electronic Storage Medium

If the application includes a sequence listing, a table, or a computer program listing submitted on a compact disc, the specification must contain an incorporation by reference of the material on the compact disc, in a separate paragraph.

Background of the Invention

The background of the invention section should include a statement of the field of endeavor to which the invention pertains. This section may also include a paraphrasing of the applicable U.S. patent classification definitions or the subject matter of the claimed invention. This section should also contain a description of information known, including references to specific documents that are related to the invention. It should contain, if applicable, references to specific problems involved in the prior art (or state of technology) that is the subject matter of the claimed invention.

Brief Summary of the Invention

The brief summary of the invention section should present the substance or general idea of the claimed invention in summarized form. The summary may point out the advantages of the invention and how it solves previously existing problems. A statement of the object of the invention may also be included.

Brief Description of the Drawings

Where drawings are included to aid the understanding of the invention, a listing of all figures by number with a brief explanation of what each figure shows must be included. The brief explanation of each figure may also account for several views of the drawings.

The brief description of the drawings should account for each labeled figure presented on the drawing sheets as filed. The USPTO will review the specification, including the brief description of the drawing, to determine if all the figures of drawing described in the specification are present.

Detailed Description of the Invention

The detailed description of the invention should explain the process of making and using the invention in full, clear, concise, and exact terms. This section should distinguish the invention from other inventions and from what is known in the art. The applicant should completely describe the process, machine, manufacture, composition of matter, or improvement invented. It is required that the description be sufficient so that any person of ordinary skill in the pertinent art, science, or area could make and use the invention without extensive experimentation. In addition, the best mode for carrying out the invention must be detailed in the description. Each element in the drawings should be accounted for in the detailed description of the invention.

Use of Hyperlinks Not Permitted

Hyperlinks and other forms of browser-executable code, especially commercial site URLs, are not included in a patent application. Incorporation by reference by hyperlink or other form of browser-executable code is not permitted. If the examiner finds hyperlinks or other forms of browser-executable code embedded in the text of the patent application, the examiner will object to the specification and indicate to applicants that the embedded hyperlinks or other forms of browser-executable code are impermissible and must be deleted.

Use of Trademarks

The use of trademarks having definite meanings is permissible in patent applications; the proprietary nature of the marks should be respected. Trademarks should be identified by capitalizing each letter of the mark (in the case of word or letter marks) or otherwise indicating the description of the mark (in the case of marks in the form of a symbol or device or other non-textual form). The applicant should make every effort to not use trademarks in a manner that might adversely affect the validity of the trademark.

Claims

A non-provisional application for a utility patent must contain at least one claim. Claims recite and define the invention in very precise, logical, and exact terms. The claims serve as the tools to determine whether an invention is patentable over prior art and whether it is infringed. Patent claims recite the "bounds" or scope of the invention. While the specification must teach how to make and use the invention, the claims must define the scope of the invention.

The claims of a patent application must begin on a separate page following the detailed description of the invention. Claims should not contain drawings or flow diagrams. If there are several claims, they must be numbered consecutively in Arabic numerals, with the least restrictive claim presented as claim number one. The claims section must begin with a statement such as:

> "What I claim as my invention is: . . ." or "I (We) claim: . . ." followed by the recitation of the particular matter that you regard as your invention.

One or more claims may be presented in dependent form, referring back to and further limiting another claim or claims in the same application. All dependent claims should be grouped together with the claim or claims to which they refer, to the extent practicable. Any dependent claim that refers to more than one other claim (a multiple dependent claim) should refer to such other claims in the alternative only. Each claim should be a single sentence, and where a claim sets forth a number of elements or steps, each element or step of the claim should be separated by a line indentation.

Types of Claims

There are three main types of claims:

- Independent Claims: Recites the minimum number of elements that are essential to the purpose of the invention, written in the broadest manner possible.
- Dependent Claims: Progressively narrow claims that provide full scope of protection for the invention. Further limits or narrows a preceding independent/dependent claim by adding restrictions, limitations, or elements. A dependent claim can depend from a multiple dependent claim, as long as that dependent claim is not a multiple dependent claim.
- Multiple Dependent Claims (MDC): A dependent claim that refers back in the alternative to more than one preceding independent or dependent claim. Multiple dependent claims cannot depend either directly or indirectly from another multiple dependent claim.

Patent claim sets start with an independent claim that is as broad as the known prior art and is followed by a series of progressively narrower claims, all of which must be supported by the disclosure as filed. Claims are narrowed by adding restrictions, elements, or limitations beyond those of the broadest claim to define the invention over the prior art. One of the components of the filing fee to be paid for a non-provisional patent application is based on the number of independent, dependent, and multiple dependent claims. In completing initial application filings and subsequent amendments of claims, support staff need to be able to accurately count claims to determine the fees due.

How to Count Claims

When filing the application, the total number of claims are counted, and if the total number of independent and dependent claims exceeds twenty, the basic filing fee is increased by an amount for each claim exceeding twenty. Next, the number of independent claims that do not refer to or depend on any other claim in the application is counted; the basic filing fee is increased by an amount for each independent claim exceeding three.

Step 1: Count the Total (T) number of claims (independent + dependent)
(Basic filing fee includes twenty total claims) T - 20
Step 2: Count the number of Independent (I) claims
(Basic filing fee includes three independent claims) I - 3

If the application contains multiple dependent claims (MDCs), calculations for determining fees become more complex. To be proper, MDCs must refer in the alternative to dependent claims (e.g., Claim 1, 2, or 3), and they must not depend either directly or indirectly from another MDC. For fee calculation purposes, each MDC is counted as a plurality of dependent claims to which it refers in the alternative. In addition, a surcharge is applied for the first presentation of MDCs in the application.

A MDC is improper if it is stated in the conjunctive (e.g., Claim 1, 2, and 3) or if it depends directly or indirectly on a prior MDC. For fee calculation purposes, improper MDCs are counted as one dependent claim.

Step 1: Count the Total (T) number of claims (independent + dependent+ mutiple dependent)
(Basic filing fee includes twenty total claims) T - 20
Step 2: Count the number of Independent (I) claims
(Basic filing fee includes three independent claims) I - 3
Step 3: Pay additional Multiple Dependent Claims (MDC) surcharge

Claim-Counting Examples

All support staff should be able to count claims for fee calculation purposes. To aid understanding, claim-counting examples are provided in Table 13 with accompanying notes on how the counts were derived.

Table 13: Claim-Counting Examples A and B

Claim Set A	Claim Count		Notes
	Independent Claims	Dependent Claims (including MDC)	
1. Independent	1		
2. Dependent on claim 1		1	
3. Dependent on claim 1		1	
4. Dependent on claim 2 and 3		1	Improper MDC using "and" instead of "or"; counts as one dependent claim.
5. Independent	1		
6. Dependent on claim 1, 2, or 5		3	MDC refers in the alternative to three dependent claims; counts as three.
7. Dependent on claim 6		3	A MDC that refers to three claims depends on claim 6; counts as three.
Total Claim Count = 11	2	9	Claim Count 2 independent claims 9 dependent claims = 11 total claims Total claims less than twenty, independent claims less than three. No additional claims fees.
Claim Set B	**Claim Count**		**Notes**
	Independent Claims	Dependent Claims (including MDC)	
1. Independent	1		

2. Dependent on claim 1		1	
3. Dependent on claim 2		1	
4. Dependent on claim 2 or 3		2	MDC refers in the alternative to two dependent claims; counts as two.
5. Dependent on claim 4		2	Refers to claim 4, which is a MDC that refers to two dependent claims; counts as two.
6. Dependent on claim 5		2	Refers indirectly to claim 5, which refers to claim 4, a MDC that refers to two dependent claims; counts as 2.
7. Dependent on claim 4, 5, or 6		1	Improper MDC, refers to another MDC 4; counts as one.
8. Dependent on claim 7		1	Improper claim as it depends on a MDC that depends on another MDC; counts as one.
9. Independent	1		
10. Dependent on claim 1 or 9		2	MDC refers in the alternative to two dependent claims; counts as two.
11. Dependent on claim 1 and 9		1	Improper MDC using "and" instead of "or"; counts as one dependent claim.
Total Claim Count = 15	2	13	Claim Count 2 independent claims 13 dependent claims = 15 total claims Total claims less than twenty, independent claims less than three. No additional claims fees.

Whenever an application or amendment is filed that increases the total number of claims above twenty or the number of independent claims above three, payment of additional claim fees are required. When an amendment is filed, the total number of claims or independent claims remaining after the amendment is subtracted from the total number of claims already paid for in the application filing fees or the previous filed amendment. A surcharge for multiple dependent claims must be paid on first presentation, either on initial filing or if multiple dependent claims are added later by amendment. For all initial application filings, the claims status identifier "original" should be placed in parentheses after the number of each claim.

Abstract

The purpose of the abstract is to enable the USPTO and the public to determine quickly the nature of invention from the technical disclosure. The abstract points out what is new in the art to which the invention pertains. It should be in narrative form and generally limited to a single paragraph, and it must begin on a separate page after the claims. An abstract should not be longer than 150 words.

Drawing Requirements

Drawings are required "where necessary for the understanding of the subject matter of the invention," or where the subject matter "admits of illustration by a drawing." The drawings must show every feature of the invention as specified in the claims. Applications that are submitted without drawings are initially inspected by the Office to determine if the applicant is entitled to the filing date without a drawing. If a drawing is referred to in the specification, but not enclosed with the application, no filing date will be given. The USPTO has set up standards for drawings that are intended to allow the public to utilize the drawings to understand the invention with minimum effort (Patent Resources Institute, Inc., 2004).

Paper and Margins

Drawings must be made on paper that is flexible, strong, white, smooth, non-shiny, and durable. All sheets must be free from cracks, creases, and folds. Only one side of the sheet may be used for the drawing. Each sheet must be reasonably free from erasures and must be free from alterations, over writings, and interlineations. The size of the sheets on which drawings are made must be 21.6 centimeters by 27.9 centimeters (8.5 by 11 inches), or 21.0 centimeters by 29.7 centimeters (DIN size A4). The margins of the drawing should be as follows:

- For letter-sized paper: 8.5 by 11-inch paper: top at least 2.5 centimeters (1 inch), left at least 2.5 centimeters (1 inch), right at least 1.5 centimeters (5/8 inch), and bottom at least 1.0 centimeters (3/8 inch) from the edge.

- For A4-sized paper: top at least 2.5 centimeters (1 inch), left at least 2.5 centimeters (1 inch), right at least 1.5 centimeters (5/8 inch), and bottom at least 1.0 centimeter. (3/8 inch) from the edge.

Presentation Mode and Content

Drawings can be submitted in black and white or color. Black-and-white drawings are most common. India ink, or its equivalent that secures black solid lines, must be used for sufficient quality to be reproducible. Drawings made by computer printer should be originals, not photocopies. On rare occasions, color drawings may be necessary as the only practical medium to represent subject matter. Submission of color drawings must include a petition explaining need for color, a fee, and triplicate copies of each color drawing. Triplicate copies of each color drawing are not required if the drawings are submitted via EFS-Web. An amendment to the drawing section of the specification should also be submitted to indicate color drawing are on file. Black-and-white photographs are generally not permitted unless they are the only practical medium to represent the subject matter. The following guidelines regarding use of shading, symbols, and reference characters should be adhered to:

- Shading: the use of shading in views is encouraged if it aids in understanding the invention and if it does not reduce legibility.
- Symbols: graphical drawing symbols may be used for conventional elements when appropriate. The elements for which such symbols and labeled representations are used must be adequately identified in the specification. Known devices should be illustrated by symbols that have a universally recognized conventional meaning and are generally accepted in the art.
- Reference Characters: numerals are preferred; sheet numbers and view numbers must be plain and legible and must not be used in association with brackets or inverted commas or enclosed within outlines (encircled). They must be oriented in the same direction as the view to avoid having to rotate the sheet. Numbers, letters, and reference characters must measure at least 0.32 centimeters (1/8 inch) in height.

Sheet and Figure Numbering

The sheets of drawings should be numbered in consecutive Arabic numerals, starting with one, within the sight usable surface. The sheet numbers must be placed in the middle of the top of the sheet but not in the margin. The numbers can be placed on the right side if the drawing extends too close to the middle of the top edge of the usable surface. The drawing sheet numbering must be clear and larger than the numbers used as reference characters to avoid confusion. The number of each sheet should be shown by two Arabic numerals placed on either side of an oblique line, with the first being the sheet number and the second being the total number of sheets of drawings.

The different views must be numbered in consecutive Arabic numerals, starting with one, independent of the numbering of the sheets and, if possible, in the order in which they appear on the drawing sheets. Partial views intended to form one complete view, on one or several sheets, must be identified by the same number followed by a capital letter (e.g., Example: FIG. 1(A), FIG. 2(B)). View numbers must be preceded by the abbreviation FIG. Where only a single view is used in an application to illustrate the claimed invention, it must not be numbered, and the abbreviation FIG. must not appear. Numbers and letters identifying the views must be simple and clear and must not be used in association with brackets, circles, or inverted commas. The view numbers must be larger than the numbers used for reference characters. The drawing must contain as many views as necessary to show the invention. The views may be plan, elevation, section, or perspective views. Detailed views of portions of elements, on a larger scale if necessary, may also be used. All views of the drawing must be grouped together and arranged on the sheets without wasting space, preferably in an upright position and clearly separated from one another. Views must not be connected by projection lines and must not contain centerlines. Waveforms of electrical signals may be connected by dashed lines to show the relative timing of the waveforms. All views on the same sheet should be oriented in the same direction to allow for vertical portrait or horizontal landscape viewing. Words must appear in horizontal, left-to-right fashion for portrait or landscape viewing.

Drawing Label

A drawing label should include the title of the invention, the inventor's name, the application number (if known), the confirmation number (if known), and the docket number (if any). The drawing label should be placed inside the top margin of each sheet of drawings, centered on the page.

Inventor Oath or Declaration

The filing requirements for the inventor oath or declaration depends on the filing date of the application. The provisions of the AIA permit non-inventor applicants to file patent applications. As a result, applicants must choose between pre-AIA or post-AIA declaration filing requirements based on their filing dates to ensure they comply with the submission requirements.

Pre-AIA Requirements

For applications filed before September 16, 2012, old language-declaration forms apply. Each inventor must make an oath or declaration that he or she is the original and first inventor of the subject matter of the application. The oath or declaration must be signed by the inventor in person or by the person entitled by law to make application on the inventor's behalf. A full first and last name with middle initial or name, if any, and the citizenship of each inventor are required. The mailing address of each inventor and foreign priority information (if any) is also required if an application data sheet is not used. Any oath or declaration must be in a language the inventor understands. If the oath or declaration used is in a language other than English, an English translation together with a statement that the translation is accurate is required. A pre-AIA inventor oath or declaration must identify all inventors in the one document, providing a separate signature block per inventor.

If the person making the oath or declaration is not the inventor, the oath or declaration must state the relationship of that person to the inventor, upon information and belief, the facts that the inventor would have been required to state, and the circumstances that render the inventor unable to sign, namely death, insanity, legal incapacity, unavailability or refusal to sign. If the inventor has refused to sign or cannot be reached to sign the declaration, then a petition under 37 C.F.R. §1.47 is required, and if there are inventors who have signed the oath or declaration, then the remaining inventors must sign the oath or declaration on behalf of the non-signing inventor. If none of the inventors will sign the oath or declaration because they refuse to do so or cannot be found or reached after diligent effort, then the oath or declaration must be signed by the party showing proprietary interest in the application, as shown in a petition under 37 C.F.R. §1.47(b). If the inventor has died or is legally incapacitated, then the legal representative of the deceased or incapacitated inventor must sign the oath or declaration on behalf of the inventor.

AIA Requirements

For an application filed on or after September 16, 2012, new language declaration forms account for non-inventor applicants. The new language declaration is required to state that the application was made or was authorized to be made by a person executing the declaration. As a result, old language declarations cannot be used in an initial application or continuing applications filed on or after September 16, 2012. In addition, an AIA inventor oath or declaration will be one document per inventor, with only one signature block. Under AIA, submission of a signed inventor declaration can be postponed until payment of the issue fee as long as the inventor's name, residence, and mailing address are provided in a signed ADS filed with the application. While delayed submission of the signed inventor declaration may be appealing, it will result in having to obtain signatures from inventors within a non-extendable three-month period to avoid abandonment of the application. It also increases the risk of not being able to find the inventor and increases the potential that the inventor may refuse to sign the declaration due if he or she has subsequently become uncooperative with a former employer. If the signature of the inventors cannot be obtained in this non-extendable period for payment of the issue fee, the only option to prevent abandonment of the application is to file a continuation application.

If the person signing the oath or declaration is not the inventor, a substitute statement in lieu of an oath or declaration may be filed by an assignee, an obligated assignee, or a party that otherwise shows sufficient proprietary interest in the application. Even if the application is filed by an assignee or an obligated assignee, a signed declaration from each inventor will still have to be filed. In addition, the assignee or obligated assignees must record documentary evidence of ownership interest no later than the date the issue fee is paid. If a non-inventor organization (juristic entity) files and prosecutes the patent application, it must be represented by a registered practitioner.

The impact of the application filing date on the inventor oath or declaration submission requirements is summarized in Table 14.

Table 14: Impact of Application Filing Date on Oath or Declaration Filing Requirements

Filing Date of Application	Before September 16, 2012 (Pre-AIA)	On or after September 16, 2012 (AIA)
Content of Oath or Declaration Document	One oath or declaration document with signature block for each inventor.	One oath or declaration document per inventor with only one inventor signature.
Identification of Other Inventors Required	Yes	No

Language of Oath or Declaration Document	First-to-Invent language. First and original inventor Reviewed and understood application. Acknowledges duty to disclose information material to patentability.	First-to-File language. Application made or authorized to be made by the person signing the oath or declaration.
Declaration Form	SB/01A	AIA/01
Citizenship Identification Required	Yes	No
Priority Claim	Can include foreign priority claim.	Cannot include a priority claim.
Options if Inventor is Unavailable or Refuses to Sign	Rule 47 practice.	Substitute statement in lieu of oath or declaration practice.

Source: Adapted from Oppedahl, (2012)

One caveat to the oath or declaration filing requirement is that under 37 C.F.R. §1.63, a person may not execute an oath or declaration unless the person has:

- reviewed and understands the content of the application; and
- is aware of the duty to disclose to the USPTO all information known to the person to be material to patentability.

While the new language of AIA declarations no longer includes the above language, the obligation remains with respect to the person signing the declaration.

Filing Date Scenarios

Support staff must be able to quickly discern which type of inventor oath or declaration form needs to be filed based on the application filing date. A review of a set of common filing date scenarios will help support staff determine which oath or declaration form to prepare for signature by the inventors (Oppedahl, 2012).

If an international application filed before September 16, 2012, enters the U.S. national phase on or after September 16, 2012, the effective filing date of the application is the international application filing date. As a result, a pre-AIA language oath or declaration (Form SB/01) should be filed in the U.S. national application. An AIA language oath or declaration (Form AIA/01A) would not be compliant with filing requirements.

If a non-provisional domestic application is filed before September 16, 2012, without an inventor oath or declaration and a Notice to File Missing Parts is received on or after September 16, 2012, a pre-AIA language oath or declaration (Form AIA/01) should be filed in the application based on the filing date. An AIA language oath or declaration would not be compliant with filing requirements.

If a continuation domestic application is filed on or after September 16, 2012, claiming priority under 35 U.S.C. to an earlier-filed domestic application filed before September 16, 2012, an AIA language declaration (Form AIA/01) should be filed based on the continuation application filing date. The pre-AIA language oath or declaration from the parent cannot be reused.

If a bypass continuation application is filed on or after September 16, 2012, off an international application that was filed before September 16, 2012, an AIA language declaration should be filed based on the continuation application filing date.

If an international application is filed before September 16, 2012, and foreign Counsel obtained a PCT Rule 4.17 declaration and the application entered the U.S. national phase on or after September 16, 2012, a copy of the PCT Rule 4.17 declaration can be filed in the U.S. national application based on the international application filing date.

Identification of Inventive Entity

The USPTO requires the correct identification of the inventive entity prior to examination of the application. The applicant may file the application and identify the inventive entity in either a signed ADS or in an inventor's oath or declaration. If a signed ADS is submitted with the application, or within the period set in a notice requesting it, the applicant can postpone submission of the signed inventor's oath or declaration until payment of the issue fee.

If the application for patent is made by a person or entity other than the inventor, any resulting patent must be granted to the real party in interest. The AIA requires that applicants other than the inventor notify the USPTO of any change in the real party in interest in a reply to a notice of allowance. Absent such notification, the USPTO will presume no change has occurred and will grant the patent to the real party in interest of record. The USPTO will continue to use the inventor's name for the application and patent identification purposes, as the inventor names tend to provide a more distinctive identification than assignee names. Correspondence directed to the USPTO concerning applications for patent should state the name of the first-filed inventor rather than the name of the applicant.

The provisions of the AIA eliminate the prohibition against modifying the application after the oath or declaration has been signed. Under the AIA, the application can be modified after the oath or declaration is signed. This change has the potential to eliminate the late-filing surcharge for filing the signed inventor oath or declaration after filing the application because changes were made to the application (Oppedahl, 2012).

Submission Options under the AIA

The AIA introduces new terminology that accounts for the different non-inventor entities that may file patent applications. An "inventor's oath or declaration" under the AIA means one of the following:

- an oath or declaration under 35 U.S.C. §115(a);
- a substitute statement under in lieu of an inventor oath or declaration under 35 U.S.C. §115(d); or
- a combined assignment-declaration under 35 U.S.C. §115(d).

All of these are executed by or with respect to an individual (whether the inventor or a joint inventor for an application) or by the inventive entity. Under the AIA, the inventor's oath or declaration need not indicate the name of each inventor if the applicant provides a signed ADS indicating the legal name, residence, and mailing address of each inventor. The AIA eliminates the requirement that an inventor's oath or declaration state that the person executing the oath or declaration has reviewed and understands the contents of the application and acknowledges the duty to disclose all information known to be material to patentability. As amended by the AIA, a person may not execute an oath or declaration for an application unless that person has reviewed and understands the contents of the application and is aware of the duty to disclose all information he or she knows to be material to patentability.

Inventor Oath or Declaration

An inventor's oath or declaration filed on or after September 16, 2012, must include statutorily mandated language that is not included on the inventor oath or declaration form available before that date. The new statutorily mandated language includes:

- a statement that "the application was made or authorized to be made by the affiant or declarant;" and
- the acknowledgment of penalties clause must refer to "imprisonment of not more than five years."

An inventor oath or declaration is no longer required to:

- state that he or she is the first inventor of the claimed invention;
- state that the application filing is made without deceptive intent; or
- provide his or her country of citizenship.

Substitute Statement in Lieu of an Oath or Declaration

AIA permits the filing of a substitute statement in lieu of an oath or declaration by an entity when the inventor is:

- deceased;
- legally incapacitated;
- unable to be found or reached after diligent effort; or
- under an obligation to assign but refuses to sign an oath or declaration.

Any of the following entities may file a substitute statement on behalf of an inventor when such a statement is permitted in a patent application:

- the inventor's legal representative;
- the assignee;
- a party to whom the inventor is under an obligation to assign; or
- a party who otherwise shows sufficient proprietary interest in the claimed invention.

When a substitute statement in lieu of an oath or declaration is used, the statement must identify the following:

- the circumstances permitting the person to execute the substitute statement in lieu of an oath or declaration (e.g., non-signing inventor who cannot be reached or refused to sign the oath or declaration);

- the relationship of the person signing the substitute statement to the non-signing inventor; and
- the last known address of the non-signing inventor.

The substitute statement in lieu of an oath or declaration must include a correspondence address to be used by the USPTO. The person signing the substitute statement must provide proof of the pertinent facts and a showing that such action is appropriate to preserve the rights of parties. The Director may require additional information where there is a question concerning ownership or interest in an application.

If an inventor is deceased or under legal incapacity, the legal representative of the inventor may file a patent application on behalf of the inventor. If an inventor dies during the time between the filing of the application and the granting of a patent, the letters patent will be issued to the legal representative.

If an application is filed by a person other than the inventor, the application must contain an ADS specifying the applicant's information. If the applicant is the assignee or obligated assignee, the documentary evidence of the ownership (e.g., assignment for an assignee, employment agreement for an obligated assignee) should be recorded no later than the date the issue fee is paid.

If the applicant is a person who otherwise shows sufficient proprietary interest in the matter, the applicant must submit a petition including:

- the fee under §1.17(g);
- a showing that such person has sufficient proprietary interest in the matter; and
- a statement that the application is filed by a person who shows sufficient proprietary interest on behalf of and as an agent for the inventor to preserve the rights of the parties.

The person signing the substitute statement must provide his or her residence and mailing address. The applicant must notify the USPTO of any change to the real party in interest, including filing a new ADS to correct or change the applicant's name.

Combination Assignment-Declaration

The AIA permits the dual purpose of a combined assignment-declaration document, allowing statements required in an oath or declaration to be included in an assignment document that can subsequently be recorded.

If there is an error in the oath or declaration portion of a combined assignment-declaration, such as in the bibliographic information, the rest of the oath or declaration is still effective and only the error need be corrected. If the combined document fails to include the statement required in a declaration, the oath or declaration must be resubmitted. If the assignment section of a combined document is found to be invalid, the combined assignment-declaration would remain effective for the oath or declaration portion, provided that the assignment contains the statements required of an oath or declaration.

The combined assignment-declaration must be clearly labeled as such and must be indicated as a combined assignment-declaration on the recordation cover sheet. This will ensure that the USPTO will know both to record the assignment in the assignment database and to place a copy of the assignment in its related application file, so that applicants will not be required to submit a separate oath or declaration in the application. The AIA encourages the use of a combined assignment-declaration, however, only if it the document is recorded at the Assignment Division. If the client prefers not to record or wishes to postpone recordation, then the assignment and declaration should not be combined into one. If a combined assignment-declaration is used, the document should be e-filed in EPAS (as an assignment) in addition to e-filing the document in EFS-Web (as a declaration). If the combination document is filed via paper, it will incur the payment of the e-filing incentive fee under the AIA (Oppedahl, 2012).

Under the provisions of the AIA, the inventive entity must be identified prior to examination on the merits to determine prior art and potential double-patenting rejections. If the USPTO grants a patent to an entity other than the inventor, the patent will be granted to the real party in interest, and applicants must notify the Office of any change in ownership no later than the date of payment of the issue fee.

If the applicant uses a combined assignment-declaration, the required content of the declaration must be included in the assignment, and the document must be clearly marked as a combined assignment-declaration. The combined assignment-declaration must be submitted both to the assignment branch and to the examining corps and must include the names of all inventors—even those assigning to different entities. The assignment recordation cover sheet should identify the document as being an assignment and declaration document. A copy of the combined assignment-declaration must be filed with the application and any continuing applications thereof; reference to a recorded reel and frame will not be sufficient. The Office will require the applicant to identify the inventive entity by providing a copy of the recordation of assignment. To facilitate the use of combined assignment-declaration documents, a practitioner with a power of attorney can sign a consent of the assignee statement under 37 C.F.R. §3.73(b). In addition, a practitioner acting in a representative capacity may change the correspondence address after the patent has issued, provided the request to change the address is accompanied by a statement and notice has been given to the applicant or owner.

Inventive Entity Forms

The USPTO has created new oath or declaration forms accounting for the submission options and containing the necessary statutorily mandated language, as shown in Table 15.

Table 15: AIA Inventor Oath or Declaration Related Forms

Form Number	Details
AIA/01	Declaration (37 C.F.R. §1.63) for Utility or Design Application using an Application Data Sheet (37 C.F.R. §1.76).
AIA/02	Substitute Statement in Lieu of an Oath or Declaration for Utility or Design Patent Application (35 U.S.C. §115(d) And 37 C.F.R. §1.64).
AIA/08	Declaration for Utility or Design Patent Application (37 C.F.R. §1.63) (declaration with multiple inventor names, usable without an ADS only if there is no domestic or foreign priority claim and there is no non-inventor applicant).
AIA/10	Supplemental Sheet for Declaration.
AIA/11	Supplemental Sheet for Substitute Statement.

Inventor Oath or Declaration Forms

For applications filed on or after September 16, 2012, the USPTO provides two declaration forms, a short form (AIA/01) and a long form (AIA/08). The long-form declaration is designed for use when an application is filed without an ADS (where there are no domestic or foreign priority claims) and includes all of the named inventors and their residential addresses. The short-form declaration is a one-page sheet prepared for each inventor. If there are joint inventors, it is not necessary to combine all the sheets into one document or to provide all sheets to the inventor for signature. The short-form declaration streamlines the signature by inventors and decreases the need to file multiple copies of declarations when the inventors sign different copies of a declaration listing all inventors. In addition, the short-form declaration will allow greater differentiation of inventors with respect to any subsequently filed continuation or divisional applications. AIA declarations do not need to include the address or citizenship of the inventor, and the inventor does not have to date the document when signing. In addition, the AIA declarations do not have to include a statement that the inventor read the application and acknowledges his or her duty of disclosure. Signed inventor declarations should be filed as soon as possible to avoid any potential negative impact on patent term adjustment.

If the person making the declaration is not the inventor, the declaration must state the relationship of the person to the inventor. If the person signing the oath or declaration is the legal representative of a deceased inventor, the declaration must include the name and address of the legal representative. A party with proprietary interest in the invention claimed in an application can sign on behalf of the inventor, if the inventor cannot be reached or refuses to join in the filing of the application. In such situations, the party with proprietary interest must provide details on their right to sign on behalf of the inventor. A declaration cannot be signed by an attorney on behalf of the inventor, even if the attorney has been given a power of attorney to do so.

Timing of Filing

Under the AIA, an applicant may file the inventor's oath or declaration either:

- on filing of the application; or
- on payment of the issue fee (provided that the applicant files a signed ADS identifying the inventive entity).

If an application contains the applicable filing fees and a signed ADS identifying the legal name, residence, and mailing address of each inventor, but does not include the inventor's oath or declaration, the USPTO will not issue an Informational Notice to the applicant indication that submission of a signed inventor oath or declaration is outstanding.

The AIA inventor oath or declaration provisions permit the Office to issue a Notice of Allowance requesting the completion of any formality matters, including identification of all inventive entities, before payment of the issues fee. In such situations, an oath or declaration, a substitute statement, or a combined assignment-declaration, with respect to each inventor, must be filed on payment of the issue fee.

If there is no inventor's oath or declaration or signed ADS naming the inventive entity, the USPTO will send a Notice to File Missing Parts requiring the submission of either the inventor's oath or declaration or a signed ADS.

Assignee as Applicant Filing

To better facilitate processing of patent applications, the AIA revises and clarifies the rules of practice for power of attorney and prosecution of an application by an assignee.

Under the AIA, a company/organization (juristic entity) may file a patent application on behalf of the company/organization rather than on behalf of the inventor. In such situations, the assignee is the applicant. However, the inventors must still execute an oath or declaration. The assignee may only execute a substitute statement in lieu of an oath or declaration where the inventor refuses to execute an oath or declaration, cannot be found or reached after diligent effort, is deceased, or is legally incapacitated.

Where the assignee is the applicant, the assignee may appoint a power of attorney to prosecute the application without having to comply with requirements to establish ownership. Juristic entities must be represented by a registered patent practitioner. If an applicant postpones submission of the inventor's oath or declaration until payment of the issues fee, the applicant must submit a signed ADS identifying the inventive entity. The ADS must identify each inventor by his or her legal name and provide a mailing address and residence for each inventor.

If an assignment is not executed prior to filing (and there is no obligation to assign or proprietary interest in the matter), the application should be filed in the name of the inventors. A party having less than the entire right, title, and interest may not on its own file the patent application.

Application Data Sheet

Use of an application data sheet (ADS) in pre-AIA provisional or non-provisional application filings is preferred but not mandatory. The ADS is used to compile bibliographic data related to the patent application and present it in a format specified by the USPTO. The specific bibliographic data included on an ADS includes applicant information, correspondence information, application information, representative information, domestic priority information, foreign priority information, and assignment information.

Under the AIA, use of an ADS is mandatory in all applications filed on or after September 16, 2012, unless there is no domestic or foreign priority claim and there is no non-inventor applicant. Under the AIA, an ADS includes a new applicant information section to account for any non-inventor applicants. The ADS must be signed and may be signed by the applicant. The provisions of the AIA also clarify that the inventor's postal address may be where the inventor works, a post office box, or other address where mail is received even if it is not the main mailing address of the inventor.

AIA Impact—ADS and Priority Claim

Effective September 16, 2012, the AIA revised the rules of practice to harmonize the practice regarding foreign priority claims with the practice regarding domestic priority benefit claims by requiring that both foreign priority claims and domestic benefit claims be made in an ADS. For applications filed on or after September 16, 2012, an ADS (Form AIA/14) will be the only medium for making a foreign or domestic priority claim. A claim to domestic or foreign priority made in a declaration or in the first sentence of the specification will no longer be sufficient to make the priority claim of record. The ADS will control with respect to any inconsistencies between the ADS and other documents related to domestic or foreign priority claims.

The USPTO has eliminated the use of the term "Supplemental ADS." Information previously submitted on an ADS may be corrected or updated until payment of the issue fee by filing a new ADS providing corrected or updated information. However, certain information cannot be changed by simply filing a new ADS. For example, changes to the named inventors must comply with the requirements of 37 C.F.R. §1.48, and correspondence address changes must comply with the requirements of 37 C.F.R. §1.33(a). A new ADS need only show the information that changed using strikethroughs and underscores; information not changed does not need to be included.

Use of the PTO PDF fillable version of the ADS form will eliminate the potential for errors in the application data when USPTO personnel hand-key the data. An extractable ADS increases the reliability and accuracy of the bibliographic data that automatically loads into PALM. If an extractable ADS is filed with the initial application through EFS-Web, applicants can use the "Publication Review" tab in private PAIR to confirm the accuracy of the date prior to publication. If an extractable ADS is not filed with the initial application but is later used, the information contained in the ADS will not be automatically loaded into PALM.

The AIA-related ADS form will also include a check box for authorization of priority document exchange (PDE) and Digital Access Service (DAS), replacing the requirement to use a separate form (SB/39) for such authorizations. An extractable ADS is never used twice. Any ADS that follows the initial ADS filed should be created using a word processor (Oppedahl, 2012).

Declarations will no longer need to identify the citizenship of the inventor; only the name and residence of each inventor will be required. Where there are inconsistencies between the declaration and the ADS, the declaration governs with respect to inventor names, and the ADS governs with respect to priority claim.

Inconsistencies Between ADS and Other Documents

For inconsistencies in information between and ADS and other documents, the USPTO applies the following rules:

- the latest submitted information will govern notwithstanding whether supplied by an ADS, an amendment to the specification, a designation of a correspondence address, or by an inventor oath or declaration;
- the information in the ADS will govern when the inconsistent information is supplied at the same time by an amendment to the specification, a designation of correspondence address, or an inventor oath or declaration, with noted exceptions as above;
- the inventor oath or declaration governs inconsistencies with the ADS in the naming of inventors;
- the USPTO will capture bibliographic information from the ADS (notwithstanding whether an oath or declaration governs the information). The USPTO will generally, for example, not look to an inventor oath or declaration to see if the bibliographic information indicated is consistent with the bibliographic information captured from an ADS (whether the inventor oath or declaration is submitted prior to or subsequent to the ADS);
- captured bibliographic information derived from an ADS containing errors may be corrected if applicant submits a new ADS.

ADS in Lieu of an Inventor's Declaration

If an ADS is used in lieu of an inventor's declaration when filing an application, the ADS must meet the following requirements:

- it must be properly signed;
- it must provide inventor(s) name and mailing address;
- it must include any claim to domestic or foreign priority;
- it must include the identification of any non-inventor applicant; and
- it must be compliant and signed if a signed inventor oath is not included.

The provision of the AIA eliminated the use of a supplemental ADS and replaced it with a corrected ADS. When changes are made to a corrected ADS, all changes must be marked-up with respect to the previously-filed ADS using strikeout or underline. The corrected ADS must be signed. Any changes to applicant or inventor names must comply with 37 C.F.R §1.46 and 37 C.F.R §1.48 respectively. A corrected ADS applies to addition or deletion of inventor names, corrections or updates to inventor names (including misspelling and name change) or changes to the order of the inventor names and requires a processing fee under 37 C.F.R §1.17(q).

Auxiliary Parts of Application

A patent application may also contain the following auxiliary parts depending on life science subject matter content and the applicant's foreign filing strategy.

Sequence Listing

Patent applications that contain disclosures of nucleotide or amino acid sequences must contain, as a separate part of the disclosure, a paper copy disclosing the nucleotide or amino acid sequences and associated information using the symbols and format in accordance with the requirements of 37 C.F.R. §1.822 and §1.823. The sequence listing can be filed in paper or electronic form, and the specification should be amended to indicate the application includes a sequence listing. Where the description or claims of a patent application discuss a sequence, the text of the description or claims must include a sequence listing identifier number (SEQ ID NO.) preceding the sequences embedded throughout the specification and claims.

Sequence Submission Software

PatentIn is the sequence listing authoring software provided by the USPTO. PatentIn allows input of raw sequence data and output of sequenced data that is compliance with the sequence listing formatting requirements. Checker is a bio-sequence verification software provided by the USPTO for preliminary evaluation of sequence listing compliance. PatentIn and Checker can be downloaded from the USPTO's website. Checker does not validate if information in free text fields is proper, but it does allow users to view error reports. Checker cannot accommodate non-English language symbols (e.g., e with an accent over it) in an inventor's or applicant's name and will produce an input file error message if non-English language symbols are detected. Users can design around this input file error message by replacing the non-English language symbol with an English language equivalent, rerunning Checker, and then replacing the English language symbol with the non-English language symbol in the outputted text file.

Sequence Listing Filing Requirements

Patent applications that contain nucleotide or amino acid sequence disclosures must include a copy of the sequence listing in accordance with the requirements in 37 C.F.R. §1.821-§1.825. The rules of practice require applicants to submit these sequence listings in a standard international format that is consistent with World Intellectual Property Organization (WIPO) Standard ST.25 (1998). The USPTO uses the sequence listings during the examination process to determine the patentability of the associated patent application.

The sequence rules require the use of standard symbols and a standard format for sequence data and submission of the data in computer-readable form. The sequence listing must be in ASCII text file with continuous pagination. The CD containing the computer-readable sequence listing should bear a printed label giving the name of the applicant, the title of the invention, the date on which the data were recorded on the computer-readable form, and the operating system used to produce the sequence listing.

Filing Methods

A sequence listing may be submitted by any one of the following methods:

- on diskette (or CD) and paper under 37 C.F.R. §1.824;
- on three CDs; or
- electronically via EFS–Web.

Sequence listings that are too large to be filed electronically through EFS-Web may be submitted on a separate CD. Applicants may file a sequence listing with an initial application filing or in response to a pre-examination Notice to Comply with Requirements for Patent Applications Containing Nucleotide and/or Amino Acid Sequence Disclosures.

If the sequence listing is filed by diskette (or CD) and paper, a copy of the sequence listing ASCII text file must be copied onto a diskette (or CD), creating a computer-readable format (CRF). The sequence listing is also printed on paper. If this method of filing is used, the sequence submission must include a statement that the CRF and paper copy are identical. If the sequence listing is being filed by this method in response to a Notice to Comply a statement that there is no new matter must also be included.

If the sequence listing is filed on three CDs, the sequence listing ASCII text file must be copied onto a CD-ROM. The CD must have read-only functionality and cannot have read-write capability—to ensure the CRF is not editable. When the CRF is finalized, it should be copied onto two additional CD-ROMs; the second CD should be labeled "Copy 1," and the third CD should be labeled "Copy 2."

If the sequence listing is filed via EFS-Web, the sequence listing ASCII text file should be added to the EFS-Web submission. If the sequence listing is filed via EFS-Web with the initial application, no paper copy or statement is required. If the sequence listing is filed in response to a Notice to Comply, a statement that there is no new matter is required. Sequence listings filed via EFS-Web that are compliant with requirements are automatically processed and placed in the Automated Biotechnology Sequence Search (ABBS). Sequence listings that are extremely long (at least three hundred pages or approximately 600 Kb) are published only in electronic format on the USPTO dedicated sequence data web page Publication Site for Issued and Published Sequences (PSIPS).

Sequence Listing Data Fields

Sequence listings should contain the following standard data identifier sequence listing caption fields:

<110> Inventor or Applicant Name
<120> Title of Invention
<130> File Reference
<140> Current Application Number (e.g., 12/125,365)

<141>	Current Filing Date (e.g., 2010-01-02)
<150>	Prior Application Number (e.g., 61/123,456)
<151>	Prior Application Filing Date (e.g., 2009-01-02)
<160>	Number of SEQ ID NOs. (e.g., twenty-five total number of sequences)
<170>	Software Application Used (e.g., PatentIn, Version 3.0)
<210>	SEQ ID NO:1
<211>	Length (e.g., ten number of bases or amino acid residues)
<212>	Type (e.g., DNA or RNA or PRT)
<213>	Organism (e.g., genus and species Homo sapiens, or artificial or unknown)
<220>	Feature (e.g., further definition for artificial or unknown)
<221>	Name/Key (e.g., further definition for artificial or unknown)
<222>	Location (e.g., further definition for artificial or unknown).
<223>	Other Information (e.g., further definition for artificial or unknown)
<300>	Publication Information
<301>	Authors
<302>	Title
<303>	Journal
<304>	Volume
<305>	Issue
<306>	Pages
<307>	Date
<308>	Database Accession Number
<309>	Database Entry Date
<310>	Patent Document Number
<311>	Patent Filing Date
<312>	Publication Date
<313>	Relevant Residues
<400>	Sequence

Sequence Listing Practice Tips

The USPTO identifies the following most common compliance issues associated with submission of sequence listings:

- the organism of each sequence must be defined at heading <213>;
- use genus/species if at all possible; if human sequence, indicate Homo sapiens;

- if "artificial" sequence or "unknown" sequence, further definition is required at headings <220> to <223>;
- use "artificial" sequence if a portion was derived from natural source; identify the source, and explain how the sequence differs from the naturally occurring material;
- use "unknown" sequence if there is no scientific name disclosed or only a partial scientific name is disclosed;
- sequence having a gap or gaps must be displayed as separate sequences in the sequence listing;
- sequences made of fragments of other sequences must be displayed as separate sequences in the sequence listing;
- use PatentIn software for the preparation of sequence listing to reduce non-compliant formatting issues;
- if filing the sequence listing with the initial application filing, no paper copy or statement is necessary;
- if filing the sequence listing in response to a Notice to Comply, a statement that there is no new matter is needed;
- the USPTO uses an in-house verification software for validation of the sequence listing; and
- sequence listings are most often rejected by the USPTO because of the information entered in field <223>. Information provided for artificial or unknown sequences must be manually verified. Field <223> must define artificial probe, expressed sequence tag, etc. Chimeric constructs should identify the source of each part. The sequence listing must include a complete explanation of any artificial or unknown sequences.

Biological Material

Every patent must contain a written description of the invention that is sufficient to enable a person of ordinary skill in the art to which the invention pertains to make and use the invention. Where the invention involves a biological material to make or use the invention in a reproducible manner, access to the biological material may be necessary to satisfy the statutory requirements of 35 U.S.C. §112. In such situations, the applicant would supplement the written disclosure of the application with a deposit of biological material that is essential to meet requirements of the statute with respect to the claimed invention. In the event that a deposit of biological material is required, examining procedures and conditions for deposit are identified under 37 C.F.R. §1.801-§1.809.

To comply with the requirements of 35 U.S.C. §112, a deposit of biological material may be made at any time before filing the application for patent or during the pendency of the application. If the deposit of biological material is made during the pendency of the application, it must be made no later than the time period set by the examiner for completion of any remaining formality matters after issuance of a Notice of Allowance. The applicant need not make a necessary deposit until the application is in condition for allowance, as long as the applicant provides written assurance that an acceptable deposit will be made on or before payment of the issue fee.

Declaration for Deposit of Biological Material

The inventor declaration for deposit of biological material should include the following statements and access information:

- Deposits of ________________were made at and accepted by the American Type Culture Collection ("ATCC"), 10801 University Blvd., Manassas, Virginia 20110-2209, on ___________, under the Budapest Treaty on the International Recognition of the Deposit of Microorganisms for the purpose of Patent Procedure;
- The deposited material has been accorded specific Accession Number: __________;
- Access to the deposited cultures will be available during the pendency of the patent application to one determined by the Commissioner of Patents and Trademarks to be entitled to access under 37 C.F.R. §1.14 and 35 U.S.C. §122;
- All restrictions on the availability to the public of the materials deposited will be irrevocably removed upon the granting of a patent;
- The deposits will be maintained for a period of thirty years from the date of deposit or for a period of five years after the date of the most recent request of a sample or for the enforceable life of the patent, whichever is longest; and
- If a culture should become nonviable, it will be replaced with a viable culture of the same kind.

Request for Non-Publication

If the invention has not been, and will not be, the subject of an application filed in another country that requires eighteen-month publication, a request for non-publication can be filed. The request for non-publication (Form SB/35) must accompany the initial application filing and cannot be submitted later. This is a statutory requirement and cannot be waived. The request for non-publication must be conspicuously requested to ensure identification and processing by the USPTO.

Initial Application Filing—Practice Tips

The USPTO offers the following practice tips for filing an initial non-provisional application (USPTO, Patent Practice Tips, 2010):

- Although use of PTO forms is not required, it is advisable to use them and not alter the language. If a form is altered by a practitioner, the statement regarding approval and the OMB number must be removed.
- Do not use combined Declaration/Power of Attorney form; use separate declaration and separate power of attorney forms.
- Any claim to domestic or foreign priority must be submitted in a signed ADS if the priority claim is to be made of record.
- Take advantage of the benefits of using an ADS. Customers using an ADS can expect improved accuracy of filing receipts and bibliographic data and more efficient processing of the application papers by the USPTO.
- An ADS can be filed to correct or update information even though no original ADS was submitted on filing the initial application.
- Avoid submitting preliminary amendments on filing. A substitute specification will be required if a preliminary amendment included on filing makes changes to the specification, except for changes to title, abstract, claims, or addition of benefit claim information to the specification.

Filing Receipt

Within six weeks of filing an application, the applicant will receive an official filing receipt from the USPTO indicating the application number and filing date assigned to the newly filed application. If the application was e-filed, the electronic acknowledgment receipt will also contain the application number assigned and indicate the date the application filing was electronically submitted. The filing receipt does contain additional information regarding particulars associated with the application. If the application was filed without a signed ADS identifying the inventors or without the filing fee, the filing receipt will be accompanied by a Notice to File Missing Parts requesting submission of the omitted ADS, the filing fee, and a surcharge fee for late filing of a formality document. The applicant will be given a two-month response period, with five-month extensions available to submit the missing parts identified in the notice (see Chapter 11 for more details on response to Notice to File Missing Parts).

The data printed on the filing receipt is taken directly from the USPTO's PALM system, which is the central reservoir of the application particulars throughout prosecution. Filing receipts should be reviewed timely for accuracy and correctness. Any errors found should be corrected quickly, to ensure that the bibliographic information of the application remains correct with respect to the application papers as filed.

Review of Filing Receipts

Support staff should immediately review the filing receipt and validate the information against the application papers as filed. Support staff should specifically check the following data fields on the filing receipt to ensure they are correct:

- Attorney Docket Number (compare to return-receipt postcard, Express Mail mailing label, or electronic acknowledgment receipt); spaces, slashes, or dashes will not be included;
- Application Number (confirm against return-receipt postcard or electronic acknowledgment receipt);
- Filing Date (confirm against Express Mail mailing label "date-in" or electronic acknowledgment receipt);
- Filing fee indicated if paid or authorized; if filing fee was not paid or authorized, it should not appear on the filing receipt unless the USPTO charged the filing fee without authorization (confirm against filing transmittal or electronic acknowledgment receipt);
- Specification pagination and claims; confirm total number of claims, total number of drawing sheets, and total number of independent claims;
- Inventor's full name, residence, city, and state; confirm format of name and inclusion of middle initial if on application filing papers (confirm against ADS or inventor oath or declaration);
- Title of the invention (confirm against front page of the specification); the USPTO will not include these filing words if they are at the beginning of the title: "an," "the," "new," "improved";
- Priority claim section; confirm priority claim benefit type (U.S. provisional or continuing priority or foreign priority), application number, and filing date for each

application claimed in priority (confirm against the ADS and front page of the specification under cross-reference to related applications);

- Entity status indicated and correct (confirm against ADS or application filing transmittal, or electronic acknowledgment receipt)
- Foreign filing license granted; confirm if required foreign filing license granted;
- Non-publication request if filed with application; confirm indicated.

Request for Corrected Filing Receipt

If typographical errors are found on the filing receipt, it is prudent to request their correction immediately. A request for a corrected filing receipt should clearly identify where on the filing receipt the error was made and should provide the corrected text. A marked-up version of the filing receipt, highlighting the error, should be included to ensure correct processing by the USPTO. The USPTO will not issue a corrected filing receipt to add the words “the,” “an,” or “new” to the beginning of the title of the invention, as the USPTO will not enter such words even if they were in the beginning of the title as filed. If an error is found in the application number or assigned filing date, correction should be requested promptly and, where necessary, supportive documentation (“date-in” Express Mail label or electronic acknowledgment receipt) should be provided.

Updated Filing Receipt

After a compliant response to the Notice to Filing Missing Parts is filed and the filing fee is paid, the USPTO will issue an updated filing receipt showing payment of filing fees. The updated filing receipt will not include any reference to the signed ADS or inventor oath or declaration filed.

CHAPTER-SPECIFIC REFERENCE MATERIAL

Reference Source	Non-Provisional Applications Applicable Rules, Regulations, and Procedures
USPTO Website Guide	Non-Provisional Patent Application Filing Guide http://www.uspto.gov/web/offices/com/iip/pdf/brochure_04.pdf
AIA Frequently Asked Questions	Inventor's Oath or Declaration *http://www.uspto.gov/aia_implementation/faq.jsp*
Title 35 of the U.S. Code	35 U.S.C. §111 Application. §112 Specification. §113 Drawings. §114 Models, specimens. §115 Oath of applicant. §119 Benefit of earlier filing date; right of priority. §120 Benefit of earlier filing date in the United States. §122 Confidential status of applications; publication of patent applications.
Title 37 of the Code of Federal Regulations	37 C.F.R. **§1.**51 General requisites of an application. §1.52 Language, paper, writing, margins, compact disc specifications. §1.53 Application number, filing date, and completion of application. §1.54 Parts of application to be filed together; filing receipt. §1.55 Claim for foreign priority. §1.56 Duty to disclose information material to patentability. §1.57 Incorporation by reference.

	Specification §1.71 Detailed description and specification of the invention. §1.72 Title and abstract. §1.73 Summary of the invention. §1.74 Reference to drawings. §1.75 Claim(s). §1.76 Application data sheet. §1.77 Arrangement of application elements. §1.78 Claiming benefit of earlier filing date and cross-references to other applications. §1.79 Reservation clauses not permitted.
	Drawings §1.81 Drawings required in patent application. §1.83 Content of drawing. §1.84 Standards for drawings. §1.85 Corrections to drawings. §1.91 Models or exhibits not generally admitted as part of application or patent. §1.93 Specimens. §1.94 Return of models, exhibit, or specimens. §1.95 Copies of exhibits. §1.96 Submission of computer program listings.
Manual of Patent Examination Procedures (MPEP, 8th Edition)	Chapter 600 Parts, Form, and Content of Application
EFS-Web Fillable Forms	http://www.uspto.gov/patents/process/file/efs/guidance/Form_fillable_pdfs_available.jsp

Chapter 9

Publication of Applications

Introduction

In 2001, the USPTO began the pre-grant publication of any patent applications filed on or after November 29, 2000. Prior to that date, essentially all U.S. applications had been kept secret throughout prosecution. With certain exceptions, non-provisional utility and plant applications for patent filed on or after November 29, 2000, were published promptly after the expiration of a period of eighteen months from the earliest filing date for which priority was claimed. Applications were pre-grant published after the expiration of a period of eighteen months from the earliest of:

- the U.S. filing date;
- the international filing date; or
- the filing date of an earlier-filed application for which priority benefit is claimed under 35 U.S.C. §119 (provisional or foreign priority), §120 (continuing application priority: continuation and continuation in part applications), §121 (divisional application), or §365 (continuing application of international application designating the United States).

Effects of Publication

Publication of patent applications at eighteen months has the following effects:

- If foreign filing is intended or has been completed, the patent application must be published at eighteen months from the U.S. filing date or the earliest claimed priority date.
- Publication serves a public-notice function; it informs competitors and the public of the invention and is also a credible showing to investors.
- Publication can provide provisional rights if the claims that issue are "substantially identical" to those that published and if actual notice is given to the infringer. If infringement is willful and it can be established that the publication of the application was used by the infringer, the damages awarded on infringement can be backdated to the publication date rather than the issue date of the patent.
- Publication releases the invention into the public knowledge base, and it creates worldwide prior art that may be applied to reject other inventions as known or obvious inventions with respect to knowledge already in the public domain.

Exceptions to Publication

The USPTO will not publish the following applications:

- Provisional applications;
- Design applications;
- Reissue applications;
- Applications recognized by the USPTO as no longer pending according to the PALM system;
- Applications under secrecy order or whose disclosure would be detrimental to national security;
- Applications that has issued as a patent before eighteen months will be removed from the publication process; and
- Applications filed with an acceptable non-publication request and a certification of no intended foreign filing.

Requirements for Publication

The USPTO will not publish an application until the application includes:

- a complete application including specification, abstract, and drawings of sufficient quality for publication;
- a sequence listing (if applicable);
- the basic filing fee (and additional application size fee, if applicable); and
- an English translation (if applicable).

If an application does not meet the requirement for publication or is not of sufficient quality for publication, the USPTO will issue a pre-examination notice requiring a substitute specification or replacement drawings. The replacement content of the applicant's reply to the notice will be used for publication. If the applicant does not provide replacement content, the USPTO will publish the application as originally filed.

Projected Publication Date

When the application is deemed complete for publication, the USPTO will identify the projected publication date on the filing receipt. The projected publication date will be the later of:

- eighteen months from the earliest claimed filing date, or
- fourteen weeks from the mailing date of the filing receipt.

The publication process takes about fourteen weeks, and applications are published on the Thursday of each week. The applicant should promptly and carefully review the filing receipt and verify the accuracy of title, inventors, priority claims, entity status, claim count, and projected publication date. If errors are found, the applicant should promptly file a request for a corrected filing receipt. If the projected publication date indicated on the filing receipt is incorrect or if a projected publication date has been assigned to an application filed with a non-publication request, the applicant should contact the Pre-Grant Publication Division. If corrections are required, they must be received by the Pre-Grant Publication Division before the technical preparation for publication has begun. The patent application publication includes a front page containing information similar to that contained on the cover page of an issued patent, the drawings (if any), and the specification including the claims.

Entry of Pre-Publication Amendments

Pre-publication amendments will only be entered and included in the published application if they are submitted in sufficient time before technical preparations for publication have begun. In general, pre-publication amendments must be submitted four months prior to the projected publication date. Any amendments filed must be in a format usable for publication; namely, amendments to the specification must be reflected in a substitute specification, amendments to the abstract must be by replacement abstract, and amendments to the claims must be reflected in a complete claim listing. Any amendments to the drawings must be incorporated in a replacement set of drawings. If the applicant wants the publication of an application to include drawings other than those originally filed with the application, replacement drawings must be filed four months prior to the projected publication date. If the applicant wants to have the publication based upon a copy of the application (specification, abstract, and drawings) as amended, the applicant must supply a substitute specification, including claims and drawings, via EFS-Web within one month of the mailing date of the filing receipt or fourteen months from the earliest claimed filing date. In such situations, the USPTO will use the electronic substitute copy of the complete application provided via EFS-Web for the publication process.

For biological applications containing long nucleotide or amino acid sequences, the sequence listing will only be published in electronic form on the USPTO sequence homepage (http://seqdata.uspto.gov) as an ASCII text file. The patent application publication will include a statement that the application contains a lengthy sequence listing and a hyperlink to the web page containing the sequence listing.

To reduce the publication processing time, the USPTO encourages applicants to avoid filing preliminary amendments. The USPTO will only enter preliminary amendments accompanying the application if they are presented in a format that is usable for publication. Otherwise, the USPTO will request that the applicant submit a substitute application via EFS-Web. To avoid submitting preliminary amendments, the applicant should incorporate any desired amendments into the text of the specification, including a new set of claims, even when the application is a continuation or divisional application of a previously filed application. If the preliminary amendment is being filed only to add or amend a priority benefit claim, a substitute specification is not required.

If the applicant would like the name of the assignee published, the assignee must be identified on the application transmittal letter or the ADS filed with the application. The applicant is still obligated to record an assignment document with the Assignment Division to confirm title rights.

Notice of Publication

Applicants will be informed of the projected publication date assigned to the application on the filing receipt. The USPTO will not mail a paper copy of the patent application publication to the applicant but will mail a Notice of Publication to the applicant indicating that the application has been published. Copies of patent application publications are available on the USPTO website.

A Notice of New or Revised Publication Date may be mailed if the publication date changes by more than six weeks due to processing delays, if a secrecy order is removed, or subsequent to the revival of an abandoned application. If the applicant timely adds or deletes a benefit or priority claim and the USPTO recognizes the correction and changes the projected publication date before the technical preparations of the application have begun, the USPTO will mail a notice (e.g., a corrected filing receipt) informing the applicant of the newly assigned projected publication date.

Early Publication

If the applicant wishes to have an application published before eighteen months from the earliest claimed priority date, the applicant may submit a request for early publication under 37 C.F.R. §1.219, including the publication fee under 37 C.F.R

§1.18(d). The USPTO will publish the application as soon as all publication requirements are met. The publication process takes approximately fourteen weeks and does not begin until the application is complete and ready for publication. The USPTO will not consider requests for publication on a certain date. If early publication is requested, the publication fee should be paid at that time, and no publication fee will be due at allowance.

Voluntary Publication

Utility and plant applications filed before November 29, 2000, will not be published. If an applicant wishes the office to publish such an application, the applicant can file a request for voluntary publication. The application must be pending, and the request for voluntary publication must include:

- a copy of the application in compliance with EFS requirements;
- the publication fee under 37 C.F.R §1.18(d); and
- the processing fee under 37 C.F.R §1.17(i).

If the applicant submits a request for voluntary publication of an application filed before November 29, 2000, but the application is later abandoned before the application publishes, the application may not be published even if the USPTO has accepted the request.

Requests for Non-Publication

If the invention disclosed in an application has not been and will not be filed in a foreign country that requires publication at eighteen months, the applicant may request that the U.S. application not be published by filing a request for non-publication with the initial application filing. The USPTO will not publish an application filed with a non-publication request. The following conditions must be satisfied for non-publication:

- a request for non-publication (Form SB/35) must accompany the application as filed; this is a statutory requirement and cannot be waived;
- the request must state in a prominent manner that the application is not to be published;
- the request must contain a certification that the invention disclosed in the application has not been and will not be the subject of an application filed in another

country (or under a multilateral international agreement) that requires eighteen-month publication; and

- the signer must have made an actual inquiry to determine that the application has not been foreign filed and at the time of filing there is no intention to foreign file.
- Rescission of Request for Non-Publication

If the applicant filed a non-publication request with the original application filing and later decides to file a counterpart foreign or international application in another country (or under a multilateral agreement) that requires eighteen-month publication, the applicant must either:

- rescind the non-publication request before filing such foreign or international application; or
- notify the USPTO of such filing no later than forty-five days after the filing date of the counterpart foreign or international application.

Failure to timely notify the USPTO of counterpart foreign filing (within forty-five days of such foreign filing) when a non-publication request has been filed will result in abandonment of the application. The recession of the non-publication request does not satisfy the timely notice requirement. If the failure to timely notify the USPTO of foreign counterpart filing was unintentional, the application may be revived on filing of a Petition to Revive under 37 C.F.R. §1.137(b), including the substantial associated fee.

The recession of non-publication form (Form SB/36) is used to rescind a non-publication request and provide notice of counterpart foreign filing. The USPTO will treat the non-publication request as annulled, and the application will be treated as if the non-publication request were never made. The USPTO will use the actual date of receipt of recession of non-publication (including notice of foreign filing, required by statute) to determine whether the non-publication request has been rescinded before or on the date of the filing of a foreign counterpart application. After either a rescission of a non-publication request or a notice of foreign filing is received by the USPTO, it is entered into the pre-examination system to schedule the application for publication. A notice regarding rescission of non-publication or notice of foreign filing will be sent to the applicant to inform the applicant of the projected publication date, and the application will be published promptly.

If the applicant made an improper certification and a corresponding foreign application was filed before the filing of the non-publication request, a request to rescind should be promptly filed. The application will not go abandoned, and the USPTO will dismiss any petition to revive as being inappropriate but will retain the large petition fee for having considered the petition. The improper certification may result in an ethics violation with respect to improper representation of information to the USPTO, and it could result in sanctions against the practitioner from the Office of Enrolment and Discipline (OED). If an improper certification was made, it is recommended to file an explanation of the circumstances in addition to the recession to clear the record and avoid any future challenge to the validity of the patent.

Redacted Publication

If a corresponding foreign application discloses less than the U.S. application, the additional disclosure material in the U.S. application may be redacted from the published application by submitting the following documents within sixteen months of the earliest effective filing date sought:

- a redacted copy of the application in electronic format suitable for electronic filing;
- a certified copy of each corresponding foreign application;
- a translation of each foreign application not in English;
- a marked-up copy of the U.S. application showing redactions in brackets; and
- a certification that the redacted copy eliminates only disclosure material not contained in any of the corresponding foreign applications.

Public Access to Published Applications

Patent application publications are publicly available in electronic format from the USPTO website. Any member of the public may also obtain application status information and view the IFW of published applications via public PAIR. Any member of the public may also request a paper copy of a published application from the Office of Public Records on payment of a fee. A copy of the complete file wrapper and contents of, or a copy of a specific paper in, any published application will be provided unless a redacted copy of the application was timely filed. If a redacted copy of the application was timely filed, a redacted copy of the file wrapper and contents will be provided.

Conversely, any member of the public cannot obtain access to the USPTO paper file, as permitting inspection of the physical file would interfere with the Office's ability to act on the application. However, members of the public may physically inspect the file of any abandoned published application provided that no redacted copy was timely submitted for publication.

Any member of the public may obtain status information concerning any published application via public PAIR or by contacting the USPTO's File Information Unit (FIU). Status information includes identification of whether the application has been published, as well as whether the application is pending, abandoned, or patented. Status information may also be obtained when the application is referred to by its application number in a U.S. or international published application. The public may also obtain continuity data for applications that have been published as a U.S. patent application publication or as a U.S. issued patent.

AIA Impact—Request for Access to Unpublished Application

Prior to publication, applications are held confidential and are inaccessible to the public. Effective September 16, 2012, under the AIA, a request for access to an application maintained in confidence under 35 U.S.C. §122(a) must be signed by:

- the applicant;
- a practitioner of record;
- the assignee or an assignee of an undivided part interest;
- the inventor or joint inventor; or
- a registered attorney or agent named in the papers accompanying the application papers filed if a power of attorney has not been appointed.

Averting Publication

If an application is filed without a request for non-publication and the applicant wants to avert publication, one of the following courses of action may be taken (Patent Resources Institute, Inc., 2004):

- File a continuation application with a request for non-publication, and abandon the parent application. Abandonment of the parent must be recognized by the USPTO in sufficient time to avoid publication at eighteen months.
- Applicant can file a petition for Express Abandonment to Avoid Publication under 37 C.F.R. §1.138(c) (Form SB/24A), including the associated fee, but if the applicant is relying on

the USPTO's declaration of abandonment, there is a risk that the abandonment may not be considered and recognized before the eighteen-month publication date.

- Convert to a provisional application, and timely file a non-provisional application claiming priority benefit to the provisional application only.

Republication and Correction of Publications

If the applicant wants to correct errors in a patent application publication or republish the application with an amended specification, including amendments or replacement drawings, or both, the applicant may file a Request for Republication under 37 C.F.R. §1.221(a). The request for republication must include:

- a copy of the application in compliance with EFS requirements;
- publication fee under 37 C.F.R. §1.18(d;) and
- processing fee under 37 C.F.R. §1.17(i).

If the applicant submits a request that does not meet the EFS requirements, the request will be dismissed. If the fees are not paid, the USPTO will send the applicant a letter requiring the fees, and republication of the application will be delayed. There is no set time limit for requesting republication, but the application must still be pending. If the application is recognized by the USPTO as abandoned or has issued as a patent, the application will be removed from the publication process and not republished, even if the USPTO accepted the request for republication.

Material Mistake

If the USPTO made a material mistake in a patent application publication that is apparent from the prosecution record, the applicant may file a request for corrected publication to correct the material mistake. A material mistake is defined as "a mistake that affects the public's ability to appreciate the technical disclosure of the patent application publication or determine the scope of the provisional rights that an applicant may seek to enforce upon issuance of the patent." An error in the claims, the effective filing date of the application, or a serious error in the written description or drawings that is necessary to support the claims may be a material error. The following are examples of material mistakes:

- the publication did not include claims that were included in the originally filed specification and not canceled by a preliminary amendment;

- the publication did not include a part of the specification that provides support for the published claims;
- the publication did not include any of the originally filed drawings; or
- the publication did not include the benefit claim to a prior-filed non-provisional application where the specific reference to the priority application made in an ADS and the specification was amended to update cross-reference to related applications.

Before submitting a request for a corrected publication, the applicant should review the PAIR IFW to determine the source of the material mistake. A request for corrected publication must be filed:

- within two months (not extendable) from the date of the patent application publication;
- including a listing of the alleged material errors made by the USPTO; and
- including a marked-up copy of the published application, indicating where in the specification as filed the relevant text appears.

If the material mistake was the applicant's error, it may be corrected by filing a request for republication, not a request for corrected publication.

Non-Material Mistake

An applicant should not file a request for corrected publication for a patent application that does not include material errors made by the USPTO. Errors in the correspondence address or the assignee information, or missing assignment information, minor typographical errors, or missing section headings are not material mistakes. The applicant should not file a request for corrected publication for the following situations:

- the publication did not include assignment information;
- the publication shows the wrong assignee, or the name of the assignee is misspelled;
- the publication did not include a benefit or priority claim to a prior application when such a claim was not timely filed in the specification or in the ADS;
- the publication did not include claims or changes submitted in an amendment; or
- the publication includes typographical errors that do not affect the interpretation of the published claims.

Where the USPTO made only non-material errors, a request for corrected publication may result in a patent term adjustment reduction.

Publication Practice Tips

The USPTO offers the following tips and suggestions related to publication (USPTO, Patent Practice Tips, 2010):

- When filing a utility or plant application, conspicuously request non-publication if the invention has not been or will not be the subject of an application filed in another country (or under a multilateral international agreement) that requires eighteen-month publication.
- A non-publication request must accompany the initial application filing; it cannot be submitted at a later date.
- Publication will generally include all preliminary amendments submitted in time to be included in the publication.
- If amendments to the specification are desired to be included in the publication, a substitute specification should be submitted.
- A request for corrected publication must be timely filed and must recite material errors.
- Assignment information must be included in the transmittal letter or ADS or else the publication will not contain such information.
- Filing receipts should be reviewed promptly so that corrections can be requested before publication or export of date for publication.

CHAPTER-SPECIFIC REFERENCE MATERIAL

Reference Source	Publication of Applications Applicable Rules, Regulations, and Procedures
Title 35 of the U.S. Code	35 U.S.C. §10 Publications.
Title 37 of the Code of Federal Regulations	37 C.F.R. §1.211 Publication of applications. §1.213 Non-publication request. §1.215 Patent application publication. §1.217 Publication of a redacted copy of an application. §1.219 Early publication. §1.221 Voluntary publication or republication of patent application publication.
Manual of Patent Examination Procedures (MPEP, 8th Edition)	*Chapter 1100* *Statutory Invention Registrations and Pre-Grant Publication*

Chapter 10

Duty of Disclosure, Citation of References, and Third-Party Pre-Issuance Submissions

Introduction

Each individual associated with the substantive filing and prosecution of a patent application has a duty of candor and good faith in dealing with the USPTO, which includes a duty to disclose all information known to be material to patentability. This duty of disclosure exists with respect to each pending claim until the claim is canceled, withdrawn from consideration, or the application status changes to abandoned. The duty of disclosure extends past allowance until a patent is granted on the application.

Who Has the Duty of Disclosure?

All individuals associated with the substantive filing or prosecution of a patent application and who are associated with the inventor, applicant, or assignee are bound by duty of disclosure requirements. More specifically, parties to the matter include the following:

- each inventor named in the application;
- each non-inventor applicant or assignee;
- each attorney/agent who prepares or prosecutes the application; and
- every other person who is substantively involved in the preparation of the application and who is associated with the inventor, with the assignee, or with anyone to whom there is an obligation to assign the application.

Individuals other than the attorney, agent, or inventor may comply with their duty by disclosing material information to the attorney, agent, or inventor, who subsequently brings such information to the attention of the examiner. Information material to patentability should be cited to the examiner on an information disclosure statement (IDS).

Definition of Material Information

The requirement for parties to the matter to disclose information material to patentability is designed to protect the public interest by ensuring that the most effective and comprehensive patent examination occurs. Material information is defined as follows:

- all prior art patents and publications related to the claimed invention known to the inventors, applicants, and assignees, including those referred to during preparation of the application and any that subsequently become known;
- information needed to carry out effective and efficient examination in a determination of patentability of the claims with respect to presently known information;
- information that a reasonable examiner would deem important in deciding whether to allow an application to issue as a patent;
- information that is material but not cumulative to information already of record or being made of record in the application;
- information that establishes by itself or in combination with other information a case of unpatentability of a claim; and
- information that refutes or is inconsistent with a position taken by the applicant, either opposing or asserting an argument for patentability.

Sources of Material Information

All individuals involved in the substantive prosecution of a patent application have the duty to disclose all material information they are aware of regardless of the sources of the information or how they become aware of the information. In effect, this means that once a practitioner or applicant becomes aware that information appearing to be material and questionable exists, he or she cannot ignore the notice in an effort to avoid the duty of disclosure. The standard of materiality controls information to be disclosed, not the circumstances under which or the sources from which the information is obtained. The duty to disclose extends to information individuals were aware of prior to, or at the time of, filing the application, and any material information they become aware of during the prosecution phase.

Support staff working with attorneys and agents need to be informed and aware of all possible sources of material information that need to be cited to the examiner. Support staff should be aware of incoming prior art generating documents (e.g., office actions, examiner reports, and search reports) in priority-related U.S. and foreign applications within the family. In addition, support staff need to be aware of subject matter related families not claimed in priority in the client portfolio to enable tracking and cross-citing of any incoming prior art generating documents. Support staff need to consult a registered practitioner to identify any subject matter related families.

Related Case Law

The USPTO relies on two distinct case law references that specifically point out the applicant's duty to disclose material information from copending U.S. applications.

In Dayco Prods., Inc. v. Total Containment, Inc., 329 F. 3d 1358 (Fed. Cir. 2003):

Details: Two families of applications were pending at the same time with substantially similar claims before two different USPTO examiners. A contrary decision of another examiner reviewing substantially similar claims meets the reasonable-examiner material test because a reasonable examiner would likely consider such a contrary decision important.

Impact: Applicant should disclose office actions from copending U.S. applications having similar subject matter even if they are unrelated by priority. Support staff should consult with the attorney/agent to identify any non-priority subject matter-related families. All issued office actions across subject matter-related families should be cross-cited. Support staff should confirm with the attorney/agent if the office actions from non-priority subject matter-related families should be cited on an SB08 form or embedded as a table in the IDS statement letter.

In McKesson Information Solutions, Inc. v. Bridge Medical Inc., 487 F. 3d 897 (Fed. Cir. 2007):

Details: Two families of U.S. applications were pending at the same time before the same examiner. When an examiner issues a notice of allowance for a parent application, the allowed claims should be identified to the examiner of the instant application.

Impact: Applicant should disclose any Notice of Allowance issued in related applications even if the applications are before the same examiner. Support staff should consult with attorney/agent to identify any non-priority subject matter-related families. All Notices of Allowance across subject matter-related families should be cross-cited. Support staff should confirm with the attorney/agent if the Notice of Allowance from non-priority subject matter-related families should be cited on an SB08 form or embedded as a table in the IDS statement letter.

The potential categories of material information, the related source documents, and their potential relevance are summarized in Table 16.

Table 16: Material Information—Categories, Sources, and Relevance

Categories of Material Information	Source Documents	Considerations
Information from Priority Related Pending U.S. Applications (within priority family)	Examiner 892 citation form. Applicant SB08 citation form. Office actions and notice of allowance issued in copending priority-related applications.	Applicant cannot assume the examiner is aware of office actions and allowed claims in a priority related U.S. application.
Information from Non-Priority Pending U.S. Applications with Related Subject Matter (across families with similar subject matter)	Examiner 892 citation form. Applicant SB08 citation form. Office actions and notice of allowance issued in copending applications with similar subject matter.	Applicant cannot assume that the examiner of a particular application is necessarily aware of other copending U.S. applications that have related subject matter. Identify inventors in copending applications with similar subject matter but patentability distinct claims.
Prior Art Cited in Related Foreign Applications (pending foreign counterpart applications in the priority family)	Prior art used in rejecting the same or similar claims in foreign counterpart applications. Prior art identified as particularly relevant in foreign search reports or by foreign patent examining office. International Search Report (ISR) and Written Opinion (WO) from foreign counterpart applications. Foreign examination and patentability reports from foreign counterpart applications.	Prior art cited in foreign search reports must be cited to the examiner by applicant. Prior art originating in a related foreign application must be cited to the USPTO within thirty days or three months of it becoming known based on the mailing date of the foreign search report or foreign office action.

Information from Related Litigation Proceedings	Evidence of possible prior public use or sales. Questions of inventorship. Allegations of fraud, inequitable conduct, and violation of duty of disclosure. Assertions made during litigation that are contradictory to position taken with the examiner.	Where the subject matter for which a patent is being sought is or has been involved in litigation, the existence of such litigation and any related material information must be brought to the attention of the examiner.
Information related to any Post-Grant Review, Interference, or Derivation proceedings	Identification of any post grant review, interference, or derivation proceedings.	Any related post grant review, interference or derivation proceedings must be brought to the attention of the examiner.

Filing Information Disclosure Statements

An IDS is the submission used to bring known material information to the attention of the patent examiner. Filing an IDS requires a review of prior art reference to be cited, preparation of an IDS letter, preparation of an IDS citation form, and submission of foreign and non-patent literature references. To be considered by the examiner, an IDS must include the following:

- a list of all patents, publications, applications, or other material information for consideration by the examiner;
- a legible copy of each foreign patent or publication and each non-patent literature reference (copies of U.S. patents or publications are not required);
- a copy of copending unpublished applications or portion of same considered relevant to the claims;
- for non-English documents, a concise explanation of the relevance of each reference; and
- an English translation of any foreign language document if it is readily available.

If the IDS does not comply with the submission requirements, it will be placed in the file but will not be considered by the examiner. The filing of an IDS cannot be construed as a representation that a search has been made and is not an admission that the information cited is, or is considered to be, material to patentability.

IDS Timing Considerations

Material information known at the time of filing should be cited in an IDS filed with the application or filed before the later of three months from the application filing date, or before the first office action on the merits (not including a restriction requirement). All references cited in a counterpart foreign application should be cited to the examiner within thirty days (to preserve patent term) or three months of citation of the references by a foreign patent office to enable a certification statement by the applicant. If an IDS is filed outside of the three-month period after the mailing date of foreign notice, payment of fees or certification statements, or both, will be required.

If an IDS is filed after the first office action on the merits but before the mailing of a final action, notice of allowance, or an action that otherwise closes prosecution in the application, the applicant must make a certification statement.

If an IDS is filed after a final office action, and the applicant is unable to make the certification statement and unable to pay the fee, then the only option to obtain consideration by the examiner is to file a Request for Continued Examination (RCE) indicating that the IDS is included as an authorized submission.

If an IDS is filed after payment of the issue fee, it must be accompanied by a petition to withdraw the application from issuance.

If, based on the timing requirements, the applicant has an option of paying a fee or making a certification statement, payment of the fee would be the more prudent option, rather than signing a certification statement on behalf of all parties to the matter. The statement and fee scenarios related to filing an IDS are summarized in Figure I.

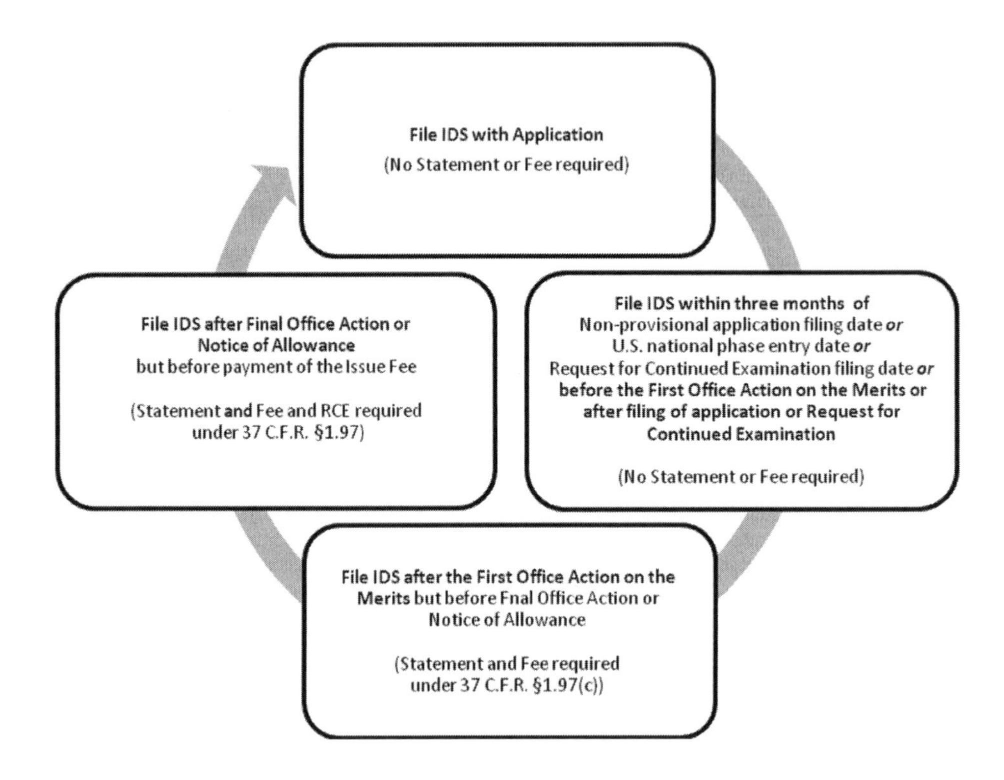

Figure I: Information Disclosure Statements--Statement and Fee Senarios

IDS Statement or Letter

If an IDS is filed after the first office action but before an action closing prosecution on the merits, the applicant must make a statement under 37 C.F.R. §1.97(e) that either:

- each item of information contained in the IDS was first cited in any communication from a foreign patent office in a counterpart foreign application not more than three months prior to the filing of the information disclosure statement; or
- no item of information contained in the IDS was cited in a communication from a foreign patent office in a counterpart foreign application and, to the knowledge of the person signing the certification, after making reasonable inquiry, no item in the IDS was known to any individual associated with the filing or prosecution of the application more than three months prior to the filing of the IDS; and
- pay the fee under 37 C.F.R. §1.17 (p).

The statement made in the IDS letter depends on the circumstance under which the IDS is being filed. The following are the circumstance-related statements that can be included in an IDS:

- This Information Disclosure Statement is being filed under 37 C.F.R. §1.97(b)(1) within three months of the filing date of the subject application. Therefore, applicant holds that no fee is due.
- This Information Disclosure Statement is being filed under 37 C.F.R. §1.97(b)(2) within three months of the date of entry of the national stage as identified in 37 C.F.R. §1.491 in an international application. Therefore, applicant holds that no fee is due.
- This Information Disclosure Statement is being filed under 37 C.F.R. §1.97(b)(3) before the mailing of a first Office Action on the merits. Therefore, applicant holds that no fee is due.
- This Information Disclosure Statement is being filed under 37 C.F.R. §1.97(b)(4) before the mailing of a first Office Action after the filing of a Request for Continued Examination under 37 C.F.R. §1.114. Therefore, applicant holds that no fee is due.
- This Information Disclosure Statement is being filed under 37 C.F.R. §1.97(c)(2) after the mailing date of the first Office Action on the merits, but before the mailing date of a Final Office Action or a Notice of Allowance. Applicant hereby authorizes the Director to charge $_____ for payment of the fee under in 37 C.F.R. §1.17(p). The Director is authorized to charge payment of any additional fee required, or credit any overpayment, in connection with this Statement to Deposit Account No. _________, under Order No. ___________.
- This Information Disclosure Statement is being filed under 37 C.F.R. §1.97(d)(1) and 37 C.F.R. §1.97(e)(1) after the mailing of a Final Office Action or a Notice of Allowance, but before payment of the issue fee. Applicant requests consideration of each item cited on this Information Disclosure Statement as first cited in a communication from a foreign patent office in a counterpart foreign application not more than three months prior to the filing of the information disclosure statement. Applicant hereby authorizes the Director to charge $_____ for payment of the fee under 37 C.F.R. §1.17(p). The Director is authorized to charge payment of any additional fee required, or credit any overpayment, in

connection with this Statement to Deposit Account No. _______ under Order No. __________.

- This Information Disclosure Statement is being filed under 37 C.F.R. §1.97(d)(1) and 37 C.F.R. §1.97(e)(2) after the mailing of a Final Office Action or a Notice of Allowance, but before payment of the issue fee. Applicant requests consideration of each item cited on this Information Disclosure Statement as first cited in a communication from a foreign patent office in a counterpart foreign application, and, to the knowledge of the person signing the certification after making reasonable inquiry, no item of information contained in the information disclosure statement was known to any individual designated in 37 C.F.R. §1.56(c) more than three months prior to the filing of the information disclosure statement. Applicant hereby authorize the Director to charge $_____ in payment of the fee under 37 C.F.R. §1.17(p). The Director is authorized to charge payment of any additional fee required, or credit any overpayment, in connection with this Statement to Deposit Account No. _____ under Order No. _______.

IDS Fees

The fee to file an IDS is under 37 C.F.R. §1.17(p); it is a flat fee and is not subject to entity size discounting. No extensions of time are available with respect to the filing of an IDS. If a fee is paid, it can be paid by credit card, EFT, or Deposit Account. If the applicant is unsure if the USPTO will deem that a fee is due, the applicant can include a general fee authorization at the end of the IDS letter rather than risk that the examiner will not consider the IDS if a fee is due and was not authorized.

There are several filing circumstances under which there is no fee to file an IDS. The no-fee IDS filing circumstances are the following:

- IDS filed with the initial application filing;
- IDS filed within three months of the application filing;
- IDS filed before the first office action on the merits;
- IDS filed within thirty days or three months of the date of citation of the art by a foreign patent office; and
- IDS filed with a RCE or before the mailing of a first office action on the merits after the filing of a RCE.

Providing Copies of References

When filing an IDS, the applicant must provide copies of foreign and non-patent references cited on the information citation form. The applicant does not have to provide copies of U.S. patent or printed publications. The applicant must provide the following:

- a legible copy of each foreign patent or publication;
- a legible copy of each non-patent literature reference;
- a legible copy of any cited, unpublished U.S. application, the application specification including the claims, and any drawing of the application, or that portion of the application that caused it to be listed, including any claims directed to that portion.

The applicant does not have to provide copies of references previously submitted in a parent application when filing an IDS in a continuation application. The applicant can include the following language in the IDS letter.

> The references cited in this Information Disclosure Statement were previously cited in U.S. Patent Application No. ______________, from which the instant application claims priority under 35 U.S.C. §120. Thus, pursuant to 37 C.F.R. §1.98(d), the applicant has not enclosed copies of the references and requests that the examiner retrieve copies of the references from the parent application file.

IDS Citation Form

The IDS SB08 form should be used to record references considered by the examiner and printed in the front page of the issued patent. The USPTO strongly encourages the use of the SB08 form, to enable the applicant to comply with requirements to list each item of information being submitted and to provide the USPTO with a uniform listing of citations and an amenable way to indicate information considered by the examiner. The SB08 form is a two-page form (SB08A and SB08B) with distinct sections for U.S. patent and publications, foreign patents, and non-patent literature citations. The USPTO has identified the following specific considerations with respect to the use of the SB08 form (USPTO, Information Disclosure Statements, 2010).

- Form SB08 should include a heading that clearly identifies it as an Information Disclosure Statement and should include a caption that identifies the attorney docket number, application number, filing date, first named inventor, and the group art unit.

- SB08A (page 1) should contain a maximum of nineteen U.S. patent document citations and six foreign patent document citations;
  - each U.S. patent listed should be identified by inventor, patent number, and issue date;
  - each U.S. application publication should be identified by applicant, publication number and publication date; and
  - each foreign patent or publication should be identified by country (or two-letter country code) or patent office, publication, or patent number, and the publication or issue date.
  - SB08B (page 2) should contain ten non-patent literature citations:
  - each non-patent literature citation should be identified by author, title, relevant pages, publisher, and date of publication.
- When each section of SB08A and SB08B fill with the maximum number of citations, the remaining citations should go in their respective sections on additional SB08A and SB08B pages.
- Office actions or notices of allowance from pending U.S. applications may be cited in the body of the IDS letter or in the non-patent literature section of the SB08B. If cited in the body of the IDS letter, it is preferable that a table format be used to allow line-item extraction for printing on the cover page of the patent.
- The SB08 form should include a column adjacent to each citation for the examiner to insert his or her initials. The form should also include a section for the examiner to e-sign and date at the end of the document. The examiner will strike through any citations not considered. A marked-up citation form will be returned to the applicant as an indication of references considered by the examiner and references not considered by the examiner.
- Unpublished, pending U.S. applications should be cited in the body of the IDS letter to prevent them being printed on the front page of the issued patent.
- Citation of material downloaded from a website should include a hyperlink to the website address.

IDS and Patent Term

The USPTO has an expectation that applicants engage in reasonable efforts to conclude prosecution in a timely manner. Delays in concluding prosecution can be caused by the USPTO or by the applicant and can affect the term of the issuing patent. When an IDS is filed containing references first cited in any communication from a foreign patent office in a counterpart application, and the IDS is filed within thirty days of the mailing date of such communications, the applicant will be considered engaged in reasonable efforts to conclude prosecution, and there will be no detrimental effect on patent term adjustment. The thirty-day period under 37 C.F.R. § 1.704(d) to cite information from foreign counterpart applications is not extendable, and failure to comply with this time period can result in a reduction in the period of adjustment of patent term.

If an IDS is filed citing reference of a foreign search report and the references are cited within thirty days of the mailing date of the foreign search report, the applicant can make the following statement:

> This Information Disclosure Statement is being filed under 37 C.F.R. §1.704(d). The applicant states that each item of information contained in the information disclosure statement was first cited in a communication from a foreign patent office in a counterpart application and that this communication was not received by any individual designated in §1.56(c) more than thirty days prior to the filing of the information disclosure statement. Thus, the applicant holds that the submission of this Statement does not affect any patent term adjustment.

Prior Art Management

Support staff dedicate extensive time and effort to preparing and submitting information disclosure statements throughout the prosecution phase. To make this task less time-consuming and labor-intensive, support staff can adopt some of the following practical strategies:

- Cite U.S. patent and publications in chronological order (from the most recent to the oldest by issue or publication date) so references are ordered how they are cited on the SB08 form. This will reduce the time spent cross-checking and accounting for all references.
- Cite non-patent literature alphabetically by author, and order the references being submitted accordingly to reduce the time spent cross-checking and accounting for all references.
- Ensure that the number of foreign or non-patent references submitted match the number of citations in each respective section on the SB08 form.

Prior Art Tracking

To help track prior art citations within priority-related families and across non-priority subject matter-related families, a centralized robust tracking system should be used. Support staff should consider compiling prior art tracking charts per client that will allow logging of prior art references received and cited in addition to noting the source matter and source date of the reference. A prior art management system should include the following steps:

- identification of the pending U.S. and foreign matters (where art must be cited to a foreign patent office) within the priority family;
- indication of the status of the U.S. and foreign matters (pending, allowed, issued)
- identification of any subject matter non-priority-related families;
- central log of all inbound prior art references (U.S., foreign, and non-patent literature) received, including notation of source matter, type of source document, and source date;
- notation of references that need to be cited in a IDS;
- notation of references that need to be forwarded to foreign agents in compliance with the foreign Patent Office duty of disclosure requirements; and
- location of file repository where copies of foreign and non-patent literature references may be retrieved.

Given that the duty of disclosure extends to foreign-filed applications, review and citing of prior art should include an awareness of citing requirements for foreign patent offices. While compiling prior art tracking charts can be time-consuming in the beginning, support staff will find them a very valuable time-saving tool as additional priority and non-priority U.S. and foreign patent applications are filed. To support understanding, a sample client-specific prior art tracking chart, created using Excel, is shown in Figure J, including interpretation guidelines.

Sample Client-Specific Prior Art Tracking Chart

	A	B	C	D	E	F	G	H	I	K	L	M	N	O	Q	R	S	T	U
1	Client Name	Prior Art Tracking Chart																	
2				Priority Family F1						Priority Family F2					Priority Family F3				
3				UTIL F1	CON	DIV	CA1	IN1	IL1	UTIL F2	DIV 2	CA1	IN1	IL1	UTIL F3	CA1	IN1	EP2	IL1
4				Similar Subject Matter to F3											Similar Subject Matter to F1				
5	Reference Details	Source	Source Date																
6	US Patents																		
7	2,258,584	892 NFOA	5/9/11	√	√	DNC	√	√	√	N/A	N/A	N/A	N/A	N/A	√	√	DNC	√	√
8	5,269,584	Inventor	1/2/10	√	DNC	√	√	√	DNC	N/A	N/A	N/A	N/A	N/A	√	DNC	√	√	√
9	2,587,147	PCT ISR	15/8/12	√	√	DNC	DNC	√	√	√	DNC	√	DNC	√	√	√	DNC	DNC	√
10	6,254,325	EP EESR	6/12/13	√	DNC	√	√	√	DNC	N/A	N/A	N/A	N/A	N/A	√	DNC	√	√	√
11	4,254,258	Inventor	1/2/11	√	DNC	DNC	√	√	√	N/A	N/A	N/A	N/A	N/A	√	DNC	DNC	√	√
12	US Publications																		
13	2003/122345	IDS filed	1/6/11	√	√	√	√	√	√	DNC	DNC	DNC	DNC	DNC	√	√	√	√	√
14	2005/142586	IDS filed		√	DNC	√	√	√	√	√	DNC	√	DNC	√	√	DNC	√	√	√
15	Foreign Patents & Publications																		
16	EP 0 254 254	PCT ISR	15/8/10	√	√	DNC	√	√	DNC	DNC	DNC	DNC	DNC	DNC	√	DNC	√	√	√
17	WO 99/25874	PCT ISR	15/8/10	√	DNC	√	√	√	√	DNC	DNC	DNC	DNC	DNC	√	√	√	√	√
18	DE 3,369,258	PCT ISR	15/8/10	√	√	√	√	√	DNC	√		√		√	√	√	√	√	√
19	Non Patent Literature																		
20	Author et al, "Name of Article" Journal Name, pp. 1-10, Month, Year	Inventor	1/2/10	√	DNC	DNC	√	DNC	DNC	N/A	N/A	N/A	N/A	N/A	√	DNC	DNC	√	DNC
21	Office Actions & Notice of Allowances																		
22	Final Office Action mailed 9/8/06, Appl. No. 12/XXX,XXX	Examiner	7/6/12	√	√	√	N/A	N/A	N/A	N/A	N/A	N/A	N/A	N/A	√	N/A	N/A	N/A	N/A
23	Notice of Allowance mailed 3/30/07, Appl. No. 12/XXX,XXX	Examiner	9/11/13	√	√	√	N/A	N/A	N/A	N/A	N/A	N/A	N/A	N/A	√	N/A	N/A	N/A	N/A

Figure J: Sample Client-Specific Prior Art Tracking Chart

Interpretation Guidelines

- Column A: references are logged under category heading (U.S. patents, U.S. publications, foreign patents and publications, non-patent literature, and U.S. office actions and notice of allowances) compatible with citation sections on a SB08 form.
- Columns B & C: the source of the reference (892 cited by examiner, ISR cited in international search report issued in PCT application, provided by inventor/applicant) and the source date of the reference to make retrieving the reference easier.
- Columns D-I: shows a priority-related family (F1) identifying all pending U.S. and foreign applications where there is an ongoing duty of disclosure (e.g., Canada, India, Israel).
- Column K-O: shows a priority-related family (F2) identifying all pending U.S. and foreign applications where there is an ongoing duty of disclosure.
- Columns Q-U: shows a priority-related family (F3) identifying all pending U.S. and foreign applications where there is an ongoing duty of disclosure.
- Subject Matter (Non-Priority) Related Families: shading shows that families F1 and F3 have non-priority subject matter related claims. References, office actions, and notices of allowance from family F1 are subject to cross-citing across family F3 and vice versa.
- References Cited/Sent to Foreign Agent: are indicated by a "√"
- References Not to be Cited: are indicated as Do Not Cite (DNC) per attorney's instructions.
- References Not Applicable to the Claimed Subject Matter: are indicated as N/A

Information Printed on Patent

References cited by the applicant on an SB08 form and considered by the examiner will be printed on the cover page of the patent under the references cited section. References cited by the examiner on form PTO892 will be noted with an asterisk; the remaining listed references will be considered as cited by the applicant. A citation listed in a separate paper equivalent to but not on a SB08 form and considered by the examiner will be printed on the cover of the patent page of the patent if the list lends itself to easy capture of the necessary information by the USPTO printing contractors. Such citations will be listed as line items under the "other publications" subheading of the references cited section. Applicants can list U.S. patent application numbers in the IDS letter to avoid the application numbers being published on the cover page of the patent. If a citation is not printed on the cover page of the patent but has been considered by the examiner, the patent file will reflect that fact.

AIA Impact—Pre-Issuance Submissions by Third Parties

Effective September 16, 2012, the AIA introduced a new option for third parties to make submissions they deem relevant to the examination of a pending application. The statutory provision of pre-issuance submissions are intended to improve the effectiveness and efficiency of patent examination by ensuring the most pertinent documents are considered by the examiner when determining the patentability of the claims. Pre-issuance submissions allow a third party to submit for consideration and inclusion in the record of a patent application any patent, published patent application, or other printed publication of potential relevance to the examination of the application.

Who Can File Pre-Issuance Submissions

Any member of the public may file a third-party submission, including private persons and corporate entities. However, the third party may not be the applicant or any individual who has a duty to disclose information with respect to the application under 37 C.F.R. §1.56.

Timing of Filing

A pre-issuance submission by a third party can be made in any non-provisional utility, design, or plant application, including continuations, but not including reissue applications or reexamination proceedings. A third-party pre-issuance submission must be statutorily submitted before the earlier of:

- the date a notice of allowance under 35 U.S.C. §151 is given or mailed in the application; or
- the later of (i) six months after the date on which the application is first published under 35 U.S.C. §122, or (ii) the date of the first rejection under 35 U.S.C. §132 of any claim by the examiner during the examination of the application.

The statutory time periods for filing third-party pre-issuance submissions cannot be waived. If the submission is deemed non-compliant, the third party will be notified electronically only if they provided an e-mail address in the pre-issuance submission (Horton, 2010).

Third parties can check public PAIR to determine if a notice of allowance has been issued in an application. If a notice of allowance has been issued, the third party cannot file a submission. If a notice of allowance has not issued, the third party can determine from PAIR if the examiner has issued a first rejection of the claims or if the application has been published for six months or longer.

If a third party files a pre-issuance submission on the same date the first rejection is mailed and the application has been published for more than six months, the submission would not be timely filed and would not be entered. All third-party submissions must be filed prior to—not on—the critical submission deadlines. Where the application has been published for more than six months and no notice of allowance has issued, the critical pre-issuance submission deadline is the mailing date of the first rejection.

Submission Requirements

To be compliant and entered into the application file, a third-party pre-issuance submission must include the following:

- Form SB/429 (or equivalent document list), identifying the publications, or portions of publications, being submitted (Form SB/429 should be used for paper submissions only; a completed form SB/429 will be automatically generated for electronic submissions);
- A concise description of the asserted relevance of each item identified in the document list;
- A legible copy of each item identified in the document list, other than U.S. patents and U.S. patent application publications;
- An English-language translation of any non-English-language item identified in the document list;
- Statements by the party making the submission that:
    - the party is not an individual who has a duty to disclose information with respect to the application under §1.56; and
    - the submission complies with the requirements of 35 U.S.C. §122(e) and §1.290; and
- Any required fee, or the statement that the fee exemption applies to the submission.

Each submission is limited to ten items of prior art. Multiple submissions, each containing ten items, may be made, as long as the fee is paid for each submission. The concise description of relevance must be more than a bare statement that the document is relevant; it must point out the sections of the references that are applicable to examination of the claims of the application. The concise description of relevance must identify facts that explain how an item listed is of potential relevance to the examination of the application. The third-party submitter must point out the relevant pages or lines of the respective document and provide a focused description to draw the examiner's attention to the relevant issues. The concise description of relevance is limited to a factual description and should not include arguments against patentability or draw conclusions about whether one or more claims are patentable.

Rather than submitting new prior art, a third party may resubmit existing prior art of record in the file, along with an explanation of additional information in that prior art. The additional information could explain a point of view not considered by the examiner and may point to parts of the prior art not discussed in any rejection or reply of record (Horton, 2010). The third party should not propose rejections of the claims or provide arguments relating to an office action or applicant's reply to an office action. The third party is not required to serve the applicant with a copy of the submission. Third parties cannot submit evidence of on-sale activities or challenges concerning inventorship, best mode, or enablement in a pre-issuance submission.

If the publication date of a printed publication filed in a pre-issuance submission is not known, the third party may include the document; however, the third party must supply evidence of publication. At minimum, the third party must provide a date of retrieval or a time frame when the document was available as a publication as well as include evidence that establishes the document as a publication. Such evidence may be in the form of affidavits, declarations, or any other appropriate format.

Filing Fees

There is no submission fee for the first three or fewer submission of documents, provided the third party makes a statement indicating that this is their first and only submission. There is a document flat fee under 37 C.F.R §1.17(p) for the submission of four to ten documents, with increasing amounts of the same fee for every fraction of ten additional documents filed. The fee under 37 C.F.R §1.17(p) is subject to small entity discounting; however, micro entity discounting does not apply. If a fee is applicable, it must accompany the pre-issuance submission at the time of filing. If the third party is submitting more than one set of ten documents (e.g., twelve documents), the contents would have to be split into two separate submissions (i.e., ten documents and two documents) and the fee paid for each submission.

If a third party has already taken advantage of the fee exemption in the application, a second third party may take advantage of the fee exemption in the same application as long as the submission includes three or fewer items and is accompanied by the "first and only" statement. However, such a statement can only be made when the third parties are not in privity with each other. If a third party has already taken advantage of the fee exemption on filing a first pre-issuance submission, they can still file a subsequent pre-issuance submission if the need for the subsequent submission was not known at the time of the earlier submission. Any subsequent submission would require payment of the appropriate fee.

Filing Methods

The USPTO strongly encourages that third-party pre-issuance submission be filed electronically under the dedicated filing category in EFS-Web. However, third-party pre-issuance submissions may also be submitted in paper via first-class mail, USPS Express Mail, or hand delivery. Paper-based submissions will be subject to processing delays related to scanning and indexing of the documents. Third-party pre-issuance submissions cannot be filed by facsimile.

The USPTO encourages the use of form SB/429 for paper submissions, as the form will help to ensure that important requirements are not overlooked, such as the document listing requirements and the required statement under §1.290. The form will also enable the third party to indicate whether a fee is due or to select the "first and only" statement where the fee exemption applies.

Use of the form will not be necessary for pre-issuance submissions filed electronically via EFS-Web, as the interface will prompt the third party to complete the fields that are provided in the form and will automatically format the information into an electronic version of the form.

Processing of Non-Compliant Submissions

The third-party pre-issuance submission will be screened for the filing requirements, and if not compliant, the submission will not be entered in the application. If the submission is deemed non-compliant, the third-party submitter will be notified, and the USPTO will identify the reasons for non-compliance. If the pre-issuance submission was filed electronically via EFS-Web, the third-party submitter can indicate through the interface under applicant data "Request for Notification of Non-Compliant Third-Party Pre-Issuance Submission" and enter an e-mail address in the box provided. The e-mail address will not be made of record in the application if the submission is deemed compliant. If the third-party submitter does not provide an e-mail address for the notification of non-compliance, no notification will be provided.

If the pre-issuance submission was filed via paper, the request for notification of a non-compliant submission must be made on a separate sheet of paper. The paper should be clearly identified as "Request for Notification of Non-Compliant Third-Party Pre-Issuance Submission" and identify the e-mail address to which the notification should be directed. The paper must be clearly labeled so the paper is not made of record in the application if the submission is deemed compliant.

Non-compliant pre-issuance submissions will not be entered in the IFW or considered by the examiner. The USPTO will not refund the required fees or toll the statutory time period for making a third-party submission if it is not compliant. The USPTO will not accept amendments to non-compliant submissions, but the third party may file another complete submission, provided the statutory time period for filing the submission has not closed.

Processing of Compliant Submissions

If the third-party pre-issuance submission meets the filing requirements and is deemed compliant, it will be entered into the application file. The examiner will consider a compliant submission in the same manner as information in an IDS filed by the applicant. If the submission is compliant and entered, the applicant will be notified of a compliant submission against the application. There is no duty on the applicant to reply to third-party pre-issuance submissions absent a request by the examiner to do so. The USPTO will directly notify the applicant of entry of the third-party pre-issuance submission. The contents of the compliant submission will be available via the IFW of the application in PAIR. In addition, the examiner will provide a copy of the listings showing which documents were considered in the next office action. Considered documents will be printed on the issued patent. The third party is not permitted to respond to an examiner's treatment of a submission.

To minimize exposure to third-party pre-issuance submissions, applicants should consider filing a request for non-publication with the application when no foreign filing is intended. The non-publication request would eliminate the opportunity for third parties to file pre-issuance submissions against an application that remains unpublished and confidential.

CHAPTER-SPECIFIC REFERENCE MATERIAL

Reference Source	Duty of Disclosure, Citation of References, and Third-Party Pre-Issuance Submission Applicable Rules, Regulations, and Procedures
AIA Implementation Frequently Asked Questions	Third Party Pre-Issuance Submissions *http://www.uspto.gov/aia_implementation/faq.jsp*
Title 35 of the U.S. Code	35 U.S.C. *§301 Citation of prior art.*
Title 37 of the Code of Federal Regulations	37 C.F.R. §1.97 Filing of information disclosure statement. §1.98 Content of information disclosure statement. §1.99 Third-party submission in published application.
Manual of Patent Examination Procedures (MPEP, 8th Edition)	*Chapter 2000* *Duty of Disclosure*

Chapter 11

Completion of Pre-Examination Filing Formalities

Introduction

When an initial application is filed, the Office of Patent Application Processing (OPAP) reviews the application for compliance with formality filing requirements and creates the record in the Patent Application Location Monitoring (PALM) system. OPAP also loads document images into the image file wrapper (IFW) and the patent application services and security (PASS) system. The PASS system converts key document into optical character recognition (OCR) format and performs an automated classification and security review based on key words and phrases. If PASS detects national security interest terms, OPAP performs a manual review. If there are color drawings or sequence listing (in ASCII text format) present in the application filing they are loaded into the supplemental complex repository for examiners (SCORE) system. Filing fees are accounted for using the revenue and accounting management (RAM) system. Black and white drawings are automatically loaded into SCORE and the IFW.

The OPAP will notify the applicant of any incomplete or missing items, setting a two-month period for response. All formality filing requirements must be completed before substantive examination can begin. The USPTO will issue a range of pre-examination notices identifying the incomplete or missing formality item.

Notice of Incomplete Application

If an application as filed is missing any of the three parts required to obtain a filing date (the description of the invention, one or more claims, and a drawing, if a drawing is necessary to understand the invention), the OPAP will not accord a filing date. The OPAP will send the applicant a Notice of Incomplete Application, setting a two-month response period for the applicant to furnish the missing part.

Response to Notice of Incomplete Application

In response to a Notice of Incomplete Application, the applicant must either file the identified missing parts or challenge the correctness of the Notice. If the applicant submits the missing description, claims, or drawings, the application will be accorded a filing date as of the date the last of those three items is filed with the USPTO.

If applicant wishes to challenge the correctness of the Notice, a petition to the Commissioner under 37 C.F.R. §1.53(e)(2) must be filed requesting review and reversal of OPAP's determination, including the fee required under 37 C.F.R. §1.17(h). In support of such a petition, the applicant must provide evidence that the application as filed was complete by including either:

- a date-stamped return-receipt postcard from the USPTO that accounts for the pages of specification, the number of claims, and the number of sheets of drawings; or
- an electronic filing acknowledgment receipt, which accounts for the pages of specification, the number of claims, and the number of sheets of drawings.

If only the drawings are identified as the missing item, the applicant may challenge that a drawing is not needed to understand the invention and request that the application be accorded a filing date as of the date of receipt of the description and claims (Patent Resources Institute, Inc., 2004).

Notice of Omitted Items

If an application was filed missing one or more pages of the specification or one or more of the figures, the OPAP will accord a filing date. The OPAP will send the applicant a Notice of Omitted Items, setting a two-month response period to furnish the omitted items.

Response to Notice of Omitted Items

In response to the Notice of Omitted Items, the applicant must either file the omitted pages of the specification or figures or challenge the correctness of the Notice. If the applicant's response to the Notice is the submission of the missing pages of the specification or figures, the filing date of the application will be the date the omitted items were filed, not the originally accorded filing date. The applicant is not obligated to respond to the Notice; however, failure to respond will be treated as the applicant's acceptance of the application as deposited without the identified missing pages of the specification or figures. In such situations, the applicant will have to file a preliminary amendment to the specification or figures to repaginate the specification or remove any reference to omitted figures and correct figure-sheet numbering if required. Such corrective preliminary amendments must be filed before the first office action in order to avoid delays in the examination of the application. If the examiner deems the omitted material essential to use of the invention or critical elements in the claims, the applicant will receive statutory rejections to patentability.

If the applicant challenges that the pages of the specification or figures said to be missing were actually filed and received by the USPTO, a petition to the Commissioner under 37 C.F.R. §1.53(e), including the fee required under 37 C.F.R. §1.17(h), must be filed. In support of such a petition, the applicant must provide evidence that the USPTO received the missing items, such as by an itemized return-receipt postcard or electronic filing acknowledgment receipt. The USPTO will refund the petition fee if it is determined that the pages of the specification or figures were received with the application as filed (Patent Resources Institute, Inc., 2004).

Notice to File Missing Parts

If the application contained all parts necessary to obtain a filing date but was missing the filing fee or an inventor declaration, OPAP will send the applicant a Notice to File Missing Parts, setting an extendable two-month period.

The two-month response period may be extendable up to five additional months on payment of associated extension fees, resulting in a potential seven-month response period. If the missing filing fee and late submission surcharge fee or signed inventor oath or declaration, or both, are not filed within seven months from the mailing date of the notice, the application will be deemed abandoned as of midnight on the last day of the set two-month response period (Patent Resources Institute, Inc., 2004).

Response to Notice to File Missing Parts

In response to the Notice to File Missing Parts, the applicant must furnish the items identified in the Notice. The most common items required to be filed in response to a Notice to File Missing Parts are the following:

- the filing fee;
- a signed declaration of inventor with respect to each inventor for applications filed before September 16, 2012;
- identification of inventive entities including inventor names and addresses for applications filed on or after September 16, 2012; or
- formal drawings.

In addition to filing one or more of the above items, the applicant must pay a surcharge for responding to the Notice. If applicant responds to the Notice beyond the two-month response period, additional extension of time fees must also be paid.

AIA Impact—Inventor Oath or Declaration Options

For original applications and related continuing applications filed on or after September 16, 2012, the declaration of the inventor can include the following options:

- a declaration form: when all inventors are available and willing to sign;
- a substitute statement: when an inventor is deceased, incapacitated, cannot be located, or refuses to sign, signed by a person with sufficient proprietary interest; or
- a combined assignment-declaration: used in lieu of a declaration when the declaration language is included in an assignment document and the assignment has been recorded. A copy of the recorded assignment must be provided for the prosecution image file wrapper and will be part of the public record.

When responding to a Notice to File Missing Parts, support staff should confirm that a signed version one of the above documents is filed with respect to each inventor. The content requirements and related forms for the declaration-related filings options are discussed in more detail in Chapter 8.

Extended Missing Parts Pilot Program

The Extended Missing Parts (EMP) pilot program allows applicants to postpone the decision of whether to pursue an application, which otherwise requires completing the desired list of claims and paying search and examination fees. The EMP pilot program provides a twelve month extension to the existing twelve month provisional application period, providing applicants additional time to find financial help, evaluate a product's worth in the marketplace or further develop the invention for commercialization. This is achieved by a change to missing parts practice that will provide twelve additional months to perfect a non-provisional patent application.

Normally applicants have a one-year period from the filing date of a provisional application to file a corresponding non-provisional application in order to claim the benefit of the provisional application. The EMP change to missing parts practice does not alter this requirement but will provide applicants with more time to reply to a missing parts notice in a non-provisional application that claims the benefit of a provisional application, as well as delay the search and examination fees associated with the non-provisional application

Filing Requirements

To take advantage of the EMP pilot program, an applicant or inventor must file a non-provisional application no later than twelve months after the filing date of the provisional application, as well as request a delay in payment of the search and examination fees. The EMP pilot program does not change the requirement that an applicant must file a non-provisional application, foreign, or PCT application within twelve months of the filing date of a provisional application. If a non-provisional application, foreign, or PCT application is filed later than twelve months from the filing date of a provisional application, it may not be entitled to the benefit of right of priority to the provisional application.

To participate in the EMP pilot program, applicant must meet the following requirements:

- File a non-provisional application (including a specification);
- Claim the benefit of the filing date of a provisional application filed within the previous twelve months in the first sentence of the specification or in an ADS;
- Include at least one claim;
- Include drawings if necessary; and
- Request a delay in payment of the search and examination fees at the time of the non-provisional application filing using form PTO/SB/421.

Both utility and plant patent applications are eligible to participate in the EMP pilot program. Utility applications can be filed either electronically, using EFS-Web, or in paper. Plant patent applications can only be filed in paper. Applications filed in paper should be filed by USPS Express Mail, or may be hand-delivered to the USPTO. A non-publication request cannot be filed with the non-provisional application because the application will be published at the eighteen month date from the earliest filing date claimed. Finally, filing date and publication requirements must be met in order to participate in the pilot program.

There are certain instances when a request to participate in the EMP pilot program will be denied. An application that is not a non-provisional utility or plant application claiming benefit of a provisional application filed as prescribed will not be eligible for this pilot program. Other instances for denial include:

- an application not entitled to a filing date;
- a certification and request submitted after the filing date of the non-provisional application;
- a non-provisional application not directly claiming benefit of a provisional application filed within the previous 12 months; and
- a non-publication request filed with the non-provisional application.

The EMP pilot program benefits applicants by permitting additional time to determine if patent protection should be sought—at a relatively low cost—and by permitting applicants to focus efforts on commercialization during this period. The EMP pilot program has been extended through the end of 2014.

Informational Notice

If an application is filed on or after September 16, 2012, with a signed ADS identifying the inventive entities but not including an oath or declaration signed by the inventors, the USPTO will issue an Informational Notice to the applicant. The Notice will indicate that no time period has been set to remedy the inventor oath or declaration deficiency. The Notice will inform that applicant of the requirement to submit a properly executed inventor oath or declaration in compliance with 37 C.F.R. §1.63, or a substitute statement in compliance with 37 C.F.R. §1.64, executed by or with respect to each actual inventor no later than payment of the issue fee. The Notice will identify the names of the inventors for which a signed oath or declaration has not been received. The Notice will encourage applicants to submit the signed inventor oath or declaration as soon as possible to avoid further processing delays.

Response to Informational Notice

The response to an Information Notice can be filed at any time up to payment of the issue fee. The response must include a signed inventor oath or declaration under 37 C.F.R. §1.63 or a substitute statement in compliance with 37 C.F.R. §1.64, executed by or with respect to each actual inventor.

Notice to Comply with Requirements for Patent Applications Containing Nucleotide or Amino Acid Sequence Disclosures

If the application as filed contains nucleotide or amino acid sequence disclosures and the sequence submission requirements are not completed on filing (or are found defective), the OPAP will send the applicant a Notice to Comply with Requirements for Patent Applications Containing Nucleotide or Amino Acid Sequence Disclosures, setting a two-month response period.

Response to Notice to Comply—Sequence Listing

In response to a Notice to Comply with requirements for patent applications containing nucleotide or amino acid sequence disclosures, the applicant must file an acceptable computer-readable format (CRF) of the sequence listing.

The Notice to comply sets a two-month response period that is extendable up to six months. If a copy of the sequence listing is not filed in a computer-readable format (CRF) within the six-month statutory deadline for response, the application will be abandoned as of midnight on the two-month response date. When a sequence listing is filed as a PDF file via EFS-Web, it satisfies only the requirement that it is equivalent only to a paper copy, as it is not a computer-readable format (CRF). In contrast, a sequence listing filed as an ASCII text file will satisfy the requirement for both the paper copy and the CRF copy. The specific filing requirements for sequence listing are discussed in more detail in Chapter 8.

If the applicant is filing a response to the Notice to Comply by providing a diskette (or CD) and paper copy of the sequence listing, the response must include the following:

- a paper copy of the sequence listing;
- a CRF copy of the sequence listing as a ASCII text file on a CD-ROM; and
- a statement that the content of the paper and computer-readable copies are the same and that no new matter is included.

If the applicant is filing a response to the Notice to Comply by filing a ASCII text file of the sequence listing via EFS-Web, no paper copy is required, but the submission should include a statement that no new matter is included in the sequence listing.

Other Considerations

The remaining formality filings that should be considered are formal drawings and recordations of assignment. Formal drawings can be filed with the application filing, in response to a Notice to File Missing Parts or in response to a Notice of Allowance where the examiner notes that acceptable formal drawings have not yet been filed. When filing formal drawings in response to a notice of allowance, they must be filed before the non-extendable three-month period that is tolled for payment of the issue fee.

Assignments can be recorded at any time during prosecution; it is possible to record assignments against issued and abandoned matters. Given that a recorded assignment is the formal nexus between the inventor and the applicant for foreign filing purposes, assignments should be recorded before any convention date for foreign filing. The requirements for recordation of assignment are discussed in more detail in Chapter 6.

CHAPTER-SPECIFIC REFERENCE MATERIAL

Reference Source	Completion of Pre-Examination Filing Formalities Applicable Rules, Regulations, and Procedures
Title 37 of the Code of Federal Regulations	37 C.F.R. §1.63 Oath or declaration. §1.64 Person making oath or declaration. §1.66 Officers authorized to administer oaths. §1.67 Supplemental oath or declaration. §1.68 Declaration in lieu of oath. §1.69 Foreign language oaths and declarations. Sequence Listings §1.821 Nucleotide and/or amino acid sequence disclosures in patent applications. §1.822 Symbols and format to be used for nucleotide and/or amino acid sequence data. §1.823 Requirements for nucleotide and/or amino acid sequences as part of the application. §1.824 Form and format for nucleotide and/or amino acid sequence submissions in computer readable form. §1.825 Amendments to or replacement of sequence listing and computer-readable copy thereof.

<table>
<tr><td></td><td>Sequence Listings
§1.821 Nucleotide and/or amino acid sequence disclosures in patent applications.
§1.822 Symbols and format to be used for nucleotide and/or amino acid sequence data.
§1.823 Requirements for nucleotide and/or amino acid sequences as part of the application.
§1.824 Form and format for nucleotide and/or amino acid sequence submissions in computer readable form.
§1.825 Amendments to or replacement of sequence listing and computer-readable copy thereof.

Biological Material
§1.801 Biological material.
§1.802 Need or opportunity to make a deposit.
§1.803 Acceptable depository.
§1.804 Time of making an original deposit.
§1.805 Replacement or supplement of deposit.
§1.806 Term of deposit.
§1.807 Viability of deposit.
§1.808 Furnishing of samples.
§1.809 Examination procedures.</td></tr>
<tr><td>Manual of Patent Examination Procedures (MPEP, 8th Edition)</td><td>Chapter 600
Parts, Form, and Content of Application
Chapter 2400
Biotechnology</td></tr>
</table>

Chapter 12
Order of Examination

The Examining Corps

All non-provisional patent applications filed are subject to a substantive examination process to determine if they contain patent-eligible subject matter. The substantive examination of the claims of a patent application with respect to the criteria for patentability is conducted by the examining corps of the USPTO. The patent examiners are assigned to technology-based examination centers based on their defined areas of technical expertise. The examiners have accumulated technical expertise in either life science or engineering subject matter that allows them to understand detailed technical disclosure documents.

To initiate formal examination, the assigned examiner conducts a keyword search for the inventive concepts claimed in the patent application. This keyword search also helps the examiner define what is already known with respect to the claimed invention. The examiner also determines if all of the elements and limitations contained in the claims are supported by the disclosure as filed. The patent examiner is responsible for applying the criteria for patentability to the claimed invention to determine if the application contains patentable subject matter.

Order of Examination

When the applicant has completed all filing formalities, the OPAP routes the application to be docketed to an examiner. Patent examiners are directed to take applications up for examination in the order of their filing dates. In the normal course of business, the examiner gives priority to examination of applications with the oldest effective U.S. filing date. However, there are circumstances when an application may be examined out of filing date order. Such applications are advanced out of filing date order for examination and given "special" status. Such special circumstances include the following:

- the Director issued an order for advance examination to expedite the business of the USPTO;

- a department of the U.S. Government deems the invention of the application to be of particular importance to the public; or
- the applicant petitions to make the application special.

The USPTO has a variety of programs through which applicants can obtain special status for their applications and obtain the benefit of an expedited examination process. The established applicant-based programs for expedited examination are as follows:

- Full First Office Action Interview Pilot Program;
- Petition to Make Special;
- Patent Prosecution Highway;
- Accelerated Examination; and
- Prioritized Examination (Track I).

The filing requirement for each of these applicant-initiated special status programs are discussed in more detail in the remainder of this chapter.

Full First Action Interview Pilot Program

The USPTO has extended the enhanced First Action Interview (FAI) pilot program, which was limited to utility applications in certain technology areas, to a full pilot program, which is open to all utility applications in all technology areas. Participants in the full FAI pilot program are permitted to conduct an interview with the examiner after reviewing a pre-interview communication providing the result of a prior art search conducted by the examiner. The full FAI pilot program provides the following advantages to participants:

- the ability to advance prosecution of an application;
- enhanced interaction between the applicant and the examiner;
- the opportunity to resolve patentability issues one-on-one with the examiner at the beginning of the prosecution process; and
- the opportunity to facilitate possible early allowance.

Filing Requirements

A grantable request for participation in the full FAI pilot program must meet the following conditions:

- the application must be an new, non-reissue utility application filed under 35 U.S.C. §111(a) or an international application that has entered the national stage in compliance with 35 U.S.C. §371(c);
- the application must contain three or fewer independent claims and twenty or fewer total claims. No multiple dependent claims are permitted;
- the request (form SB/413C) must be filed electronically using EFS-Web;
- the claims must be directed to a single invention or, if the USPTO issues a restriction requirement, the applicant must make an election without traverse;
- the request must be filed at least one day before a first Office action on the merits appears in PAIR; and
- the request for a full FAI must include a statement that the applicant agrees not to file a request for a refund of the search fee and any excess claims fees paid in the application after the mailing or notification of the Pre-Interview Communication. Any petition for express abandonment under 37 C.F.R. §1.138(d), and request for a refund of the search fee and any excess claims fees filed after the mailing or notification of the Pre-Interview Communication will not be granted.

There are no additional fees required for participation in the full FAI pilot program. Any duly appointed representatives of the inventors or the assignee of record of the entire interest may sign the request.

If an amendment is proposed, it must accompany the Applicant-Initiated Interview Request form (PTOL-413A) or equivalent paper to schedule the interview. The applicant can file a preliminary amendment concurrently with the request to conform the claims to requirements. Claims cannot be canceled or withdrawn to conform to requirements. If a proposed amendment is denied entry, the proposed amendment will be placed in the application file, but it will not be considered by the examiner. If the applicant still wishes to make the changes (e.g., amendments to the claims) in the proposed amendment after the interview, the applicant may resubmit the changes in an amendment filed in response to a FAI Office Action in compliance with 37 C.F.R. §1.121 and §1.111.

The forecasting mechanism in private PAIR that projects the time until issuance of a first office action on the merits is the best way to estimate when the applicant will get a Pre-Interview Communication. When the procedure outlined in the FAI pilot program is exhausted then practice and procedure for initial patent examination governs. The FAI pilot program is exhausted after the applicant receives a Notice of Allowance or timely responds to the FAI office action. The FAI office action follows the interview, should the applicant elect to have an interview. All further prosecution is governed by current policy, practice, and procedure for initial patent examination.

An application can only be withdrawn from the pilot if a Pre-Interview Communication has been not issued by the Office. Once a Pre-Interview Communication has issued, withdrawal from the program is not permitted. Any request for withdrawal from the FAI program received after the Office has issued a Pre-Interview Communication will be treated as a request to not conduct an interview. Failure to conduct an interview will result in withdrawal from the program. Accordingly, the examiner will, in due course, issue an FAI office action and the applicant will then have the shortened thirty-day time period, extendable for an additional thirty days, to respond.

It is the responsibility of the applicant to make the substance of the interview of record in the application file. If the applicant fails to file a statement of the substance of the interview, the examiner will determine whether the record of the substance of an interview is complete. It depends on whether the examiner previously provided a written summary of the interview and whether the examiner's summary is a sufficient record of the substance of the interview. If the record is not complete, the examiner may give the applicant one month to file the statement of the substance of the interview to complete the reply under 37 C.F.R. §1.135(c).

Petitions to Make Special

The vast majority of advanced order examinations are attributable to the applicant filing a Petition to Make Special under one of the twelve supported grounds. The criteria, basis, and showing required for Petitions to Make Special are shown in Table 17. Petitions to Make Special under 37 C.F.R. §1.102(c) do not required payment of a fee; however, Petitions to Make Special under 37 C.F.R. §1.102(d) require payment of a fee.

Table 17: Petitions to Make Special

Criteria	Basis of Petition	Showing Required	Fee Required
Applicant's Health	Applicant's health is diminished to such an extent that he or she may not be available to assist in the prosecution of the application if subject to normal examination order.	Doctor's certificate giving evidence of diminished health.	No
Applicant's Age	Applicant is sixty-five or older.	Birth certificate giving evidence of applicant's age.	No
Environmental Quality	The invention materially enhances the quality of the environment.	A statement explaining how the invention contributes to the restoration or maintenance of air, water, or soil.	No
Energy Resources	The invention materially contributes to energy resources, utilization, or conservation.	A statement explaining how the invention materially contributes to utilization or conservation of energy resources.	No
Superconductivity	The invention is related to superconductivity.	A statement that the invention involves superconductive materials.	No
Prospective Manufacture	Manufacture of the invention is dependent upon allowance or issuance of a patent.	Provide evidence that: ▪ sufficient capital and facilities are or will be available upon grant of the patent to manufacture the invention in quantity	Yes
		▪ the manufacturer will not increase or license the manufacture until the patent is granted ▪ the manufacturer is obligated to manufacture the invention in quantity immediately upon grant of the patent to protect investment, and ▪ the applicant or assignee has made a thorough search of the prior art.	

Marketplace Infringement	The claims of the invention are being infringed in the marketplace.	A statement that: ▪ there is an infringing product/method on the market ▪ based on a rigid comparison of the market product/method to the claims of the application, some of the claims are unquestionably infringed ▪ the applicant or assignee has made a thorough search of the prior art and provides copies of the most closely related art.	Yes
Recombinant DNA	The invention relates to safety of research in the field of recombinant DNA.	A statement explaining how the invention relates to safety of research in the field of recombinant DNA.	Yes
Accelerated Examination is Requested	Applicant requests accelerated examination and meets filing requirements.	A statement that: ▪ all the claims are directed to a single invention or applicant will elect without traverse ▪ a pre-examination search was made, including listing the field of search by class and subclass ▪ copies of the most closely related art are provided ▪ a detailed discussion of the references, particularly pointing out how the claims are patentably distinguishable from the prior art.	Yes
HIV/AIDS or Cancer	The invention relates to the diagnosis, treatment, or prevention of HIV/AIDS or cancer.	A statement explaining how the invention contributes to the diagnosis, treatment, or prevention of HIV/AIDS or cancer.	Yes

Counter Terrorism	The invention relates to counter-terrorism technology.	A statement explaining how the invention contributes to the counter-terrorism technology.	Yes
Biotechnology–Small Entity	The invention relates to biotechnology, and the applicant is a small entity.	A statement that: ▪ small entity status exists and is entitled ▪ the invention is a major asset of the small entity ▪ an explanation of how development of the technology will be significantly impaired if examination is delayed.	Yes

Filing Requirements

Any petition to make special must:

- be in writing (use web-based form SB/130 for petition to make special based on age);
- identify the application by application number and filing date;
- identify the ground for which special status is claimed, including any supportive documentation required;
- include the petition fee (where applicable).

Applications that have been made special will be advanced out of turn for examination and will continue to be treated as special throughout the entire prosecution in the Office. Each petition to make special, regardless of the ground upon which the petition is based and the nature of the decision, is made of record in the application file, together with the decision on the petition.

Patent Prosecution Highway

The Patent Prosecution Highway (PPH) can speed up the examination process for corresponding applications filed in participating countries by allowing the examiner to leverage examination and search results. The PPH is a work-sharing program that lets examiners use the search and examination results from other offices for applications filed in multiple jurisdictions under both Paris Convention and PCT routes. The PPH program is being used in all technical areas and offers concrete benefits that include accelerated examination, fewer actions per disposal, and an overall allowance rate of more than double the rate for non-PPH cases. The PPH program provides an alternative way for U.S.-based applicants to get their U.S. patents issued more quickly and provides applicants who might not otherwise consider foreign filing with an alternative to the Accelerated Examination procedures, at reduced savings, with respect to cost and risk (USPTO, Overview of the Patent Prosecution Highway (Video), 2010). The USPTO has waived the petition fee for participation in the PPH program.

Under the PPH, an applicant receiving a ruling from an Office of First Filing (OFF) that at least one claim is patentable may request that the Office of Second Filing (OSF) fast-track the examination of the claims in a corresponding application filed in an OSF. All claims in the OSF application must sufficiently correspond to the allowable claims in the OFF application. A request for benefit of the PPH cannot be filed after substantive U.S. examination has begun (not including restriction requirement) (USPTO, Expedited Examination, 2009). The OSF can use the search and examination results of the OFF. The scope of the claims filed in the OSF is more focused, and the number of claims filed in the OSF are often reduced.

Benefits of the Patent Prosecution Highway

The primary benefits of the PPH are as follows:

- Predictable examination process and lowers costs: PPH users can obtain the best, most cost-effective examination. Examination will begin within two to three months from the grant of the PPH request, provided the application has completed all its pre-exam processing and is ready for examination.
- Provides greater efficiency: More than 90 percent of PPH cases are allowed. The allowance rate for non-PPH cases is less than 50 percent.
- Decreases costs of prosecution: PPH cases have fewer actions per disposal when compared to non-PPH cases, saving applicants both time and expense.
- Reduces pendency: PPH enables applications filed in multiple jurisdictions to be fast-tracked based on another Office's work product.

Participating Countries

As of the end of 2013, the USPTO has PPH agreements with the following twenty-five countries and organizations: Australia, Austria, Canada, China, Columbia, Czech Republic, Denmark, the European Patent Office, Finland, Germany, Hungary, Iceland, Israel, Japan, Korea, Mexico, Norway, Philippines, Portugal, Russia, Singapore, Spain, Sweden, Taiwan, and the United Kingdom. The USPTO is actively seeking PPH agreements with other IP offices, and it is likely that the list of PPH member countries will continue to grow.

Eligibility Criteria

To qualify for PPH in the USPTO, the U.S. application must meet one of the following criteria:

- A Paris Convention application that either:
    - claims priority under 35 U.S.C. §119(a) and 37 C.F.R. §1.55 to one or more applications filed with the OFF; or
    - claims priority under 35 U.S.C. §119(a)/ §365(a) to a PCT application that contains no priority claims.

- A national stage entry in the U.S. under §371 from a PCT application that:
    - claims priority under 35 U.S.C. §365(b) to an application filed with the OFF; or
    - claims priority under 35 U.S.C. §365(b) to a PCT application that contains no priority claims; or
    - contains no priority claim.
- A so-called "bypass application" filed under 35 U.S.C. §111(a) that claims benefit under 35 U.S.C. §120 to a PCT application that:
    - claims priority under 35 U.S.C. §365(b) to an application filed with the OFF; or
    - claims priority under 35 U.S.C. §365(b) to a PCT application that contains no priority claims; or
    - contains no priority claims.

Decision on the Request

If the PPH request is not granted, the applicant will be notified, and the defects will be identified in the decision. The applicant will be given one opportunity to perfect the request in a renewed request for participation. If the renewed request is perfected and examination has not begun, the request and special status will be granted. The applicant will be notified, and the U.S. application will be placed on an accelerated examination track. The application will be examined about two to three months from the grant of the PPH request, provided the applicant has completed all pre-examination filing requirements and the application is ready for examination. If the request is not perfected, the applicant will be notified, and the application will await action in its regular turn based on the filing date.

Requirements After Acceptance of the Request

When an application has been accepted to qualify to participate in the PPH, there are additional requirements that must be completed with respect to the claims and provision of documentation related to prosecution in the OFF.

- The claims in the U.S. application for which a request for PPH participation is filed must sufficiently correspond, or be amended to sufficiently correspond, to the allowable claims in the OFF application. Claims will be considered to sufficiently correspond where, accounting for differences due to translations and claim format requirements, the claims are of the same or similar scope.

- Applicant must fill out the claims correspondence table in English in the PPH request form indicating how all the claims in the U.S. application correspond to the allowable claims in the OFF application.
- Applicant must submit a copy of the allowable claims from the OFF application, along with an English translation and a statement that the English translation is accurate, if the claims are not in the English language.
- Applicant must submit a copy of all the office actions that are relevant to patentability from each of the OFF applications containing the allowable claims, along with an English translation and a statement that the English translation is accurate, if the Office actions are not in the English language. For the USPTO-EPO PPH pilot program, if no EP office action has been issued yet, the applicant may rely on and submit a positive Extended European Search Report (EESR) and explain how the EESR establishes allowability of the EP claims.
- Applicant must submit an IDS listing the documents cited by the examiner in the OFF (unless such an IDS has already been filed in the U.S. application).
- Applicant must submit copies of the documents listed in the IDS (except for U.S. patents or U.S. patent application publications).
- Applicant must file a request for participation in the PPH/Petition to Make Special. Applicants are encouraged to use the appropriate USPTO request form for participation in the PPH.
- The request for participation in the PPH and all supporting documents must be submitted to the USPTO via EFS-Web and be indexed with the appropriate document description.

Patent Cooperation Treaty—Patent Prosecution Highway

The PCT-PPH program is limited to the utilization of search and examination results of national applications between cross-filings under the Paris Convention. As part of a trilateral effort to expand the potential of the PPH program by drawing on PCT work products of PCT applications, the Trilateral Offices (European Patent Office, Japan Patent Office, and United States Patent and Trademark Office) agreed to launch a PCT-PPH pilot program based on positive PCT work products. The PCT-PPH pilot program started on January 29, 2010, for a trial period of two years and was extended a further two years. On June 1, 2010, a PCT-PPH pilot was started with the Korean Intellectual Property Office based on the same framework. An applicant who has received the following can use the PCT-PPH pilot program:

- a Written Opinion from an International Searching Authority (WO/ISA) (ISA must be in the PCT-PPH program);
- a Written Opinion from an International Preliminary Examining Authority (WO/IPEA) (IPEA must be in the PCT-PPH Program); or
- an International Preliminary Report on Patentability (IPRP) from an International Preliminary Examining Authority (IPEA) (IPEA must be in the PCT-PPH Program).

If the Written Opinion or Preliminary Report on Patentability indicates that at least one claim in the PCT application has novelty, inventive step, and industrial applicability, the applicant may file a request to participate in the PCT-PPH pilot program in a corresponding U.S. application and have the U.S. application placed on an accelerated examination track. The requirements for requesting participation in the PCT-PPH pilot program are similar (but not identical) to the PPH requirements.

Enhanced Patent Prosecution Highway 2.0

An enhanced PPH 2.0 program makes it possible for an U.S. applicant to advance prosecution of a U.S. case based on an allowance in a corresponding foreign case, even if the foreign case was filed after the U.S. case. This enables U.S. inventors to exploit the higher speed, lower cost, and increased grant rate of the PPH for their U.S. applications. The PPH 2.0 removed limitations related to the requirement to have a priority claim either directly or via the PCT to the allowed foreign application. The PPH 2.0 program eliminated the priority claim limitation to allow U.S. applications to benefit from the PPH program. The PPH 2.0 guidelines have been adopted between the United States and the patent offices of Australia, Canada, Europe, Finland, Japan, Korea, Russia, Spain, and the United Kingdom.

Under the PPH 2.0 guidelines, it is possible to advance examination of a U.S. application based on a favorable office action in a corresponding foreign application, regardless of whether the foreign application was filed before, after, or concurrently with the U.S. application. This system allows a U.S. inventor to use the PPH in the USPTO without having to file abroad before filing in the U.S. It also allows U.S. inventors to exploit the inexpensive protection afforded by provisional applications without sacrificing the opportunity to use the PPH program in the United States and other participating countries. The PPH 2.0 program offers many ways for U.S. inventors to lower prosecution costs and reduce prosecution time (Colice et al, PPH 2.0 Offers Ways To Reduce Prosecution Time and Costs, 2013).

Accelerated Examination

On August 25, 2006, the USPTO introduced an Accelerated Examination (AE) program to allow applicants to obtain patents quicker than the average pendency period of three to five years. The goal of AE is to arrive at a final decision on patentability within twelve months of the application filing date. While a final decision under the twelve-month period can include a final rejection, a Notice of Allowance, the filing of a RCE, or abandonment of the application, the USPTO continues the examination of such actions on a fast track (Jewik, 2010). In order to meet the twelve-month goal, the applicant will be required to provide additional information with the petition for AE and comply with procedures throughout the examination process to assist the examiner in expeditiously arriving at a final disposition.

Filing Requirements

To qualify for the AE program, the applicant must comply with the following filing requirements:

- file the request with respect to an application filed under 35 U.S.C. §111(a);
- file the application and all follow-on submissions via EFS-Web;
- file a complete application complying with 37 C.F.R. §1.51;
- file three or fewer independent claims and no more than twenty claims total;
- file an application for a single invention or agree to elect without traverse a single invention for examination;
- submit the petition and fee (where appropriate);
- agree to an interview with the examiner to discuss any outstanding issues arising in the examination process;
- conduct a pre-examination search; and
- provide an accelerated examination support document (AESD).

Requirements for Accelerated Examination

A new application filing may be granted AE status under the following conditions:

- Application type: The application must be a non-reissue utility or design application filed under 35 U.S.C. §111(a).
- Petition requirement: The application must be filed with a Petition to Make Special under the AE program, accompanied by either the fee under 37 C.F.R. §1.17(h) or a statement that the claimed subject matter is directed to environmental quality, the development or conservation of energy resources, or countering terrorism.
- Application form: Applicant should use form SB/28 for filing the petition.
- Filing method: The application, petition, and required fees must be filed electronically using EFS-Web.
- Fees and declaration: At the time of filing, the application must be complete with respect to all filing formalities, including payment of all filing fees (search fee, examination fee, and application size fees), if applicable. An executed declaration must be included.
- Claims: The application must contain three or fewer independent claims and twenty or fewer total claims. Multiple dependent claims are not permitted. Under AE, the applicant is agreeing to have the dependent claims grouped with the independent claims for examination purposes. The petition must include a statement that the applicant will agree not to separately argue the patentability of any dependent claims during any appeal of the application. Claims must be directed to a single invention, or application must make an election without traverse in a telephone interview. The petition must include a statement that applicant will agree to make an election without traverse in a telephone interview.
- Examiner interview: The applicant must be willing to have an interview with the examiner to discuss the prior art and any potential rejections or objections to help clarify and resolve any issues with respect to patentability.
- Pre-Examination search: At time of filing, the applicant must provide a statement that a pre-examination search was conducted, including an identification of the field of search (by class and subclass), the date of the search, the search logic (or chemical structure or sequences used in the query), the name of the file or files searched, and the database services used. The pre-examination search must include U.S. patents and publications, foreign patent documents, and non-patent literature. The pre-examination search must be directed to the claimed invention (including any amendments) and encompass all of the features/elements of the claims. Any

statement in support of the petition for AE must be based on good faith that the pre-examination search was conducted in compliance with requirements.

- Examination support document: At time of filing, applicant must provide an Accelerated Examination Support Document (AESD), which includes an IDS statement citing each reference deemed most closely related to the subject matter of each of the claims. For each reference cited, the AESD must include an identification of all the limitations in the claims that are disclosed by the reference, specifying where the limitation is disclosed in the cited reference. The AESD must include a detailed explanation of how each of the claims is patentable over the references cited, a concise statement regarding utility of the invention, and a showing of where each limitation of the claims finds support in the written description of the specification.

Twelve-Month Goal

The goal of the AE program is to issue a final disposition on patentability within twelve months of filing of the application. The goal of AE is successfully achieved when one of the following dispositions occur:

- Notice of Allowance;
- Final Office Action;
- Notice of Appeal;
- Request for Continued Examination; or
- Abandonment.

If there is a failure to meet the twelve-month goal, or other issues relating to the goal of the AE program, the applicant does not have the option to petition on or appeal the issues (USPTO, Revised Accelerated Examination Program and Petition to Make Special Prodedures, 2006).

Processing of Accelerated Examination Applications

The applicant will be notified of the decision to grant AE. If the application or petition does not meet all the requirements, the applicant will be notified of the defects, and the application will remain in the status of new, awaiting action in its regular turn. The applicant will be given a single opportunity to perfect the petition or AESD within a time period of one month (no extensions available). This opportunity does not apply to applications that are not in condition for examination on filing. If the document is corrected in a timely manner, the petition will then be granted, but the final disposition of the application may occur later than twelve months from the filing date of the application.

When the application is granted special status, the application will be docketed and taken up for action expeditiously, usually within two weeks of the granting of the special status. If all claims present are not directed to a single invention, the examiner will request a telephone interview with the applicant for election of claims. If the examiner determines that a possible rejection of other issues must be addressed, the examiner will contact the applicant by telephone to discuss the issue and any possible amendments needed to resolve such issues. The examiner will not issue an office action (other than a notice of allowance) unless either an interview was conducted but did not result in the application being placed in condition for allowance or there is a determination that an interview is unlikely to result in the application being placed in condition for allowance.

Reply to Office Actions

If an office action other than a Notice of Allowance or a final office action is issued, a shortened statutory period of two months (as amended under the Patent Law Treaty (PLT) effective December 18, 2013) will be set for response. No extensions of this shortened statutory period under 37 C.F.R. §1.136(a) will be permitted. Failure to timely file a reply will result in abandonment of the application. Applicant's reply must be limited to the rejections, objections, and requirements stipulated by the examiner. Any attempt to add claims beyond the number permitted, present claims not encompassed by the pre-examination search, or present claims that are directed to a non-elected invention will be treated as not fully responsive and will not be entered. For any amendments to the claims or addition of new claims that are not encompassed by the AESD filed, the applicant is required to provide an updated AESD that encompasses the amended claims or the newly added claims at the time of amending or adding the claims. Failure to provide an updated AESD at the amendment will cause the amendment to be treated as not fully responsive, and it and will not be entered. Any reply or other papers must be filed electronically via EFS-Web to ensure that the papers are expeditiously processed and considered. If the papers are not filed via EFS-Web or the reply is not fully responsive, the final disposition of the application may occur later than twelve months from the application filing date.

Final Disposition under Accelerated Examination

The mailing of a Notice of Allowance is a final disposition for the twelve-month goal of AE. In response to a Notice of Allowance, the applicant must pay the issue fee within one month of the date of mailing of the notice of allowance to ensure that the application is expeditiously issued as a patent. The applicant must not file any post-allowance papers that are not required by the examiner.

The mailing of a final office action or the filing of a Notice of Appeal, whichever is earlier, is the final disposition for the purposes of the twelve-month goal period. Prior to the mailing of a final office action, the USPTO will conduct a conference to review the rejections in the final office action. In order for the application to be expeditiously forwarded to the Board for a decision, the applicant must promptly file the notice of appeal, appeal brief, and appeal fees, but is prohibited from requesting a pre-appeal conference. During the appeal process, the application will be treated in accordance with normal appeal procedures. The USPTO will continue to treat the application as special under the AE program after the decision from the Board.

If the applicant files a RCE with a submission and fee, it is considered a final disposition with respect to the AE program. The application will retain its special status and remain in the AE program. Any subsequent replies filed must meet the requirements of the AE program. The new goal of the AE will then be to reach a final disposition of the application within twelve months from the filing of the RCE.

There is no provision for withdrawal from special status under the AE program beyond the applicant abandoning the application in favor of a continuing application. Granting of special status does not transfer from parent to continuing applications. Each application must meet all the requirements for the AE program.

Accelerated Examination Practice Tips

The USPTO identifies the following common pitfalls related to filing a petition for AE (USPTO, Patent Practice Tips, 2010):

- failure to provide the text search logic; a mere listing of terms will not suffice;
- failure to search the claimed invention; the petition for AE may be dismissed if the search is not commensurate in scope with the claims;
- failure to show support in the specification or drawings, or both, for each limitation of each claim;

- failure to show support in the specification or drawings, or both, for each limitation of each claim for every document whose benefit is claimed; and
- failure to specifically identify the limitations in each claim that are disclosed in each reference.

One caveat to the AE program is that if a request is denied, the accelerated examination support document, which includes a characterization of the closest prior art, the claims, and the application's priority, will remain in the image file wrapper and can create possible unwanted prosecution history (Colice et al, Beware Risks When Expediting USPTO Examination, 2013).

AIA Impact—Prioritized Examination

The AIA contains provisions for a Track I Prioritized Examination (PE) program that allows applicants to receive an expedited review of a patent application for an additional fee. In return, the USPTO will provide a final disposition within twelve months of prioritized status being granted. Prioritized examination is available for any original utility or plant patent application but does not apply to international, design, reissue, or provisional applications or reexamination proceedings. PE may be requested for a continuing application after the filing of a RCE.

While the PE program prioritizes an application for prosecution ahead of standard filings, the AE program prioritizes and accelerates the actual prosecution of the application. The PE and AE programs coexisted as of September 16, 2011. Both routes are viable examination routes for applicants, and the decision on which route to take depends on the portfolio strategy and tactics of the applicant (Witchey et al, 2011). The fee for a request for PE under 37 C.F.R. §1.17(c) is subject to a small entity discount; the micro entity discount does not apply. A request for PE will reduce the pendency or examination time from the usual two to three years down to about one year.

Filing Requirements

A certification and request for a Track 1 Prioritized Examination under 37 C.F.R. §1.102(e) must include the following:

- a certification and request for PE using form AIA/424;
- payment of all required fees (see filing fee details);

- an application that contains (or is amended to contain) no more than four independent claims, no more than thirty total claims, and no multiple dependent claims.;
- an indication if this is an original request for Track I PE or a request for Track I PE after the filing of a RCE;
- an executed inventor's oath or declaration under 37 C.F.R. §1.63 or 37 C.F.R. §1.64 for each inventor, or an ADS meeting the conditions specified in 37 CFR §1.53(f)(3)(i) (for original requests for Track I PE);
- an indication that this certification is being filed prior to the mailing of a first Office action responsive to the RCE and that no prior RCE has been granted prioritized examination status under 37 C.F.R. §1.102(e)(2). (for request for Track I PE after the filing of a RCE; and
- the certification and request for PE must be filed via EFS-Web.

Filing Fees

The following filing fees must be paid on filing a Track I PE application:

- Basic filing fee under 37 C.F.R. §1.16(a), or for a plant application, 37 C.F.R. §1.16(c);
- Search fee under 37 C.F.R. §1.16(k), or for a plant application, 37 C.F.R. §1.16(m);
- Examination fee under 37 C.F.R. §1.16(o), or for a plant application, 37 C.F.R. §1.16(q);
- Publication fee under 37 C.F.R. 1. 18(d), even if a request for non-publication is included;
- Track I processing fee under 37 C.F.R. §1.17(i);
- Track I prioritized examination fee under 37 C.F.R. §1.17(c);
- If applicable, any application size fee due because the specification and drawings exceed one hundred sheets of paper under 37 C.F.R. §1.16(s);
- If applicable, any excess independent claim fee due because the number of independent claims exceeds three under 37 C.F.R. §1.16(h); and
- If applicable, any excess claim fee due because the number of claims exceeds twenty under 37 C.F.R. §1.16(i).

If any fee is unpaid at the time of filing of the application, the request for Track I PE will be dismissed. However, if an explicit general authorization to charge any additional required fees has been provided in the papers accompanying the application and the request, the fees will be charged in accordance with the authorization, and the request will not be dismissed for non-payment of fees.

Prioritized Examination After the Filing of a Request for Continued Examination

On December 19, 2011, the USPTO published final rules to implement a PE program for applications in which a RCE has been filed. Applicants with pending applications may file a RCE to trigger eligibility for Track I PE. An application is eligible for the PE program if one RCE has been filed for the application. The PE rules will apply to any patent application in which a proper RCE has been filed on or after December 19, 2011. When requesting RCE-related PE, applicants must meet the following requirements:

- the RCE is for an original utility or plant non-provisional application or a U.S. national stage application;
- the request for PE is filed electronically using request form SB/424; the request may be filed with, or after, the filing of the RCE but must be filed before the first office action after the RCE;
- at the time of the request for PE, the application must contain or be amended to contain no more than four independent claims, no more than thirty total claims, and no multiple dependent claims;
- the request for PE must be accompanied by the prioritized examination fee and the processing fee, and, if not previously paid, the publication fee; and
- the request must be one of the 10,000 for the fiscal-year limit.

The limit on the number of requests includes requests for PE for initial examination and requests for PE after the filing of a RCE. The PE after a RCE differs from that a Track I PE in two ways (Gomez, 2012):

- a U.S. national stage application in which a RCE has been filed is eligible for the PE program, such an application is not eligible for the Track I PE program; and
- a request for PE can be filed after a RCE has been filed, in the Track I PE program; a request must be filed at the same time the application is filed.

Processing of Application

An application accorded special status after filing a RCE will be placed on the examiner's special docket throughout its entire course of continued prosecution before the examiner until a final disposition is reached in the application. An application under PE, however, would not be accorded special status throughout its entire course or before the Board, or after the filing of a subsequent RCE. The goal of the program is to provide a final disposition within twelve months of the PE status being granted (Gomez, 2012). The PE program grants special status to the application until one of the following applicant-initiated or examiner-initiated actions occur:

- applicant files a petition for extension of time to extend the time period for filing a reply;
- applicant files an amendment to amend the application to contain more than four independent claims, more than thirty total claims, or a multiple dependent claim;
- applicant files a subsequent RCE;
- applicant files a Notice of Appeal;
- applicant files a Request for Suspension of Action;
- the examiner issues a final office action;
- the examiner issues a Notice of Allowance;
- the application is abandoned; or
- examination is completed, as defined in 37 C.F.R. §41.102.

Dismissal of Request

If the applicant receives a decision dismissing a request for PE and believes the decision is improper, the applicant can file a petition under 37 C.F.R. §1.181. Before filing such a petition, the applicant should review the reasons stated in the decision dismissing the request and make a determination that an error was made by the USPTO in not granting the request. If the request for PE is dismissed, only the PE fee will be refunded upon dismissal of the original request. The fee will be refunded automatically without the need for the applicant to request such a refund. The PE processing fee, filing fee, search fee, examination fee, and any excess claims or application size fees will not be refunded. The applicant may request a refund of the search fee and any excess claims fees by filing a Petition for Express abandonment of the application. In addition, the applicant may also request a refund of the publication fee if the application did not publish.

Filing an amendment in the application that results in more than four independent claims, more than thirty total claims, or a multiple dependent claim will remove the application from the PE program. An applicant will not receive any refund of the PE fee if prioritized examination is terminated (Gomez, 2012).

Final Disposition under PE

A final disposition under the PE program is considered to have been reached when any of the following events have occurred:

- mailing of a Notice of Allowance;
- mailing of a Final office action;
- filing of a Notice of Appeal;
- completion of examination as defined under 37 C.F.R §41.102 pertaining to interference;
- filing of a RCE; or
- abandonment of the application.

The aim of the PE program is to reach a final disposition within twelve months of the filing date. A final disposition does not necessarily mean that prosecution has been completely concluded, and the twelve-month goal is not always attained. The Track I PE program offers applicants expedited examination, higher issuance rates than regular applications, and fewer office actions and RCEs, which can translate to saved attorney time, reduced USPTO fees, and a shorter prosecution history (Gaudry, 2013).

Differences Between Accelerated Examination and Prioritized Examination

One of the major differences between the programs is that the PE program does not require a pre-examination search document. While the time spent searching for related art and improving and focusing the claims tend to yield stronger claim sets for the AE program, it also significantly adds to pre-filing costs. In contrast, the time and costs related to preparing responses to overcome examiner rejections when there is no pre-filing thorough analysis of the claims under the PE program can result in significant post-filing costs before obtaining a Notice of Allowance. The AE program allows for fewer claims and is less expensive. PE allows for more claims but is more expensive, and micro entity discounts do not apply.

The prosecution phase turnaround times are also different. AE stipulates a two-month response period on a non-final office action, and failure to meet that strict time requirement results in abandonment of the application. The PE program adheres to the normal three-month response periods, which can be extended as usual, though doing so results in the application being removed from the PE program and reverting to the examiner's standard docket. The AE program returns faster results than the PE program but also has more severe consequences if response dates are missed. While the PE program is also limited to ten thousand applications (Track I PE and RCE-related PE) per USPTO fiscal year, there is no formal limit to the number of AE applications (Witchey et al, 2011). The notable differences between the accelerated examination and prioritized examination programs are identified in Table 18.

Table 18: Differences Between Accelerated Examination and Prioritized Examination

	Accelerated Examination (AE)	Prioritized Examination (PE)
Type of Application	Available for non-provisional utility or plant applications filed on or after August 26, 2006.	Available for original non-provisional utility or plant applications filed on or after September 26, 2011. Available for continuation, continuation-in-part, and divisional applications. Not available for design, provisional, U.S. national stage or PCT international applications, reissue or reexamination proceedings.
Filing Requirements	Must be filed via EFS-Web with a Petition to Make Special along with required petition fee or a statement that the claimed invention is directed to environmental quality, development or conservation of energy resources, or counterterrorism. The application must be complete and in condition for examination on filing. The petition must include a statement agreeing to an examiner interview. Applicant must provide a statement that a pre-examination search was conducted that meets certain requirements.	Must be filed via EFS-Web unless for plant patent applications, which must be filed by paper. Request for PE must be present on initial filing. File Certification and Request for Prioritized Examination (Track I) using Form SB/424 to ensure recognition of request and to avoid processing delays. Executed inventor declaration must be filed with the application. Any deficiencies in the application or failure to pay all fees and include a signed inventor declaration will delay a decision on the request for prioritized examination and result in a notice to file corrected papers.
	Applicant must provide an accelerated examination support document that satisfies certain requirements.	Any request for an extension of time prior to the granting of a request for prioritized examination will remove the application from the PE program.

Filing Fees	Fees under 37 C.F.R. §1.17(h) must be paid on filing application and include the following: ▪ Basic filing fee; ▪ Search fee; ▪ Any required excess claims fees; ▪ Any required application size fee; ▪ Publication fee; ▪ AE processing fee; and ▪ AE examination fee. Small entity discount applies. Micro entity discount does not apply.	Fees under 37 C.F.R .§1.17(c) must be paid on filing application and include the following: ▪ Basic filing fee; ▪ Search fee; ▪ Any required excess claims fees; ▪ Any required application size fee; ▪ Publication fee (even if non-publication request included); ▪ PE processing fee; and ▪ PE examination fee. Small entity discount applies. Micro entity discount does not apply.
Number of Claims	No more than three independent claims. No more than twenty total claims. No multiple dependent claims.	No more than four independent claims. No more than thirty total claims. No multiple dependent claims.
Required Supportive Documents	Requires a pre-examination search document (PESD) and an accelerated examination support document (AESD).	No pre-examination search or examination support documents required.
	Requires prior art searching and analysis by the applicant.	
Examination Process	Prioritizes and accelerates the actual prosecution of the application. Final deposition (i.e., final rejection or allowance) within twelve months.	Prioritizes an application for prosecution ahead of standard filings. Final deposition (i.e., final rejection or allowance) within twelve months.

Response Periods	Three-month response period. Extensions of time available; if taken, application returns to the regular examination track.	Two-month response period. No extensions of time available.
Imposed Limitations	No limit on number of applications per fiscal year.	Available for a maximum of ten thousand applications per USPTO fiscal year.
Advantages	Higher pre-filing costs, strategic set of claims required, claims issue quickly.	Cost-effective, immediate feedback, early start on prosecution.

Suspension of Examination

An applicant may request and receive suspension of action by the USPTO for a period of up to six months by submitting a showing of good cause for requesting suspension of action, specifying the period of suspension, and paying the fee under 37 C.F.R. §1.17(h). The USPTO will only suspend Office-issued actions and will not suspend any outstanding applicant reply to an already issued office action. When filing a RCE, the applicant may request a suspension of action by the USPTO of up to three months by requesting the suspension at the time of filing the RCE, specifying the period of suspension, and paying the fee under 37 C.F.R. §1.17(i). This suspension period allows the applicant time to prepare and file supplemental submissions in support of patentability.

Deferred Examination

An applicant may defer examination for a period of up to three years from the earliest filing date claimed if no Non-Publication Request has been filed or rescinded in the application, the application is in condition for publication, and the USPTO has not issued an office action or Notice of Allowance. Deferral of examination requires filing a request specifying the period of deferral, accompanied by the publication fee under 37 C.F.R. §1.18(d) and the processing fee under 37 C.F.R. §1.103(d).

CHAPTER-SPECIFIC REFERENCE MATERIAL

Reference Source	Order of Examination Applicable Rules, Regulations, and Procedures
AIA Guides	Prioritized Examination Track I—Quick Start Guide http://www.uspto.gov/aia_implementation/track-1-quickstart-guide.pdf Prioritized Examination http://www.uspto.gov/aia_implementation/faq.jsp
USPTO Guides	Patent Prosecution Highway http://www.uspto.gov/patents/init_events/pph/index.jsp http://www.uspto.gov/patents/init_events/pph/pphbrochure.pdf

	http://www.uspto.gov/patents/init_events/pph/pph_faqs.pdf
Title 37 of the Code of Federal Regulations	37 C.F.R. §1.102 Advancement of examination. §1.103 Suspension of action by the Office.
Manual of Patent Examination Procedures (MPEP, 8th Edition)	708 Order of Examination §708. 01 List of Special Cases §708. 02 Petition To Make Special §708. 02(a) Accelerated Examination

Chapter 13

Examination and the Criteria for Patentability

Introduction

This overview of the examination process and the criteria for patentability is designed to give support staff a basic understanding of the terminology and procedures related to formal examination of patent applications. Patent examiners are tasked with an initial review of the application as filed against statutory disclosure and formality filing requirements and then a more substantive review of the application against the criteria for patentability. As the examiner applies the criteria for patentability against the disclosure and claims of the application, the examiner provides the applicant with a written argument against patentability based on statutory non-prior art disclosure-based rejections and prior art-based rejections for lack of novelty and obviousness.

Formal patent examination is a complex process that is very fact-dependent and subject to differing interpretations of specification disclosure requirements against the applicability of applied prior art-based rejections. Applicant responses can introduce further layers of complexity based on client portfolio strategy and the scope of claim coverage pursued. The legal argument of patent prosecution involves an application of advanced subject matter knowledge, in addition to the legal argument to overcome rejections based on the criteria for patentability. The level of complexity in the examination process mandates that applicants retain a registered practitioner to represent them before the USPTO.

From a support staff perspective, formal examination involves substantive legal argument and subject-matter expertise and is the remit of experienced patent attorneys and agents. Support staff are more removed from the examination process but can still offer time efficiencies to practitioners by helping them to manage the logistics of responses and related deadlines.

The Terminology of Examination

Support staff should have an understanding of the basic terminology associated with the examination phase. Examiners apply the criteria for patentability against the application as filed; they formulate their arguments against patentability in an office action that details the basis of any objections and rejections. Each patent application is framed against the level of public knowledge already established in the related technology. Some technologies are more defined, while other technologies are less defined. The knowledge level of a person of ordinary skill in the technology to which the invention relates is the standard the applicant must overcome to prove that his or her invention is new and not obvious from what is already known. An exhaustive review of all the subtle variations of the examination process is beyond the scope of this book and its intended support staff audience. The most common terminology related to the examination phase will be discussed in more detail in this chapter.

The Examination Process

After the application has been read and the claimed invention understood by the examiner, the examiner conducts a prior art search of the claimed invention. The examiner reviews the patent application against the state of the prior art to determine whether the claims define a useful, novel, non-obvious, and enabled invention that is clearly supported by the specification. From the applicant's perspective, the claims of the application must be distinguished from the known prior art and the applicant must argue the examiner's rejections or amend the claims, or both, to define the claimed invention over the asserted prior art.

The Criteria for Patentability

The criteria for patentability in the United States are novelty, utility, and non-obviousness. First, an invention is novel if it differs from what is already known in the field of the invention. The invention must be unique from what currently exists in the public knowledge base if it is to be patentable. If the invention is not new, it is not patentable. Second, an invention is useful if it produces an effect that is desirable to society. If the invention is useful or solves an existing problem, there will be market demand to make or sell it. Third, and perhaps the most complex criteria for patentability, is the degree to which the invention differs from the totality of established knowledge. If the invention is obvious, it would be anticipated by a person of ordinary skill in the field of the invention. The invention must offer a distinct evolutionary step that distinguishes it from established knowledge.

The patent examiner can object to or reject the claimed invention over statutory disclosure requirements or over asserted prior art reference that purport to show that the invention lacks novelty and is obvious. While rejections for non-statutory subject matters or lack of utility are more rare, rejections based on written description requirements, lack of novelty, and obviousness requirements are most common and form the basis for substantive rejections of the claims or specification. The progressive application of the criteria for patentability is summarized in Figure K. To be patentable, the claimed invention must pass all the criteria for patentability.

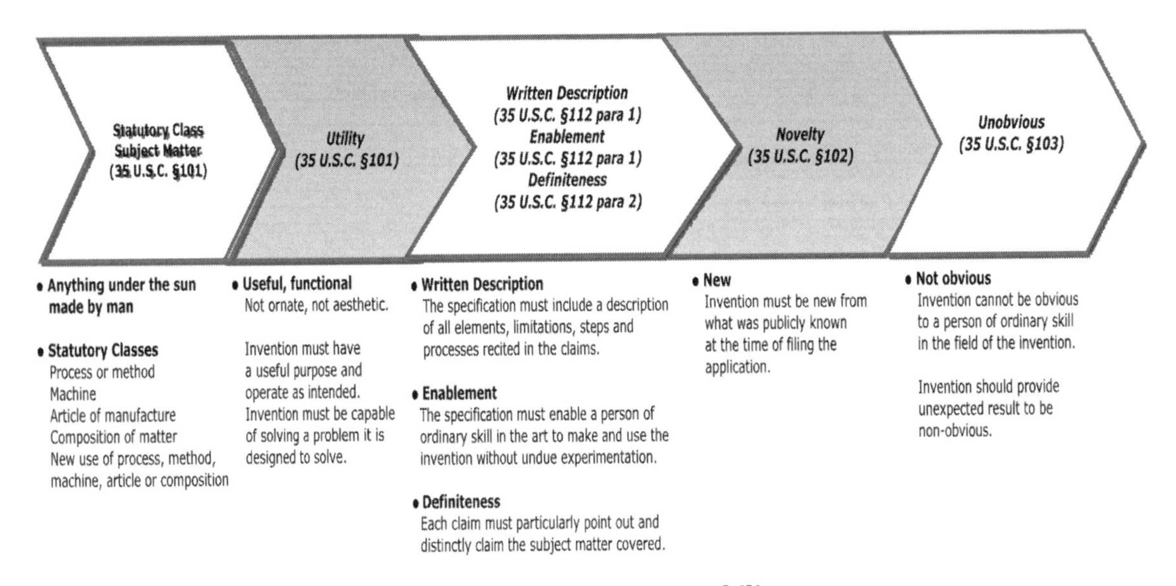

Figure K: Criteria for Patentability

Objections and Rejections

The examiner's office action may contain objections to the form of the claims or rejections of the substance of the claims, or both. Objections are non-prior art-related and focus on the improper form of the claim rather than the substance of the claim. Rejections are based on the substance of the claim, and the examiner may apply statutory rejections or prior art-based rejections. Examiner-asserted objections and rejections are compared and contrasted in Table 19. In general, if the invention is not considered patentable, or not considered patentable as claimed, the claims, or those considered unpatentable, will be rejected. In rejecting the claims for want of novelty or for obviousness, the examiner must cite the best references available. If the pertinence of the references is not apparent, it must be explained for each rejected claim (Patent Resources Institute, Inc., 2004).

Table 19: Objections vs. Rejections	
Objections	**Rejections**
Involves the improper form of the claim.	Involves the substance of the claim.
Non-prior art-based.	May be prior art or non-prior art-based, or both.
Subject to review by petition to the Director.	Subject to review by the Patent Trial and Appeal Board.

Non-Prior Art-Based Rejections

Many rejections of claims are not based on prior art references cited by the examiner. The examiner can reject the claims on the basis that they fail to comply with the statutory subject matter or utility requirements under 35 U.S.C. §101 or the written disclosure requirements under 35 U.S.C. §112. The non-prior art-based statutory rejections are summarized in Table 20 and are discussed in more detail in the following non-prior art-based rejections section.

Table 20: Non-Prior Art-Based Statutory Rejections		
Rejection under U.S.C. §101 (Non-Statutory Subject Matter)	**Rejection under U.S.C. §101 (Lack of Utility)**	**Rejections under §112 (Supportive Specification)**
A patent can be granted for new and useful processes, machine, manufacture, or composition of matter, or any new and useful improvement thereof.	To be patentable, an invention must have a specific utility. The utility of the invention must be disclosed in the application as filed. The examiner must establish an evidentiary basis for concluding the claimed invention has no specific and substantial credible utility.	The specification must contain a written description of the invention, and of the manner and process of making and using it, in such full, clear, concise, and exact terms as to enable any person skilled in the art to which it pertains, or with which it is most nearly connected, to make and use the invention, and should include the best mode contemplated by the inventor.

		The application as filed must meet the written description, enablement, definiteness and best mode requirements. All claim elements and limitations must be supported by the specification. All claim terminology must be defined in the specification.
Inventions related to laws of nature, physical phenomena, abstract ideas, literary, dramatic, musical, and artistic works are not patentable.	An invention lacks utility if its sole purpose is to deceive the public or if it is directed to an illegal or immoral purpose. Inventions that lack utility are not patentable.	If the specification as filed does not fully support the claimed invention it is unpatentable.

Rejections Based on Non-Statutory Subject Matter

Rejections based on non-statutory subject matter include rejection of claims that define over the prior art only by the arrangement of printed matter, or the printed matter per se recited in the claims are rejected as not being within the statutory classes. While an article that occurs in nature may not be patented in that unaltered, naturally occurring form, it may be patented if it is given a new form, quality, or property by means of a purification process. Business methods are statutory subject matter under §101. A scientific principle or law of nature per se falls outside of the statutory classes and cannot be patented. Process patent claims containing mathematical algorithms are patentable subject matter when they apply the algorithm to produce a useful, concrete, tangible result without preempting other uses (Patent Resources Institute, Inc., 2004).

Rejections Based on Lack of Utility

The statutory basis for a rejection of claimed subject matter as lacking utility is also found in §101. A process, machine, manufacture, or composition of matter or any improvement thereof must be useful to be patentable. If the examiner attacks the usefulness of the claimed subject matter, the applicant must provide evidence extraneous to the patent application demonstrating that the claimed subject matter does in fact have sufficient utility. Practical utility can be used to attribute a real-world value to the claimed subject matter. If one skilled in the art can use a claimed discovery in a manner that provides some immediate benefit to the public, then the invention is considered useful. An invention is said to lack utility if its sole purpose is to deceive the public. If an invention is directed to an illegal or immoral purpose, it also lacks utility under §101. If a claimed invention is not capable of operation, it cannot, by definition, have utility. An invention may be inoperative either for the reasons that it inherently will not work or that it is disclosed and claimed in an inoperative manner. In such a situation, a rejection under §112 is more appropriate than a rejection for lack of utility (Patent Resources Institute, Inc., 2004).

Rejections Based on Statutory Requirements for the Specification

All applications as filed must comply with three distinct statutory requirements under the first paragraph of 35 U.S.C. §112, as follows:

> The specification shall contain a written description of the invention, and of the manner and process of making and using it, in such full, clear, concise, and exact terms as to enable any person skilled in the art to which it pertains, or with which it is most nearly connected, to make and use the same, and shall set forth the best mode contemplated by the inventor of carrying out his invention.

The function of the written description requirement is to ensure that the inventor has possession of the subject matter claimed in the invention as of the filing date. It further ensures that the public receives something in return for the exclusionary rights granted to the inventor. The function of the best mode requirement is to restrain inventors from applying for patents while concealing from the public the preferred embodiment of their invention. The written description and best mode must be disclosed in a sufficient manner to allow a person of ordinary skill in the art to practice it. Under 35 U.S.C. §112, each claim as filed must satisfy the written description, enablement, and best mode requirements. Failure to satisfy any of the three requirements will render the claims fatally defective and invalid (Patent Resources Institute, Inc., 2004).

Written Description Requirement

The written description must clearly convey the claimed invention and must describe the technology claimed. A patent specification must describe the claimed invention in sufficient detail that one skilled in the art can reasonably conclude that the inventor had full possession of the invention that is claimed. There is a strong presumption that an adequate written description of the disclosure is present when the application is filed. The original application as filed should provide adequate support for the claims and will also be used to determine if material added by subsequent amendments is deemed new matter, which is prohibited. The claims as filed must be supported by the disclosure as filed; the specification and drawings can be amended to support aspects in the claims as filed. The scope of description must be commensurate with the scope of the claims. The more that is known by one of ordinary skill in the art, and the greater the predictability, the less disclosure that is required, and vice versa.

The specification is considered defective, inadequate, or not supportive if it does not include a description of all limitations, elements, steps, and processes recited in the claims. The claims—not the specification—define the subject matter that the applicant regards as the invention. To conform to the claims as filed, the specification and the drawings may be amended to include a description of all elements in the claims as initially filed. Addition of new matter is not permitted. If a limitation or element was not disclosed in the application as filed, the rejection may be overcome by deleting the undisclosed element or limitation from the claim.

Enablement Requirement

To assert an enablement rejection, the examiner must establish on the record a reasonable basis for questioning the adequacy of the disclosure to enable a person of ordinary skill in the art to make and use the claimed invention without resorting to undue experimentation. When the examiner has advanced a reasonable basis for questioning the adequacy of the disclosure, the applicant must rebut the challenge and factually demonstrate that the application disclosure is sufficient.

Publications as of the filing date of the application can be used as evidence of the state of the art at the time of filing. The examiner may cite technical publications to support his or her stance; to defeat enablement, the examiner may use publications after the filing date to support a non-enablement-based rejection as representing what a person of ordinary skill in the art would have known as of the application's effective filing date.

Definiteness

The primary purpose of the definiteness requirement of claim language is to ensure that the scope of the claims is clear so that the public is informed of the boundaries of the claimed invention. If indefinite terminology is used in the claims, and the specification does not provide the examiner with a specific definition of the terminology, then the boundaries of the claim are not clear to the examiner. Each claim must be sufficiently definite to apprise the public of the boundaries of protection circumscribed by the claim, i.e., which products and process will literally infringe the claims and which will not.

The drawings must show every feature of the invention as specified in the claims. However, conventional features disclosed in the description and claims, where their detailed illustration is not essential for a proper understanding of the invention, should be illustrated in the drawing in the form of a graphical drawing symbol or a labeled representation (e.g., a labeled rectangular box). In addition, tables and sequence listings that are included in the specification are not permitted to be included in the drawings.

The specification should act as a dictionary of terminology used in the claims. The descriptive specification gives the scope and meaning of the claims. Terminology and elements recited in the claims must have clear definition and support in the specification. Terms used contrary to their ordinary meaning must be clearly redefined in the written description.

Best Mode Requirement

The purpose of the best mode requirement is to restrain inventors from applying for patents while at the same time concealing from the public the preferred embodiment of their inventions that they have in fact conceived. There are two factual inquiries that are made to determine whether the specification satisfies the best mode requirement. First, there must be a subjective determination as to whether at the time the application was filed, the inventor knew of a best mode of practicing the invention. Second, if the inventor has a best mode of practicing the invention in mind, there must be an objective determination as to whether that best mode was disclosed in sufficient detail to allow one skilled in the art to practice it.

Prior Art-Based Rejections

For pre-AIA applications, any publication, including a patent from anywhere in the world, in any language, is valid prior art against an applicant's patent, provided it was published before the applicant's filing date or before the applicant's earliest provable date of invention, up to one year before the applicant's filing date. The effective date of any U.S. patent and published application reference is its filing date, and the effective date of any other reference is its publication date. If the issue date of the patent or the publication date of the application is later than the applicant's filing date, the reference is not good against the applicant's claims unless it is a U.S. patent or published application that was filed before the applicant's application. Any patent of any country is enforceable only within the geographical area of that country and has no enforceability elsewhere; however, it is good as a prior art reference in the United States and can be used to establish what was already known with respect to the field of the invention.

Rejections Based on Lack of Novelty

Both the USPTO and the Federal Circuit require that for a claimed invention to be properly rejected under 37 C.F.R. §102 based upon a prior art reference, the claimed invention must be completed described or illustrated within the four corners of that reference to be anticipated by a single reference. It is improper for an examiner to enter a rejection under §102 based on a combination of prior art references. More than one reference may be cited in a §102 rejection, but only one may be applied. The non-applied references may be cited evidence that the claimed invention is, in fact, fully anticipated by the applied reference. The examiner can hold that a claimed limitation not explicitly described in the applied reference is inherently disclosed to one of ordinary skill in the art. For a proper rejection under §102, there must be no differences whatsoever between the claimed subject matter and the prior art reference. To be anticipated under §102, a claim must literally read on a single prior art reference. The reference applied must provide an enabling disclosure sufficient to support an anticipatory rejection under §102 (Patent Resources Institute, Inc., 2004).

Under a pre-AIA first-to-invent system, a §102 rejection can be applied if the invention was either patented or described in a printed publication in either the U.S. or a foreign country before the applicant's invention; then the invention is not patentable. A printed publication must have been available to or accessible by the public. If the invention was first described in a thesis that was indexed and catalogued in a library system, it is deemed accessible to the public. If the publication or issue date of the reference is more than one year prior to the effective filing date of the application, patentability is statutorily barred. The inventor may statutorily lose patent rights if the application was not filed within one year of the grace period. In addition, if the inventor expressly or impliedly abandoned the invention, patentability is statutorily barred. If the same invention was described in a foreign application filed more than one year before the effective U.S. filing date, patentability is statutorily barred. If the inventor did not invent the subject matter being claimed but derived it from the true inventor, then proof of conception and communication to another party would have to be established by the true inventor.

AIA Impact—First-Inventor-To-File System

On March 16, 2013, the U.S. patent system transitioned from a first-to-invent system to a first-to-file system. Under the first-to-file patent system, patents are granted to the first inventor to file a patent application regardless of who was the first to invent. Any application or patent that contains, or at any time contained, a claimed invention having an effective filing date on or after March 16, 2013, will be subject to the first-to-file system (Venable LLP, 2013). The first-to-file patent system will increase the amount of prior art available to reject the claims for lack of novelty under §102.

The AIA eliminates seven separate conditions for patentability under §102 in favor of a more simplified structure defining two types of information that can be used as prior art to defeat patentability, along with exceptions to each (Coyne, 2011). Under the AIA, amended 35 U.S.C. §102 prior art includes:

> anything patented, described in a printed publication, or in public use, on sale, or otherwise available to the public before the effective filing date of the claimed invention.

This includes submarine prior art, namely, published patent applications and issued patents that were filed before the effective filing date and published or issued after the applicant's filing date. The AIA permitted some prior art-based exceptions; more specifically, the inventor's public disclosure (or a disclosure by one who derived the subject matter) within one year before the filing date is not prior art. In addition, the AIA creates a one-year grace period based on the inventor's own public disclosure. Furthermore, the ability to antedate (swear behind) prior art has been eliminated except where:

- the art was derived from the patentee, or
- there is a prior public disclosure by an inventor within one year of the filing date.

Limited Grace Period

Under the first-to-file system, the AIA granted the inventor a one-year grace period. The intent of the grace period is to allow the inventor to disclose the invention prior to filing. Any subsequent intervening inventor disclosure would not result in rejections under §102 if the subject matter of the intervening disclosure was a more general description of the subject that was previously publicly disclosed by the inventor. However, any public disclosure prior to filing an application can be a bar to patentability in foreign counties that apply the absolute novelty standard.

Redefinition of Prior Art

The AIA introduced a new standard of "otherwise available to the public" to further define the one-year grace period that is applied to avoid a statutory filing bar. The new standard will add further limits to invalidating prior art because it was known, used, patented, or described in a printed publication, in public use, or on sale more than a year before the applicant's filing date. In addition, the prior art sale or offer to sell bar has been expanded to include sales and offers anywhere in the world, not just in the United States. Furthermore, all patents or published patent applications will be considered prior art as of the filing date of the first application filed anywhere in the world to which priority is claimed.

Prior Art Expansion

The AIA overhaul of §102 effectively means that a published U.S. patent or application is available as prior art back to its effective filing date, which includes any priority claims under §119, §121, and §365. As a result, U.S. provisional applications, international PCT applications, and foreign national applications are added to an expanded redefinition of prior art. These changes put foreign applicants and domestic applicants with foreign research and development sites on equal footing with traditional U.S. applicants. Furthermore, any foreign application filed in a WTO member country serves as prior art against others, provided that it becomes a validly claimed priority document of a U.S. or international PCT application. The AIA preserves the one-year grace period of §102(b) where it is the inventor himself or herself who disclosed the invention. It also allows an inventor to use such a pre-filing disclosure as a shield against the later disclosures of others prior to his or her application filing date. The AIA also preserves and expands the preferential treatment given to entities engaged in joint research. For many years, §103(c) has disqualified commonly owned prior-filed patents and applications from being used to show obviousness of the claimed invention. Under the 2004 Create Act, this disqualification was expanded to include prior-filed patents and applications of entities working together under a joint research agreement. The AIA expands these protections to include the realm of novelty; §102 itself now disqualifies commonly owned patents and applications and those owned by parties to a joint research agreement. However, the doctrine of obviousness type-double patenting limits the extent to which this exception can be exploited to obtain extended patent terms (Halstead, 2011).

The legal arguments to overcome novelty-based rejections vary from arguing the rejections or amending the claim to distinguishing over the prior art to perfecting priority claims or filing an affidavit or declaration making a showing of facts to support an argument. The patent attorney or agent assigned to the application must apply his or her knowledge of the subject matter of the invention against the rejections raised by the examiner and identify the best way to proceed.

Importance of the Filing Date

As the U.S. patent system moves to a first-to-file system, an inventor will be denied patent protection if the invention was disclosed in a prior art reference dated before the filing date of the inventor's patent application. Under a first-to-file patent system, a greater scope of prior art can be asserted against the inventor's application, which will require the inventor to overcome more prior art-based rejections of the claims. Under the AIA, the USPTO will deny patent protection if the invention is described in a printed publication, is in public use, is on sale, or is available to the public anywhere in the world prior to the filing date of the inventor's application. The inventor's application will also be unpatentable if it was described in an issued patent or patent application publication that was filed before the filing date of the inventor's application. In addition, a patent application filed on or after March 16, 2013, will be subject to post-grant review proceedings (post-grant review and *inter partes* review), where the validity of the patent can be challenged by third parties. The impact of the filing date of the application on the examination process is summarized in Table 21.

Table 21: Impact of the Filing Date on Examination Process		
	Filing Date Before March 16, 2013	Filing Date on or After March 16, 2013
Applicable Examination Rules	Pre-AIA First-to-Invent rules apply.	AIA First-to-File rules apply.
Patentability Criteria	Patentability can be supported by ability to assert an invention-conception date prior to the effective reference date. Inventor can to swear behind a prior art reference by producing evidence of earlier invention-conception date.	Patentability denied if invention disclosed in a printed publication, is in public use, is on sale, or is available to the public anywhere in the world prior to the filing date of the inventor's application. Inventor can rely only on his or her own publication within a year of filing to overcome subsequent publications by others.
Rejection Basis	Oral disclosures not deemed prior art. Use or sale of invention limited to within the United States. Published patents or patent applications that claim priority to foreign patent applications will be deemed prior art as of their effective U.S. filing date.	Prior art includes not only written but oral public disclosures. Use or sale rejections can be anywhere in the world. Published patents or patent applications that claim priority to foreign patent applications will be deemed prior art as of their foreign priority date.
Continuing Applications	Parent application filed before March 16, 2013, can be relied upon for continuing applications filed on or after March 16, 2013. Continuing applications will be examined under the pre-AIA first-to-invent prior art rules.	Parent application filed on or after March 16, 2013, can be relied upon for continuing applications filed after March 16, 2013. Parent and continuing applications will be examined under the AIA first-to-file prior art rules.
Impact of Case Law	Applicants can rely on a significant body of case law when interpreting patentability requirements under first-to-invent system.	Lack of case law creates uncertainty regarding the scope of enforcement of patents issued under first-to-file system.

Third-Party Challenges	Validity of issued patent can be challenged in *inter partes* or *ex parte* reexamination.	Validity of issued patent can be challenged under *ex parte* reexamination and AIA post-grant review proceedings. *Inter partes* review (replaced *inter partes* reexamination).

Source: Adapted from Mollaaghababa, (2013)

Transition Applications

As with any extensive patent rules changes, the AIA introduces a transition period where examiners and applicants must be able to determine if an application should be examined under the first-to-invent or the first-to-file rules. Under the AIA, a new patent application filed on or after March 16, 2013, will be examined under the first-to-file rules as long as the new application contains at least one claim that has an effective filing date of on or after March 16, 2013. Under the AIA rules, the USPTO requires that patent applicants help the Office determine whether a new application should be examined under first-to-file rules. More specifically, the applicant must tell the Office when it is requesting examination of a patent application that claims priority to a pre-AIA filing but that it includes (or once included) at least one claim that has a AIA priority date. The revised ADS forms have a section where this statement can be made by checking a box.

The potential impact of the transition effect and need to make a statement would apply to a situation where a provisional application was filed pre-AIA and was converted to a non-provisional application filed after March 16, 2013, with new matter added to the claims on filing of the non-provisional application. Under the AIA rules, if any of the claims in the non-provisional application lacked sufficient support in the provisional application then the entire application should be examined under the first-to-file system. The USPTO relies on the applicant to make this determination and include a transition application statement where applicable (Crouch, AIA Changeover: Claiming Subject Matter Not Found in the Provisional Application, 2013).

Rejections Based on Obviousness

When the examiner does not find a single prior art reference that anticipates that claimed invention under §102 but finds one or more prior art reference that would have rendered the claimed invention obvious to a person of ordinary skill in the relevant art at the time the invention was made, a rejection under §103 is proper. The examiner bears the initial burden of factually supporting a prima facie (first sight) case of obviousness. A prima facie case of obviousness is established when it appears that the teachings of the prior art relied upon by the examiner are sufficient for one of ordinary skill in the relevant art to make the modification to the prior art or combine the teaching of the prior art in the manner proposed by the examiner. If the examiner meets the threshold of a showing that establishes obviousness, the burden then shifts to the applicant to produce evidence or argument to prove non-obviousness. When the examiner asserts a rejection under §103, the examiner must explain the rejection by identifying:

- the relevant teaching of the prior art relied upon;
- the differences of the claimed subject matter over the applied references;
- the proposed modifications of the applied reference that are necessary to meet the claimed subject matter; and
- an explanation of why such proposed modifications would have been obvious to a person having ordinary skill in the art at the time the invention was made.

The purpose of prima facie obviousness is to protect the applicant by ensuring the examiner does not use hindsight based on the applicant's own disclosure. To establish a prima facie case of obviousness the examiner must step back in time to when the invention was unknown and just before it was made. Knowledge of the applicant's disclosure must be put aside, and only facts gleamed from the prior art may be used to establish obviousness. The U.S. Supreme has established objective indicia of non-obviousness, known as the Graham factors, that can be used to interpret and argue against rejections under §103.

Strategies for arguing against rejections under §103 range from attacking the interpretation of the reference, or the combination of references used, to arguing unexpected results of the invention. If the new and unexpected results of the invention are marginal, secondary factors can be used to establish nonobviousness. If applicant considers the feature of the invention to be obvious, the claims must be amended to add more features from the specification as filed to define the existing elements more narrowly. Rejections under §103 are often more difficult to overcome, and the patent attorney or agent assigned to the application must apply his or her knowledge of the subject matter of the invention against the rejections under §103 and decide the best way to proceed.

Rejections Based on Common Knowledge

An obviousness rejection may be based on an examiner's assertion that an element or limitation recited in a claim is "common knowledge" in the art or well-known prior art. Such an assertion may be challenged by the applicant, in which case the examiner should cite a reference to show that the element claimed is indeed in the prior art. Similarly, a rejection may be based on facts within the personal knowledge of the examiner—again, subject to challenge by the applicant.

To adequately traverse such an assertion of common knowledge, an applicant must specifically point out the supposed errors in the examiner's argument, which would include stating why the noticed fact is not considered to be common knowledge or well known in the art. If applicant adequately traverses the examiner's assertion, the examiner must provide documentary evidence in the next office action if the rejection is to be maintained. If the applicant does not traverse the examiner's assertion of common knowledge or statement that a fact is well known in the art, it is taken as admitted prior art.

Differences Between Novelty and Obviousness Rejections

The prior art-based rejections of novelty and obviousness are the dominant rejections asserted by examiners in rejecting the patentability of a claimed invention. While it is most likely that applicants will first have to overcome novelty rejections, it is also likely they will then face a more elaborate process in overcoming rejections based on obviousness. The difference between prior art-based rejections based on novelty and obviousness are shown in Table 22.

Table 22: Distinctions Between Rejections Based on Novelty and Obviousness	
Novelty Rejection under 35 U.S.C. §102	**Obviousness Rejection under U.S.C. §103**
Claim is anticipated by the reference.	Claim is obvious over reference A or in view of reference B.
Only single reference may be applied.	Several references applied in combination.
The reference must teach every aspect (all elements, all limitations) of the claimed invention either explicitly or impliedly.	The reference teachings are modified/combined in order to meet the claims.
Claimed invention must be completely described or illustrated within the four corners of the reference.	The modification/combination of the references must be obvious to a person of ordinary skill in the art at the time the invention was made.
No question of obviousness is present.	The initial burden is on the examiner to establish a *prima facie* case of obviousness.

Overcoming Rejections with Declarations

Whenever an applicant seeks to respond to an office action by pointing out facts not evident from the application and cited references, a written personal statement identifying the pertinent facts must be filed. Such written personal statements should be based on practical or personal firsthand knowledge and signed by the person testifying to the facts. If the signing of the statement is notarized, the document is called an affidavit or oath made by an affiant. If the signed statement simply includes acknowledgment of the consequence of false statements, the statement is acceptable as a declaration made by a declarant. Both affidavits and declarations are treated by the USPTO as verified documents entitled to evidentiary status. The three most commonly used declarations are (Patent Resources Institute, Inc., 2004):

- Declaration under 37 C.F.R. §1.131: used to overcome a prior art rejection based on a reference whose prior art date is prior to the applicant's filing date but after the applicant's actual date of invention. This declaration can be used in a pre-AIA application to swear behind or antedate and remove the reference as prior art against applicant under a first-to-invent system.
- Declaration under 37 C.F.R. §1.132: used to overcome rejections or objections in a variety of circumstances not otherwise provided for.
- Declaration under 37 C.F.R. §1.130: used to disqualify commonly owned patents or published applications as prior art. This declaration is used only in the rare instances

where a claim in an application is rejected over a reference in the form of a U.S. patent or published application that is owned by the same party who owns the application under rejections and claims an obvious variant of the invention claimed in the rejected claim. The declaration should be accompanied by a terminal disclaimer to overcome an obviousness-type double-patenting rejection.

Claiming an Earlier Date of Invention

Under the pre-AIA first-to-invent system, the only invention date the examiner is aware of is the effective filing date of the application. The application filing date is the only date on record relating to the applicant's date of invention. As a result, the examiner is entitled to assert a reference as prior art against the applicant if the effective date of the reference is prior to the applicant's invention date of record. For applications filed before March 16, 2013, the applicant can overcome and swear behind the asserted reference by a showing of facts to establish an earlier reduction to practice prior to the effective date of the reference.

For AIA applications filed on or after March 16, 2013, the applicant will be bound by his or her effective filing date and will not be able to swear behind references with an earlier filing date.

Difference Between Declarations Under §1.131 and §1.132

The context and use of declarations §1.131 and §1.132 are compared and contrasted in Table 23. An applicant may remove a reference underlying a §102 or §103 rejection by showing prior completion of less than the invention claimed and less than the reference discloses if the portion of the invention completed prior to the reference renders the subject matter of the reference obvious or otherwise evidences the applicant's prior possession of the subject matter disclosed in the reference (Patent Resources Institute, Inc., 2004).

Table 23: Differences Between Declarations Under 37 C.F.R. §1.131 and §1.132

	Declaration Under 37 C.F.R. §1.131	Declaration Under 37 C.F.R. §1.132
Grounds for Filing	Used to overcome a prior art rejection based on the first-to-invent patent system. Used to swear behind a prior art reference by asserting an earlier date of invention than the effective date of the applied reference. Used to show completion of applicant's invention in a "qualified" country (in United States only prior to 12/8/93), in North American Free Trade (NAFTA country after 12/8/93), or World Trade Organization (WTO country after 1/1/96) before the effective date of the reference.	Used to overcome any rejection of or objection to a claim on a basis that is not otherwise provided for. Used to remove a reference used to reject a claim by identifying facts establishing that the relevant subject matter disclosed in the reference was attributable to the applicant, i.e., the reference is describing the applicant's own work. Used to remove a published article authored by an entity other than the inventive entity of the rejected claims when the relevant subject matter disclosed in the article was invented by the applicant. Used to remove a patent or published application naming an inventive entity other than the inventive entity of the rejected claims by establishing facts that the applicant both invented the relevant subject matter in the reference patent sought to be removed and disclosed it to the patentee.
Content Requirements	Declaration must be supported by additional evidence, e.g., dated notebook entries. Facts asserted by the declarant will go uncontroverted, as prosecution is a non-adversarial proceeding. Applicant must make a *prima facie* showing of prior invention by stating facts and providing supporting documentary evidence that infer that the invention was completed before the reference effective date. Applicant does not have to corroborate evidence of facts supporting an earlier date of invention.	Facts asserted in the declaration to remove a reference authored by an entity other than the inventive entity named in the application is an evidentiary issue. Where the publication does not reveal inventorship, and the applicant is only one of the authors, it is incumbent on the applicant to provide a satisfactory showing that would lead to a reasonable conclusion that he or she is the sole inventor.

		Facts asserted by the declarant must support that the inventor named in the application invented the relevant subject matter disclosed in the article. To be of probative value, any objective evidence presented in a declaration should be supported by actual proof.
Filing Requirements	Declaration is presented as a separate document and accompanies a reply to office action that refers to the declaration. Declaration should not refer to the reference it is attempting to overcome. Generally, the declaration only refers to the date of the reference because the declaration is effective to remove all references having effective dates after the invention date established by the declaration, not just the reference cited by the examiner.	Declaration is presented as a separate document and accompanies a reply to office action that refers to the declaration.
Signature	Declaration must be signed by all inventors named in the application. If any of the inventors are not available to sign due to death, the remaining inventors can sign the declaration.	Declaration can be signed by applicant, coauthors, independent experts, or others. Declaration can be signed by the non-inventor authors, disclaiming invention of the relevant subject matter disclosed in the article and attributing such inventorship to the applicant.
Timing of Filing	After final rejection: Declaration can only be considered after a final office action when presented with a first response after a final rejection for the purpose of overcoming a new ground of rejection or requirement made in the final rejection. After appeal: Declaration can only be considered after filing an appeal with a showing of good and sufficient reason why it was not presented earlier.	Failure to file supporting evidence in a declaration form while the case is in initial prosecution precludes filing and consideration of such evidence on appeal, and the only way to have it considered is to file a request for continued examination or a continuation application.

Impact on Examination	The examiner must take the declaration and stated facts at face value. The USPTO will rely on the truthfulness of the declarant and on the accuracy of the facts in the declaration.	A declaration may be used to overcome rejections in the following circumstances: to attack the reference; to provide expert testimony; to challenge the relevancy of the reference; to challenge the operability of the reference; to present comparative test results; to present a showing of commercial success and long-felt need; to challenge the sufficiency of the disclosure of the reference; or to provide substantive support for the Graham factors of obviousness.
Review Options	The examiner determines if the declaration is effective and acknowledges or comments on the declaration filed in the next succeeding office action. If the examiner refuses to consider the declaration on formal sufficiency, the decision is reviewable by petition to the Commissioner. If the applicant disagrees with a holding on the merits of a declaration that the facts shown are insufficient to overcome the rejection, applicant may appeal the rejection to the Board.	The examiner determines if the declaration is effective and acknowledges or comments on the declaration filed in the next succeeding office action. The weight to be given to a declaration depends on whether it presents allegations, opinions, or facts. The weight to be given to a declaration is a judgment call by the examiner based on consideration of the entire record and preponderance of the evidence. Review of the examiner's decision that the declaration does not overcome a rejection is appealable to the Board.

Use Limitations	Cannot be used to overcome rejections based on same patentable invention (interference proceeding). Cannot be used to overcome a reference issued more than a year before the effective date of the rejected claims. Cannot be used to overcome a reference issued to a U.S. applicant for the same invention prior to the filing date of the U.S. application filed more than twelve months before the filing date of the application. Cannot be used to overcome a double-patenting rejection. Cannot be used to overcome a non-prior art rejection when the reference has an effective date prior to the filing date of the application but the claims are entitled to the benefit of an earlier filing date of a parent, provisional, or foreign application prior to the effective date of the reference. Cannot be used to overcome a rejection based on a reference that the applicant has clearly admitted to be prior art. Cannot be used to overcome a rejection if the invention was derived from another and not made by the applicant.	Cannot be used to overcome rejections that are otherwise provided for by the filing of a declaration under §1.131 or §1.130.

Adapted from (Patent Resources Institute, Inc., 2004)

Double Patenting

Under 35 U.S.C. §101, whoever invents or discovers any new and useful process, machine, manufacture, or composition of matter, or any new and useful improvement thereof may obtain a patent for the invention. The language could be interpreted to imply that an inventor is limited to one patent per invention. The doctrine of double patenting seeks to prevent the unjustified extension of patent exclusivity beyond the term of a patent. The public policy behind this doctrine ensures that the public can assume that it is free to use the invention upon expiration of the patent term. A double-patenting rejection arises when an inventor files more than one application claiming the same invention. In addition to examining the application for compliance with requirements under §101, §112, §102, and §103, the examiner will compare applications known to be related to determine whether more than one application has claims directed to the same invention. The examiner ensures that such claims, if patentable, are allowed in only one such application. Any claims in the other related applications that are directed to the same invention will be rejected on the grounds of double patenting over claims of the allowed application when it issues as a patent. Copending applications and patents are "related" if they are:

- filed by the same inventive entity;
- assigned to the same assignee; or
- have at least one common inventor.

However, application claims cannot be rejected over a previously issued patent of the same inventive entity under §102(e), because the patent is not that of "another." In such circumstances, a double-patenting rejection can be used to prevent the issuance of a second patent on the same invention to the same inventive entity. Double patenting is prohibited to prevent inventors from obtaining a series of patents covering the same invention to extend the exclusionary term beyond the twenty-year patent term limit.

Terminal Disclaimers

A terminal disclaimer can be used to obviate a provisional double-patenting rejection over a pending referenced application or over a prior patent. Each terminal disclaimer should indicate that the patent that issues subject to the terminal disclaimer is to run for the complete statutory period of the first patent, whether or not the first patent itself may prematurely expire or effectively expire for any reason (e.g., failure to pay maintenance fees).

When a terminal disclaimer is filed, it must include a provision that any patent granted on that application will be enforceable only for the period that the patent is commonly owned with the application or patent that formed the basis of the rejection. Terminal disclaimers function to dedicate to the public the part of a patent term that would extend beyond the permitted twenty-year patent term where an obviousness-type double-patenting rejection has been asserted and maintained. Terminal disclaimers cannot be restricted to certain claims; it must disclaim the terminal portion of the term of the entire patent. Where some claims are free of a double-patenting rejection and some are not, the preferable procedure is not to file a terminal disclaimer in the rejected application but to instead file a divisional application containing the claims rejected for double patenting, canceling those claims from the parent, and filing a terminal disclaimer in the divisional application. The patent that would issue on the parent application would then be operative for its entire term, and only the divisional application would have a reduced term.

Terminal Disclaimer Forms

Support staff should be able to discern the correct terminal disclaimer form to use. The USPTO provides pre-AIA and AIA terminal disclaimer forms that are based on the filing date of the application. The terminal disclaimer form selected also depends on whether the applicant is disclaiming a pending application or an issued patent. The variations of the terminal disclaimer forms are summarized in Table 24.

Table 24: Terminal Disclaimer Forms

Form Number	Use Guidelines
SB/25	Use for applications filed before March 16, 2013. Terminal Disclaimer to Obviate a Provisional Double Patenting Rejection Over a Pending Second Application.
SB/26	Use for applications filed before March 16, 2013. Terminal Disclaimer to Obviate a Double Patenting Rejection Over a Prior Patent.
AIA/25	Use for applications filed on or after March 16, 2013. Terminal Disclaimer to Obviate a Provisional Double Patenting Rejection Over a Pending "Reference" Application.
AIA/26	Use for applications filed on or after March 16, 2013. Terminal Disclaimer to Obviate a Double Patenting Rejection Over a "Prior" Patent.

Alternatively, an e-terminal disclaimer can be filed via EFS-Web for non-provisional applications by completing a series of web-screen forms. Each e-terminal disclaimer filed requires a single terminal disclaimer fee but can include up to fifty reference applications or patents. The e-terminal disclaimer must be personally filed by the attorney or agent of record and cannot be delegated to support staff. If the filing requirements for the e-terminal disclaimer are completed, the terminal disclaimer will be auto-processed and approved immediately on submission (see Chapter 3 for more details on e-petitions).

Filing Requirements

The filing requirements for terminal disclaimers are as follows:

- must be signed by the applicant where no assignee of record exists, or by the applicant and assignee of record of an undivided part interest, or by the assignee of record of the entire interest, or by the attorney or agent of record;
- must specify the portion of the term of the patent being disclaimed;
- must state the present extent of the applicant's or assignee's ownership interest in the patent to be granted; and
- must include the fee under 37 C.F.R. §1.20(d).

Terminal disclaimers can be filed by attorneys or agents of record, as well as by the owner of the patent or application. However, the signing attorney or agent must have power of attorney in the application. A person acting in representative capacity cannot sign a terminal disclaimer (Patent Resources Institute, Inc., 2004).

Combining Applications

Given that it is proper to list a plurality of applicants on an application, even though such persons are joint inventors of fewer than all of the claims or none of the claims, it permits combining of technology-related applications to avoid double-patenting rejections. If there is adequate disclosure for the claims present in the application, in which both claim sets are to be included, entitlement to the earlier filing date is established. When a continuation-in-part application is filed to add new matter and the specification as well as the claims of the parent are combined in one continuation-in-part application, a single patent will issue with two sets of claims entitled to different earlier filing dates, the parent filing date and the continuation-in-part filing date, respectively. If the examiner imposes a restriction requirement between the claims of the two inventions now combined in the continuation-in-part application, one invention may be divided out to restore the former two-application status but with the advantage that no double-patenting rejection can be issued because of the protective shield afforded by the restriction requirement. Such an action would extend prosecution time and diminish patent term concomitantly and would have to be weighed against the amount of term that would be lost by filing a terminal disclaimer (Patent Resources Institute, Inc., 2004).

Double Patenting and Divisional Applications

Under restriction requirement practice, the USPTO can require that an application that claims two or more independent and distinct inventions be restricted to one of those inventions for instant prosecution. The applicant will have the opportunity to file one or more divisional applications on the non-elected claims before issuance of the parent application. Any subsequently filed divisional applications will be entitled to the benefit of the filing date of the original application under 35 U.S.C. §121. An examiner-initiated restriction requirement precludes a double-patenting rejection in subsequently filed divisional applications. The protective shield of the divisional application also precludes either the parent or the divisional application from being used as a reference against each other (see Chapter 14 for more details on response to restriction requirement).

The protective shield of a divisional application does not apply to any voluntary applicant-initialed divisional application filings or any divisional applications filed to claim inventions that were disclosed but not claimed in the parent application. Only the non-elected claims that result from an examiner-initiated restriction requirement can benefit from the protections afforded from a divisional application filing. In addition, for the prohibition against double-patenting rejections to apply, the examiner-initialed restriction requirement must remain in effect. If the restriction requirement was withdrawn (or was erroneously made by the examiner and election was made without traverse) after the filing of a divisional application, the prohibition against a double-patenting rejection does not apply (Patent Resources Institute, Inc., 2004).

Conflicting Claims of Different Inventive Entities

Where two applications or an application and a patent having different inventive entities have conflicting claims, a determination of priority will be required unless the record shows that the two applications were commonly owned at the time of the later invention. If they were commonly owned or subject to an obligation of common ownership at the time, they cannot be used as prior art against each other, as they are not by "another."

When there is no common ownership of the conflicting claims and the different inventive entities are overlapping, the examiner will issue a double-patenting rejection for the conflicting claims. The examiner will not accept a terminal disclaimer to rectify the situation as he or she would if there has been a common assignee of the different but overlapping inventive entities. When there is an inventorship question and several company employees have contributed in an area of development, a single application may be filed naming multiple inventors and containing a set of claims for each inventor or inventive entity, or both. If the claims are allowable in that single application, then no double-patenting problem exists. If the application is subject to a restriction requirement, a divisional application may be filed claiming priority back to the earlier-filed application even if the inventorship designation is now different between the divisional and the parent application. In addition, as the divisional application was filed in response to an examiner-initialed restriction requirement, it is protected from a double-patenting rejection.

CHAPTER-SPECIFIC REFERENCE MATERIAL

Reference Source	Examination and the Criteria for Patentability Applicable Rules, Regulations, and Procedures
AIA Frequently Asked Questions	First-Inventor-To-File http://www.uspto.gov/aia_implementation/faq.jsp
Title 35 of the U.S. Code	35 U.S.C. §100 Definitions. §101 Inventions patentable. §102 Conditions for patentability; novelty and loss of right to patent. §103 Conditions for patentability; non-obvious subject matter. §131 Examination of application. §132 Notice of rejection; reexamination. §133 Time for prosecuting application.

Title 37 of the Code of Federal Regulations	37 C.F.R. §1.104 Nature of examination. §1.105 Requirements for information.
Manual of Patent Examination Procedures (MPEP, 8th Edition)	Chapter 700 Examination of Applications Chapter 2100 Patentability

Chapter 14

Office Actions and Responses, Request for Continued Examination, Appeal, and Abandonment

Office Actions

An office action is an official written communication from the examiner detailing objections and rejections to the patentability of the claimed invention. The office action sets a period of reply for the applicant to file a response that addresses all objections and rejections raised by the examiner. Office actions and applicants' respective responses form the substantive record of patent prosecution.

Types of Office Actions

There are four types of office actions issued by an examiner:

- a restriction requirement;
- a non-final office action;
- a final office action; and
- an advisory action.

A restriction requirement is issued by an examiner when the application as filed contains independent and distinct inventions. The examiner will require the applicant to make an election of species or groups of claims for instant examination. A restriction requirement is not considered an office action on the merits as the examiner has not yet conducted a search on the keywords of the invention.

A non-final office action is usually considered the first office action on the merits in which the examiner details prior art and non-prior-based objections or rejections, or both, with respect to the criteria for patentability. A non-final office action raises patentability issues for the first time. The prosecution record of an application can contain one or more non-final office actions.

A final office action is issued by an examiner when the applicant's response to the previous office action fails to address or overcome the rejections raised. When a final office action is issued, the applicant's options to proceed are more limited. The applicant can no longer make substantive amendments to the claims. A reply to a final office action must include cancellation of, or appeal of the rejection of, each rejected claim. If any claim stands allowed, the reply to a final rejection must comply with any requirements or objections as to form with respect to the allowed claims.

An advisory action is issued by an examiner to inform the applicant that the response to the final office action filed will not be entered, as it raises new issues or would require additional searching or consideration, or both. The advisory action is usually issued by the examiner during the response period for the final office action.

First Office Action on the Merits

The examiner's first office action on the merits will be a statement of the examiner's position on patentability of the claimed invention and is the primary action to establish the issues. The first action must be comprehensive and address all issues as to the prior art patents and printed publications. The office action will clearly identify each ground of rejection and of objection and the reasons supporting the grounds, including providing copies of any foreign patent and non-patent literature asserted against the claims. Comprehensive reasons for patentability must be given for each determination favorable to patentability of claims.

If a third party has made a pre-issuance submission that has been made of record, the examiner must address the rejections proposed by the third party, including an indication of each rejection that the examiner enters.

Requirements for Replies to Office Actions

A "reply" is a document filed by an applicant in response to an office action issued by the examiner. Office action replies may include an amendment to the specification, drawing, or claims, or may just contain argument against the examiner's rejection of the claims over prior art with no amendments. The applicant's reply to the examiner's office action must address every ground of objection and rejection and may do so with or without amendment. Replies to office actions must be filed in a timely manner to avoid abandonment of the application. A reply to an office action on the merits must satisfy the following requirements in order to entitle the application to further examination:

- The reply must be in writing; an interview with the examiner does not constitute a reply. Every ground of objection and rejection raised by the examiner must be addressed with specificity. A general allegation that the claims are patentable will not suffice. The reply must present arguments pointing out the specific distinctions believed to render the claims, including any newly presented claims, patentable over the applied references.
- An amendment to the description or claims, or both, standing alone, does not constitute an adequate reply. The applicant must clearly point out the patentable novelty of the claims in view of the state of the art disclosed by the references cited or the objections made, and how the amendment overcomes such rejections or objections.
- When a reply to an office action adds claims to the application so as to increase the number of claims beyond the number previously paid for, the fee required for the additional claims must accompany the reply. If it does not, the reply will be regarded as not responsive to the office action.

The reply must constitute a bona fide (good faith) attempt to advance the application to a final office action. Filing a reply that the examiner considers not a bona fide attempt to advance the prosecution of the application can result in abandonment of the application.

Preparation of Office Action Response Shells

Support staff can improve the efficiency of the patent attorney or agent by preparing office action response shells that contain an outline of the issues to be addressed in a response to an office action. Support staff should complete the following steps when preparing an office action response shell:

- Prepare a matter-specific response document in Word that contains a matter-specific USPTO caption, including header information, and save the document to a document management system.
- Verify that the matter-specific caption contains the correct examiner name, technology center and confirmation number as indicated on the front page of the office action.
- Verify the correct Mail Stop Address is indicated even if filing the response via EFS-Web.

- Ensure that the first page of the office action indicates the type of office action (restriction requirements, non-final office action, or final office action) and the mailing date of the office action.
- Review the office action headings, and create separate section headings per page for amendments to the specification, drawings, or claims.
- For each objection raised in the office action copy, include the indicated section from the specification in the office action response shell.
- Copy the most recent set of claims from either the application as filed or from the last response to office action filed; update the claim status identifiers as needed.
- In the remarks section of the response shell, include a statement of the current standing of the claims as indicated in the office action.
- For each rejection raised in the office action, create a subheading in the remarks section (e.g., Objections to the Drawings, Claim Rejections Under 35 U.S.C. §102, Claim Rejections Under 35 U.S.C. §103)
- Consult the attorney or agent regarding any auxiliary filing documents (e.g., inventor declarations including any exhibits, terminal disclaimers, replacement drawings, information disclosure statements) that may be required to accompany the response to office action.
- Provide the attorney or agent with a copy of the office action (annotated to show the three-month and six-month response deadlines), a copy of any prior art references cited by the examiner in the office action, and a copy of the office action response shell document created.

Format of Amendments

The USPTO mandates the requirements for making amendments in an application. These formatting requirements ensure that the format of the applicant's amendment is compatible with the requirement for documents stored in the IFW system. The USPTO stipulates that amendments to the specification, claims, drawings, and accompanying applicant remarks all begin on separate sheets in the amendment document.

Amendments to the Specification

Amendments to the specification must be presented on a separate sheet entitled "Amendments to the Specification." Amendments to the specification that include addition or deletion of a paragraph should include a directive instruction (e.g., "Please delete the paragraph beginning on page 10, line 20, and ending on page 11, line 12," or "Please add the follow new paragraph after the paragraph ending on line 14 of page 15"). If the applicant wants to amend text within a paragraph or section, a replacement paragraph or section marked up to show all changes made from the previous version should be included. Text added should be underlined; text deleted should be annotated with strikethrough. It is not necessary to include a clean version of the replacement paragraph. When a specification is amended extensively, the applicant should submit a clean version of the substitute specification, an instruction to replace the prior version, a marked-up version showing all changes from the prior version, and a statement that the substitute specification does not include new matter.

Amendments to the Claims

Amendment to the claims must be presented on a separate sheet entitled "Amendments to the Claims." Any amendment changing, adding, or canceling a claim requires a complete listing of all claims presented, including the text of all pending and withdrawn claims. The text of claims that have been canceled or not entered should not be shown. In listing all claims, the status of each claim must be identified in parentheses after each claim number by using one of the following status identifiers:

- (Original): claim as originally filed; no amendments made.
- (Currently Amended): claim being amended in the present amendment; marked-up text included showing changes, underline additions, and strikethrough deletions.
- (Canceled): claim canceled; text of claim should not be included.
- (Withdrawn): set aside, may be rejoined later, remain in claim count; text of claim should be included.
- (Withdrawn—Currently Amended): withdrawn claims should be amended according to prosecution to ensure if rejoinder is possible, the claim will overcome any rejections or objections that were previously raised.
- (Previously Presented): claim was amended in the most previous amendment.
- (New): newly added claim.
- (Not Entered): text of claim should not be included.

Claims must be presented in ascending numerical order. Consecutive claims that are canceled or not entered can be grouped together into one statement, such as: "Claims 5-9 (Canceled)." All claims being currently amended must be marked-up to show additions by underline and deletions by strikethrough. If deleting five or fewer consecutive characters, double brackets placed before and after the deleted characters can be used to mark up the changes. The text of all pending claims not being currently amended must be presented in the claim listing without underlining, strikethrough, or brackets. Claims not being currently amended should have status identifiers of original, withdrawn, or previously presented. The text of claims that are canceled, or not entered should not be included. Previously canceled claims may only be reinstated by adding them as "new" claims with new claim numbers at the end of the numbered claims. When an amendment is submitted that adds claims in excess of the number of claims previously paid for, the additional claim fees must be submitted with the amendment. If the additional claim fees are not submitted, the amendment will not be entered, and the USPTO will notify the applicant of the claim fee deficiency and set a period of one month or thirty days, whichever is longer, to pay the required fees.

Failure to account for the full set of claims, failure to include the correct status identifier, or failure to mark up currently amended claims as required can result in the examiner issuing a claims-related non-compliant amendment, giving the applicant two months (as amended by the Patent Law Treaty) to correct the amendment formatting errors.

Amendments to the Drawings

Amendments to the drawings should be explained on a separate sheet entitled "Amendments to the Drawings" or within the remarks section of the amendment. Any amendment to the drawings must include:

- a replacement sheet of drawings containing the amended figures, labeled "Replacement Sheet"; and
- a detailed explanation of each change made.

If a figure is deleted or added, the other figures of the drawings must be renumbered if necessary to preserve continuity of the figure-numbering sequence. Renumbering of the figures can be achieved by submitting a new sheet containing the renumbered figures. Any amended replacement drawing sheets must include all the figures appearing on the immediate prior version of the sheet even if only one figure is amended. If the changes to the figures are extensive, the examiner can request that the applicant file a set of marked-up drawings showing the changes made. If the amendments to the drawings are not acceptable to the examiner, the applicant will be notified in the next office action and will be required to make further corrections.

Failure to label the replacement sheet of drawings as "Replacement Sheet" outside the margins of the scanable area is a common reason for an examiner to issue a drawing-related notice of non-compliant amendment.

Preliminary Amendment

An amendment to the specification, claims, or drawings of an application may be submitted by the applicant at any time during prosecution. Such preliminary amendments may be submitted with the application as filed or as a standalone submission when no reply to an office action is outstanding. A preliminary amendment may be filed with the application, before the first office action or after an application has been allowed. Preliminary amendments are filed to:

- correct errors in the specification or drawings of the application;
- add, cancel, or amend claims;
- add subject matter in a separate paper filed at the time of filing the application; or
- update priority claim information in continuing applications.

The objective of filing a preliminary amendment before the first office action on the merits is to address objections or rejections that would otherwise be part of the examiner's first office action. Preliminary amendments most often address errors that were not discovered until after the application was filed or to correct known errors that were not addressed due to time pressure to secure a filing date. In addition, a preliminary amendment may be used to make changes to the claims based on material information that has become known from related foreign applications that may render some of the claims unpatentable.

Preliminary Amendment Filed with Application

A preliminary amendment filed with the application that does not contain new matter will be considered part of the original disclosure if either:

- an inventor declaration is filed with the application and indicates that the inventor has reviewed and understands both the application and the preliminary amendment; or
- the application and preliminary amendment are filed without an inventor declaration and the subsequently filed inventor declaration refers to both.

If the preliminary amendment is filed with the application and the inventor declaration does not make reference to the preliminary amendment, the amendment will not be considered part of the disclosure; the subject matter will be considered new matter, and the applicant will be required to delete it.

If a preliminary amendment is used to add an incorporation by reference statement to the specification it must be filed with the initial application filing to be considered part of the original disclosure. An incorporation by reference statement added after an application filing date is not effective because no new matter can be added to an application after its filing date.

Preliminary Amendment Filed After Filing Date

A preliminary amendment filed after the filing date of an application will be entered prior to the examiner's first office action if either of the following conditions are satisfied:

- the preliminary amendment is filed no later than three months from the filing date of the application; or
- the preliminary amendment will not unduly interfere with the examiner's preparation of first office action.

In deciding if the preliminary amendment would unduly interfere with the examiner's preparation of the first office action, the USPTO considers both the state of the examiner's preparation of the office action on the date the preliminary amendment was received and the nature of the changes contained in the preliminary amendment. If the examiner has already spent significant time preparing the first office action and the entry of the preliminary amendment would require significant additional time in revising the office action, the examiner may deny entry of the preliminary amendment. In such situations, the first office action would be based on the application as filed.

Signature Requirement

Every reply to an office action or applicant-initiated amendment must be signed by a person having authority to prosecute the application. Amendments may be signed by the following individuals or entities:

- a registered attorney or agent of record in the application;
- a registered attorney or agent not of record in the application, but who represents that he or she is authorized to act in a representative capacity;
- an assignee of the entire interest, or all partial assignees; or
- all of the inventors unless there is an assignee of the entire interest and such assignee has already joined prosecution.

An unsigned or improperly signed amendment will not be entered. The signer of the amendment should include his or her USPTO registration number and telephone number.

Time Periods for Reply to Office Actions

The statutory time period for replying to an office action is six months from the mailing date of the office action. However, the USPTO is authorized to set a shortened statutory period of one, two, or three months, but not less than thirty days, for a response. The period for reply is computed from the mailing date of the office action as indicated on the front page of the document. If the shortened statutory response date falls on a Saturday, Sunday, or Federal holiday within the District of Columbia, the reply will be considered timely filed on the next business day. A summary of the response periods and the potential extensions of time available for common office actions are shown in Table 25.

Table 25: Office Action Response Periods and Extensions of Time

Type of Office Action	Shortened Response Period	Extensions of Time Available
Response to Restriction	*Two months	Four months
Non-Final Office Action	Three months	Three months
Notice of Non-Compliant Amendment	*Two months	Four months

Final Office Action	Three months	Three months
Appeal Brief after Notice of Appeal	Two months	Five months
Ex Parte Quayle Action (Closing prosecution on merits but allowing correction for formal matters)	Two months	None
Notice Allowance—Issue Fee Due	Three months	None

*(as amended by the Patent Law Treaty effective December 18, 2013)

Under the provisions of the Patent Law Treaty (PLT), which became effective on December 18, 2013 one month (or thirty days, whichever is longer) response periods were replaced by a minimum two month response period consistent with international standards. A one month response period will only be maintained for pre-appeal brief conference program and the pre-first office action on the merits interview program.

Support staff should be aware of anomalies related to the calendar year when calculating the three-month response deadline when the mailing date of the office action is at the end of a calendar month. In addition, particular attention should be paid to response deadlines falling in the end of February in a leap year (Patent Resources Institute, Inc., 2004). Notable anomalies in the calculation of the office action response deadline are shown in Table 26.

Table 26: Anomalies in Calculation of Office Action Response Deadlines

Office Action Mailing Date	Shortened Statutory Response Period Deadline
January 31	April 30 (not May 1; thirty days in month of April) Assuming April 30 is not a Saturday, Sunday, or Federal holiday within the District of Columbia
February 28	May 28 (not the last day of May) Assuming April 30 is not a Saturday, Sunday, or Federal holiday within the District of Columbia
November 30	February 28 (if falls in leap year) Assuming April 30 is not a Saturday, Sunday, or Federal holiday within the District of Columbia

Extensions of Time

The six-month statutory period for response to an office action cannot be extended, and failure to respond before the six-month deadline will result in abandonment of the application. There are two distinct procedures for extending two and three-month shortened statutory periods. Firstly, automatic extensions of time under 37 C.F.R. §1.136(a) allow an applicant to extend a shortened period for reply by filing a petition for an extension of time and paying the associated fee. No cause or need for the extensions of time need to be stated. Secondly, extension of time under 37 C.F.R. §1.136(b) permits an applicant to request an extension of time for cause but only when automatic extensions of time are not available (Patent Resources Institute, Inc., 2004).

Automatic Extensions of Time

Under 37 C.F.R. §1.136(a), the applicant may extend the time period for replying to an office action to the earlier of the expiration of the six-month statutory period or five months after the time period set for reply by filing a petition that requests the appropriate monthly extensions of time, including payment of the fee specified under 37 C.F.R. §1.17(a). Fees for monthly extensions of time are graduated according to the number of months of time requested; the fees increase per month up to the limit. Fees for extensions of time are entitled to a 50 percent reduction if small entity status is claimed and a 75 percent discount if micro-entity status is claimed. Petitions for automatic extensions of time under 37 C.F.R. §1.136(a) may be filed retroactively after the shortened statutory period for reply has expired when accompanied by response to the outstanding action. Granting of a petition for an extension of time under 37 C.F.R. §1.136(a) is retroactive and automatic as long as the statutory response deadline has not passed. If the applicant fails to respond to an outstanding office action setting a shortened statutory period, the application is abandoned after midnight on the last day of the shortened statutory period, not the extended statutory period. The applicant should specify the number of extensions of time required and pay the associated fee by either authorizing a deposit account charge or credit card payment. Under 37 C.F.R. §1.36(a)(3), the USPTO provides for a constructive petition for an extension of time if authorization is provided to charge all required fees; this covers for any miscalculation by applicant of the amount of fees due and ensures that the application is not abandoned. The USPTO will forgive the failure to file a petition but will not forgive failure to authorize payment of required extension fees.

Extensions of Time for Cause

When an automatic extension of time is not available, an extension of time for cause may be considered under 37 C.F.R. §1.36(b); however, the period for response cannot be extended beyond the statutory six months. Extensions of time for cause may not be filed retroactively; they must be filed on or before the day on which the reply is due. The Director of the technology center reviews a request for an extension of time for cause and either grants it in full or in part or denies it. The mere filing of a request for an extension of time for cause will not affect an extension. The request may be granted in part, and the extent of the extension will be indicated. If the request is denied, the reason for denial will be indicated (Patent Resources Institute, Inc., 2004).

No Extensions of Time Available

When a notice of allowability requires the submission of a signed inventor oath or declaration, corrected or formal drawings, or deposit of biological material, no extensions of time are available. When an examiner issues a notice of allowance, applicant has a three-month non-extendable period to comply with the stipulated formality requirements.

Timeliness of Reply Based on Filing Method

In determining whether a reply to an office action was timely filed, the standard of proof depends on the filing method used.

- Reply Filed by First-Class U.S. Mail: A reply to an office action sent by first-class mail will be considered timely filed if it is mailed to the USPTO prior to the expiration of the set response deadline and is mailed in an envelope addressed to the Commissioner for Patent and deposited with the USPS within the set period for reply with sufficient postage. The reply must include a Rule 1.8 certification of mailing stating that the date of deposit with the USPS was prior to the expiration of the period for reply, and the certificate must be signed by a person having reasonable basis to expect that the correspondence would be mailed on or before the date indicated. If the first-class mail filing requirements are not met, the actual date of receipt in the USPTO will be considered the filing date of the reply. In addition, Rule 1.8 certificates of mailing only apply to correspondence mailed within the United States.

- Reply Filed by Express Mail: A reply to an office action may be sent to the USPTO using the Express Mail post office-to-addressee service of the USPS. When the reply is filed by Express Mail and adheres to the requirements, it is considered timely filed in the USPTO on the date of deposit with the USPS as entered by a mail counter employee as "date-in" on the Express Mail mailing label. If the USPTO cannot determine the "date-in" from the Express Mail mailing label, the filing date of the correspondence will be the date of receipt by the USPTO. If a discrepancy arises between the filing date accorded by the USPTO and the date-in on the Express Mail label due to an error in the entry of the date-in by the USPS employee or if the reply was never received by the USPTO, the applicant can seek recourse by Rule 1.10 petition. In order for Express Mail-related petitions to be granted, the applicant must promptly file the petition as soon as they become aware of the discrepancy or error. A copy of the Express Mail mailing label must be provided, showing the date-in, a copy of the itemized return-receipt postcard, and proof that the Express Mail mailing label number was affixed to the front page of each document filed. Supplemental supportive documentation may be required, which can include a statement from the person who deposited the reply, a copy of an Express Mail log that existed prior to the deposit and was completed within one day of the deposit showing the Express Mail entry, or a copy of the USPS corporate account statement showing the associated matter-specific Express Mail charge.
- Reply Filed by Facsimile: A reply to office action sent by facsimile is accorded a receipt date on which the complete transmission is received by the USPTO in the eastern time zone. If a certificate of fax transmission is appended to the reply, the time zone used to determine the timeliness of the reply is the time zone from where the reply was faxed. If a Rule 1.8 certificate is included identifying the date of fax transmission and is signed by a person having reasonable basis to expect that the correspondence would be transmitted on or before the date indicated, it will be considered timely filed on the date of the certificate of transmission.
- Reply Filed by EFS-Web: A reply to an office action that is electronically filed using EFS-Web will be accorded the filing date as indicated on the instantaneous electronic acknowledgment receipt produced by the EFS-Web interface when the documents are submitted.
- Reply Filed by Hand Delivery, Courier, or without a Certificate of Mail: A reply to an office action hand-delivered or sent by courier or sent without a certificate of mailing will be accorded a filing date as of the date the USPTO receives the reply.

Supplemental Replies to Office Actions

The USPTO encourages applicants to make their replies to office actions complete. However, supplemental follow-on replies to office actions will be entered if they are received before the mailing date of the next office action. Second and subsequent supplemental replies may also be entered if entry does not unduly interfere with an office action that is already being prepared in response to the first reply and first supplemental reply. The factors the USPTO considers in determining if entry of supplemental replies interferes with the preparation of an office action that is in progress are the same factors considered in determining if a preliminary amendment will be entered or not. The examiner can deny entry of the supplemental replies if the examiner determines that a significant amount of time has already been dedicated to preparation of an office action and that entry of the supplemental reply would require signification additional time in revision of the office action (Patent Resources Institute, Inc., 2004).

Telephone Interviews with the Examiner

Applicants may schedule an interview with the examiner to discuss prior art-based rejections and proposed amendments to overcome them. Interviews are not granted before the first office action unless the application is a continuing application. The USPTO encourages applicants to request telephone interviews with the examiner to help advance prosecution or to aid the examiner's understanding of the subject matter of the invention.

Following a telephone interview with the examiner, a complete written statement as to the substance of the interview with regard to the merits of the application must be made of record in the application, whether or not agreement was reached. The applicant is responsible for making the substance of an interview of record in the application file, unless the interview was initiated by the examiner. The recordation of the substance of the interview should include an identification of the claims discussed, an identification of specific prior art discussed, identification of proposed amendments, identification of the principal arguments of the applicant and examiner, and a notation of the general results or outcome of the interview. If the examiner initiates the telephone interview, the examiner must complete an interview summary form if a matter of substance was discussed and send the applicant a copy of the completed form for review (Patent Resources Institute, Inc., 2004).

Order of Office Actions

Examiner-issued office actions follow the chronological order of the examination phase. The first action issued by the examiner may be a restriction requirement or a non-final office action. Toward the end of the examination phase, the examiner can issue a final office action with or without an subsequent advisory action.

Restriction Requirement

The laws of double patenting guard against more than one invention being claimed in a patent application. In general, patents cover a single invention, but it is possible to have two separate inventions in one patent as long as there is an allowable generic claim or the subject matter is sufficiently related to each other that examination together does not require separate searching by the examiner. When the applicant files a patent application that potentially covers multiple inventions, the USPTO uses restriction requirement practice as a discretionary tool to limit the examination of a patent to only one invention. In order to issue a restriction requirement, the examiner must find that two independent (unrelated to each other) or distinct (unobvious relative to each other) inventions have been claimed and that simultaneous examination of both would be burdensome on the examiner. (Crouch, USPTO Releases Notes on Restriction Practice, 2004). Under 35 U.S.C. §121, the USPTO has authority to restrict the claims in a patent application where the claims are too distinct to justify coexamination. Restriction requirement practice facilitates effective examination of inventions and ensures that the Office obtains the filing fee and maintenance fee revenues for each independent and distinct invention. If restriction is required by the USPTO, any subsequently filed divisional applications would be immune from double-patenting rejections under the statutory protection of 35 U.S.C. §121.

A restriction requirement is not considered an office action on the merits, as the examiner is requiring that the applicant elect a set of claims before a prior art search is completed. Alternatively, a restriction requirement can be done by telephone, and elections made by the applicant can be included in the first office action on the merits (Crouch, Rise in Restriction Requirement: A Response from USPTO, 2010). If issued in writing, the restriction requirement will detail the grouping of claims and will identify the claims assigned to each group.

Response to Restriction Requirement

Whether an applicant agrees with the restriction requirement or not, claims to one invention must be elected provisionally. If the applicant disagrees with the requirement for restriction, a request for reconsideration and withdrawal or modification of the requirement giving reasons may be filed; however, the request must include a provisional election of claims or species. A broad allegation that the restriction requirement is wrongly issued does not comply with requirements to support a traversal (reconsideration). The election with traverse should specifically point out why the claimed inventions are not distinct. If election of claims is made without traverse, the applicant loses the right to petition for review of the propriety of the restriction requirement. If the examiner finds that the election requirement was incorrect, the restriction requirement will be withdrawn, and the examiner will examine all claims as if no election were ever made.

If the restriction requirement is maintained in the next office action after an election with traverse, or if election is made without traverse, only the claims to the elected invention will be examined. The remaining claims will be considered non-elected claims and are withdrawn from prosecution. Where there is no linking allowable generic claim, the applicant will have the option to pursue non-elected claims in a divisional application filed prior to issuance of the parent application (see Chapter 16 for more details on divisional applications). The election of claims or species may be filed within two months of the mailing date of the requirement for restriction. The response period may be extended, by up to four months by payment of extension fees, to the statutory six-month response deadline. The election of claims becomes fixed when the examiner issues an office action on the merits of the elected claims, and further shifting of the elected invention is not permitted unless it results in no additional examining effort. The applicant's response to a restriction requirement must include an election of a species or groups detailed in the restriction requirement, including an identification of the claims that read on the elected species or groups.

Petition if Restriction Requirement Improper

The propriety of a restriction requirement is reviewable by petition rather than by appeal. After a final requirement for restriction is made by the examiner, and the applicant has traversed the requirement, the applicant can petition the Director for withdrawal of an improper restriction requirement under 37 C.F.R. §1.144 to review the requirement for restriction or election. The applicant cannot petition to review a restriction requirement unless election was made with traverse and reconsideration has already been requested and the requirement made final. Filing the petition will not stop any period of response that may be running against the application. The filing of the petition for withdrawal of an improper restriction requirement may be deferred until after a final office action or notice of allowance, but it must be filed no later than a notice of appeal.

Non-Final Office Action

The first office action on the merits issued by the examiner will be given a status of non-final and will contain all prior art-based and non-prior art-based rejections and/or objections with respect to the specification and claims. The examiner will detail rejections against prior art citations and will enclose copies of any non-patent literature asserted against the claims. The applicant will be given a three-month shortened statutory period for response that is extendable up to the statutory six-month response deadline on payment of monthly extension of time fees.

Notice of Non-Compliant Amendment

When a preliminary amendment, supplemental amendment, or non-final amendment is filed, it is reviewed by USPTO technical support staff for compliance with formatting requirements. If the amendment is not compliant with requirements, a Notice of Non-Compliant Amendment is sent to the applicant pointing out all of the reasons for noncompliance. The most common causes of a notice of non-compliant amendment are:

- amendment does not contain the separate page sections required for amendments to the specification, amendments to the drawings, amendment to the claims and remarks;
- amendments to the specification are not completed with marked-up paragraphs using strikethrough and underlining to show changes within the paragraph;
- the directive insertion point indicated for a replacement paragraph in the specification was incorrect;

- a clean copy of a substitute specification is filed and not labeled "Substitute Specification" and an additional copy of the marked-up specification showing all changes is not included;
- amendments to the drawings did not include a new set of amended drawings with "Replacement Sheet" added within the margins of each sheet;
- amendment does not contain a complete listing of the claims;
- currently amended claims do not show changes made from the most previous of the claim using strikethrough and underline markups, preferably completed using the black-and-white "track changes" feature in Microsoft Word;
- amendment to the claims section does not include status identifiers for each claim, or the status identifiers included are not the acceptable status identifiers;
- in a response to restriction requirement, the applicant elected species/groups that did not correspond to species/groups detailed in the restriction requirement, or the applicant did not identify the claims readable on the elected species/groups;
- in a response to restriction requirements, non-elected claims did not have the status identifier "withdrawn" and/or the text of the claim was not included, or both; or
- in a preliminary amendment, full set of claims was not accounted for or status identifier "New" was not used for claims added by the preliminary amendment.

On June 1, 2005, the USPTO waived certain requirements under 37 C.F.R. §1.121 to reduce the incidence of non-compliant amendments. As a result of this waiver, the USPTO agreed to accept amendments that include:

- the text of canceled or non-entered (withdrawn) claims; and
- certain variations of status identifiers.

The USPTO deemed that certain amendment filing requirements were not essential and that waiver of certain provisions would still allow examiners to clearly understand exactly what amendments have been made of record. More specifically, the USPTO deemed that claims listings that include the text of a canceled or non-entered claim, if the amendment otherwise complied with requirements including the use of the correct status identifier "canceled" or "not entered" respectively, would be acceptable. In addition, the USPTO permitted some acceptable alternative to the status identifiers under 37 C.F.R. §1.121(c), as shown in Table 27. The USPTO directed that the technical support staff and examiners should only issue a Notice of Non-Compliant Amendment when the status of the amended claims is not accurate and clear in view of the application file record.

Table 27: Claim Status Identifiers and Acceptable Variations	
Status Identifiers	Acceptable Variations
Original	Original Claim Originally Filed Claim
Currently Amended	Presently Amended Currently Amended Claim
Canceled	Canceled Without Prejudice Cancel Canceled Canceled Herein Previously Canceled Canceled Claim Deleted
Withdrawn	Withdrawn From Consideration Withdrawn—New Withdrawn Claim Withdrawn—Currently Amended
Previously Presented	Previously Amended Previously Added Previously Submitted Previously Presented Claim
New	Newly Added New Claim
Not Entered	Not Entered Claim

Response to Notice of Non-Compliant Amendment

The cause of the non-compliant amendment will determine whether the applicant will be given a period of time in which to comply with the rule and whether the applicant's reply to the notice should consist of the corrected section of the amendment instead of the entire corrected amendment. The cause and effect of a non-compliant amendments are detailed as follows:

- A preliminary amendment that is filed with the application: the OPAP will send the applicant a Notice to File Corrected Application Papers, which sets a time period of two months for reply, and extensions of time are available up to the six-month end of statutory period. Failure to reply to the OPAP notice will result in abandonment of the application. Applicant's reply is required to include either a substitute specification if the amendment is to the specification, or a complete claim listing if the amendment is to the claims.
- A preliminary amendment filed after the filing date of the application: the OPAP will send the applicant a Notice of Non-Compliant Amendment, which sets a time period of two months (effective December 18, 2013 under the Patent Law Treaty) for reply, no extensions of time are available. Failure to submit a timely reply will result in the application being examined without entry of the preliminary amendment. Applicant's reply is required to include the corrected section of the amendment.
- A non-final amendment including an amendment filed as a submission for a RCE: the OPAP will send the applicant a Notice of Non-Compliant Amendment, which sets a time period of two months (effective December 18, 2013 under the Patent Law Treaty) for reply; extensions of time are available up to the six-month end of statutory period. Failure to reply to this notice will result in abandonment of the application. Applicant's reply is required to include the corrected section of the amendment.
- An after final amendment: the amendment will be forwarded in unentered status to the examiner. In addition to providing reasons for non-entry when the amendment is not in compliance, the examiner should also indicate in the advisory action any non-compliance in the after final amendment. The examiner should attach a Notice of Non-Compliant Amendment to the advisory action. The notice provides no new time period for correcting the non-compliance. The time period for reply continues to run from the mailing of the final office action. Applicant still needs to respond to the final Office action to avoid abandonment of the application. If the applicant wishes to file another after final amendment, the entire corrected amendment must be submitted within the time period identified in the final Office action.
- An amendment filed in response to an *ex parte quayle* action: the OPAP will send the notice that sets a time period of two months for reply; no extensions of time are available. Failure to reply to this notice will result in abandonment of the application. Applicant's reply is required to include the corrected section of the amendment.

- An after allowance amendment will be forwarded to the examiner: Amendments after allowance are not entered as matter of right. The examiner will notify the applicant if the amendment is not approved for entry. The examiner may attach a Notice of Non-Compliant Amendment to the response to an after allowance communication. The notice provides no new time period. If applicant wishes to file another after allowance amendment, the entire corrected amendment must be submitted before the payment of the issue fee.

Final Office Action

A final office action is usually the second action on the merits that an applicant receives. The examiner may properly issue a final office action when:

- previous arguments are unpersuasive;
- a new ground of rejection is required by amendments made to the claims in the previous response; or
- a new ground of rejection is required by a reference in an IDS submitted after the first action.

An examiner can also make a first action after the filing of a continuing application final if the claims are drawn to the same invention as the parent application and would have been finally rejected on the art of record in the next office action issued in the parent application.

Options After Final Office Action

When the examiner has issued a properly made final office action, the applicant has a range o options to consider. First, the applicant should consider scheduling an interview with the examiner to help better understand the examiner's position or to clarify the applicant's position on the rejected claims. The examiner has the right to grant or deny an interview request after a final office action. If there is an agreement between the applicant and the examiner on a misunderstanding in interpreting the claims, a simple claim amendment could resolve the issues and overcome the rejections. The applicant will also be able to evaluate if a declaration or data supporting patentability may be useful.

If agreement cannot be reached on the claims, the applicant must consider next steps. It is very rare that an applicant would consider abandoning the application at this stage due to the significant time and monies already invested in prosecution. The applicant may further narrow the claims by amendment to define over the prior art to obtain allowance of a set of claims with some valuable scope.

If the applicant believes the rejections raised by the examiner are incorrect and the facts are in favor of the applicant's stance, applicant can file an appeal. The appeals process before the Board is expensive and time-consuming.

The applicant can also decide to continue prosecution with the examiner rather than appeal to the Board. In such situations, the applicant can file a continuation application for final rejected claims and permit any allowed claims to proceed to issuance. The applicant can also consider filing a request for continued examination with the required submission to have the examiner consider and enter further amendments.

Another new option is participation in the After Final Consideration pilot program. This program is designed to reduce the need to file a RCE. To participate in the After Final Consideration program, the applicant must respond to the final office action and amend at least one independent claim without broadening the scope of the independent claim in any way. The applicant must also be willing to participate in an examiner interview (Tu et al, 2013).

The options for proceeding after the final office action are shown in Figure L. The options to file a response to the final office action, participate in the After Final Consideration pilot program, request for continued examination, filing appeal, and abandonment are discussed in more detail in the remainder of this chapter. The option to file a continuing application is discussed in Chapter 16.

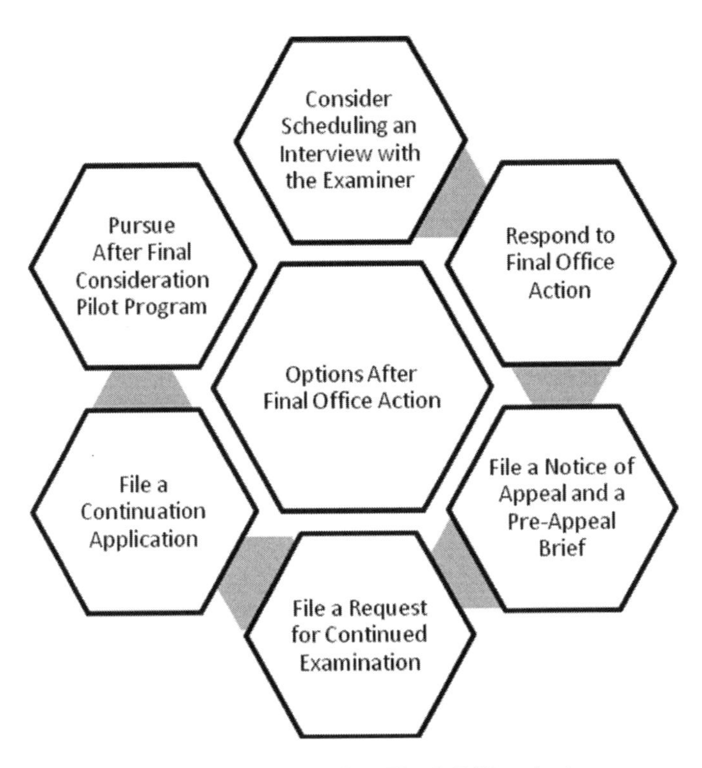

Figure L: Options after Final Office Action

Response to Final Office Action

If an applicant files an amendment narrowing the claims in an effort to overcome an obviousness rejection, entry of such an amendment is at the examiner's discretion. The examiner will consider the amendment to determine whether it places the claims in condition for allowance or in better condition for appeal, or both. Amendments that show a good and sufficient reason why they are necessary and were not presented earlier may be admitted by the examiner, although this option would not be favored by the applicant as it is a high standard to comply with (Patent Resources Institute, Inc., 2004). An amendment after final office action will not be entered if it:

- does not place the application in condition for allowance or in better condition for appeal;
- raises a new matter issue;
- presents a new issue requiring further consideration or search; or
- presents additional claims without canceling any finally rejected claims.

Non-Entry of Response to Final Office Action—Advisory Action

If a response to a final office action is not entered by the examiner, the application will go abandoned unless the applicant timely files an acceptable reply before the six-month statutory deadline. Any reply filed beyond the three-month shortened statutory response period must be accompanied by an automatic retroactive petition for an extension time and associated fee. When a reply to a final office action is not entered, the examiner is supposed to send an advisory action to the applicant indicating that entry of the reply was denied. If the applicant does not receive an advisory action from the examiner, the applicant should not assume that the reply to final office action was entered. If the reply was not entered, the application will go abandoned. When the applicant files a response to a final office action, the applicant should telephone the examiner well within the statutory period to find out the status of reply and ensure precautionary measures are taken to avoid abandonment. To ensure the application remains pending, the applicant should file a precautionary notice of appeal prior to expiration of the six-month statutory period for response to the final office action. It is the applicant's responsibility to be aware that the final office action response period tolls to the six-month deadline in absence of an affirmative indication by the examiner that the reply to final office action has been entered.

Response Period for Final Office Action

Responses to final office actions are subject to expedited processing under 37 C.F.R. §1.116 to place the application in condition for allowance or appeal in a timely manner. If the applicant replies to a final office action within two months of the mailing date of the final action, and an advisory action from the examiner indicating the reply was not entered is mailed after the three-month shortened statutory period, the expiration of the shortened statutory period will be automatically shifted to the mailing date of the advisory action. As a result, the extensions of time needed and fees required to file a request for continued examination or notice of appeal will be calculated from the mailing date of the advisory action rather than the earlier, three-month shortened statutory response date. However, the shifting of the expiration date of the shortened statutory period affects only the number of months of extensions of time needed to timely file a further reply. It does not shift the end of the six-month statutory response deadline.

When a complete reply to a final office action has been filed within two months, an examiner's amendment may be made to place the application in condition for allowance without having to pay an extension of time fee, even if the examiner's amendment is made more than three months after the mailing date of the final office action. If a complete reply to a final office action is filed more than two months after the final office action, an applicant's authorization for an examiner's amendment to place the application in condition for allowance must be made within the three-month shortened statutory period. If an examiner's amendment is required after the shortened statutory period, the applicant must file a petition for an extension of time, including payment of associated fees.

After Final Consideration Program 2.0

The After Final Consideration Program (AFCP 2.0) is designed to advance the goal of compact prosecution to allowance without undue burden on the examiner or the applicant. The AFCP authorizes additional time for examiners to search or consider responses after final rejection, or both. Under AFCP 2.0, the examiner will also use the additional time to schedule and conduct an interview with the applicant to discuss the results of his or her search or consideration, or both. The AFCP is designed to encourage greater communication between examiners and applicants after a final office action to reduce the number of requests for continued examination filed. To be eligible for consideration under AFCP 2.0, an applicant must file:

- a request for consideration under the AFC program (Form SB/434), including a statement that the applicant is willing to participate in an interview with the examiner; and
- a response to final office action and amendment to at least one independent claim that does not broaden the scope of the independent claim in any aspect.

There is no additional fee for filing the request to participate in AFCP; however, the applicant should ensure that any required extensions of time fees for the final office action response period are authorized. The AFCP is advantageous when the applicant is prepared to amend an independent claim and expects the response will lead to allowance of the application with only limited further searching or consideration, or both, by the examiner. The AFCP may also be used to submit a "perfected" affidavit or declaration if previously submitted before the final office action.

If the examiner reviews the response and determines that additional search or consideration is required and could not be completed within the three-hour time period allotted by the AFCP, the examiner treats the submission in a way that is consistent with current practices after final rejection. If the examiner reviews the response and determines that any additional search or consideration can be completed within the three-hour time period or that no additional searching is required, then the examiner considers whether the amendment places the application in condition for allowance. If not, the examiner will contact the applicant and request an interview (Tu et al, 2013). The AFCP has been extended until September 30, 2014.

Request for Continued Examination

If an application is under a final rejection, appeal, or notice of allowance and prosecution on the merits is closed, the applicant can file a request for continued examination (RCE) under 37 C.F.R. §1.114. The options of filing a RCE applies to utility (including international applications) or plant applications filed on or after June 8, 1995. The RCE provisions do not apply to:

- provisional applications;
- utility (including international applications) or plant applications filed before June 8, 1995;
- design application; or
- a patent under reexamination.

Filing Requirements

An applicant can file a RCE when prosecution on the merits is closed by filing the following:

- RCE form SB/30;
- an acceptable submission; and
- the fee under 37 C.F.R. §1.17(e).

An acceptable submission to accompany a RCE filing includes but is not limited to:

- an information disclosure statement;
- an amendment to the written description, claims, drawings; or
- new arguments or evidence in support of patentability.

An applicant can file a RCE with only an IDS submission after a notice of allowance when the applicant wants the examiner to consider prior art references that have not been cited. However, if there is an outstanding final rejection, *ex parte quayle,* or the application is under appeal, the filing of an IDS would not be considered an acceptable RCE submission as substantive rejections are still in effect. The substantive submission accompanying a RCE can include arguments previously filed in an appeal brief or appeal reply or a statement that incorporates such material by reference. The distinct opportunities to file a RCE based on the status of the application are shown in Table 28.

Table 28: Opportunities to File a Request for Continued Examination

Status of the Application	Submission Requirement
After Final Rejection	RCE must include a reply that is fully responsive to the outstanding final office action or request entry of a previously filed reply to the final office action.
After *Ex Parte Quayle* Action (Amendment after Allowance)	RCE must include a reply that is fully responsive to the outstanding *ex parte quayle* action.
After Appeal	RCE must include a reply that is fully responsive to the outstanding final office action. Applicant must advise the Board that a RCE has been filed.
After Allowance	RCE must include an IDS, amendment, new arguments, or new evidence in support of patentability.
After Payment of the Issue Fee	RCE must include a petition to withdraw from issuance.

Attributes of a Request for Continued Examination

An applicant can only file a RCE in an application where prosecution is closed. Requests for continued examination have the following notable attributes:

- a RCE is a continued examination of the same application with the original application number and filing date;
- a RCE is entitled to the benefit of a certificate of mailing under Rule 1.8;
- the fee for filing a RCE is set at the amount equal to the basis filing fee of a utility application; payment of the RCE fee cannot be deferred and must be paid on filing the RCE;
- when there is an outstanding office action, the amendment filed must attempt to advance prosecution of the application;
- there is no limit on the number of RCEs that the applicant may file to obtain continued examination;

- the filing of a RCE does not abandon the pending application: appeals to the Board are dismissed on filing of a RCE, but any pending court action must be dismissed to restore jurisdiction of the application to the USPTO.

Treatment of Improper Request for Continued Examination

If one or more conditions for filing a RCE have not been met, the applicant will be notified of the discrepancy in a Notice of Improper Request for Continued Examination. An improper RCE will not operate to toll the running of any time period for response set in the most previous office action. If the amendment filed with the RCE is not fully responsive to the final office action and is a bona fide attempt to advance prosecution, it will be treated as a proper RCE but a Notice of Non-Compliant Amendment will be sent to the applicant, giving a period of two months (effective December 18, 2013 under the Patent Law Treaty), to file a corrective response.

Prosecution After the Filing of a Request for Continued Examination

Prior to submitting the RCE, the final rejection continues as modified by the advisory action. The RCE may or may not be accompanied by new arguments or amendments. The fact that the previously submitted arguments were not found persuasive does not preclude them as an acceptable RCE submission, provided that such arguments are responsive to the last office action.

When a proper RCE is filed, including the fee and an acceptable submission, the finality of the last office action is withdrawn. Any previously filed, unentered amendments, amendments filed with the RCE, and any amendments filed prior to the mailing of the first office action after the filing of a RCE will be entered. Absent specific instructions for entry, all amendments filed as of the date the RCE is filed are entered in the order in which they were filed.

If the application is under final rejection, a response to the final office action must be timely filed to continue prosecution of the application. Filing a RCE without a response to the outstanding final office action will not toll the running of any time period set in the previous final office action.

If the application has been allowed, the filing of a proper RCE will reopen prosecution. If the issue fee has been paid, however, the filing of a RCE without a petition under 37 C.F.R. §1.313 to withdraw the application from issuance will not avoid issuance of the application as a patent. If a petition to withdraw from issuance accompanies the filing of the RCE, prosecution will be reopened. The applicant will not receive a refund of the issue fee paid.

If the application is under appeal, the filing of a proper RCE after the filing of a notice of appeal but prior to a decision on appeal will be treated as a request by the applicant to withdraw the appeal, irrespective of whether the RCE included the appropriate fee or a submission. Withdrawal of the appeal reopens the prosecution of the application before the examiner. If a RCE is filed in an application after appeal but the request does not include the fee or submission required, the examiner will withdraw the appeal. The proceedings as to the rejected claims are considered terminated. Therefore, if no claim is allowed, the application is abandoned. If there is at least one allowed claim, the application should be passed to issue on the allowed claims. If there is at least one allowed claim but formal matters are outstanding, the applicant should be given a shortened statutory period of one month or thirty days, whichever is longer, in which to correct the formal matters.

Notice of Appeal

Under 37 C.F.R. §41.31(a)(1), an applicant for a patent whose claims have been twice rejected by a patent examiner, can appeal to the Patent Trial and Appeal Board (PTAB) for review of the examiner's rejection. An appeal to the PTAB is initiated by filing a notice of appeal, including the required fee under 37 C.F.R. §41.20(b)(1). A notice of appeal may be filed after any of the claims has been twice rejected in the present application, or if any claims were rejected in a parent application and the claims were again rejected in the first office action after the filing of a continuing application.

Response Period

The applicant must file an appeal brief within two months from the date of receipt of the notice of appeal by the USPTO (not the date of mailing by applicant; Rule §1.8 certificate of mailing does not apply). When the applicant timely files a complaint notice of appeal, the time period for reply to the final office action is tolled and is no longer relevant. The two-month response period set for filing a reply brief is extendable by a further five months, giving a total potential appeal response period of seven months. Given the response period for the appeal period (two months and five-month extensions) is activated by responding to the final office action response period (three months and three-month extensions), it creates the longest prosecution response period of thirteen months from beginning to end, as shown in Figure M.

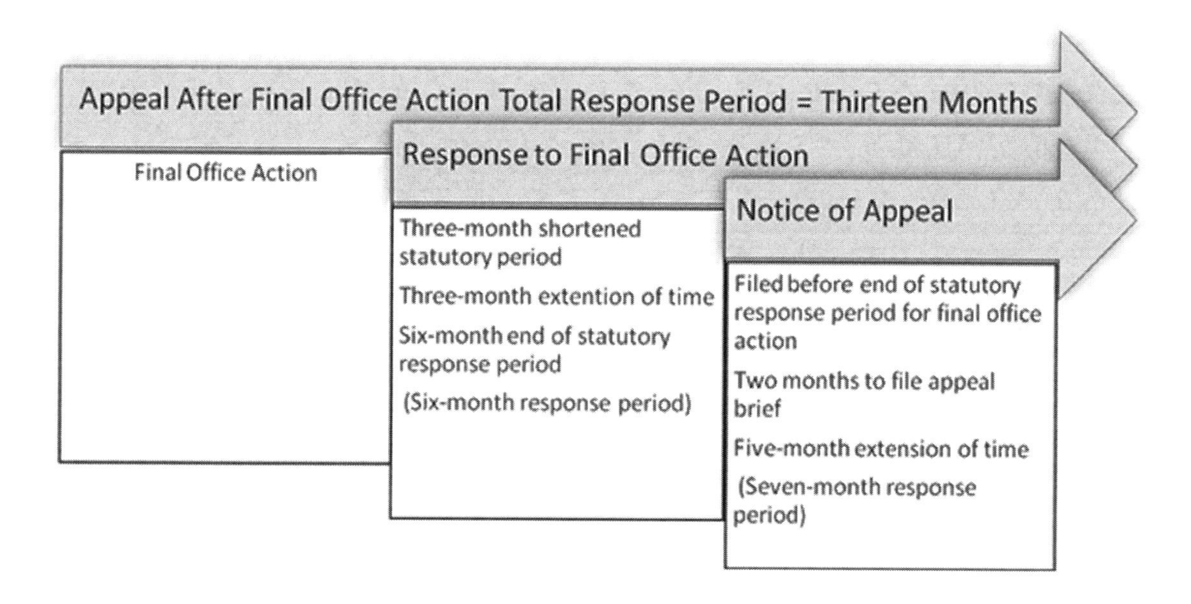

Figure M: After Final Office Action—Notice of Appeal Response Period

Filing Requirements

The notice of appeal must be filed within the period for reply set in the last office action. If the notice of appeal is filed after a final office action, it must be filed before the six-month statutory deadline for response to avoid abandonment of the application. A notice of appeal is a single-page PTO form (SB/31) that does not have to be signed when filed as a standalone submission. However, if the notice of appeal includes authorization to charge fees then it must be signed to be acceptable. The mailing date of the outstanding final office action should be indicated, the final rejected claims being appealed should be identified, and the applicant should authorize payment of the appeal fee and any extension of time required (small entity and micro entity discounts apply) to ensure the application remains pending. If the applicant filed a previous reply outside of the three-month shortened statutory period set for reply to the final office action and previously paid some extension of time fees, the amount of fees previously paid should be deducted from the extensions of time fees due when filing a notice of appeal at the six-month statutory deadline.

AIA Impact—Appeal Forms

For applications filed on or after September 16, 2012, the following AIA-related appeal forms should be used:

- Form AIA/31: Notice of Appeal form
- Form AIA/32: Request for Oral Hearing Before the PTAB form
- Form AIA/33: Pre-Appeal Brief Request for Review form

Revised Rules of Practice Before the Board of Appeals

On January 23, 2011, the USPTO effected new rules of practice before the Board of Appeal in *ex parte* appeals, aimed at streamlining the process. The new rules apply to any appeal that includes a notice of appeal filed on or after January 23, 2011. A certificate of mailing or transmission in compliance with §1.8 will be applicable to determine whether the notice of appeal was filed prior to the effective date and if the revised rules apply.

Objectives of Appeal Rule Changes

The objectives of the revision to the rules of practice before the Board of Appeals are as follows (USPTO, Rules of Practice Before the BPAI in *Ex Parte* Appeals, 2012):

- ensure that the Board has adequate information to decide the *ex parte* appeal on the merits without unduly burdening applicants and examiners with unnecessary briefing requirements;
- reduce the number of non-compliant appeal briefs and examiner answers;
- eliminate any gap in time from the end of the briefing to the commencement of the Board's jurisdiction;
- clarify and simplify petition practice on appeal;
- reduce confusion as to which claims are on appeal;
- avoid unintended cancellation of claims by the USPTO due to appellant's mistake in listing of the claims in either the notice of appeal or the appeal brief; and
- provide procedures under which appellant may seek review of the USPTO's failure to designate a new ground of rejection in either the examiner answer under §41.39 or Board decision under §41.50.

Process Improvement During Appeals

The USPTO identified the following process improvements with respect to *ex parte* appeals (USPTO, Rules of Practice Before the BPAI in *Ex Parte* Appeals, 2012):

- the Board will presume that an appeal is taken from the rejections of all claims under rejection unless canceled by an amendment filed by the appellant and entered by the USPTO;
- the Board will assume jurisdiction upon the earlier of the filing of a reply brief or expiration of the time to file a reply brief;
- the Board will reduce instances of non-compliant briefs by applying the default assumptions if a brief omits a statement of real party-in-interest or a statement of related cases;
- the USPTO will toll appellant's time to file a reply brief until the issuance of a petition decision determining whether the examiner failed to designate a rejection in the answer as a new ground of rejection; and
- the rules reduce the amount of time that the application is under appeal by eliminating the examiner's response to reply brief.

Patent Appeal Process

The patent appeal process affords applicants an option to have an adverse decision of the examiner reviewed before a Board of five members of advanced administrative and technically competent judges. The distinct process components and outcome potentialities of the patent appeal process are summarized in Figure N.

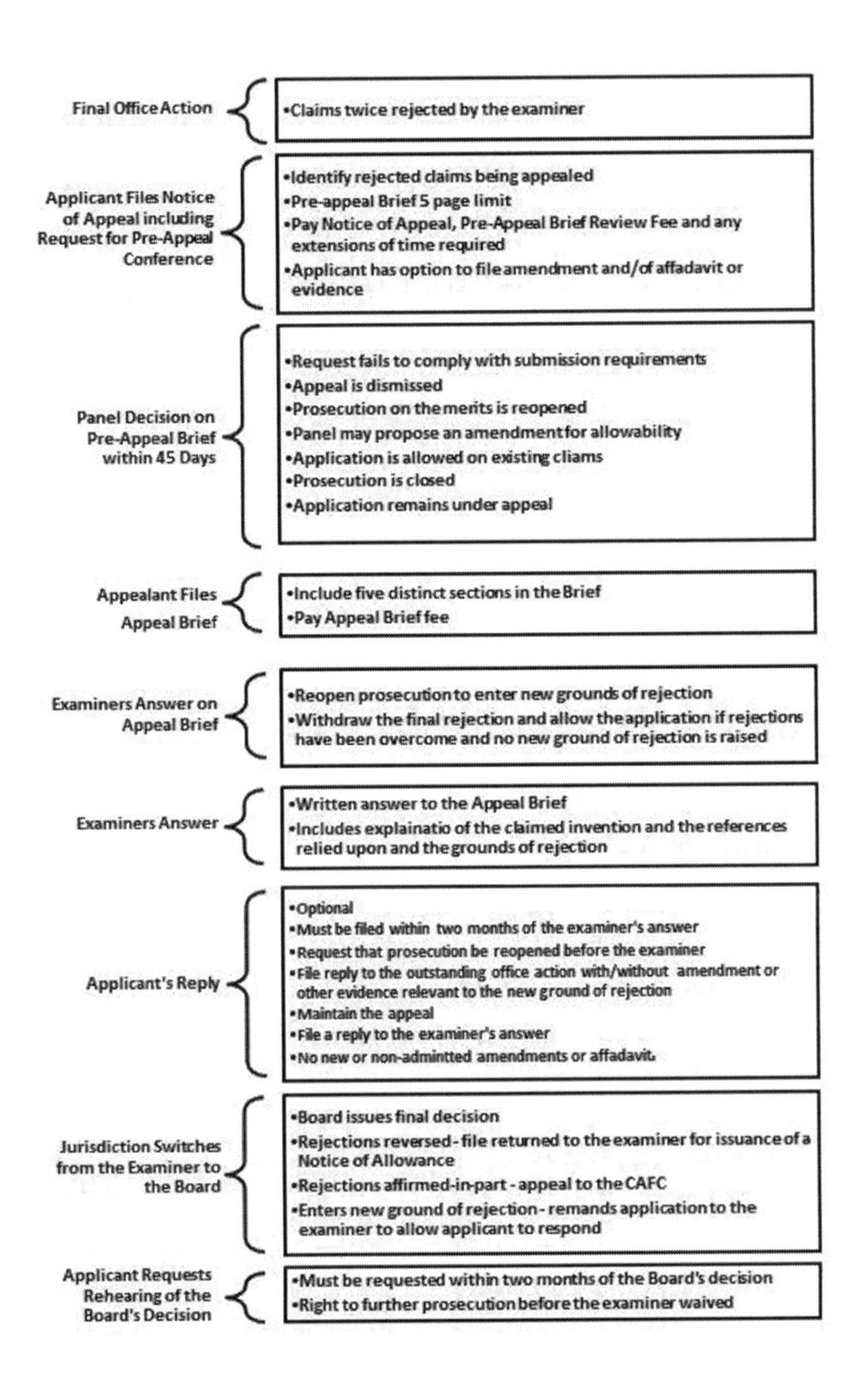

Figure N: Processing Under Appeal

Entry of Amendments and Affidavits After Appeal

Amendments filed with the notice of appeal or after the notice of appeal cannot raise any new matter, necessitate a new search, or present additional claims without canceling a corresponding number of final rejected claims. Amendments filed after the filing of a notice of appeal but before the filing of an appeal brief will only be entered if they:

- cancel claims;
- comply with a requirement of form identified in the previous office action;
- present rejected claims in better form for consideration of appeal; or
- amend the specification or claims upon a showing of good and sufficient reasons why the amendment is necessary and was not presented earlier.

Amendments filed on or after the filing of an appeal brief will only be entered if they:

- cancel claims without affecting the scope of any other pending claims under appeal; or
- rewrite dependent claims into independent form.

Affidavits or other evidence submitted after filing a notice of appeal will only be entered if they overcome all rejections under appeal and include a showing of good and sufficient reasons why they were not presented earlier. Any new amendment, new affidavit, or other new evidence must be submitted in a separate paper. The applicant can also submit new evidence in support of patentability. However, the mere filing of an amendment or evidence after a notice of appeal does not ensure acceptance and entry by the examiner. The examiner may accept the new evidence if it overcomes a rejection, but only if "good cause" exists why the evidence was not submitted earlier. The USPTO strictly enforces the "good cause" requirement. If the examiner determines that an affidavit or other evidence clearly places the application in condition for allowance, the examiner can enter the affidavit or evidence and allow the application. If the examiner declines to admit the new amendment or new evidence, the applicant cannot include that refusal in the appeal and cannot rely on the new amendment or new evidence. If the applicant is not satisfied by an examiner's refusal to allow the amendment or the new evidence, the applicant can file a petition under 37 C.F.R §1.181 asking the Director to review the examiner's decision, file a RCE under 37 C.F.R §1.114, or file a continuing application to bring the new amendments and evidence to the examiner's attention (Yarbrough, 2008).

Pre-Appeal Brief Conference

In February 2006, a pre-appeal brief conference pilot program was extended indefinitely. Under the pre-appeal brief conference program, the applicant may request at the time of filing a notice of appeal that the pending rejections be reviewed by a panel of examiners knowledgeable in the art. The panel of examiners can elect to reopen prosecution, to allow the pending claims while leaving prosecution closed, to allow the application to remain on appeal, or to reject the request on procedural grounds. The pre-appeal brief conference offers a relatively low-cost mechanism to obtain review of an examiner's decision by someone other than the examiner. The requirements for the pilot program are considerably less involved than preparation of an appeal brief. Under the pre-appeal conference rules, the applicant must limit arguments to a five-page document. The pre-appeal brief conference can be used when the applicant does not believe that the examiner is competent or willing to evaluate fairly the applicant's arguments. If issues remain unresolved after a pre-appeal brief conference, the appellant prepares and files an appeal brief.

Processing Under Appeal

The appellant submits the appeal brief to the examiner, who initially determines whether the brief meets technical requirements and standards. If the examiner refuses to accept the appeal brief, the applicant will be given one more opportunity to correct the brief. If the examiner maintains his or her acceptance refusal on the corrected appeal brief, the examiner will find that the applicant failed to file an appeal brief in a timely fashion, and the appeal and the application will be deemed abandoned. The applicant can then petition to revive the application under 37 C.F.R. §1.137 for unavoidable or unintentional abandonment or can petition the Director under 37 C.F.R. §1.181 to review the examiner's decision. After an appeal brief has been filed and the examiner has considered the issues on appeal, the examiner can take one of the following steps:

- reopen prosecution and issue a new office action containing a new ground of rejection with approval from the supervisory patent examiner;
- withdraw the final rejection and allow the application if all grounds of rejection have been overcome and no new ground of rejection is appropriate; or
- maintain the appeal by conducting an appeal conference.

Appeal Conference

An appeal conference is mandatory in all cases in which an acceptable appeal brief has been filed unless the examiner concludes that the appeal should not go forward. Appeal conferences should include at least three conferees: the primary examiner, the supervisory examiner, and another examiner considered knowledgeable on the merits of the issues on appeal. If after reviewing appellant's brief, rejections are not resolved, the examiner accepts the appeal brief filed, and jurisdiction now passes to the Board. The Board will issue a docket notice formally accepting jurisdiction. The examiner responsible for preparing the examiner's answer will weigh the arguments of the other examiners during the appeal conference. If it is determined that the rejections should be maintained, the examiner prepares the examiner's answer. The examiner must send the appellant a written statement in answer to the appellant's brief within two months of receipt of the appeal brief. If the examiner's answer contains a new ground of rejection, the appellant must be given a two-month period to respond. The examiner's answer must respond to the arguments presented in the appeal brief.

Contents of the Appeal Brief

An appellant's brief must be responsive to every ground of rejection stated by the examiner that the appellant is presenting for review on appeal. The appeal brief must comply with formatting and content requirements. The majority of the appeal brief is directed toward identifying the issues presented for review and the arguments regarding each issue (Gallagher, 2003). The appeal brief must be double-spaced with fourteen-point type; only one copy of the brief is required. The grounds for rejection, statement of facts, and arguments cannot exceed thirty pages. Due to the imposed page limitations, the applicant must reduce the issues to a bare minimum. Under the revised appeal rules, an appeal brief should contain five sections:

- Statement of the real party at interest under §41.37(c)(1)(i): the named inventors will be assumed, allowing appellants to omit this information. Information will be used by the board members to determine whether a conflict exists requiring recusal of a Board member.
- Statement of related appeals and interferences under §41.37(c)(1)(ii): appellant may eliminate this section if there are no related appeals or interferences.

Information will be used to identify other cases that would affect the Board's decision, such as a continuation application that would have the effect of withdrawing the appeal.

- Summary of claimed subject matter under §41.37(c)(1)(iii): increased detail required. Must include references to the specification in the record by page and line number or by paragraph number, and to the drawings, if any, by reference characters.
- Appellant's argument under §41.37(c)(1)(iv): appellant must explain why the examiner erred as to each ground of rejection contested by the appellant. Separate headings are required for each ground or rejection contested by the appellant. Separate subheadings are requested for any claims argued separately or as a subgroup. The new rule omits the presumption of examiner correctness in the original rejection.
- Claims appendix under §41.37(c)(1)(v): containing a copy of the claims involved in the appeal.

While an evidence appendix is no longer required, the USPTO recommends that appellants clearly identify in the appeal brief the evidence relied upon (e.g., providing a list of the evidence that includes a clear description of the evidence along with the date of entry of the evidence into the record.) Under amended 37 C.F.R. §41.37(c)(2), the procedure for review of an examiner's refusal to admit an amendment or evidence is by a petition to the Director under 37 C.F.R. §1.181. Such petitions for refusal to enter an amendment or evidence are decided in the technology center.

Assumptions Regarding Appeal Brief

In order to minimize the number of appeal briefs deemed non-compliant, the USPTO will assume the following:

- if there is no statement as to real party in interest, it will be assumed that the inventors are the real party in interest;
- if there is no statement of related appeals and interferences, it will be assumed that no such related appeals or interferences exist; and
- the USPTO will not hold a brief defective if an appellant not represented by a registered practitioner fails to include a brief summary of the claimed subject matter; such an appellant need only substantially comply with the remaining appeal brief requirements.

Non-Compliant Appeal Briefs

The PTAB has identified the following top eight reasons for non-compliant appeal briefs:

- Related proceedings: Appellant must provide a statement identifying by application, appeal, or interference number all other prior and pending appeals, interferences, or judicial proceedings known to appellant, the appellant's legal representative, or assignee that may be related to, directly affect, or be directly affected by having a bearing on the Board's decision in the pending appeal.
- Status of claims: Appellant must provide a statement of the status of all claims in the proceeding (e.g., rejected, allowed or confirmed, withdrawn, objected, or canceled) and an identification of those claims that are being appealed.
- Status of the amendments: Appellant must provide a statement of the status of any amendment filed subsequent to the final rejection in the brief. Any amendments that have not been entered by the examiner should not be presented as entered at the time of filing of the brief.
- Summary of claimed subject matters: Appellant must provide a concise explanation of the subject matter defined in each of the independent claims involved in the appeal, which must refer to the specification by page and line number or to the drawing by reference character. For each independent claim involved in the appeal and for each dependent claim argued separately, every means-plus-function and step-plus-function support must be referenced to the specification by page and line number or in the drawing by reference character.
- Claims appendix: Appellant must provide an appendix containing a copy of the claims involved in appeal.
- Evidence filed: Any affidavit or other evidence filed after the date of filing of an appeal and prior to the date of filing of the brief may be admitted if the examiner determines that it overcomes all rejections under appeal and that a showing of good and sufficient reasons why it was not presented earlier has been made.
- Evidence appendix: In the brief, the appellant must provide an appendix containing copies of any evidence submitted or of any other evidence entered by the examiner and relied upon by the appellant in the appeal, along with a statement identifying where in the record that evidence was entered in the record by the examiner.
- Related proceeding appendix: Appellant must provide an appendix containing copies of decisions rendered by a court or the Board in any proceeding identified.

If the appellant does not file an amended brief within the set time period, correcting all of the reasons for non-compliance, the appeal will be dismissed. An appellant who disagrees with the determination of non-compliance may petition the Chief Administrative Patent Judge under 37 C.F.R. §41.3.

Petitions During Appeal

Under the amended appeal rules, any petition (or information disclosure statement) filed while the Board possesses jurisdiction over the proceeding will be held in abeyance until the Board's jurisdiction ends and will not be considered "of record" in the appeal. The primary exception to this is with regard to a petition seeking review of an examiner's failure to designate a rejection in the answer as a new ground of rejection prior to filing a reply brief. In that case, the applicant can await the petition decision and thereby avoid having to file a request for extension of time in which to file the reply brief (Crouch, New BPAI Final Rules, 2011).

An appellant who receives a decision granting the petition under §1.181 will have two months from the decision to file a reply under §1.111(a). Failure to file the reply within two months will result in dismissal of the appeal. An appellant who receives a decision refusing to grant the petition under §1.181 will have two months from the decision to file a reply brief under §41.41. An appellant may file only a single reply brief; failure to timely file a reply brief will not result in dismissal of the appeal.

If the appellant files a reply brief prior to the decision on the petition under §1.181, the reply brief will be deemed a request to withdraw the petition and to maintain the appeal. An extension of time to file the petition or reply brief must be filed under 37 C.F.R. §1.136(b) for sufficient cause; extensions of time under 37 C.F.R. §1.136(a) are not available (USPTO, Rules of Practice Before the BPAI in *Ex Parte* Appeals, 2012).

Examiner's Answer

The primary examiner may furnish a written answer to the appeal within such time as directed by the Director. The examiner's answer is deemed to incorporate all of the ground of rejection in the office action from which the appeal is taken (as modified by any advisory action and pre-appeal brief conference decision) unless the examiner expressly indicates in the examiner's answer that a ground of rejection has been withdrawn. The examiner has the ability to raise a new ground or rejection in the examiner's answer. The Director must approve of the filing of a new ground of rejection in the examiner's answer.

New Grounds of Rejection

The amended appeal rules clarify that an argument in the examiner's answer that uses evidence that was not relied upon in the office action will be considered a new ground of rejection. In addition, a rejection will be considered "new grounds" when the "basic thrust" of the rejection as presented in the examiner's answer or the Board's decision is different than that presented in the office action. However, an examiner or Board's use of certain extrinsic evidence such as dictionaries will not, according to the new rules, automatically result in a new ground of rejection. The rules also include a loosening of the requirements on requests for rehearing so that an applicant can present new arguments that respond to the merits of a new ground of rejection and allows the applicant to request rehearing for the purposes of arguing that the Board's decision contains an undesignated new ground of rejection (Crouch, New BPAI Final Rules, 2011).

Appellant Reply

The appellant is given the right to file a reply (with or without amendments, submission, affidavits, or evidence) or a reply brief in response to any new grounds of rejection raised by the examiner. The appellant must file any reply or reply brief within two months from the date of the examiner's answer to avoid dismissal of the appeal as to the claims subject to the new grounds of rejection. If a reply is filed, prosecution is reopened, and each new ground of rejection must be addressed. If a reply brief is filed addressing the new grounds of rejection, the appeal is maintained but no additional amendments can accompany the reply brief. In addition, the appellant may request an oral hearing of the appeal by the Board. Generally, an oral hearing should only be requested when necessary or desirable for a complete presentation of the appeal (Gallagher, 2003). Arguments raised in the reply brief that were not raised in the appeal brief or are not responsive to arguments raised in the examiner's answer will not be considered except for good cause. The examiner will not review the reply brief or acknowledge receipt and entry. The revised patent appeal rules eliminated the examiner's response to the reply brief to shorten the appeal period.

Jurisdiction of the Board

Jurisdiction of the application is normally transferred from the technology center to the board after two months from the examiner's answer or supplemental answer (if no reply brief is filed), or after the examiner has notified the appellant in writing that the reply brief has been entered and considered and forwarded to the Board. The Board may affirm or reverse an examiner's decision in whole or in part, or remand to the examiner. If a substitute examiner's amendment is written in response to the Board's remand for further consideration of a rejection, the appellant must elect one of two options to avoid dismissal of the appeal as to the remanded claims. The appellant must elect to either request reopening of prosecution or request to maintain the appeal.

Final Decision by the Board

The Board then considers the briefs and oral arguments, if any, and writes a decision. The decision may affirm or reverse the examiner's rejection in whole or in part, or remand the application to the examiner for further consideration before rendering its decision. The decision must include specific findings of fact and conclusions of law sufficient for review, should the decision be appealed. The Board will frequently restrict the decision to a review of the rejections made by the examiner (Gallagher, 2003).

The Board relinquishes jurisdiction by issuing a final decision or a remand of the appeal. The Board will remand where an appellant elects further prosecution in response to a new ground of rejection or where the Board determines that clarification of facts or law is required. The Board also loses jurisdiction when an express abandonment or a RCE under 37 C.F.R §1.114 is filed. The applicant may file a RCE up until the time of filing an appeal from a final decision of the Board to the Federal Circuit. This allows the applicant to present new evidence and arguments to the examiner where the applicant receives an unfavorable decision in an appeal or where the applicant determines that his or her position would be strengthened by additional evidence or argument (Yarbrough, 2008).

If the Board affirms any of the grounds specified, the Board's decision constitutes a general affirmance of the decision by the examiner on the claim, except as to any ground specifically reversed. The Board may enter a new ground of rejection of any pending claims, even claims that stood allowed as of the appeal. If the Board does enter a new ground of rejection, the appellant has three options:

- submit an appropriate amendment or showing of facts, or both, in a Rule §1.131 or §1.132 declaration to overcome the rejection, thereby remanding the application to the examiner;
- request rehearing by the Board; or
- abandon the rejected claims.

Any amendment or request for rehearing must be filed within the non-extendable period of two months from the Board's decision. If an applicant amends the claims or submits a new showing of facts, or both, and the application is remanded to the examiner for consideration, the examiner is bound by the new ground of rejection raised by the Board. The examiner may allow the claims involved if the amendments or showing of facts, or both, overcome the Board's new grounds of rejection. If the new ground of rejection applies to some but not all of the claims, prosecution is reopened only on the subject matter to which the new rejection was applied.

Rehearing of Board's Decision

If the appellant requests rehearing, the request must address the new ground of rejection and state the points believed to have been misrepresented or overlooked in rendering the decision and also state all other grounds upon which rehearing is sought. If the appellant requests rehearing, the right for further prosecution before the examiner is waived. An appellant faced with an unfavorable Board decision, both on the merits and on a matter other than the merits of the appeal, should consider judicial review of both decisions. An appeal of the Board's decision on the merits may be filed in the United States Court of Appeal for the Federal Circuit or the United States District Court for the District of Columbia. An appeal taken directly from the Board to the Federal Circuit is decided based on the record generated in the USPTO, and no new evidence may be filed. In contrast, in an action in the D.C. District Court, the appellant may introduce evidence not presented in the USPTO.

Procedure Following Decision by the Board

Following the Board's decision, the application is returned to the examiner, subject to the applicant's right of further review by the Federal or D.C. District Court. If, after the Board's decision, no claims stand allowed, the application is no longer considered pending. Accordingly, the application will be stamped abandoned even if there are claims in the application that were indicated as allowable prior to appeal except for their dependency from rejected claims. As a precaution to losing dependent claims that depend on rejected independent claims, the dependent claims should be rewritten in independent form prior to appeal. If, following the Board's decision, any claim stands allowed, the examiner will issue an action appropriate to the status of the claims.

Abandonment of Applications

After a final office action, if the applicant does not want to pursue the final rejected claims, the application can be passively or actively abandoned. An application may be abandoned passively by not responding to an outstanding office action or actively when the applicant expressly requests abandonment. Applications can be abandoned in favor of a copending continuing application or because the inventor or owner of the patent rights do not wish to pursue prosecution of the final rejected claims.

Express Abandonment

An application may be expressly abandoned by filing a request for express abandonment under 37 C.F.R. §1.138(a). A request for express abandonment can be signed by any of the following parties:

- all of the inventors, unless there is an assignee of record who has actively joined prosecution of the application; if there is an assignee of record, an express abandonment is effective only if the assignee consents;
- an assignee of the entire interest;
- a registered attorney or agent of record in the application who has been appointed by all inventors or the assignee of the entire interest; or
- a registered attorney or agent not of record in the application, but only when concurrently filing a continuing application and abandoning the parent application as of the filing date granted to the continuing application.

A request for express abandonment properly signed becomes effective when acted on by the USPTO unless the request specifies a different date (e.g., on or after a filing date has been granted to a concurrently filed continuing application). To avoid USPTO processing delays, if an applicant wants to expressly abandon an application to avoid publication, the applicant must file a petition under 37 C.F.R. §1.138(c) requesting express abandonment including the fee under 37 C.F.R. §1.17(h) in sufficient time to permit the USPTO to recognize the abandonment and remove the application from the publication process.

An application may be expressly abandoned after allowance if the applicant wants to file a RCE or a continuing application in order to have prior art not of record in the application considered during the prosecution. If the issue fee has been paid and the applicant wishes to abandon the application, the express abandonment should be accompanied by a petition to withdraw the application from issue under 37 C.F.R. §1.313, including the fee under 37 C.F.R. §1.17(h). The petition for express abandonment should be filed in sufficient time to allow the USPTO to act on the petition and remove the application from the issue process. The USPTO will acknowledge the request for express abandonment after the petition is granted.

Abandonment for Failure to Timely Respond

If an applicant fails to adequately reply to an outstanding office action within the time period set for reply, the application will be passively abandoned for failure to timely respond. If the applicant fails to timely reply or files a reply that is not fully responsive to all objections and rejections asserted by the examiner, the application will become abandoned at midnight on the date of the shortened statutory period set for reply. However, if the examiner determines that the applicant's response was a bona fide (genuine) attempt to advance prosecution, the examiner can give the applicant two months (effective December 18, 2013 under the Patent Law Treaty), to correct the deficiencies in the reply. If the applicant fails to correct the deficiencies in the reply within the one-month or thirty-day period, the application will go abandoned (Patent Resources Institute, Inc., 2004).

Abandonment for Failure to Notify of Foreign Filing

If, on initially filing the application, the applicant included a request for non-publication based on a certification that the application has not or will not be subject to foreign filing, the USPTO must be timely notified of any subsequent foreign filing. If the application is subsequently foreign filed, the applicant has forty-five days from the date of foreign filing to notify the USPTO of foreign counterpart filing and request recession of the non-publication request. Failure to notify the USPTO of a subsequently foreign-filed application within forty-five days will result in abandonment of the application unless the applicant can prove the delay in submitting the notice of foreign filing was unintentional. The only remedial action available in such circumstances is to file an unintentional petition for revival, including payment of the substantial associated fee. A petition for revival of an application for failure to notify the Office of a foreign or international filing can be e-filed using form SB/64A or may alternatively be filed as a web-based e-Petition.

AIA Impact—Abandonment Forms

For applications filed on or after September 16, 2012, the following AIA-related abandonment forms should be used:

- Form AIA/24: Express Abandonment under 37 C.F.R. §1.138;
- Form AIA/24A: Petition for Express Abandonment to Avoid Publication under 37 C.F.R. §1.138(c); and
- Form AIA/24B: Petition for Express Abandonment to Obtain a Refund under 37 C.F.R. §1.138(d).

Remedial Action After Abandonment

When the USPTO holds that an application is abandoned, one of three remedial courses of action are available to the applicant, depending on the circumstances that caused the holding of abandonment. The remedial actions that can be pursued after the holding of abandonment are as follows (Patent Resources Institute, Inc., 2004):

- request reconsideration of the holding of abandonment;
- petition to have the holding of abandonment withdrawn; or
- petition to revive the abandoned application.

Request for Reconsideration

If the applicant disagrees with the holding of abandonment, reconsideration of the holding may be requested. Where the holding of abandonment is based on a determination that the applicant's timely reply to a non-final office action was insufficient, the applicant can request reconsideration on the grounds that the reply was complete. If the examiner agrees, the holding of abandonment may be reversed, and prosecution will proceed. If the basis of the holding of abandonment was that no reply was received within the set period for reply, the applicant may request reconsideration based on a presumption that the USPTO incorrectly calculated the period for reply.

Petition to Withdraw Holding of Abandonment

A holding of abandonment for failure to timely respond to an office action may be overcome by a petition under 37 C.F.R. §1.181, if the applicant's practitioner can demonstrate that the office action was never received by the applicant. Such a petition requires a showing from the applicant stating that the office action was never received and attesting to the fact that a search of the relevant files indicates that the office action was not received. To support such a petition, the applicant's practitioner would have to provide a copy of the docket record for the date on which the office action would have been received and would have been entered, had it been received, to support the statement.

Petition to Revive

An abandoned application may be revived by way of petition to revive under 37 C.F.R. §1.137, where an applicant's failure to timely reply to an office action is demonstrated to have been unavoidable or unintentional.

Unintentional Abandonment

A petition to revive an application for unintentional abandonment is less complicated and less expensive to prepare as it requires a statement rather than a showing. A petition to revive due to an unintentional delay under 37 C.F.R. §1.137(b) must include:

- petition form SB/64;
- the required reply, unless it was previously filed and deemed late;
- the petition fee under 37 C.F.R. §1.17(m);
- a statement that the entire delay in filing the required reply from the due date of the reply until the filing of a grantable petition was unintentional; and
- any terminal disclaimer required under 37 C.F.R. §1.137(d).

Petitions to revive for an unintentional delay are easier to have granted than petitions for unavoidable delay. The USPTO relies upon the applicant's duty of candor and good faith and accepts the statement without requiring further information. However, providing an inappropriate statement in support of the petition to revive may have an adverse effect when attempting to enforce any resulting patent. In addition, if a petition to revive for unavoidable delay is denied, the applicant can then file a petition to revive due to unintentional delay. When a petition to revive is granted, prosecution continues as if abandonment never happened.

Unavoidable Abandonment

An application will be held as abandoned if the applicant fails to prosecute the application within the period set for reply, unless it can be shown to the satisfaction of the Director that such delay was unavoidable. A petition to revive due to an unavoidable delay under 37 C.F.R. §1.137(a) must include:

- petition form SB/61;
- the required reply, unless it was previously filed and deemed late;
- the petition fee under 37 C.F.R. §1.17(l);
- a showing that the entire delay in filing the required reply from the due date of the reply until the filing of a grantable petition was unavoidable; and
- any terminal disclaimer required under 37 C.F.R. §1.137(d).

Petitions to revive based on unavoidable delay are generally more expensive to file and prepare and do not have as high of a grant rate due to the requirement for a showing, including supportive documentation. If the cause of the unavoidable delay was a clerical error that either omitted or miscalculated a response date, a statement of the facts can support a petition to revive if it is shown that:

- the clerical error was the cause of the delay at issue;
- there was in place a business routine for performing the clerical function that could be relied upon to avoid errors in performance of the function; and
- that the employee was sufficiently trained and experienced with regard to the function and routine for his or her performance that reliance upon such employee represented the excise of due care.

A delay resulting from lack of knowledge or improper application of patent statute, rules of practice, or the MPEP would not constitute an unavoidable delay.

CHAPTER-SPECIFIC REFERENCE MATERIAL

Reference Source	Amendments and Reponses to Office Actions Applicable Rules, Regulations, and Procedures
Title 35 of the U.S. Code	35 U.S.C. §131 Examination of application. §132 Notice of rejection; reexamination. §133 Time for prosecuting application. §134 Appeal to the Board of Patent Appeals and Interferences. §141 Appeal to Court of Appeals for the Federal Circuit. §142 Notice of appeal. §143 Proceedings on appeal. §144 Decision on appeal.
Title 37 of the Code of Federal Regulations	37 C.F.R. §1.111 Reply by applicant or patent owner to a non-final office action. §1.112 Reconsideration before final action. §1.113 Final rejection or action. §1.114 Request for continued examination. §1.115 Preliminary amendments. §1.116 Amendments and affidavits or other evidence after final action and prior to appeal. §1.125 Substitute specification. §1.126 Numbering of claims. §1.127 Petition from refusal to admit amendment.
	§1.130 Affidavit or declaration to disqualify commonly owned patent or published application as prior art. §1.131 Affidavit or declaration of prior invention. §1.132 Affidavits or declarations traversing rejections or objections. §1.134 Time period for reply to an office action. §1.135 Abandonment for failure to reply within time period. §1.136 Extensions of time. §1.137 Revival of abandoned application, terminated reexamination proceeding, or lapsed patent. §1.138 Express abandonment. §1.141 Different inventions in one national application. §1.142 Requirement for restriction. §1.143 Reconsideration of requirement. §1.144 Petition from requirement for restriction. §1.145 Subsequent presentation of claims for different invention.

	§1.146 Election of species. §1.191 Appeal to Board of Patent Appeals and Interferences. §1.197 Return of jurisdiction from the Board of Patent Appeals and Interferences; termination of proceedings. §1.198 Reopening after a final decision of the Board of Patent Appeals and Interferences §1.301 Appeal to U.S. Court of Appeals for the Federal Circuit. §1.302 Notice of appeal. §1.303 Civil action under 35 U.S.C. 145, 146, 306. §1.304 Time for appeal or civil action. §1.321 Statutory disclaimers, including terminal disclaimers.
Manual of Patent Examination Procedures (MPEP, 8th Edition)	Chapter 700 Examination of Applications Chapter 800 Restriction in Applications Filed Under 35 U.S.C. 111; Double Patenting Chapter 1200 Appeal Chapter 2100 Patentability

Chapter 15
Allowance, Issuance, and Maintenance

Examiner Review at Allowance

When an application is in condition for allowance, the application will be considered special, and prompt action must be taken to resolve any outstanding formality matters. The examiner will review the application filed to ensure that all formal and substantive requirements have been completed and that the language of the allowable claims is enabled by an adequate disclosure as originally filed. Frequently, the invention as originally described and claimed may now be more defined in the allowed claims and the examiner may require the applicant to modify the brief summary of the invention and restrict the descriptive matter to align with the scope of the allowed claims. When the examiner determines that all of the claims in an application satisfy the requirements for patentability, the examiner promptly notifies the applicant that the claims are allowable. The form of such a notice depends on whether or not there are objectionable formal matters between the drawings and the specification that require correction. If such formal inaccuracies are present, the examiner will issue an *ex parte quayle* action, which closes prosecution on the merits but permits correction of the formal inadequacies within a non-extendable shortened statutory period of two months.

Ex Parte Quayle Action

An *ex parte quayle* action is an office action noting that all claims are allowable and the application is in condition for allowance except as to matters of form, such as correction of the specification or the requirement to submit an signed oath or declaration, substitute statement, or a combined assignment-declaration with respect to each inventor. An *ex parte quayle* action closes prosecution on the merits. A proper response from the applicant to an *ex parte quayle* action is limited to correcting formality matters.

Notice of Allowability and Notice of Allowance

When the examiner determines that both the substantive and formal requirements for patentability have been satisfied, a combined notice of allowability and notice of allowance are sent to the applicant. The notice of allowance specifies the amount of the issue fee (which may include a publication fee if not previously paid), which must be paid within three months of the mailing date of the notice of allowance to avoid abandonment of the application. The three-month period for payment of the issue fee is non-extendable. In general, the examiner will state the reasons for allowance.

Examiner's Amendment

A formal examiner's amendment may be used to correct informalities in the body of the specification and errors or omissions in the claims. A formal examiner's amendment must be signed by the primary examiner and placed in the file, and a copy must be sent to the applicant. The applicant should be provided with a copy of the examiner's amendment, including an indication if any of the changes or additions are unacceptable to the applicant. An applicant amendment after allowance may be filed no later than payment of the issue fee. An examiner's amendment can be created by the examiner using a paragraph or claim replacement with authorization from the applicant. Alternatively, the examiner's amendment can also be created from a facsimile or e-mailed amendment received by the examiner and referenced in the examiner's amendment, with a copy of the amendment attached. When the applicant submits an amendment in response to a request from the examiner, the examiner should indicate "requested" on the entire attachment to avoid reduction in patent term adjustment. The amendment or cancellation of claims by formal examiner's amendment can be authorized by the applicant in a telephone or personal interview. In such circumstances, the examiner's amendment should indicate that the changes were authorized via telephone or personal interview, naming the individual who authorized and the date of the interview. In order to expedite the issuance of the patent, an examiner's amendment may be used to make a charge against a deposit account or credit card when an amendment to the claims results in additional fees being owed. The most common uses of a formal examiner's amendment are as follows:

- to correct the title of the invention to align with the allowed claims;
- to amend the abstract to align with the scope of the allowed claims;
- to cancel non statutory claims;
- to cancel non-elected claims;
- to cancel claims rejected after appeal; or
- to correct drawings redlined by the examiner.

Reasons For Allowance

The prosecution file history of the application should clearly reflect the reasons why the application was allowed. The practice of stating the reasons for allowance aids in the evaluation of the scope and strength of a patent by the patentee and the public and may help avoid or simplify any subsequent litigation of the patent. The examiner's authority to state the reasons for allowance provides applicants or patent owners an opportunity to comment upon the statement of the examiner. Identifying the reasons for allowance is not mandatory but is deemed an important step in the completeness of the prosecution file history. If the examiner deems that the reasons for allowance are evident from the record, no statement is necessary. When the examiner does make a statement of reasons for allowance, it must be accurate, precise, and not place unwarranted interpretations upon the claims. In most cases, the examiner's statement on reasons for allowance should include the major difference in the claims not found in the prior art of record and the reasons why the difference is considered to define patentability over the prior art.

Applicant's Comment on the Reasons for Allowance

The examiner's statement of reasons for allowance is the personal opinion of the examiner as to why the claims are allowable. The failure of the applicant to comment on the examiner's reasons for allowance cannot be treated as acquiescence to the examiner's statement. The applicant can comment on the examiner's statement if the applicant disagrees with the examiner's reasons for allowance. Any applicant comments on the examiner's statement of reasons for allowance should be submitted no later than the payment of the issue fee to avoid processing delays. The applicant's submission should be clearly labeled "Comments on Statement of Reasons for Allowance." The office of publication will enter the comments in the application file and will notate the file wrapper accordingly. The application is generally not returned to the examiner after the entry of the applicant's comments. As a result, the lack of a response from the examiner on the applicant's comments does not mean that the examiner agrees or acquiesces to the applicant's reasoning.

Notice of Allowance and Fees Due

A notice of allowance and fees due and notice of allowability are sent simultaneously to the applicant with the official mailing date recorded on the paper or the

IFW table of contents. If a publication fee for the application has not been previously paid, it will be due in addition to the issue fee in response to the notice of allowance. The notice of allowance will indicate the amount of the issue fee and publication fee (if any) due, including an indication if the applicant claimed an entity-size discount of fees during the prosecution phase. The notice of allowance will indicate that prosecution on the merits is closed and any outstanding fees must be paid within a non-extendable three months from the date of the notice of allowance to avoid abandonment of the application. If an oath or declaration, substitute statement, or combined assignment-declaration, executed with respect to each inventor, has not yet been filed in the application, the notice of allowance will identify this as an outstanding formality requirement.

AIA Impact—Submission of Signed Papers Accounting for all Inventive Entities

Under the AIA Technical Corrections Bill, if an application is in condition for allowance and does not include an oath or declaration in compliance with 35 U.S.C. §1.63, or a substitute statement in compliance with 35 U.S.C. §1.64, or a combined assignment-declaration under 35 U.S.C. §115(d), executed with respect to each inventor, the examiner will identify this outstanding requirement in the notice of allowance. The applicant will be given a three-month non-extendable period to file an oath or declaration, a substitute statement, or a combined assignment-declaration, executed by or with respect to each actual inventor, with payment of the issue fee to avoid abandonment of the application (see Chapter 8 for more details on accounting for inventive entities).

Amendment After Allowance

After the applicant has been notified that the claims are allowable, further prosecution on the merits of the application is a matter of grace and not a right. After an *ex parte quayle* action, a notice of allowability or notice of allowance has been issued, the examiner can refuse to enter an amendment filed by the applicant. After mailing of an *ex parte quayle* action, amendments touching the merits are treated in a manner similar to amendments after final rejection, although the prosecution may be continued as to the formal matters. Any amendments touching the merits, such as substantive claims amendments, are ordinarily refused entry if they raise a new issue of patentability or require further searching.

Any amendment after allowance but before payment of the issue fee is governed by 37 C.F.R. §1.312 and may be entered on the recommendation of the primary examiner and approved by the Director without withdrawing the application from issue. When the notice of allowance has been mailed, the application is no longer under the jurisdiction of the primary examiner. However, the examiner may still take one of the following actions:

- make an examiner's amendment to correct obvious formal errors or omissions (e.g., to correct misspellings or grammatical errors or to update status information concerning an application referred to); and
- enter amendments that correct formal matters or cancel claims.

However, amendments that pertain to substantive matters or change the scope of the claims require approval by the supervisory patent examiner. Accordingly, amendments filed after allowance under Rule §1.312 are sent to the Publishing Division which, in turn, forward the proposed amendment to the technology center that allowed the application. In the technology center, the amendment is considered by the examiner who allowed the application who then recommends entry or non-entry of the amendment. Amendments after allowance may be entered on the recommendation of the primary examiner if they are one of the following:

- needed for proper disclosure or protection of the invention; and
- require no substantial amount of additional work on the part of the Office.

The remarks accompanying amendments after allowance affecting the disclosure or scope of any claims, or adding claims, must clearly and fully explain:

- why the amendment is necessary;
- why no additional search or examination is required;
- why the claims are patentable; and
- why amendments were not presented earlier.

If an amendment requires an additional search or more than a cursory review of the prosecution record by the examiner or involves significant additional editorial work by the Office, the primary examiner may recommend against entry of the amendment without providing a detailed explanation (Patent Resources Institute, Inc., 2004).

Issue Fee Payment

The response due to the notice of allowance is payment of the issue fee and any required publication fee. The time period for payment of the issue fee is not extendable, and failure to pay the fees due within the three-month deadline will result in abandonment of the application. Intentional failure to pay the issue fee within three months of the notice of allowance does not amount to unavoidable or unintentional delay in making payments.

If an issue fee has previously been paid in the application as reflected in the notice of allowance, the return of the fees transmittal form will be considered a request to reapply the previously paid issue fee toward the issue fee that is now due. If the application was allowed and the issue fee paid, but the applicant withdrew the application from issue to file a request for continued examination (RCE) and the application was later allowed, the notice of allowance should reflect the issue fee amount that is due and the issue fee that was previously paid. The amount due at the time the issue fee is paid may differ from the amount indicated on the notice of allowance if the fees have changed in the interim. If the issue fee is paid after a fee rate change, the new issue fee amount must be paid. Issue fee payments are subject to reduction for entitlement to entity size discount. The USPTO encourages applicants to use the issue fee transmittal form (PTOL-85B) provided with the notice of allowance when submitting their issue fee payments. To ensure that that applicant pays the correct issue fee and any required publication fee, an applicant should use a general authorization to charge any overages of fees to a deposit account. Providing a general authorization to charge the issue fees is an important safeguard to prevent abandonment of the application after the non-extendable three-month deadline.

If an applicant fails to pay the issue fee within the three-month period, the application will become abandoned at midnight on the three-month deadline. When abandoned for failure to timely pay the issue fee, the applicant may petition for revival and acceptance of late payment of the fee under 37 C.F.R. §1.137. Such a petition may be granted if the delay in payment is shown to have been either unavoidable under 37 C.F.R. §1.137(a) or unintentional under 37 C.F.R. §1.137(b) (See Chapter 14 for more details on petitions to revive.)

Late Issue Fee Payment Under the Patent Law Treaty

Effective December 18, 2013 under the Patent Law Treaty, the USPTO can accept last payment of issue and or publication fees. The applicant must show that the delay in payment of the fees was unintentional and pay a petition fee and the balance due for issuance (Johnson et al, 2013).

Quick Path Information Disclosure Statement Pilot Program

The Quick Path Information Disclosure Statement (QPIDS) is a pilot program designed to reduce pendency by eliminating the requirement to file an RCE after payment of the issue fee to have reference considered by the examiner. Where the examiner determines that no item of information in the IDS necessitates reopening prosecution, the USPTO will issue a corrected notice of allowability. In the QPIDS pilot, IDS submissions will be considered by the examiner before determining whether prosecution should be reopened. Prosecution will only be reopened where the examiner determines that reopening prosecution is necessary to address an item of information in the IDS. When the items of information in the IDS do not require prosecution to be reopened, the application will return to issue, thereby eliminating the delays and costs associated with RCE practice. The QPIDS program has been extended through September 30, 2014.

Filing Requirements

A request for participation in QPIDS pilot program must include the following:

- a transmittal form that designates the submission as a QPIDS submission, such as form SB/09 or a web-based e-Petition to withdraw from issue under 37 C.F.R. §1.313(c)(2), including the petition fee under 37 C.F.R. §1.17(h);
- an IDS, including a timeliness statement as identified in 37 C.F.R. §1.97(e) and the IDS under 37 C.F.R. §1.17(p);
- a RCE, including the RCE fee under 37 C.F.R. §1.17(e).

Deferring Issuance of a Patent

A petition to defer issuance of a patent is not appropriate until the issue fee is paid. Issuance of a patent cannot be deferred after an allowed application receives a patent number and issue date unless the application is withdrawn from issue under 37 C.F.R. §1.313(b) or (c). Issuance of the patent can be deferred for a period of up to one month only in the absence of extraordinary circumstance or requirement of regulations. Situations like negotiation of licenses, time for filing in foreign countries, collection of data for filing a continuation-in-part application, or desire for simultaneous issuance of related applications are not considered to amount to extraordinary circumstances. In order to facilitate consideration of the petition for deferment of issue, the petition should be firmly attached to the fee transmittal form and clearly labeled as a petition to defer issuance and addressed to the attention of the Office of Petitions.

Withdrawal From Issue

An application is considered to be in the process of issuance when a notice of allowance has been sent to the applicant. The mailing of the notice of allowance begins the USPTO's formal process of issuing a patent. An allowed application may be withdrawn from the process of issuance under 37 C.F.R. §1.313 to prevent it from maturing into a patent either prior to or after the applicant's payment of the issue fee. However, the grounds for withdrawal from issuance after payment of the issue fee are more limited.

Withdrawal Prior to Payment of the Issue Fee

If the applicant wishes to have an application withdrawn from issue, the applicant must take one of the following steps:

- petition the Director under 37 C.F.R. §1.313(b) for withdrawal from issuance prior to payment of the issue fee;
- file a request for continued examination (RCE) under 37 C.F.R. §1.114 with an acceptable submission and a fee under 37 C.F.R. §1.17(e); or
- file a continuing application on or before the issue fee payment deadline and permit the parent application to go abandoned for failure to pay the issue fee.

Applications may be withdrawn from issuance for further action at the request of the Ofice or on petition by the applicant. Applicant-initiated petitions to withdraw an application from issuance under 37 C.F.R. §1.313(b) prior to payment of the issue fee should be directed to the technology center Director and should include the following:

- a petition under 37 C.F.R. §1.313(b);
- the petition fee under 37 C.F.R. §1.17(h); and
- a showing of good and sufficient reasons why withdrawal of the application from issue is necessary.

While there is no apparent reason for an applicant to petition to withdrawal prior to payment of the issue fee, if the applicant desires to prevent issuance for any reason, the applicant can simply not pay the issue fee and allow the application to go abandoned. If the applicant wants to continue the prosecution process to have newly discovered prior art considered by the examiner, the applicant may file a RCE or a continuing application without incurring the additional expense of the petition process (Patent Resources Institute, Inc., 2004). If the applicant files a RCE, the issue fee does not have to be paid to avoid abandonment of the application. However, the USPTO cautions against filing a RCE prior to payment of the issue fee and subsequently paying the issue fee before the RCE is acted on by the examiner because doing so may result in issuance of the patent without consideration of the RCE.

The USPTO may independently withdraw an application from issuance and reopen prosecution to reject previously allowed claims based on newly discovered prior art or to initiate an interference proceeding. However, a previously allowed claim may only be rejected after the proposed rejection has been submitted to and approved by the primary examiner. In such situations, the Director of the technology center will notify the applicant of the withdrawal and provide detailed reasons (Patent Resources Institute, Inc., 2004).

Withdrawal From Issue After Payment of the Issue Fee

When the issue fee is paid, withdrawal by an applicant-initiated petition is only permitted for the limited reasons under 37 C.F.R. §1.313(c), namely:

- unpatentability of one or more claims the petition must be accompanied by a unequivocal statement that one or more claims are unpatentable, an amendment to such claims, and an explanation as to how the amendment causes such claims to be patentable;
- consideration of a request for continued examination (RCE) under 37 C.F.R. §1.114; or
- express abandonment of the application in favor of a continuing application.

Petitions for withdrawal after payment of the issue fee under 37 C.F.R. §1.313(c) should be directed to the Office of Petitions. The USPTO cautions applicants intending to file a petition to withdraw that such a petition may not be effective unless it is actually received and granted before the set issue date of the patent. As a result, use of a petition to withdraw from issue may not be effective to avoid publication of application information. In order to ensure sufficient time to stop the issuance process, such a petition should be clearly marked and submitted by facsimile or hand-carried to the Office of Petitions (Patent Resources Institute, Inc., 2004). When the issue fee has been paid, the USPTO will not withdraw the application unless one of the following circumstances applies:

- a mistake on the part of the USPTO;
- a violation of 37 C.F.R. §1.56 or illegality in the application;
- unpatentability of one of more claims; or
- a declaration of an interference or derivation proceeding.

Applicant Review at Allowance

The applicant should timely review the prosecution file on receipt of a notice of allowance and validate the following critical information:

- confirm that formal drawings have been filed and accepted by the examiner;
- confirm if a signed oath or declaration, substitute statement, or combined assignment-declaration, with respect to each inventor, has been filed; if a signed oath or declaration, substitute statement, or combined assignment-declaration has not been filed it must be filed before payment of the issue fee;
- confirm examiner has entered and considered references cited by applicant; review priority-related and subject matter-related U.S. and foreign pending matters to confirm all relevant prior art has been cited;
- confirm any domestic or foreign priority claim made has been entered, confirm application or patent number, filing or issue date, and status of each priority claimed under cross-reference to related applications in the specification and ADS filed against the continuity data tab in PAIR;
- consider if an amendment after allowance under 37 C.F.R. §1.312 should be filed or, if it was filed, confirm it was entered and considered by the examiner;
- confirm if claim for entitlement to reduce fees was made under small or micro entity status and if such entitlement still applies on payment of the issue fee;
- if there is an assignee of record, confirm name of Assignee is correct, verify against Assignment Division records, and note reel and frame number; if application is to be assigned and no assignment has yet been recorded, the assignment should be recorded before payment of the issue fee;

- confirm patent term adjustment (PTA); if indicated on notice of allowance, independently verify against prosecution record. If PTA is not correct, consider if a request for reconsideration or petition under 37 C.F.R. §1.702-7.705 should be filed;
- consider if continuing applications are to be filed; confirm if restriction requirement was issued and if non-elected claims should be pursued in a divisional application. Consider if additional subject matter can be claimed in a continuation application and if any new improvements to the invention can be claimed in a continuation-in-part application.

Issuance to an Assignee or Owner

The exclusive rights associated with a patent may be assigned by the inventor to an assignee or non-inventor applicant prior to issuance of a patent. If the patent is to issue in the name of the assignee or non-inventor applicant, a request for such issuance must be submitted on payment of the issue fee and must be supported by an assignment document recorded with the Assignment Division or by proof of sufficient proprietary interest. If the assignment has not been previously recorded, the request to issue the patent in the name of the assignee should be accompanied by a copy of the assignment and a direction to record the assignment or a statement under 37 C.F.R. §3.73(b). A patent will issue in the name of the inventors unless the assignee or non-inventor applicant is named on the issue fee transmittal form.

The USPTO requires that the attributable owner of the title to the application be identified upon payment of a patent issue fee. The USPTO has proposed rules that would require the periodic reporting of application and patent ownership. Under the January 24, 2014 proposed rules, the USPTO would require patent applicants and owners to regularly update ownership information when they are involved in proceedings before the Office. The USPTO would require identification of the ultimate parent entity in control of the patent or application.

Post-Allowance Practice Tips

The USPTO offers the following post-allowance tips and suggestions (USPTO, Patent Practice Tips, 2010):

- Avoid filing an Information Disclosure Statement (IDS) after payment of the issue fee. If an IDS has to be filed after payment of the issue fee, it must be accompanied by a Petition to Withdraw from Issue and a Request for Continued Examination (RCE).

- Avoid delays in paying the issue fee; ensure the payment is received by the USPTO within the non-extendable period of three months from the mailing date of the notice of allowance.
- Petitions to Withdraw from Issuance must be directly filed with the Office of Petitions.
- Provide a Deposit Account Number and authorization for payment of the issue fee. Be clear with payment authorization statements; avoid contradictory payment statements on filing component documents. Ensure Deposit Account contains sufficient funds for fees authorized.
- Include a general Deposit Account fee authorization to account for any potential miscalculation of fees due.

Issue Notification

When the issue fee is received by the USPTO, the patent will issue within about four weeks. A patent number and issue date will be assigned to the application, and an issue notification will be mailed less than two weeks before the application is expected to issue as a patent. Any intended continuing applications must be filed before issuance of the parent patent to meet the copendency requirement.

The Patent Grant

On the date the patent is actually issued, the official original letters patent will be mailed to the correspondence address of record. The formal patent grant is physically attached to a bond paper copy of the specification, drawing, and claims by a blue ribbon, and the attachment is secured under the red seal of the Patent and Trademark Office. The issued patent has a standardized front page format, as shown in Figure O, which summarizes key data related to the invention.

(12) **United States Patent**
Camble et al.

(10) **Patent No.: US 6,999,999 B2**
(45) **Date of Patent: *Feb. 14, 2006**

(54) **SYSTEM AND METHOD FOR SECURING FIBER CHANNEL DRIVE ACCESS IN A PARTITIONED DATA LIBRARY**

(75) Inventors: **Peter Thomas Camble**, Bristol (GB); **Stephen Gold**, Bristol (GB); **Ian Peter Crighton**, Bristol (GB)

(73) Assignee: **Hewlett-Packard Development Company, L.P.**, Houston, TX (US)

(*) Notice: Subject to any disclaimer, the term of this patent is extended or adjusted under 35 U.S.C. 154(b) by 908 days.

This patent is subject to a terminal disclaimer.

(21) Appl. No.: **10/033,010**

(22) Filed: **Dec. 28, 2001**

(65) **Prior Publication Data**

US 2003/0126360 A1 Jul. 3, 2003

(51) **Int. Cl.**
G06F 15/167 (2006.01)
G06F 13/00 (2006.01)

(52) **U.S. Cl.** **709/215**; 711/112; 711/114; 711/154

(58) **Field of Classification Search** 709/213, 709/214, 215, 226; 711/112, 114, 154
See application file for complete search history.

(56) **References Cited**

U.S. PATENT DOCUMENTS

5,070,404 A	12/1991	Bullock et al.	
5,164,909 A	11/1992	Leonhardt et al.	
5,303,214 A	4/1994	Kulakowski et al.	
5,367,669 A	11/1994	Holland et al.	
5,416,914 A	5/1995	Korngiebel et al.	
5,442,771 A	8/1995	Filepp et al.	
5,734,859 A	3/1998	Yorimitsu et al.	
5,802,278 A	9/1998	Isfeld et al.	
5,805,864 A	9/1998	Carlson et al.	
5,819,309 A	10/1998	Gray	
5,835,940 A	11/1998	Yorimitsu et al.	
5,867,335 A	2/1999	Ozue et al.	
5,867,736 A	2/1999	Jantz	
5,890,014 A	3/1999	Long	
5,943,688 A	8/1999	Fisher et al.	
5,970,030 A	10/1999	Dimitri et al.	
6,009,481 A *	12/1999	Mayer	710/33

(Continued)

FOREIGN PATENT DOCUMENTS

EP 0859308 8/1998

(Continued)

OTHER PUBLICATIONS

European Search Report issued for EP 02 25 8806, dated Jan. 4, 2005.

(Continued)

Primary Examiner—Ario Etienne

(57) **ABSTRACT**

A storage area network associated data library partitioning system comprises a plurality of storage slot elements adapted to store data storage media, at least one set of at least one of the slots is assigned to one partition of a plurality of partitions, and a plurality of data transfer elements that are adapted to receive the media and transfer data to and from the media, each of at least one set of at least one of the data transfer elements is assigned to one of the partitions, at least one data transfer element of each of the partitions hosts a logical element designation of a virtual controller for each of the partitions, the virtual controllers restricting movement of the media to between the set of slots and the set of data transfer elements assigned to a same of the partitions.

24 Claims, 2 Drawing Sheets

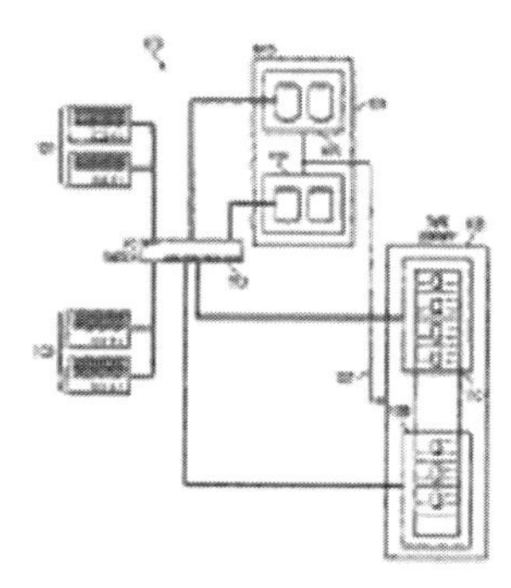

Figure O: U.S. Patent Front Page––Standard Format

Support staff should be familiar with the information on the front page of the patent and should cross-check the informational fields against the prosecution record. More specifically, the front page of a patent includes the following numeric informational fields:

- Field No. <10>: the patent number;
- Field No. <45>: the date of patent (the issue date);
- Field No. <54>: the title of the invention;
- Field No. <75>: the inventors names and residential city and state (and citizenship for applications filed pre-AIA);
- Field No. <73>: the assignee of record, name, and city and state;
- *Notice: subject to any disclaimer, the term of the patent is extended or adjusted under 35 U.S.C.§154(b) by X days, and an indication of the patent is subject to a terminal disclaimer
- Field No. <21>: the application number;
- Field No. <22>: the application filing date;
- Field No. <65>: prior publication data;
- Field No. <62>: related U.S. application data, which includes the details of the applications claimed in the priority family;
- Field No. <51>: international classification codes;
- Field No. <52>: U.S. classification codes;
- Field No. <58>: Field of classification search;
- Field No. <56>: references cited, including U.S., foreign, and non-patent literature documents, including a notation of references cited by the examiner; and
- Field No. <57>: abstract of invention, including the number of claims and number of drawing sheets.

The *Notice filed and Field No. 62 will only be present if they are applicable—that is, if the patent is subject to a terminal disclaimer and if the application contained a priority claim. The front page of the patent also includes a drawing considered to be representative of the invention. In addition, the names of the examiners and attorneys or agents involved in the prosecution of the patent will be indicated.

The Issue Date

The date on which an application matures into a patent is the issue date. On this date, the U.S. patent rights attach and become enforceable against potential infringers. The rights of the patent owner to collect a reasonable royalty for pre-issuance use of the patented invention does not vest until the patent issues. On the issue date, certain rights of the patentee are foreclosed. The specification, drawing, and entire prosecution file history of an unpublished application become publicly available. The patentee can no longer assert claims based upon any trade secret information contained in the patent. After the issue date, the patentee can no longer file a continuing application under 35 U.S.C. §120. The issue date also starts the two-year period within which a patentee may file a broadening reissue application under 35 U.S.C. §251. An interference proceeding with a patent cannot be initiated unless a claim interfering with one or more of the patent claims is present in or is copied into a pending application within one year following the patent's issuance. Patent rights are statutorily presumed to have been validly granted as of the issue date. After a patent has issued, it may be amended, corrected, or modified only by way of a certificate of correction, reissue patent, or disclaimer, or it may be statutorily reexamined (Patent Resources Institute, Inc., 2004). The issue date also opens the window of opportunity for filing of a post-grant review proceeding under the AIA.

Post-Issuance Maintenance Fees

All utility patents, including reissues issued from applications filed on or after December 12, 1980, are subject to payment of post-issuance maintenance fees under 37 C.F.R. §1.362. Maintenance fees must be paid during the term of the patent for the patent to be maintained in force and effect. A patent issuing from a continuing application of a reissue application is subject to maintenance fees only if the original non-reissue patent was subject to such fees. Maintenance fees are not required for a plant or design patent, for a reissue patent if its parent did not require maintenance fees, or for any patent where the actual application filing date was prior to December 12, 1980. The fact that an application may be entitled to an earlier effective filing date under 35 U.S.C. §119, §120, or §365 is immaterial for purposes of determining the obligation to pay maintenance fees.

While the USPTO has no duty to notify the patentee when a maintenance fee is due and assumes no responsibility for the failure of the patentee to timely pay the fee, the USPTO will provide a reminder notice to a patentee who fails to make payment during the fee payment due period. A reminder is sent as a courtesy after the six-month grace period has begun, to aid the patentee in preventing early expiration of the patent. However, the USPTO will not accept any responsibility for the failure to send such maintenance fee reminder notices, and non-receipt of a reminder notice will not relieve the patentee from the responsibility to monitor and timely pay maintenance fees. The maintenance fee reminder notice is sent to the correspondence address on the prosecution record unless a maintenance fee address has been designated.

Maintenance Fee Address

The maintenance fee address of a patent is the same as the prosecution correspondence fee address unless the applicant has filed a fee address indication form electing a different address to be used for maintenance fee notifications. For pending matters, the maintenance fee address of record cannot be viewed until after the issue fee is paid. The maintenance fee address for all issued patents is viewable through the fee address tab in PAIR.

Payment of Maintenance Fees

The fees to maintain a utility patent in force and effect beyond the four years, eight years, and twelve years must be submitted between three-and-a-half years, seven-and-a-half years and eleven-and-a-half years from the original patent grant date, or within a six-month grace period of those dates, subject to the payment of a surcharge. Payments will not be accepted for any of the three maintenance fee payment periods earlier than the initial threshold payment dates (i.e., not earlier than three years for the four-year fee, not earlier than seven years for the eight-year fee, and not earlier than eleven years for the twelve-year fee). The amounts of the maintenance fees due are identified under 37 C.F.R. §1.20(e)-(g). A certificate of mailing and Express Mail procedures under 37 C.F.R. §1.8 and §1.10, respectively, may be used when paying maintenance fee and surcharges. Maintenance or surcharge fees due on a Saturday or Sunday or Federal Holiday in the District of Columbia may be timely paid on the next succeeding business day. Any person or organization may pay a maintenance fee and any surcharge on behalf of the patentee; proof of authorization from the patentee is not required by the USPTO.

On payment of each maintenance fee, the payee should review the entity status of all parties to the matter to ensure that intermittent sale or license of patent rights does not result in loss of entitlement to discounted fees with respect to payment of the next maintenance fee. In addition, if the status of the patent owner changes from a small or micro entity to a large entity or from a large entity to a small or micro entity, a written assertion of the claim to a change in entity status entitlement must accompany the payment of the next maintenance fee.

Effects of Failure to Pay Maintenance Fees

Failure to timely pay maintenance fees will result in expiration of the patent grant. The surcharge for payment of the maintenance fee during the six-month grace period is identified under 37 C.F.R. §1.20(h). The Director may accept payment of the required maintenance fee after the six-month grace period if the patentee submits:

- form SB/65;
- a petition showing that the delay in payment was unavoidable or unintentional;
- a surcharge fee under 37 C.F.R. §1.20(i); and
- the scheduled maintenance fee due.

The surcharge fee due for an unintentional delayed payment is much greater than that for unavoidable delayed payment. Upon granting of the petition and acceptance of the maintenance fee and surcharge, the patent is considered not to have expired at the end of the six-month grace period.

Reinstating a patent after expiration for unavoidable failure to pay a maintenance fee can be done at any time after the six-month grace period. The Petition for Unavoidable Failure to Pay a Maintenance Fee under 37 C.F.R. §1.378(c) must include the following:

- form SB/66;
- payment of the required maintenance fee;
- payment of the surcharge fee under 37 C.F.R. §1.20(i)(1); and
- a showing that the delay was unavoidable because reasonable care had been taken for timely payment and that the petition to reinstate was promptly filed after the patentee became aware of the expiration of the patent.

Reinstatement of a patent after expiration due to unintentional failure to pay a maintenance fee requires filing a petition. The Petition for Unintentional Failure to Pay a Maintenance Fee under 37 C.F.R. §1.378(c) must include the following:

- a petition that must be filed within twenty-four months after the six-month grace period for payment of the maintenance fee;
- payment of the required maintenance fee;
- payment of a substantial surcharge fee under 37 C.F.R. §1.20(i)(2); and
- a statement that the delay in payment of the maintenance fee was unintentional.

Effective December 18, 2013 the Patent Law Treaty eliminated the use of the unavoidable standard in favor of the unintentional standard.

Late Maintenance Fee Payments Under the Patent Law Treaty

For any application filed before, on, or after December 18, 2013, and for any patent issuing from such an application the Patent Law Treaty permits the USPTO to accept late maintenance fee payments at any time under the unintentional standard. The Patent Law Treaty eliminated the unavoidable standard applicable to missed maintenance fee payments giving patentees wider leeway to reinstate expired patents. Applicant must show that the delay in payment of the maintenance fee was unintentional and pay a petition fee and the outstanding maintenance fee required (Johnson et al, 2013).

CHAPTER-SPECIFIC REFERENCE MATERIAL

Reference Source	Allowance, Issuance, and Maintenance Applicable Rules, Regulations, and Procedures
AIA Implementation Frequently Asked Questions	Inventor's Oath or Declaration http://www.uspto.gov/aia_implementation/faq.jsp
Title 35 of the U.S. Code	35 U.S.C. §151 Issue of patent. §152 Issue of patent to assignee.
	§153 How issued. §154 Contents and term of patent; provisional rights.
Title 37 of the Code of Federal Regulations	37 C.F.R. §1.311 Notice of Allowance. §1.312 Amendments after allowance. §1.313 Withdrawal from issue. §1.314 Issuance of patent. §1.315 Delivery of patent. §1.316 Application abandoned for failure to pay issue fee. §1.317 Lapsed patents; delayed payment of balance of issue fee. §1.362 Time for payment of maintenance fees. §1.363 Fee address for maintenance fee purposes. §1.366 Submission of maintenance fees. §1.377 Review of decision refusing to accept and record payment of a maintenance fee filed prior to expiration of patent. §1.378 Acceptance of delayed payment of maintenance fee in expired patent to reinstate patent.
Manual of Patent Examination Procedures (MPEP, 8th Edition)	Chapter 1300 Allowance and Issue Chapter 2500 Maintenance Fees

Chapter 16

Continuing Applications

Definition of Continuing Application

A continuing application is a patent application filed by an applicant who wants to pursue additional claims to an invention disclosed in an earlier application of the applicant (the "parent" application) that has not yet been issued or abandoned. The continuing application uses the same specification as the pending parent application, claims the priority based on the filing date of the parent, and must name at least one of the inventors named in the parent application. This type of application is useful when a patent examiner allowed some, but rejected other, claims in an application or where an applicant may not have exhausted all useful ways of claiming different embodiments of the invention (Patent Lens). There are three distinct types of continuing applications, namely: a continuation, a divisional and a continuation-in-part application.

Differences Between a Continuing Application and a Request for Continued Examination

Support staff should be aware of the subtle differences between continuing applications and a request for continued examination (RCE). A continuing application is a newly filed application that is assigned a new application number and filing date. A RCE is a continued examination of an existing application that is under final rejection. A RCE does not result in a new application number and filing date.

Nature of Continuing Applications

Continuing application are statutorily authorized under 35 U.S.C. §120 and have the effect of giving a later-filed application the effective filing date of an earlier-filed application claimed in priority. A non-provisional application that claims priority to an earlier-filed non-provisional application is called a continuing application. The earlier-filed application is referred to as the "parent" application and the later-filed application as the "child" application. If a third continuing application is filed, the first-filed application is a third-generation application and is referred to as a "grandparent" application. In general, each earlier-filed priority application is called an "ancestral" application within a priority-related application family. There is no limit to the number of continuing applications an applicant may file, as long as each application in the family meets the filing requirement. Each continuing application in the family must constitute a bona fide effort to advance prosecution of the application toward issuance of a patent. Continuing applications can be used to expand or contract the disclosure of a parent application when no new matter is added, without sacrificing the benefit of the filing date of the parent application for claims in the continuing application that are supported by the parent disclosure (Patent Resources Institute, Inc., 2004).

Advantages of Continuing Applications

Assuming all procedural requirements are met, and the applicant is entitled to claim priority benefit to an earlier-filed application, the ability to file a continuing application offers an applicant the following advantages:

- The filing date of the priority application is the effective filing date of the claims in the later-filed application.
- Any novelty events under §102 occurring after the filing date of the earlier-filed application cannot defeat patentability of the claims in the later-filed application, even if such events occurred prior to the filing date of the later application.
- It provides a viable option to pursue an invention disclosed but not claimed in the parent application.
- It allows the applicant to extract rejected claims from an parent application to ensure the indicated allowable claims can proceed to issuance.

Requirements for Continuing Applications

There are four prerequisites for claims in a later-filed application to be entitled to the benefit of the filing date of an earlier-filed application, namely (Patent Resources Institute, Inc., 2004):

- Continuity of Disclosure: The subject matter for the claims in the later-filed application must be disclosed by the written description requirements of 35 U.S.C. §112, first paragraph.
- Continuity of Inventorship: The later-filed application must be filed by an inventor or inventors named in the previously filed application.

- Continuity of Prosecution: The later-filed application must be filed before the patenting or abandonment of or termination of proceedings on the first-filed application.
- Reference to Earlier-Filed Application: The later-filed application must contain a specific reference to the earlier-filed application.

Continuity of Disclosure

The first paragraph of 35 U.S.C §112 imposes three separate specification requirements, specifically: describe the claimed invention, enable one of ordinary skill in the art to make and use the claimed invention, and identify the best mode for carrying out the claimed invention. When the specification, drawings, and claims meet these requirements for each claim, the application supports the claims. For continuing applications filed under 35 U.S.C. §120, the same three requirements are imposed on any continuing application claiming benefit to an earlier-filed parent application. More specifically, for any claim in a continuing application to be entitled to the benefit of the filing date of an earlier-filed application, the earlier-filed application must satisfy the written description, enablement, and best mode requirements for the invention covered by the claim. A continuing application may eliminate certain information disclosed in the parent application, and such elimination will not deprive the continuing application of the benefit of the filing date of the parent, as long as the claims in the continuing application are supported by both the parent disclosure and the modified disclosure in the continuing application.

Continuity of Inventorship

Continuity of inventorship is satisfied when one or more of the inventors named in the continuing application is also named as an inventor in the earlier-filed application. In general, the continuity of inventorship requirement can be met by only a single common inventor. The one exception to this rule is divisional applications. If a restriction requirement is issued by the examiner and the filing of a divisional application results in the inventive entities in the parent and the divisional applications being entirely different, but there is one inventor named in the divisional who was an inventor named in the parent as originally filed, the continuity of inventorship requirements is satisfied.

Continuity of Prosecution

A continuing application must be filed while the earlier-filed application is still pending. Any breaks in the continuity of prosecution will prevent the claims in the later-filed application from being entitled to the filing date of the parent application. A continuing application must be filed before the patenting or abandonment or termination of proceedings on the earlier-filed application. Failure to file the continuing application before any of these events will preclude the claims in the later-filed application from being entitled to the benefit of the filing date of the parent application. An applicant may file a continuing application at any time, including the issue date of the earlier-filed application.

Abandonment of a pending application can occur under several circumstances, including the applicant's failure to respond in a timely manner to an outstanding action. If applicant fails to respond in a timely manner, the application is considered abandoned on the day following the last day of the shortened statutory period for reply. Abandonment can also result from an applicant's withdrawal of or failure to actively prosecute an appeal to the Board. Termination of proceedings may result from other events, such as a decision by the Court of Appeals for the Federal Circuit affirming the rejection of all claims in the application. Such proceedings are considered terminated on the date the USPTO receives the Court's certified copy of the decision. Termination of proceedings can also occur after a decision by the Board when no further appeal is taken by the appellant. An interference or derivation proceeding is terminated when all claims are lost by one party and the time for appeal or review has elapsed.

Reference to Earlier-Filed Application

For continuing applications filed before September 16, 2012, the application must contain or be amended to contain a specific reference to the earlier-filed application. The specific reference to the earlier-filed application may be made in either an application data sheet (ADS) or in the first sentence of the specification. For continuing applications filed on or after September 16, 2012, the priority claim must be made in a signed ADS to be made of record by the USPTO. For applications filed on or after September 16, 2012, it is no longer sufficient to just make reference to the earlier-filed application in the specification to have the priority claim acknowledged and entered by the USPTO. An incorporation by reference statement added after an application's filing date is not effective because no new matter can be added to an application after its filing date.

The request for priority claims must identify the earlier application by its application number and filing date, indicate the status (patented or abandoned), and indicate the specific relationship of the continuing application to the earlier-filed application (continuation, division, or continuation-in-part). If a benefit claim involves a chain of non-provisional applications, the relationship must be stated for each application in the chain relative to the immediate prior application to establish copendency throughout the entire chain. As shown in the following example, precise words must be used to describe the relationship between applications:

Example of Reference to Chain of Related Applications:
This application is a continuation of Application No. ________, filed on ___________, which is a continuation-in-part of Application No. ___________, filed on ______________, which is a divisional application of Application No. ____________, filed on ___________, now Patent No. ________, the entire contents of which is incorporated by reference herein.

If on filing the continuing application, a request for benefit of an earlier-filed application is not included, the applicant has four months from the application filing date or sixteen months from the earliest claimed filing date to request and perfect the priority claim (see Chapter 8 for details on the requirements to claim priority). The time period for making a benefit claim to an earlier-filed application is not extendable. If the applicant fails to submit a proper priority benefit claim within the four- or sixteen-month period, the right to claim the priority benefit will be considered waived. However, if a proper priority claim is presented after the time limit, it may be accepted if the delayed claim is filed with a petition under 37 C.F.R. §1.78(a)(3) to accept it, a surcharge for delayed presentation, and a statement that the entire delay between the date the claim was due and the date it was filed was unintentional.

Types of Continuing Applications

The term continuing application is an umbrella term used to cover three distinct types of continuing applications, namely:

- a divisional (DIV) application under 35 U.S.C. §121;
- a continuation (CON) application under 35 U.S.C. §120; and
- a continuation-in-part (CIP) application under 35 U.S.C. §120.

Each type of continuing application has distinct filing requirements to ensure that the priority claim benefit to an earlier-filed application is secured.

Divisional Applications

A divisional application filed under 35 U.S.C. §121 discloses only information that is disclosed in the parent application; no new matter is permitted. A divisional application claims an invention different from the invention claimed in the parent. A divisional application is most commonly filed following a restriction requirement issued by the examiner in the parent application. In issuing a restriction requirement, the examiner holds that there were two or more independent (unrelated to each other) and distinct (unobvious relative to each other) inventions claimed in the parent application. When responding to a restriction requirement, the applicant must elect claims for current examination and will have the option to pursue non-elected claims in one or more divisional applications. Any such divisional applications must be filed before the parent application is patented or abandoned. An example of the presentation of a divisional application filing decision is shown in Figure P.

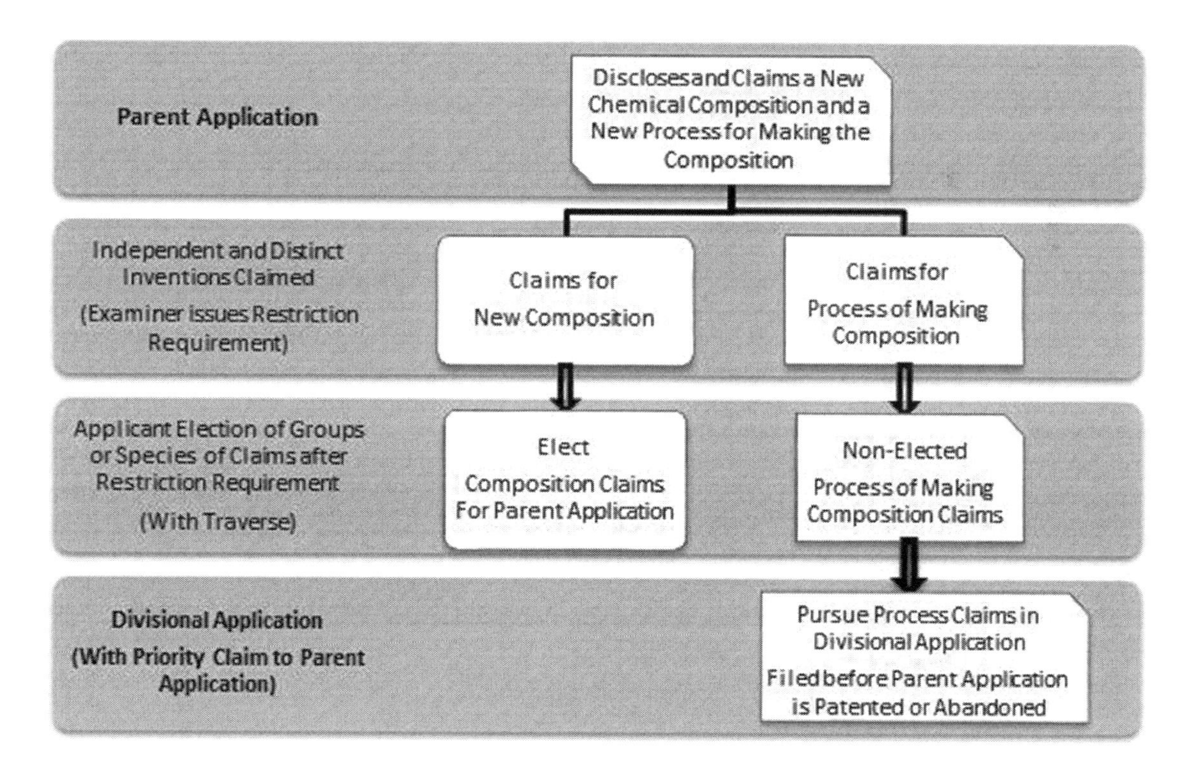

Figure P: Divisional Application Filing Decision

If the procedural requirements for filing a divisional application are satisfied, the effective filing date of the divisional application will be the filing date of the parent application. With referncnce to Figure P, if claims to both the independent and distinct inventions are patentable, two separate patents will issue, one with claims to the new composition and the other with claims to the new process; the claims in both will have the same effective filing date accorded to the parent application. A divisional application can be filed voluntarily by an applicant with claims to an invention disclosed but not claimed in the parent application.

Filing Requirements

Divisional applications filed on or after September 16, 2012, should include the following:

- a specification, including drawings and claims (drawn to non-elected groups restricted out in the parent application); and
- a signed ADS containing a claim to priority under 35 U.S.C. §121 to an earlier-filed U.S. application.

A utility application transmittal form (SB/05) can be filed with the divisional application indicating that the type of continuing application is a divisional. The use of form SB/05 is optional, as the equivalent functionality can be achieved using an ADS. A divisional application can only be filed when a restriction requirement was received in the parent application. The claims of a divisional application are non-elected claims from the parent application that have not been previously examined.

When preparing divisional application filing papers, support staff should review the parent application with respect to the presence of a non-publication request, a sequence listing, information disclosure statements, and any recorded assignment. In particular, if a request for non-publication was filed in the parent application, it should be repeated in the divisional application. Any request for non-publication must accompany the divisional application filing and cannot be submitted at a later date. The request for non-publication can be made in the ADS or in a separate paper conspicuously named as such a request.

A preliminary amendment should be filed with the divisional application to make reference to an earlier-filed application claimed in priority and should also include an incorporation by reference statement to ensure the entire disclosure of the parent application is claimed. In a divisional application, the applicant can pursue non-elected claims from the parent that were restricted out by the examiner. The claim to priority benefit for a divisional application under 35 U.S.C. §121 must be included in a signed ADS if it is to be made of record in the application. Reference to an earlier-filed application in the specification is no longer sufficient to enter the priority claim on the record. An incorporation by reference statement added after the divisional application filing date is not effective because no new matter can be added to an application after its filing date.

The divisional application filing fees may be paid on filing or may be deferred and paid in response to a Notice to File Missing Parts. Any required extensions of time to keep the parent application pending must be filed in the parent application before or concurrently with the divisional application filing.

An oath or declaration executed with respect to each inventor can be filed with the application or can be filed before payment of the issue fee at the latest. A copy of an oath or declaration from the parent application cannot be used in a divisonal application filed on or after September 16, 2012, unless the parent application declaration includes the statements required under the AIA. The controlling date for whether a pre-AIA or AIA declaration should be filed is the filing date of the divisional application not the parent application.

Continuation Applications

A continuation application filed under 35 U.S.C. §120 discloses only information that is also disclosed in the parent application; no new matter is permitted. While the claims in the continuation application may differ in scope from the claims in the parent application, the claims must be directed to the same subject matter. A continuation application is typically filed in one of the two following situations:

- The examiner has finally rejected all of the claims in the parent application, and the applicant does not want to appeal the rejection. The applicant may want to make further claim amendments, make additional arguments, or submit further evidence. The applicant can file a continuation application, allow the parent to go abandoned and submit the further evidence, claim amendments, or arguments for patentability in the continuation application. The effective filing date of the claims in the continuation application will be the filing date of the parent.

- The examiner has allowed some claims—usually the narrower claims—but finally rejects broader claims, and the applicant wants to obtain an issued patent for the allowed claims. The applicant can file a continuation application containing the broad, previously rejected claims, and file additional evidence or arguments for patentability in the continuation application. The applicant can cancel the broader rejected claims in the parent and allow the narrower allowed claims to issue in the parent application. The effective filing date of the claims in the continuation application will be the filing date of the parent application. If the applicant is successful in overcoming the rejections in the continuation application, a separate patent will be issued, and the applicant will have two patents, each with the same effective filing date.

If the applicant elects to file a continuation application in response to an office action having a shortened response period, which is less than six months, a continuation application may be filed after the shortened period has expired and before the statutory six months if a request for extension of time under Rule 1.136 and the requisite fee are filed in the parent application before or concurrently with the filing of the continuing application.

Filing Requirements

Continuation applications filed on or after September 16, 2012, should include the following:

- a specification, including drawings and claims (which include correction of any objections raised during the prosecution of the parent application); and
- a signed ADS containing a claim to priority under 35 U.S.C. §120 to an earlier-filed U.S. application.

A utility application transmittal form (SB/05) can be filed with the continuation application, indicating the type of continuing application to be a continuation. The use of form SB/05 is optional, as the equivalent functionality can be achieved using an ADS. When preparing continuation application filing papers, support staff should review the parent application with respect to the presence of a non-publication request, a sequence listing, information disclosure statements, and any recorded assignment. In particular, if a request for non-publication was filed in the parent application, it should be repeated in the continuation application. Any request for non-publication must accompany the continuation application filing and cannot be submitted at a later date. The request for non-publication can be made in the ADS or in a separate paper conspicuously named as such a request.

A preliminary amendment should be filed with the continuation application to make reference to an earlier-filed application claimed in priority and should also include an incorporation by reference statement to ensure the entire disclosure of the parent application is claimed. An incorporation by reference statement added after the continuation application filing date is not effective because no new matter can be added to an application after its filing date. The claim to priority benefit for a continuation application under 35 U.S.C. §120 must be included in a signed ADS if it is to be made of record in the application.

The continuation application filing fees may be paid on filing or may be deferred and paid in response to a Notice to File Missing Parts. Any required extensions of time to keep the parent application pending until the continuation application is filed must be paid in the parent application prior to or concurrently with the filing of the continuation application. An oath or declaration executed with respect to each inventor can be filed with the application or can be filed before payment of the issue fee at the latest. A copy of an oath or declaration from the parent application cannot be used in a continuation application filed on or after September 16, 2012, unless the parent application declaration includes the statements required under the AIA. The controlling date for whether a pre-AIA or AIA declaration should be filed is the filing date of the continuation application not the parent application.

Continuation-in-Part Applications

A continuation-in-part application filed under 35 U.S.C. §120 discloses both subject matter disclosed in the parent application and subject matter not disclosed in the parent application. Continuation-in-part applications are usually filed when an applicant who has already filed a patent application on an invention wishes to disclose and claim an additional improvement, embodiment, or other variation of the invention. A continuation-in-part application may disclose more subject matter than its parent application and is the only type of continuing application that accommodates new matter. A continuation-in-part application can contain the following claims:

- claims directed to both the commonly disclosed subject matter and the newly added subject matter;
- claims directed only to the newly added subject matter; or
- claims directed only to the commonly disclosed subject matter.

Claims supported by the parent's disclosure are entitled to the effective filing date of the parent application. Claims requiring the supplemental disclosure of the continuation-in-part application are entitled to the filing date of the continuation-in-part application. If the continuation-in-part application only claims newly added subject matter, the effective date of all claims will be the filing date of the continuation-in-part application.

Filing Requirements

Continuation-in-part applications filed on or after September 16, 2012, should include the following:

- a specification, including drawings and claims; and
- a signed ADS containing a claim to priority under 35 U.S.C. §120 to an earlier-filed U.S. application

A utility application transmittal form (SB/05) can be filed with the continuation-in-part application indicating the type of continuing application to be a continuation-in-part. The use of form SB/05 is optional, as the equivalent functionality can be achieved using an ADS. When preparing continuation-in-part application filing papers, support staff should review the parent application with respect to the presence of a non-publication request, a sequence listing, information disclosure statements, and any recorded assignment. In particular, if a request for non-publication was filed in the parent application, it should be repeated in the continuation-in-part application. Any request for non-publication must accompany the continuation-in-part application filing and cannot be submitted at a later date. The request for non-publication can be made in the ADS or in a separate paper conspicuously named as such a request.

A preliminary amendment can be filed with the continuation-in-part application to make reference to an earlier-filed application claimed in priority and should also include an incorporation by reference statement to ensure the entire disclosure of the parent application is claimed. The claim to priority benefit for a continuation-in-part application under 35 U.S.C. §120 must be included in a signed ADS if it is to be made of record in the application.

The continuation-in-part application filing fees may be paid on filing or may be deferred and paid in response to a Notice to File Missing Parts. Any required extensions of time to keep the parent application pending until the continuation-in-part application is filed must be paid in the parent application prior to or concurrently with the filing of the continuation-in-part application.

Given that a continuation-in-part application contains new matter, it necessitates that new formal papers be prepared to cover the new matter added. A copy of the signed inventor oath or declaration from the parent application cannot be filed in a continuation-in-part application as it does not include new matter added to the continuation-in-part application claims.

Incorporation by Reference in Continuing Applications

An applicant may file a copy of the parent or prior application, including copies of the specification and drawings as originally filed (not as later amended), when filing any type of continuing (continuation or divisional) application. To address the potential adverse consequences of an omitted page in the specification or drawings of the parent application, the applicant should include an incorporation by reference statement in the continuing application. The disclosure of priority application can only be effectively incorporated by reference at the time of filing the continuing application. An incorporation by reference statement added by way of an amendment after the filing of the continuing application is ineffective. As no new matter can be added to the application after its filing date, any inadvertently omitted pages added after the initial filing would constitute new matter and be subject to rejection by the examiner. Alternatively, a continuing application can be filed with a new specification and/or drawings rather than a true copy of the parent application, as long as any differences from the parent application do not constitute new matter.

AIA Impact—Accounting for Inventive Entities

Under the AIA, an oath or declaration, substitute statement, or combined assignment-declaration, executed with respect to each inventor, can be filed with a divisional or continuation application or may be filed at a later date, but it must be filed before payment of the issue fee. A copy of an oath or declaration from the parent application cannot be used in divisional or continuation applications filed on or after September 16, 2012, unless the parent application declaration includes the statements required under the AIA.

As a continuation-in-part application claims new matter, new formal papers must be prepared and signed with respect to each inventor. An oath or declaration, substitute statement, or combined assignment-declaration, with respect to each inventor, can be filed with the continuation-in-part application or can be filed later, but it must be filed no later than payment of the issue fee.

If an applicant files a continuation-in-part application on or after September 16, 2012, naming inventors X and Y, and the parent application named only inventor X, the applicant can use a copy of the declaration filed in the parent and a signed ADS in the continuation-in-part application (either before or with the copy of the parent declaration) naming the inventive entity (X and Y). An oath or declaration signed by the additional inventor Y in the continuation-in-part application would also be required. However, as long as a signed ADS was filed naming the inventive entity (X and Y) in the continuation-in-part application, the oath or declaration executed by the additional inventor Y in the continuation-in-part application would not need to identify inventor X.

Request for Non-Publication

Support staff should review the parent application as filed to confirm if a request for non-publication was filed. If a request for non-publication was filed in the parent it is most likely that one should also be filed in the continuing application claiming priority to the parent application. Any request for non-publication must be made on filing and can be made in an ADS or in a separate form SB/35 filed with the application.

Inventorship in Continuing Applications

The continuity of inventorship requirement for filing a continuing application can be met even if there is only one inventor in common between the parent application and the continuing application.

For divisional and continuation applications filed before September 16, 2012, a newly executed inventor oath or declaration is not required if:

- the parent contained a proper oath or declaration;

- the divisional or continuation is filed by all or fewer than all of the inventors named in the parent;
- there is no new matter in the divisional or continuation; and
- a copy of the signed oath executed in the parent is submitted.

Where the divisional or continuation application is filed by fewer than all of the inventors named in the parent, a statement requesting deletion of the name of each inventor named in the parent application who is not an inventor of any subject matter in the divisional or continuation application must also be filed.

For divisional or continuation applications filed on or after September 16, 2012, the AIA-related forms that account for inventor and non-inventor entities must be used. A copy of a signed oath or declaration from a parent application filed before September 16, 2012, cannot be filed in a divisional or continuation application filed on or after September 16, 2012.

Continuing Applications—Similarities and Differences

An at-a-glance summary of similarities and differences between divisional, continuation, and continuation-in-part applications is shown in Figure Q. In executive summary, divisional applications can only be filed when a restriction requirement was issued by the examiner in the parent application. In a divisional application, the applicant can pursue non-elected claims from the parent application. A continuation application is most often an applicant-initiated filing decision that is one of the options after a final rejection, which would allow any indicated allowable claims to proceed to issue. In a continuation application, the applicant can continue to try to overcome the examiner's final rejection of broader claims from the parent application. All of the continuing application types have the copendency, common inventor, continuity of disclosure, and priority claim requirements. A continuation-in-part application is the only continuing application that can accommodate new matter related to a new improvement or additional embodiment.

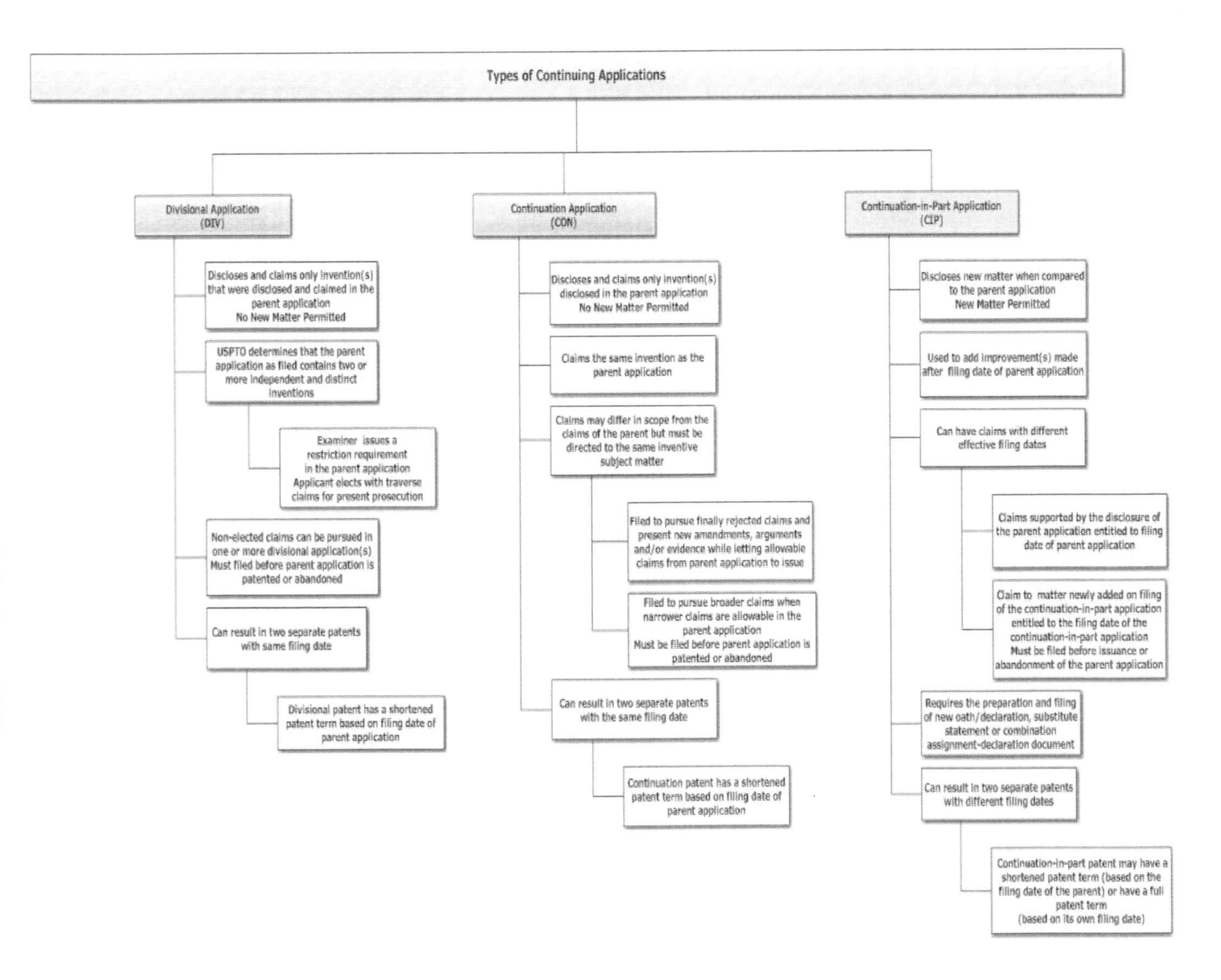

Figure Q: Continuing Applications—Similarities and Differences

Continuity Data in PAIR

Continuity data is information about continuation applications that may have been filed based on a parent application. The continuity data tab in PAIR contains information related to any child continuing application including an indication as to whether the child application is a continuation, divisional or continuation-in-part application of the parent. The application numbers and filing dates of the child continuing application will also be indicated. Support staff should be able to locate and understand continuity data to enable them to validate priority chain data or to be able to derive the order and sequence of applications in a family of continuing applications.

CHAPTER-SPECIFIC REFERENCE MATERIAL

Reference Source	Continuing Applications
Manual of Patent Examination Procedures (MPEP, 8th Edition)	Chapter 200 Types of Applications Chapter 800 Restriction Requirement and Double Patenting

Chapter 17
Patent Term—Duration, Adjustment, and Extension

Patent Term

The term of a patent dictates how long the patentee maintains rights to the invention. When the patent term expires, any member of the public has the right to make and use the invention. For utility applications filed before June 8, 1995, the term of the resulting patent is seventeen years from the date of issue or twenty years from the filing date, whichever is longer. For utility applications filed on or after June 8, 1995, the term of the resulting patent is twenty years from the filing date. If the application contains a specific reference to an earlier-filed application under 35 U.S.C. §120 (continuation or continuation-in-part application), §121 (divisional application), or §365(c) (international application designation in the United States under §371), then the term is calculated from the earliest claimed filing date. When the patent term is twenty years from the application filing date, the first several years of that term are spent prosecuting the application. The exact duration of patent terms depends on the type of patent issued, as shown in Table 29.

Table 29: Patent Term Duration

Type of Patent	Date Impact	Duration of Term
Utility Patent	Issued before June 8, 1995 No priority claim or priority claim to a U.S. provisional application	The longer of: ▪ Seventeen years from the issue date or ▪ Twenty years from the filing date
	Issued before June 8, 1995 Priority claim under §120, §121, or §365(c) to an earlier-filed application	The longer of: ▪ Seventeen years from the issue date or ▪ Twenty years from the earliest claimed filing date

	Application filed on or before June 8, 1995 Priority claim under §120, §121, or §365(c) to an earlier-filed application	The longer of: ▪ Seventeen years from the issue date or ▪ Twenty years the earliest filing date
	Application filed on or after June 8, 1995 Priority claim under §120, §121, or §365(c) to an earlier-filed application	Twenty years from the earliest filing date
Plant Patent	All dates	Twenty years from the filing date
Design Patent	All dates	Fourteen years from the issue date

Exceptions to the Patent Term Regulations

A patent granted on a continuation, divisional, or continuation-in-part application that was filed on or after June 8, 1995, will have a term that ends twenty years from the filing date of the earlier-filed application for which benefit is claimed, regardless of whether the application for which benefit is claimed was filed prior to June 8, 1995.

A patent granted on an international application filed on or after June 8, 1995, that enters the national stage under 35 U.S.C. §371 will have a term that ends twenty years from the filing date of the international application. A continuation or continuation-in-part application claiming benefit to an international application filed under 35 U.S.C. §363(c) or an international application filed under 35 U.S.C. §363 designating the United States will have a term that ends twenty years from the filing date of the parent international application.

Foreign priority under 35 U.S.C. §119(a)-(d), §365(a), or §365(b) is not considered in determining the term of a patent. An application claiming such priorities has a term that ends twenty years from the filing date of the application in the United States and not the prior international or foreign application. Domestic priority under 35 U.S.C. §119(e) to one or more provisional applications is not considered in the calculation of patent term.

The expiration date of a patent subject to a terminal disclaimer can be determined by referring to the language of the terminal disclaimer filed. If the terminal disclaimer disclaims the terminal portion of the term of the patent that would extend beyond the expiration date of an earlier issued patent, then the expiration date of the later-filed patent (in which the terminal disclaimer was filed), is the expiration date of the parent patent. If the terminal disclaimer filed disclaims the terminal portion of the patent subsequent to a specific date without reference to the full statutory term of the referenced patent, then the expiration date is the date specified. In such situations, the USPTO will consider any discrepancies in the patent term as the applicant dedicating the term to the public.

Determinants of Patent Term

The terms of certain patents may be subject to extension or adjustment. Such extensions or adjustments result from certain specified types of delays that may occur while an application is pending before the Office. The following equation represents the determinants of patent term:

Patent Term = 20 Years From Filing Date (Patent Term Guarantee under AIPA)
+ (USPTO Delay – Applicant Delay) (Patent Term Adjustment under U.S.C. §154(b))
+ Regulatory Delay (Patent Term Extension under under 35 U.S.C. §156 which includes PTE for interferences, secrecy orders, and administrative appeals)

Patent Term Guarantee

The 1999 American Inventors Protection Act (AIPA) contained a patent term guarantee provision that provides patent term adjustments for the net effects of USPTO-based and applicant-based prosecution delays. Prior to the AIPA, the term of a utility or plant patent ended seventeen years from the date of patent grant. To comply with the Uruguay Round Agreements of the General Agreement on Tariffs and Trade (GATT), the United States was required to establish a minimum term for patent protection ending no earlier than twenty years from the date the application was filed.

As a result of GATT, the USPTO amended 35 U.S.C. §154 on June of 1995 to change the term of utility and plant patents from ending seventeen years from the date of patent grant to ending twenty years from the filing date of the application (or twenty years from the earliest filing date claimed under 35 U.S.C. §120, §121, or §369(c)). Under the AIPA, 35 U.S.C. §154 was further amended to provide for patent term extension in the event that issuance of the application as a patent was delayed due to secrecy order, interference, or successful appellate review. Any applicable patent term extension was subject to a five-year cap under 35 U.S.C. §154(b). The AIPA amended 35 U.S.C. §154(b) to expand the list of administrative delays that may give rise to patent term adjustment. The patent term guarantee provisions of the AIPA established three main bases for adjusting the term of a utility or plant patent (USPTO, Patent Term Guarantee, 2009):

- if the USPTO fails to take certain actions within specified time frames;
- if the USPTO fails to issue a patent within three years of the actual filing date of the application; or
- for delays due to interference, secrecy order, or successful appellate review.

Original utility and plant patents issuing from applications filed on or after May 29, 2000, are eligible for patent term adjustment if issuance of the patent is delayed due to one or more of the identified administrative delays.

Patent Term Adjustment

The patent term adjustment (PTA) provisions of the AIPA apply to original (non-reissue) utility and plant applications filed on or after May 29, 2000, which include continuing applications. A request for continued examination (RCE) under 35 U.S.C. §132(b) and 37 C.F.R. §1.114 is not a new application, and filing a RCE in an application filed before May 29, 2000, will not cause the application to be eligible for the patent term adjustment provisions. The PTA provisions of the AIPA provided the following three categories of patent term guarantee:

- "A" guarantee assures that the USPTO will promptly respond to applicant submissions, including an initial office action within fourteen months of the application filing date and subsequent office actions within four months of the applicant's last response. For every day of USPTO delay beyond these deadlines, the patentee receives one day of term adjustment. See 35 U.S.C. §157(b)(1)(A), 37 C.F.R. §1.702(a), and 1.703(a).
- "B" guarantee is a no-fault backstop assurance of at least a seventeen-year term from issuance (the pre-GATT term). If an application has not issued as a patent after three years, then the patentee receives a day of term adjustment for every day of PTO delay after the three years. See 35 U.S.C. §157(b)(1)(B), 37 C.F.R. §1.702(b), and 1.703(b).

- "C" guarantee delays deal with extraordinary situations, such as interferences, secrecy orders, and administrative appeals. See 35 U.S.C. §157(b)(1)(C), 37 C.F.R. §1.702(c)-(e), and 1.703(c)-(e).

However, the AIPA limited PTA in two ways. First, if the applicant fails to act diligently in prosecuting the application, then the applicant's delay is subtracted from any term adjustment. Second, where periods of "A" (Fourteen or four months to respond to applicant's filing), "B" (issue a patent within three years of the application filing date), or "C" (interference, secrecy orders, and administrative appeals) delay overlap, the net PTA is limited to the actual number of days the issuance of the patent was delayed to prevent double counting. According to the USPTO, a patentee was due only the greater of any "A" or "B" adjustment, but not both. The USPTO reasoned that the "A" delay necessarily contributed to the "B" delay, and the USPTO held that the Office calculation systems prevented constructive double-counting of PTA.

The patent term extension provisions under U.S.C. §154 for "C" delays due to secrecy order, interference, or successful appellate review continue to apply to utility and plant applications filed on or after June 7, 1995, and before May 29, 2000.

Patent Term Extension

All patents, whether their terms are seventeen years from the issue date or twenty years from the filing date, can have their terms extended under 35 U.S.C. §156 if their effective terms have been truncated because of delays due to regulatory review by the Food and Drug Administration (FDA) or the U.S. Department of Agriculture (USDA). This form of extension was enacted on September 24, 1984, relative to FDA review and on November 19, 1988, relative to USDA review. All patents that issue on applications filed after June 7, 1995, are entitled to have their terms extended under 35 U.S.C. §154(b) for reasons specified either under amendment to the section under the URAA agreement or amendments imposed by the AIPA, effective May 29, 2000. The patent term extension (PTE) under §154 (whether derived from the URAA or AIPA amendments) and extensions under §156 (FDA or USDA) are not mutually exclusive. One can be added to the other but only under very limiting constraints.

Regulatory Agency Delay

Patented human drug products (including those that are biotechnology-generated), medical devices, food additives, and color additives are subject to regulatory review for their safety and efficacy prior to commercial sale or use and are subject to patent term extension caused by regulatory agency review delay. Patent term extension under 35 U.S.C. §156 extends the term of a patent up to a maximum of five years to offset time lost in the patent's term due to FDA review. To obtain an extension of patent term, the patentee must submit an application for patent term extension due to regulatory agent delay to the Director and include the following:

- a verification that the patented invention is for the type of human drug or medical device or recombinant DNA process for making a product, or method of using such a product, subject to FDA regulatory review or that the patented invention is for the type of animal product subject to USDA regulatory review;
- an indication that the term of the patent has not yet expired;
- a verification that the product or device has been subject to regulatory review before its commercial marketing or use; and
- a verification that the commercial marketing, use, or production of the product or device after the regulatory review was the first such commercial activity permitted by law.

If the regulatory review has not yet been completed and the patent is about to expire, the Director can grant an interim one-year extension of the patent, renewable four more times under 35 U.S.C. §156(d)(5)(c). Extension of term is not possible when the patent expires, and preemptive action must be taken by the patentee to keep the patent alive.

Patent term extension under 35 U.S.C. §156 imposes a limit that the patent term remaining after extension cannot be more than fourteen total years irrespective of how much patent term was sacrificed due to regulatory review delay. Patent term guarantee extensions under 35 U.S.C. §154(b) are in addition to the extension permitted under 35 U.S.C. §156 for regulatory agency delays (which are diminished to a limit of fourteen years from the date of commercial marketing approval by the regulatory agency). Thus, irrespective of how long an extension may be available due to patent term guarantee, if it is tacked onto a regulatory delay extension, the combined extension cannot exceed the fourteen years from marketing approval limit.

Components of Patent Term Adjustment

Any net patent term adjustment accrued is derived from the USPTO-based delays less applicant-based delay under 35 U.S.C. §154(b)(2)(C). The USPTO-based delay is derived with respect to four distinct time frames that the Office must adhere to during the prosecution phase. Applicant-based delay is derived with respect to the shortened statutory period set for response to any outstanding notices or office actions. More specifically, when an applicant requests an extension of time to respond to an outstanding notice or office action, the USPTO deems this to not be a reasonable effort to conclude prosecution. The determinants of USPTO-delay and applicant-delay are discussed in more detail in the following sections.

USPTO Delays

The first main basis for patent term adjustment establishes four "time clocks" for certain actions by the USPTO. If the USPTO fails to meet any of the enumerated time clocks, the term of the patent is adjusted one day for each day by which the USPTO misses the time frame. The four time clocks are as follows:

- The USPTO must issue an initial action in an application within fourteen months of its filing date or the date on which a U.S. national phase application fulfilled the requirements of 35 U.S.C. §371. An initial action can be a restriction requirement, a first office action on the merits, or a notice of allowance, but it does not include preexamination formality notifications.
- The USPTO must respond to an office action reply or to an appeal taken within four months of the date on which the reply was filed or the appeal brief was filed.
- The USPTO must act on an application within four months of the date of a decision by the Board or a decision by a Federal Court in an application where allowable claims remain. Allowable claims are considered to remain in an application when there are claims indicated as allowable or there are claims with no outstanding objection or rejection. A dependent claim that has been indicated prior to an appeal as objected to, but allowable if rewritten into independent form, is not considered an allowable claim.
- The USPTO must issue a patent within four months after the date on which the issue fee was paid and all outstanding formal requirements are met. If the notice of allowability requires completion of formality matters (submission of formal drawings or signed inventor oath or declaration), this time clock does not begin until the

date the issue fee is paid or the date the formality filings are completed, whichever date is later.

The second main basis for PTA requires that the USPTO issue a patent within three years of the actual filing date of the application. The actual filing date of an international application is the date of commencement of the national stage under 35 U.S.C. §371(b) or (f). In addition, the three-year period begins with the actual filing date of the application, not any earlier-filed application for which priority benefit is claimed under 35 U.S.C. §120, §121, or §365(c). Thus, if an application is filed on May 29, 2000, and a continuation of that application is filed on June 5, 2002, the three-year period is measured from June 5, 2002, not May 29, 2000. Certain periods of time during processing or examination of an application do not count against this three-year period. For example, any time consumed by continued examination, imposition of a secrecy order, declaration of an interference, appellate review, or applicant-requested delays does not count against the three-year period. Although filing a request for continued examination (RCE) cuts off any additional patent term adjustment due to failure of the USPTO to issue a patent within three years, an applicant may continue to accrue patent term adjustment for events after the filing of the RCE. The following fact-impact pattern is provided as an illustrative example of the impact of filing a RCE on patent term.

Fact Pattern

If an applicant files an application on June 1, 2000, the USPTO must issue a patent within three years of the filing date (before June 1, 2003). However, if applicant files a RCE on August 1, 2003, the USPTO must respond to the filing of the RCE within four months (before December 1, 2003). The USPTO responds to the filing of the RCE, and issues the next office action on January 1, 2004 (five months after the filing of the RCE). The patent issues on August 1, 2004 (two months later than the three years from the application filing date).

Under the above fact pattern, the applicant would be entitled to a PTA of three months: two months from the USPTO's failure to issue a patent within three years of the application filing date ("B" delay), plus one month from the USPTO's failure to respond within four months of the applicant's filing of a RCE ("A" delay).

The third main basis for PTA accounts for term adjustment due to delays caused by an interference proceeding, imposition of a secrecy order, or a successful appellate review. Unlike the provisions applying to applications filed before May 29, 2000, however, there is no five-year cap, no preclusion from patent term adjustment for a successful appellate review if the patent is subject to an obviousness-type double-patenting terminal disclaimer, or provision for a minimum pendency of three years before patent term adjustment may accrue for a successful appellate review (USPTO, Patent Term Guarntee, 2009).

Applicant Delay

The period of adjustment of the term of a patent will be reduced by a period equal to the period of time during which the applicant failed to engage in reasonable efforts to conclude prosecution of the application. An applicant is deemed to have failed to engage in reasonable efforts to conclude prosecution of an application for the cumulative total of any periods of time in excess of the shortened statutory period of three months that was taken to reply to any notice or action. The three-month shortened statutory period is calculated from the mailing date of the notice or action. The amount of PTA will be reduced by the number of days, if any, beginning on the day the shortened statutory period for response ended and ending on the date the reply was filed. If the notice or action issued by the Office identified a response period that is less than a three-month shortened statutory period, it will have no bearing on the calculation of the three-month period with respect to PTA (Bellis, 2012).

A non-exclusive list of activities that constitute failure by the applicant to engage in reasonable efforts to conclude prosecution includes the following:

- Suspension of action: The period of adjustment will be reduced by the number of days, if any, beginning on the date a request for suspension of action was filed and ending on the date of the termination of the suspension.
- Deferral of issuance: The period of adjustment will be reduced by the number of days, if any, beginning on the date a request for deferral of issuance of a patent was filed and ending on the date the patent was issued.
- Abandonment of the application or late payment of the issue fee: The period of adjustment will be reduced by the number of days, if any, beginning on the date of abandonment or the date after the date the issue fee was due and ending on the earlier of:

    - the date of mailing of the decision reviving the application or accepting late payment of the issue fee; or
    - the date that is four months after the date the grantable petition to revive the application or accept late payment of the issue fee was filed.
- Failure to file a Petition to Withdraw the Holding of Abandonment: For the applicant's failure to revive an application within two months from the mailing date of a notice of abandonment, the period of adjustment will be reduced by the number of days, if any, beginning on the day after the date two months from the mailing date of a notice of abandonment and ending on the date a petition to withdraw the holding of abandonment or to revive the application was filed.
- Conversion of a provisional application to a non-provisional application: The period of adjustment will be reduced by the number of days, if any, beginning on the date the application was filed and ending on the date a request to convert the provisional application into a non-provisional application was filed.
- Submission of a preliminary amendment less than one month before the mailing of an office action or notice of allowance: The period of adjustment will be reduced by the lesser of:
    - the number of days, if any, beginning on the day after the mailing date of the original office action or notice of allowance and ending on the date of mailing of the supplemental office action or notice of allowance; or
    - four months.
- Submission of a reply having an omission: The period of adjustment will be reduced by the number of days, if any, beginning on the day after the date the reply having an omission was filed and ending on the date that the reply or other paper correcting the omission was filed.
- Submission of a supplemental reply: The period of adjustment will be reduced by the number of days, if any, beginning on the day after the date the initial reply was filed and ending on the date that the supplemental reply or other such paper was filed.
- Submission of an amendment after a decision by the Board or a Federal Court: The period of adjustment will be reduced by the lesser of:
    - the number of days, if any, beginning on the day after the mailing date of the original office action or notice of allowance and ending on the mailing date of the supplemental office action or notice of allowance; or

    - four months.
- Submission of an amendment after allowance: The period of adjustment will be reduced by the lesser of:
    - the number of days, if any, beginning on the date the amendment after allowance and ending on the mailing date of the office action or notice in response to the amendment after allowance; or
    - four months.
- Further prosecution via a continuing application: The period of adjustment will not include any period that is prior to the actual filing date of the application that resulted in the patent.

A paper containing only an information disclosure statement (IDS) will not be considered a failure to engage in reasonable efforts to conclude prosecution if it is accompanied by a statement that each item of information (references and office actions issued in related copending international, foreign, or domestic applications of record) contained in the IDS was first cited in a communication from a foreign patent office in a counterpart application and that this communication was not received by any individual with a duty to disclose more than thirty days prior to the filing of the information disclosure statement. This thirty-day period is not extendable. Submission of an application for patent term adjustment (with or without request for reinstatement of reduced patent term adjustment) will not be considered a failure to engage in reasonable efforts to conclude prosecution of the application.

Due Care Showing

The USPTO will consider some justifications for the applicant's failure to meet the three-month response period. If the applicant can make a showing that the failure in responding within the three-month shortened statutory period was "in spite of all due care," the USPTO will reinstate the patent term adjustment, but for no more than a period of three months. Some examples of showings that may establish the applicant was unable to respond within the three-month shortened statutory period in spite of all due care include the following:

- a showing that the three-month period was insufficient to obtain the test data necessary for an affidavit or declaration under 37 C.F.R. §1.132;

- a showing that the applicant was unable to respond within the three-month period due to a natural disaster;
- a showing that the applicant was unable to respond within the three-month period because testing was required to reply to the office action and the testing took longer than three months; or
- a showing that the applicant was unable to reply within the three-month period due to illness or death of a sole practitioner of record who was responsible for prosecuting the application.

Challenges to USPTO PTA Calculation System

There have been several court challenges to the system that the USPTO uses for calculating PTA. The resulting court decisions and impact on applicants is discussed in more detail in the following sections.

Wyeth Challenge—Overlapping Time Periods

Wyeth challenged the USPTO's PTA calculation system, more specifically the Office's interpretation of overlapping "A" and "B" delays. Wyeth argued that the statute clearly limited overlap to any "A" and "B" delays falling on the same calendar day, i.e., that "overlap" could only occur when the "A" delays occurred more than three years after the initial filing date. Wyeth held that the USPTO had been under calculating the amount of PTA due under the provisions of the AIPA. Under Wyeth's interpretation, patentees should often receive adjustments under both the "A" and "B" guarantees. On appeal to the Federal Circuit, the court ruled in Wyeth's favor, holding that the language of the statute was unambiguous and that both the "A" and "B" delays must be counted unless they fall on the same calendar day.

Impact of Wyeth Challenge

On January 21, 2010, the USPTO released guidelines for expediting requests for recalculation of PTA in light of Wyeth for patents issued before March 2, 2010. As a result of the Wyeth ruling, applicants who were still engaged in substantive prosecution and who aligned with the Wyeth fact pattern were entitled to the benefit of the decision without further action. Applicants whose applications were allowed or issued before March 2, 2010, had to follow certain procedures and meet specific time limits to preserve rights to additional PTA under Wyeth. The USPTO explicitly reminded applicants and patentees that they must seek review of PTA determinations according to the statutory and regulatory scheme (Ashbrook et al., 2010).

Exelixis Challenge—RCE Filing

In November 2012, Exelixis challenged how the USPTO calculates B-type delays when a Request for Continued Examination (RCE) is filed after the three-year critical deadline. Exelixis challenged that if a RCE is filed after the three-year critical date, the USPTO calculates the B-type delay from the critical date through the filing date of the RCE, thereby eliminating any PTA that would have accumulated between the filing date of the RCE and the issuance of the patent. Exelixis contested that B-type delays should not be tolled by a RCE filed beyond the three-year critical date. Exelixis argued that the filing of a RCE has no effect on PTA if it was filed after the three-year deadline.

The Eastern District Court of Virginia ruled that any event past the three-year critical date had no impact on the PTA. Consequently, if a RCE is filed beyond the statutory three-year period, it cannot toll the B-type delay for PTA calculations. The Court found the language of §154 was clear and unambiguous and that the tolling of a B-type delay modified the determination of the three-year statutory period, not the PTA remedy. The Court explicitly ruled that filing a RCE only tolls the B-type delay PTA calculation when it is filed before the three-year critical deadline (Kilpatrick Townsend & Stockton LLP, 2012).

Impact of Exelixis Challenge

If the District Court ruling stands, the patent term may be extended for a significant number of applicants who have filed a RCE after the three-year critical deadline and had B-type PTA tolled. If applicants wish to avail of the Exelixis court ruling, they would need to review the Office's PTA determination to ensure they received the maximum patent term if a RCE was filed after the three-year deadline. From a practice perspective, applicants should avoid filing a RCE before the three-year deadline to ensure they maximize patent term. Remedies for improper calculation of PTA are available under 37 C.F.R. §1.705 and 35 U.S.C. §154(b)(4)(a). If the patent has issued in the past two months, the applicant can request reconsideration of PTA under 37 C.F.R. §1.705(d). If the patent has issued in the last 180 days, the applicant must file a civil action in the Eastern District of Virginia to request reconsideration of PTA under 35 U.S.C. §154(b)(4)(a) (Kilpatrick Townsend & Stockton LLP, 2012).

Novartis Challenge—Time Between Allowance and Issuance

In a ruling in Novartis AG v. Lee case the Federal Circuit resolved the issues raised in the Exelixis decisions regarding the effect of a RCE filing on PTA. The Federal Circuit's ruling states that although a RCE filed more than three years after an application's filing date will continue to have an impact on PTA, the time period after allowance until issuance should not necessarily be precluded from any B-type delay calculation. Prior to this decision, the USPTO interpreted the statute to read that the filing of any RCE would preclude any additional B-type delay. Thus, once a RCE was filed, an application would no longer be eligible for any B-type adjustment. Thus, once a RCE was filed, an application would no longer be eligible for any B-type adjustment.

At issue in the Novartis case was whether or not PTA should be reduced by the time attributable to a RCE when the RCE is filed after expiration of the three-year date from filing. The Court partially upheld and partially reversed the USPTO's interpretation of the statute. The Court agreed with the USPTO that no adjustment of time is available for any time consumed by continued examination, even if the continued examination was initiated more than three years after the application's filing date. Thus, even if the first RCE for an application is filed more than three years after the application's filing date, no PTA is available under B-type delay during the time consumed by continued examination (Armstrong Teasdale LLP, 2014).

Impact of Novartis Challenge

The Court, however, rejected the USPTO's argument that the time between allowance and issuance is considered "time consumed by continued examination" and therefore would be excluded from PTA. The Court ruled that "examination" presumptively ends at allowance because prosecution is closed and there is normally no further examination on the merits. Thus, the Court ruled that unless examination on the merits resumes, the time period from the notice of allowance until the application issues is eligible for consideration under B-term delay.

Accordingly, the effect of the Court's decision on a RCE is that instead of a RCE terminating the B-delay "clock," a RCE merely tolls the B-delay clock from the time a RCE was filed until the application is allowed (Armstrong Teasdale LLP, 2014).

Notation of Patent Term Adjustment

The USPTO does not print the expiration date on issued patents because the actual date a patent will expire is dependent upon a number of future events. The actual date any particular patent will expire is dependent upon the following variants:

- if all maintenance fees are timely paid;
- if the patent is disclaimed, either by a statutory disclaimer of all claims or a terminal disclaimer;
- if all of the claims of the patent are canceled during a reexamination proceeding; or
- if term extension under 35 U.S.C. §156 is granted.

Since less than 40 percent of patentees pay all three maintenance fees, an expiration date based upon a calculation of twenty years from the earliest filing date under 35 U.S.C. §111(a), §120, §121, §363, or §365(c) plus any calculated extension under 35 U.S.C. §154(b) would be incorrect and misleading more than 60 percent of the time. However, the front page of the patent will indicate the number of days of PTA to which the patent is entitled.

Applicants can view the calculated PTA of a patent under a dedicated tab in PAIR. The USPTO uses a computer program to determine the amount of adjustment to the term of patent under 35 U.S.C. §154(b) and 37 C.F.R. §1.702-1.705. For patents that have issued before January 14, 2013, the computer program will perform the PTA calculations twice. The first calculation will be performed when the Office enters or mails the notice of allowance, and the second calculation will be performed when the Office enters or mails the issue notification. The PAIR screen displays a series of entries related to the specific application that is being evaluated to ascertain whether the application will receive an adjustment to the term of the patent.

Request for Reconsideration of Patent Term Adjustment

After receiving the initial determination of the PTA on the notice of allowance, applicants have one opportunity to request reconsideration of the determination. Any request for reconsideration of PTA must be filed with or before payment of the issue fee and cannot be filed before the mailing date of the notice of allowance. An application for patent term adjustment must be accompanied by:

- the fee under §1.18(e);
- a statement of the facts specifically identifying:

- the correct patent term adjustment and the basis or bases under §1.702 for the adjustment;
- the relevant dates as specified in §1.703(a)-(e) for which an adjustment is sought, and the adjustment as specified in §1.703(f) to which the patent is entitled;
- whether the patent is subject to a terminal disclaimer, and any expiration date specified in the terminal disclaimer; and
- any circumstances during the prosecution of the application that constitutes a failure to engage in reasonable efforts to conclude prosecution, or state that there are no circumstances that constitute failure to engage in reasonable efforts to conclude prosecution.

In addition to the above requirements, any request for reconsideration of PTA that requests reinstatement of all or part of the period of adjustment reduced under §1.704(b) for the applicant's failure to reply to a rejection, objection, argument, or other request within the three-month, shortened statutory period must also be accompanied by:

- the fee under §1.18(f); and
- a showing to the satisfaction of the Director that, in spite of all due care, the applicant was unable to reply to the rejection, objection, argument, or other request within three month shortened statutory period. However, the Office will not grant any request for reinstatement for more than three additional months for each reply beyond the three-month shortened statutory period for reply.

If there is a revision to the patent term adjustment indicated in the notice of allowance, the patent will indicate the revised patent term adjustment. If the patent indicates or should have indicated a revised patent term adjustment, any request for reconsideration of the patent term adjustment must be filed within two months of the date the patent issued.

About two weeks before the patent is issued, a final PTA calculation will be made and printed on the issue notification. This final calculation will be made when the issue date of the patent is known (i.e., whether the patent is issued within four months of issue fee payment or within three years of the actual filing date of the application). The patent will also include the USPTO's final adjustment determination, and applicants will have thirty days after the date of patent grant to request reconsideration. The applicant should compare the PTA indicated in the issue notification with that indicated on the notice of allowance. This short time period is necessary to permit any applicant dissatisfied with the PTA determination to file a civil action in the United States District Court for the District of Columbia within 180 days after the grant of the patent. If requests for reconsideration were not required to be filed promptly after patent grant, the USPTO would not have time to evaluate the request, send the applicant a decision, and allow the applicant a suitable amount of time to seek judicial review. Third parties may not challenge or appeal the patent term adjustment determination before the USPTO (USPTO, Patent Term Guarntee, 2009).

AIA Impact—Calculation of Sixty-Day Period

Effective September 16, 2013, section 37 of the AIA required that calculation of the sixty-day period for PTE begin on the date of marketing approval, which should be the next business day if the time of transmission of the approval is after 4:30 p.m. EST. The rule change applies to any application for term extension pending on, filed after, or as to which a decision regarding the application is subject to judicial review on the date of enactment.

AIA Technical Corrections Bill—Patent Term Adjustment Rules

The AIA patent term adjustment rules clarify when the USPTO must issue its calculations of patent term adjustment, the time added to the life of a patent to compensate for delays in examination, and how applicants can challenge those determinations. The AIA patent term adjustment rules apply to any patent issued on or after January 14, 2013. The changes to the patent term adjustment rules eliminate inefficiencies that existed under the previous system, including a provision that in some cases required applicants to sue the USPTO in Federal Court to challenge a patent term adjustment before the Office had finalized its ruling.

Under the previous patent term adjustment rules, the USPTO would determine the amount of patent term adjustment an applicant was entitled to when it issued a notice of allowance for a patent. If the applicant wanted to challenge the calculation, the applicant had to pay the issue fee and wait until the patent issued before requesting reconsideration.

Under the AIA patent term adjustment rules, the USPTO will tell the applicant the amount of patent term adjustment they are entitled to only when the patent issues. The AIA rules also give applicants more time to request reconsideration of the patent term adjustment. While the two-month (from the date the patent was granted) time limit to request reconsideration has been retained, applicants will be able to extend that period for an additional five months upon request. Any applicant who is still dissatisfied with the USPTO reconsideration decision has 180 days from the decision date to file a civil action in the District Court.

Under the AIA rules, the 180-day time period for filing a suit in the District Court begins running after the Office rules on the request for reconsideration. Under the AIA rules, applicants have an alternative other than filing a lawsuit when an applicant is dissatisfied with the decision on the request for reconsideration. Under the AIA PTA rules, an unsuccessful request for reconsideration by the USPTO is a prerequisite to a judicial challenge.

In addition, the AIA PTA rules clarify that international applications filed in the United States under the PCT will be treated the same way as applications that originated in the United States with respect to patent term adjustment (Davis, 2013). Under the AIA patent term rules, U.S. national phase applicants can delay submission of formal documents without being subject to loss of patent term adjustment.

Time Limits for Requesting Patent Term Extension

An informal application for patent term extension must be filed within the sixty days of marketing approval and must be filed before the patent expires. This statutory time period is not extendable and cannot be waived or excused. If the product is not approved before the patent is due to expire, the applicant can apply for an interim extension of patent term under 35 U.S.C. §156(d)(5). The initial application for interim extension of patent term must be filed at least three months before the patent term is due to expire. Each subsequent application for interim extension must be filed during the period beginning sixty days before and ending thirty days before the expiration of the preceding interim extension.

Processing of Request for Patent Term Extension

When the USPTO receives an application for patent term extension, a determination is made as to whether the patent is eligible for an extension based on the information provided. The USPTO will communicate with the regulatory agency to determine the length of the regulatory review period. When a final determination has been made on the request for patent term extension, a notice will be mailed to the applicant containing the determination as to eligibility of the patent for extension and the period of time of extension given (if any). The applicant has one opportunity to request reconsideration of the determination, which must be filed within one month or within a period of time specified in the notice. If no request for reconsideration is filed within the permitted period, the certificate of patent term extension, under seal, will be issued to the patent owner in due course. Most patent term extension applications and grants are available for viewing in public PAIR.

Steps in Calculating Patent Term

The following steps can be used to determine if an issued patent is still in force and effect (Crouch, Calculating Patent Term, 2010):

- Calculate the original patent term: Twenty years from filing date or seventeen years from issue date depending upon the timing of the application and issuance.
- Calculate any term adjustment for PTO-based delays (+PTA).
- Calculate any term adjustment for applicant-based delay (-PTA).
- Calculate any term adjustment for regulatory approval delays (+PTE).
- Determine whether there are any terminal disclaimers and, if so, calculate the term of the linked-to patent (-TD).
- Determine whether patent term has been disclaimed for any other reason (-D).
- Determine whether claims were eliminated or changed based on reexamination or reissue.
- Confirm the status of the patent in PAIR to see if the patent status is abandoned.

Given the complexity of calculating patent term adjustments and extensions and the prevalence of overlapping time periods, support staff should validate all patent term-related calculations with a registered practitioner before communicating patent expiration dates to the client or patent owner.

USPTO Patent Term Calculator

The USPTO does not calculate expiration dates of patents but has provided a downloadable patent term calculator as a resource to help the public estimate the expiration dates of patents. The calculator can be used to estimate the expiration dates of utility, plant, or design patents. The calculator contains prompts to enter specific information related to the patent. The USPTO patent term calculator can be downloaded from the website at http://www.uspto.gov/patents/law/patent_term_calculator.jsp. Support staff need to be aware that the USPTO patent term calculator is only an educational tool and should not be relied upon when providing patent expiration dates to clients. All patent term calculations should be reviewed and approved by a registered patent practitioner.

Practice Tips on Patent Term Adjustment

As a result of the patent term adjustment provisions, applicants should take the following practical steps to avoid negative impact on patent term (Kamholz, 2009):

- avoid extensions of time beyond the three-month shortened statutory period for reply to an office action or notice (extensions of time are deemed failure to engage in reasonable efforts to conclude prosecution);
- make elections of species in response to a restriction requirement by telephone (the fourteen-month-to-first-office action is tolled by the issuance of a paper restriction or election requirement);
- avoid submitting a preliminary or supplemental amendment/response (unless requested by the examiner);
- avoid terminal disclaimers, as they specify the patent expiration in terms of another application or patent (any PTA cannot extend beyond the term of the earlier patent's expiration date);
- file an IDS with a reply (if an IDS is filed by itself, it is considered a supplemental reply);
- ensure responses are compliant (notice of non-compliance can negatively affect PTA);
- review PAIR for calculation of PTA, including verifying the response periods related to USPTO delay deadlines; request informal corrections before allowance;
- file formal drawings and a signed inventor oath or declaration, substitute statement, or assignment-declaration with the initial application or during examination phase (do not delay until payment of the issue fee);
- appeal rejections (time spent in a successful appeal will count toward PTA);
- consider filing a continuation-in-part (CIP) application instead of a continuation (CON) application (a CIP is docketed for examination based on its actual filing date, not its effective parent filing date, and resets the fourteen-month-to-first-action patent guarantee period);

- avoid filing papers after allowance (amendments after allowance are deemed failure to engage in reasonable efforts to conclude prosecution);
- independently confirm the USPTO's calculation of PTA as indicated in the notice of allowance;
- request reconsideration of the PTA indicated in the notice of allowance before paying the issue fee;
- if the request for reconsideration of the PTA indicated in the notice of allowance includes a request to reinstate a portion of PTA reduced for failure to reply to an office action or notice within the three-month shortened statutory period, the request must include both fees and a showing that despite all due care the applicant was unable to reply within the three-month period;
- recalculate PTA when the issue notification is received (any request for reconsideration of PTA after issuance must be filed within two months of issuance); and
- request correction of PTA errors in the patentee's favor; if the time period for correcting the PTA has passed, the patentee should independently confirm that it is entitled to the PTA period to be enforced.

CHAPTER-SPECIFIC REFERENCE MATERIAL

Reference Source	Patent Term—Duration, Adjustment, and Extension Applicable Rules, Regulations, and Procedures
Title 35 of the U.S. Code	35 U.S.C. §155 Patent term extension. §155 A patent term restoration. §156 Extension of patent term.
Title 37 of the Code of Federal Regulations	37 C.F.R. Patent Term Adjustment
	§1.701 Extension of patent term due to examination delay under the Uruguay Round Agreements Act (original applications, other than designs, filed on or after June 8, 1995, and before May 29, 2000). §1.702 Grounds for adjustment of patent term due to examination delay under the Patent Term Guarantee Act of 1999 (original applications, other than designs, filed on or after May 29, 2000). §1.703 Period of adjustment of patent term due to examination delay. §1.704 Reduction of period of adjustment of patent term. §1.705 Patent term adjustment determination. Patent Term Extension §1.710 Patents subject to extension of the patent term. §1.720 Conditions for extension of patent term. §1.730 Applicant for extension of patent term; signature requirements. §1.740 Formal requirements for application for extension of patent term; correction of informalities. §1.741 Complete application given a filing date; petition procedure. §1.750 Determination of eligibility for extension of patent term. §1.760 Interim extension of patent term under 35 U.S.C. 156(e)(2). §1.765 Duty of disclosure in patent term extension proceedings. §1.770 Express withdrawal of application for extension of patent term.

	§1.779 Calculation of patent term extension for a veterinary biological product. §1.780 Certificate or order of extension of patent term. §1.785 Multiple applications for extension of term of the same patent or of different patents for the same regulatory review period for a product. §1.790 Interim extension of patent term under 35 U.S.C. 156(d)(5) §1.791 Termination of interim extension granted prior to regulatory approval of a product for commercial marketing or use.
Manual of Patent Examination Procedures (MPEP, 8th Edition)	Chapter 2700 Patent Terms and Extensions

Chapter 18
U.S. National Phase Entry From An International Application

Types of U.S. National Applications

There are three types of U.S. national applications that originate from different sources, and each type of application has distinctive attributes:

- a provisional application filed under 35 U.S.C. §111(b);
- a regular domestic national application filed under 35 U.S.C. §111(a); and
- a national stage application under the Patent Corporation Treaty (PCT) (an application that entered the national stage in the United States from an international application under 35 U.S.C. §371).

The filing requirements for a U.S. national stage application under 35 U.S.C. §371 filed off an international application are discussed in more detail in this chapter.

The Patent Corporation Treaty

The Patent Cooperation Treaty (PCT) is an international patent law treaty that provides a unified procedure for filing patent applications to protect inventions in each of its contracting states. A patent application filed under the PCT is called an international application, or PCT application. Under the PCT, an international application is filed with a Receiving Office (RO) in one of the acceptable languages. The applicant-elected International Searching Authority (ISA) performs a search of the keywords of the invention and issues an International Search Report (ISR) and Written Opinion (WO) regarding the patentability of the invention.

PCT applicants have an additional option to request a preliminary examination of the subject matter of the application, which is carried out by the International Preliminary Examining Authority (IPEA). The IPEA issues an International Preliminary Report on Patentability (IPRP), which is a more detailed analysis of the patentability of the claims with respect to the prior art. If the applicant does not file a demand for international preliminary examination, the WO becomes the basis from which the national offices will commence examination.

The PCT does not grant a patent; it is an international central processing unit for applications that may be subsequently nationalized in contracting member states. When the international stage is completed, the application progresses to national or regional entry, or both, where applicants must meet the requirements of the foreign or domestic patent offices, or both. It is the domestic or foreign patent offices, or both, that will grant any related patent based on the patentability of the claims and the fulfillment of national procedural filing requirements, which may include translation requirements.

Advantages of Filing Under the Patent Corporation Treaty

The PCT is administered by the World Intellectual Property Organization (WIPO), as are other international treaties in the field of industrial property, such as the Paris Convention. Filing an application under the PCT system offers the following advantages to applicants:

- ability to complete all formality filing requirements prior to entry into the national phase;
- the ISR and WO gives applicant a preliminary assessment on the question of whether the claimed invention appears to be novel, to involve an inventive step (to be non-obvious), and to be industrially applicable;
- reassurance that the contracting states will honor the patentability assessment of the international phase;
- ability to complete defensive international publication;
- option to obtain a more detailed international preliminary examination and an IPRP under Chapter II processing;
- ability to delay expenditure of translation costs and national fees until thirty months, when the applicant can make a more informed national phase entry decision;
- provides the applicant additional time for research and evaluation of financial, marketing, commercial, and other considerations.

Identification of the U.S. National Phase Application

The USPTO requires that documents submitted by the applicant be clearly identified as being for entry into the national phase under the PCT; otherwise, the documents will be treated as having been filed for a domestic patent application under §111(a). The identification requirement is usually complied with if the U.S. National

Phase Entry Transmittal Form (SB/1390) is used. The identification of the international application, in the declaration or oath of the inventor or otherwise, as a prior filed application for priority purposes is not considered to be a sufficient indication of an intention to enter the national phase under the PCT. When an international application entering the U.S. national phase has been accorded a U.S. application number, that number should be used whenever papers or other communications are directed to the USPTO regarding the national stage application.

Commencement and Entry

Commencement of the U.S. national stage occurs upon expiration of the applicable time limit of no later than the expiration of thirty months from the priority date. The national stage may commence earlier than thirty months from the priority date, provided the applicant makes an express request for early processing and has complied with the applicable procedural requirements under 35 U.S.C. §371(c).

To begin entry into the national stage, the applicant must pay the basic national fee and ensure that a copy of the international application has been received by the U.S. Designated (DO) or Elected Office (EO) prior to expiration of thirty months from the priority date. Where the international application was filed with the United States Receiving Office (USRO) as the competent receiving Office, the copy of the international application is not required. A copy of the international application is provided to the DO or EO by the International Bureau (IB) at about eighteen months from the priority date. The IB also mails a confirmation to the applicant (Form PCT/IB/308), indicating to which Offices the international application was transmitted.

Filing Requirements

To enter the U.S. national stage under 35 U.S.C. §371 off an international application, the following items must be submitted:

- form SB/1390 (Transmittal letter to the United States Designated/Elected office (DO/EO/US) Concerning a Submission under 35 U.S.C. §371);
- a copy of the international application, unless it has been previously transmitted by the IB or unless it was originally filed in the USRO; and
- the basic national fee under 37 C.F.R §1.492(a).

To complete the filing requirements of the U.S. national stage application, the following items must be filed:

- a translation of the international application, as filed, into the English language if it was originally filed in another language;
- an signed oath or declaration of the inventor, if a declaration of inventorship has not been previously submitted in the international application within the time limits provided;
- a copy of any amendments to the claims made under PCT Article 19, and a translation of those amendments into English if they were made in another language. Article 19 amendments that are not received by the expiration of thirty months from the priority date will be considered to be canceled.

AIA Impact—Inventor Oath or Declaration and Priority Claim

For international applications filed before September 16, 2012, the pre-AIA declaration forms can be used, and a priority claim can be made on the front page of the specification and in the signed inventor declaration or ADS. For international applications filed on or after September 16, 2012, an signed AIA language oath or declaration, substitute statement, or combined assignment-declaration must be filed with respect to each inventor. Any claim to priority must be made in a signed ADS to be made of record in the application. The critical date for deciding whether to use pre-AIA or AIA forms is the international filing date, not the U.S. national filing date.

Completing the U.S. National Phase Transmittal

To complete the request for entry into the U.S. national stage under 35 U.S.C. §371, support staff need to be able to interpret PCT forms from the international phase. The filing of an international application automatically designates all PCT member states, including the United States. When completing the U.S. National Phase transmittal (Form SB/1390), the international filing date and any priority date claimed should be entered using the day/month/year international format. For an English-language application, the U.S. National Phase transmittal should be completed as follows:

- Box 1: Check as this is the first submission of items concerning a submission under 35 U.S.C. §371.
- Box 3: Should only be checked if an express request includes a signed inventor declaration and basic filing fee in the first submission under 35 U.S.C. §371.

- Box 5: Check a copy of the International Application as filed.
- Box 5a: Check only if application has not been communicated the IB and is attached.
- Box 5b: Check only if application has been communicated by the IB (confirm on form PCT/IB/308; United States indicated in list of designated countries communicated to by the IB).
- Box 5c: Check only if application transmittal is not required as the application was filed in the RO/US.
- Box 7: Check amendments to the claims of the International Application under PCT Article 19.
- Box 7d: Check if amendments under Article 19 have not and will not be made (confirm if Article 19 amendments were filed in response to the ISR/WO).
- Box 9: Check only if a signed oath or declaration is enclosed (confirm Box 3 is also checked).

Optional Enclosures

Items 11 to 20 on the transmittal form relate to optional enclosures, documents, or information included. The following are the most common optional enclosures for a first submission:

- Box 11: Check only if an IDS with a copy of the ISR is included.
- Box 12: Check only if an assignment document for recordation including a recordation cover sheet, is included.
- Box 13: Check only if a preliminary amendment is included.
- Box 14: Check only if an ADS is included.

A signed inventor oath or declaration, IDS including an ISR, assignment, sequence listing, and formal drawings can all be filed at a later date as part of a second submission.

Filing Fees

The filing fees for a U.S. national phase entry under 35 U.S.C. §371 includes a basic filing fee, an examination fee, a search fee, and additional sheet and excess claim fees, if applicable. The basis national fee must be paid on the first submission under 35 U.S.C. §371 and within thirty months from the priority date. The applicable time limit may not be extended. If the basic national fee is not paid on filing the U.S. national phase application, the application becomes abandoned as to the United States. The fees are accounted for in items 21 through 23 on the transmittal form.

If the written opinion was prepared by the ISA/U.S. or if the IPRP prepared by the IPEA/U.S. indicates all claims satisfy the provisions of PCT Article 33 (1)(4) then a reduced examination fee can be paid. For all other situations, the full examination fee must be paid.

If the written opinion of the ISA/U.S. or the IPRP prepared by the IPEA/U.S. indicates all claims satisfy the provisions of PCT Article 33 (1)(4) (see Box V of the ISR/WO, must have all Yes for all claims under Novelty, Inventive Step, and Industrial Applicability) then examination and search fees do not have to be paid. If a search fee has been paid on the international application to the USPTO as the international searching authority or the international search report was prepared by an ISA other than the U.S. (EP or AU) and provided to the office or previously communicated to the United States by the IB then a reduced search fee can be paid. For all other situations, the full search fee must be paid.

An additional sheet fee charge must be paid for specification and drawings filed in paper over one hundred sheets, excluding sequence listing or computer program listings in an electronic medium. An additional fee must be paid for each additional fifty sheets of paper or fraction thereof.

If the claim count in the application exceeds three independent or twenty total claims, additional fees must be paid for excess claims. There is also a multiple dependent claim fee surcharge if the application contains multiple dependent claims. All fees are subject to entity size discounting if the applicant is entitled to claim such status.

The examination fee, search fee, additional sheets, and multiple dependent claims fee can be paid in a subsequent submission in response to a Notice of Missing Requirement subject to payment of a surcharge.

Preliminary Amendment

A preliminary amendment should be filed with the first submission under 35 U.S.C. §371. The preliminary amendment should insert or update the priority claim in the paragraph on page one of the specification regarding cross reference to related applications. An example of the text of the preliminary amendment is as follows:

On Page 1, please amend the following paragraph immediately after the title:

Cross Reference to Related Applications

This application is a national state filing under 35 U.S.C. §371 of International Application No. PCT/US[Year]/XXXXXX, file on __________, which claims the benefit of the filing date under 35 U.S.C. §119(e) to U.S. Provisional Application No. XX/XX,XXX, filed on ____________, the entire disclosure of which is incorporated by reference herein. International Application No. PCT/US[Year]/XXXXXX was published in English under PCT Article 21(2).

In addition, the preliminary amendment should add an abstract as the last page of the specification, immediately after the claims. A preliminary amendment may also be used to reduce the total number of claims or number of independent claims or remove multiple dependent claims on entry into the U.S. national phase.

For international applications filed on or after September 16, 2012, any domestic or foreign priority claim must be made in a signed ADS if it is to be made of record by the USPTO.

Recording Changes During the International Phase

The file of the international application should be reviewed for any changes to the application, applicant, or inventor information during the international stage. Support staff should be looking for any changes to the address or the applicant or inventors, including the addition or removal of any applicants or inventors. If changes were made during the international phase, such filings would have been made under PCT Rules 91 (Rectification of Obvious Mistakes) or 92Bis (Recording of a Change). If changes are not reflected in the published PCT application, such changes will need to be made during the U.S. national phase. Support staff preparing U.S. national phase filing papers should confirm if there were Notifications of Recordation of a Change issued in the international phase and validate if such changes were reflected in the front page of the PCT published application. Support staff can review the bibliographic information and the published documents on the WIPO website.

Notification of Missing Requirements

If the basic national fee has been paid and the copy of the international application (if required) has been received by expiration of thirty months from the priority date, but the required oath or declaration, translation, search fee, examination fee, or application size fee have not been filed prior to commencement of the national stage, the Office will send the applicant a Notification of Missing Requirements (Form PCT/DO/EO/905). The notification will set a time period to correct any missing or defective requirements and to submit the surcharge fee required under 37 C.F.R. §1.492(h). The time period is thirty-two months from the priority date or two months from the date of the notice, whichever expires later. The time period may be extended for up to five additional months, as provided in 37 C.F.R. §1.136(a). For the purposes of U.S. national phase entry, the inventors are the applicant. Failure to timely file the required signed inventor oath or declaration will result in abandonment of the application. Support staff should ensure that the correct pre-AIA or AIA inventor oath or declaration forms are used based on the filing date of the international application.

Sequence Listing Submission Requirements

If the international application contains a sequence listing, the Office encourages applicants to submit the sequence listing upon U.S. national stage entry. Applicants should file a sequence listing text file via EFS-Web regardless of the format in which the sequence listing was originally filed in the international application. The sequence listing ASCII text file serves both as part of the application and the CRF format requirement. If the sequence listing was not part of the international application, it must be filed as an amendment in the national stage. No statement of identity is required, and the sequence listing text file is excluded when determining the application size fee. The specification of the national stage application should be amended to include a statement in a separate paragraph that incorporates by reference the sequence listing text file.

If the international application was filed with the USRO and includes a sequence listing in paper or PDF format and a compliant CRF, a sequence listing transfer request may be filed. When the international application enters the U.S. national stage, a PDF copy of the sequence listing is include in the IFW of the U.S. national stage application as provided by the International Bureau or by the applicant. The applicant can request transfer of the CRF compliant sequence listing from the international application to the U.S. national stage application as long as the international application is completely identified and a statement is provided that the CRF from the international application is identical to the PDF copy of the sequence listing contained in the U.S. national stage application. However, sequence listing transfer requests are effective only for the transfer of the compliant CRF, not the sequence listing part of the application. The applicant cannot state that the CRF from the other application is identical to the paper copy of the sequence listing contained in the new application, since the new application was filed with no sequence listing part of the application. A request for transfer of a sequence listing under such a circumstance would be improper and would not be granted. The USPTO encourages applicants to provide a sequence listing text file rather than a request for sequence listing transfer from another application. When a sequence listing text file is filed by the applicant, it serves both as part of the application and meets the CRF requirement, and no statement of identity is required.

Sequence listing text files can be retrieved from the supplemental content tab in PAIR if the sequence listing text file was filed after April 2007. The USPTO will update the sequence listing text file fields <140> to reflect the application number and filing date of the U.S. national stage application. The sequence listing text file can also be downloaded from the documents tab in Patentscope if the sequence listing text file was part of the international application filed with the International Bureau.

Filing Date

An international application designating the United States has two stages (international and national) with the filing date being the same in both stages. The filing date of the international stage application is also the filing date for the national stage application. When the USPTO makes a determination that all the filing requirements for national stage entry have been met, it will issue a Notification of Acceptance of Application under 35 U.S.C. §371 and 37 C.F.R. §1.495, indicating the date of completion of all filing requirements. The filing receipt of the national stage application will be mailed concurrently with the acceptance notification. The national stage application filing date is the date of receipt of the 35 U.S.C. §371(c)(1), (c)(2), and (c)(4) requirements. The national stage application completion date is the latest of:

- the date of submission of the basic national fee;
- the date of submission or communication of the copy of the international application;
- the date of submission of the translation of the international application if the international application is not in the English language;

- the date of submission of an oath or declaration of the inventor in compliance with 35 U.S.C. §371(c)(4);
- the earlier of thirty months from the priority date or the date of request for early processing under 35 U.S.C. §371(f);
- if a request for early processing has not been requested prior to thirty months from the priority date, the date of submission of any translation of the annexes to the international preliminary examination report if the translation of the annexes are filed within the time period set in a Notification of Missing Requirements (Form PCT/DO/EO/905), requiring either an English translation of the international application or an oath or declaration; and
- the date of submission of any surcharge for submitting the oath or declaration later than thirty months from the priority date.

Applicants should not request a corrected filing receipt based on the assumption that the indicated filing date is incorrect. For most legal purposes, the effective filing date of a U.S. national phase application is the PCT international filing date.

Filing Methods

Facsimile transmission is not acceptable for submission of the basic national fee or the copy of the international application. The certificate of mailing procedures of 37 C.F.R. §1.8 do not apply to the filing of the copy of the international application and payment of the basic national fee. Applicants may file national stage applications via EFS-Web or USPS Express Mail.

Priority Claim

A U.S. national stage application may be entitled to the priority benefit of an earlier-filed foreign or domestic application. More specifically, a U.S. national stage application may be entitled to the following priorities:

- a foreign/international priority claim under 35 U.S.C. §119(a) and §365(b) to an earlier-filed foreign or international application designating at least one country other than the United States; and
- a domestic priority claim under 35 U.S.C. §119(e) or 35 U.S.C. §120 and §365(c) to an earlier-filed U.S. national application or international application designating the United States.

Foreign/International Priority Claim

For a U.S. national phase application to benefit from an earlier-filed foreign or international application, the priority benefit must have been timely claimed in the international stage of the international application. If priority was properly claimed in the international stage, the claim for priority is acknowledged and the national stage application file is checked for a certified copy of the priority document submitted to the IB. International applications filed on or after April 1, 2007, are subject to amended PCT rules permitting restoration of a right of priority. Consequently, international applications filed on or after April 1, 2007, may claim priority to a foreign application filed more than twelve months before the filing date of the international application. While such priority claims are permitted in the international stage, the right of priority will not be effective in the U.S. national stage, as 35 U.S.C. §119(a) does not permit a priority period that exceeds twelve months. If the priority claim in the national stage application is to an application, the priority of which was not claimed in the international stage, the claim for priority will be denied for failing to meet the requirements of the international phase.

Certified Copy

The requirement for a certified copy of the foreign priority application is normally fulfilled by the applicant providing a certified copy to the receiving Office or to the IB or by applicant requesting that the receiving Office prepare and transmit the priority document to the IB if the receiving Office issued the priority document. The applicant must submit the certified copy or must request that the receiving Office prepare and transmit the certified copy within sixteen months from the priority date. Where the applicant complied with priority claiming requirements during the international phase, the IB will forward a copy of the certified priority document to each Designated Office that has requested it with an indication that the priority document was submitted in compliance with the requirements of the international phase. This indication may be in the form of either a cover sheet attached to the copy of the priority document or a WIPO stamp on the face of the certified copy that will indicate the date the IB received the document. The USPTO will normally request the IB to furnish the copy of the certified priority document upon receipt of the applicant's submission under 35 U.S.C. §371, to enter the U.S. national phase. The certified copy from the IB is placed in the U.S. national stage file. The examiner should acknowledge in the next Office action that the copy of the certified copy of the foreign priority document has been received.

If the IB is unable to forward a copy of the certified priority document to the USPTO because the applicant failed to comply with priority claiming requirements, then the applicant will have to provide a certified copy of the priority document during the national stage to fulfill the requirement of 37 C.F.R. §1.55(a)(2).

Domestic Priority Claim

A U.S. national stage application may include a benefit claim under 35 U.S.C. §119(e) or §120 and §365(c) to a prior U.S. national application or under 35 U.S.C. §120 and §365(c) to a prior international application designating the United States.

In order for a national stage application to obtain benefit under 35 U.S.C. §119(e) of a prior U.S. provisional application, the national stage application must comply with the requirements for claiming benefit of an earlier-filed application. The filing requirements for the provisional application must have been completed. The provisional application must name as an inventor at least one inventor named in the later-filed international application and disclose the named inventor's invention claimed in at least one claim of the national stage application in compliance with requirements under 35 U.S.C. §112. The national stage application must contain:

- a reference to the provisional application (either in an ADS, or in the first sentences of the specification must be a signed ADS for international applications filed on or after September 16, 2012); and
- the reference must identify the provisional application and include the provisional application number and filing date.

The required reference to the earlier-filed provisional application must be submitted within the later of four months from the date on which the national stage commenced under 35 U.S.C. §371(b) or (f) in the later-filed international application or sixteen months from the filing date of the prior-filed provisional application. This time period is not extendable. However, if the entire delay—between the date the claim was due under 37 C.F.R. §1.78(a)(5)(ii) and the date the claim was filed—was unintentional, a petition under 37 C.F.R. §1.78(a)(6) may be filed to accept the delayed claim.

In order for a national stage application to obtain benefit under 35 U.S.C. §120 and §365(c) of a prior-filed copending non-provisional application or prior-filed copending international application designating the United States, the national stage application must comply with the requirements for claiming benefit of an earlier-filed application. The prior non-provisional application or international application must name as an inventor at least one inventor named in the later-filed international application and disclose the named inventor's invention claimed in at least one claim of the national stage application in compliance with requirements under 35 U.S.C. §112. The national stage application must contain a reference to the prior non-provisional or international application, identifying it by application number or international application number and international filing date and indicating the relationship of the applications. The required reference to the earlier-filed application must be submitted within the later of four months from the date on which the national stage commenced or sixteen months from the filing date of the prior-filed application. This time period is not extendable, and failure to timely submit the required reference to the earlier-filed application will be considered a waiver of any benefit under 35 U.S.C. §120, §121, or §365(c) to such application. However, if the entire delay—between the date the claim was due under 37 C.F.R. §1.78(a)(2)(ii) and the date the claim was filed—was unintentional, a petition under 37 C.F.R. §1.78(a)(3) may be filed to accept the delayed claim.

A prior-filed non-provisional application is copending with the national stage application if the prior U.S. national application was pending on the international filing date of the national stage application. A prior-filed international application designating the United States is copending with the national stage application if the prior international application was not abandoned or withdrawn, either generally or as to the United States, on the international filing date of the national stage application.

A national stage application submitted under 35 U.S.C. §371 cannot claim benefit of the filing date of the international application of which it is the national stage since its filing date is the international filing date of the international application. The international application is not an earlier application (it has the same filing date as the national stage); a benefit claim under 35 U.S.C. §120 in the national stage to the international application is inappropriate and may result in the submission being treated as an application filed under 35 U.S.C. §111(a).

Duty of Disclosure

When an international application is filed under the PCT, prior art documents may be cited in the ISR and WO or the IPRP. The applicant must cite prior art documents from the ISR to the examiner by filing an IDS with three months of the filing of the national stage application. Under U.S. duty of disclosure requirements, the applicant is required to disclose to the examiner all information material to patentability.

When all the requirements for a national stage application have been completed, the applicant is notified in form PCT/DO/EO/903 of the acceptance of the application under 35 U.S.C. §371, including an itemized list of the items received. The itemized list includes an indication of whether a copy of the ISR and copies of the cited references are present in the national stage file. The examiner will consider the documents cited in the ISR, without any further action by applicant under 37 C.F.R. §1.97 and §1.98, when both the international search report and copies of the documents are indicated to be present in the national stage file. The examiner will note the consideration in the first office action.

Examination of Application

A national stage application will be forwarded to the appropriate Technology Center (TC) for examination in turn based on the 35 U.S.C. §371(c) filing date. If the WO or the IPRP issued during the international phase states that the criteria of novelty, inventive step (non-obviousness), and industrial applicability have been satisfied for all of the claims presented in the application entering the national stage, the national stage search fee and examination fee are reduced. Such applications may be amended only to the extent necessary to eliminate objections as to form or cancel rejected claims, and such applications will be advanced out of turn for examination. When the national stage application has been taken up by the examiner, prosecution proceeds in the same manner as for a domestic application.

Abandonment of Application

If the requirements for the submission of the basic national fee and a copy of the international application (if necessary) are not satisfied prior to the expiration of thirty months from the priority date, then the international application becomes abandoned as to the United States at thirty months from the priority date. If the requirements under 37 C.F.R. §1.495(b) are timely met, but the requirements under

37 C.F.R. §1.495(c) for an English translation of the international application, signed oath or declaration, search fee, examination fee, and application size fee are not met within a time period set in a notice provided by the Office, then the application will become abandoned upon expiration of the time period set in the notice. Applicants should be aware that sometimes papers filed for the national stage are deficient, and abandonment results. For example, if on filing the U.S. national phase application, the basic filing fee is not paid, the application is abandoned at thirty months. The applicant may file a petition to revive an abandoned application in accordance with the provisions of 37 C.F.R. §1.137. The applicant may use either form SB/61PCT (unavoidably abandoned application) or form SB/64PCT (unintentionally abandoned application), as appropriate.

Continuation or Continuation-in-Part Applications

Instead of filing an national stage application, the applicant may file a continuing (continuation or continuation-in-part) application under 35 U.S.C. §120, provided the international application designating the United States is not considered withdrawn or abandoned at the time of filing. The filing of continuing applications of an international application designating the United States is used primarily in instances where there was difficulty in obtaining a signed oath or declaration by the expiration of the time for entry into the national stage. Such continuation applications allow applicants to bypass the requirements of 35 U.S.C. §371, and they are often referred to as "bypass" applications. The normal procedure for filing continuing applications applies (see Chapter 16 for more details on continuation and continuation-in-part applications).

The applicant must claim the benefit of the international filing date of the international application designating the United States of America. The first sentence of the description following the title must contain a reference to the international application, identifying it by the international application number and the international filing date, and must indicate the relationship of the applications, unless such information has been included in an ADS. This reference to the international application must be submitted during the pendency of the continuing application, and within the later of four months from the actual filing date of the continuing application or sixteen months from the filing date of the international application. This time period is not extendable. For international applications filed on or after September 16, 2012, any foreign or domestic or priority benefit claim must be made in a signed ADS filed with the application.

The USPTO may require the filing of a certified copy of the international application together with a translation if the application was not filed in English. If, at the time of filing the continuing application, the basic filing fee has not been paid or the signed inventor oath or declaration has not been furnished, the requirement may still be completed in response to a Notice of Missing Parts on payment of a surcharge.

Continuation-in-part applications are generally filed in instances where the applicant seeks to add matter to the disclosure that is not supported by the disclosure of the international application as originally filed. In such applications, new formal papers (declaration and assignment) should be prepared to cover the new matter added.

Comparison of National Stage and National Domestic Applications

The differences between a U.S. national application filed under 35 U.S.C. §111(a) (including those claiming benefit of a PCT application under 35 U.S.C. §120) and a U.S. national stage application filed under 35 U.S.C. §371 are summarized in Table 30.

Table 30: Differences Between U.S. National Domestic and U.S. National Stage Applications

Criteria	U.S. National Domestic Application Filed Under 35 U.S.C. §111(a)	U.S. National Stage Application Filed Under 35 U.S.C. §371
Filing Date	Deposit date of specification, claims, and any necessary drawings.	International filing date of PCT application.
Priority Claim Requirement	Certified copy of foreign priority document provided by the applicant or by a foreign patent office.	Certified copy of priority document provided by IB during the international stage.
Unity of Invention	Subject to U.S. restriction requirement practice.	Subject to PCT unity of invention practice.
Copendency Requirement	Applicant provides proof copendency.	Not applicable.

Most notably, a U.S. national stage application differs from a domestic national application in the following manner:

- A U.S. national stage application is filed later in the prosecution, at thirty months from a claimed priority date. A domestic application must be filed within twelve months of any domestic application claimed in priority.
- A U.S. national stage is filed after the applicant has received a preliminary assessment of the patentability of the claims during the international phase. A domestic application is filed without any preliminary assessment of the patentability of the claims by an independent body.

Recordation of Assignment Documents

The USPTO will record assignments relating to international patent applications that designate the United States. The U.S. national phase assignment must identify the application by the international application number and filing date. Each document submitted for recording must be accompanied by a cover sheet referring to the international application.

CHAPTER-SPECIFIC REFERENCE MATERIAL

Reference Source	U.S. National Phase Entry Under U.S.C. §371 Applicable Rules, Regulations, and Procedures
Guides	PCT Applicants' Guide–USPTO as a Designated Office–U.S. National Phase http://www.wipo.int/pct/guide/en/gdvol2/annexes/us.pdf
Title 35 of the U.S. Code	U.S.C. §371 National stage: Commencement. §372 National stage: Requirements and procedure. §373 Improper applicant. §374 Publication of international application. §375 Patent issued on international application: Effect. §376 Fees.
Title 37 of the Code of Federal Regulations	37 C.F.R. §1.491 National stage commencement and entry. §1.492 National stage fees. §1.495 Entering the national stage in the United States of America. §1.496 Examination of international applications in the national stage. §1.497 Oath or declaration under 35 U.S.C. 371(c)(4). §1.499 Unity of invention during the national stage.
Manual of Patent Examination Procedures (MPEP, 8th Edition)	Chapter 1800 Patent Corporation Treaty §1893 National Stage (U.S. National Application Filed Under 35 U.S.C. 371)

Chapter 19
Correction of Patents—Reissue Applications and Certificates of Correction

Introduction

There are two primary vehicles for correcting defective patents, namely:

- reissue applications; and
- certificates of correction.

The reissue application process is designed to allow a patent holder to correct a defective patent and is nestled between certificates of correction (minor clerical or typographical errors) and reexamination (novelty and obviousness issues) (Crouch, Reissue Applications Over Time, 2009). The specific filing requirements of reissue applications and certificates of correction are discussed in more detail in this chapter.

Reissue Applications

A reissue patent application is filed post-grant to correct an error in an issued patent where the error renders the patent wholly or partially inoperable or invalid. The provisions of 35 U.S.C. §251 permit the reissue of a patent to correct an error made in the patent without any deceptive intention.

Grounds for Filing

A reissue application can be filed to correct an error in the patent that was made without any deceptive intention that has resulted in the patent being deemed wholly or partly inoperative or invalid. The error in the patent was caused by conduct during the preparation or prosecution, or both, of the application that became the patent. There must be at least one error in the patent to provide grounds for reissue. The error must be one that causes the patent to be deemed wholly or partially inoperative or invalid as a result of one of the following:

- a defective specification or drawing; or
- the patentee claiming more or less than they have a right to claim.

Reissue applications should not be used to correct spelling, grammatical, typographical, editorial, or clerical errors that do not cause the patent to be deemed wholly or partly inoperative or invalid. The most common bases for filing a reissue application are:

- the claims are too narrow or too broad;
- the disclosure contains inaccuracies (substantive error in the specification or drawings);
- correction of inventorship;
- correction of problem with patent oath or declaration;
- applicant failed to or incorrectly claimed foreign priority; and
- applicant failed to make reference to or incorrectly made reference to prior copending applications.

It is no longer required that the applicant physically surrender the original patent. In addition, the requirement for the assignee to consent to filing a reissue no longer includes a requirement for the applicant to order a title report with the filing of the reissue application.

Defective Specification or Drawing

A reissue application is an appropriate means to correct defects in the specification or drawings only when such errors render the patent wholly or partially inoperative or invalid. The correction to the specification or drawing must be substantive in nature. A non-substantive drawing change (e.g., reference numeral correction or addition, addition of shading, or even the addition of an additional figure merely to clarify the disclosure) is not sufficient grounds for filing a reissue application. In addition, a spelling, grammatical, typographical, editorial, or clerical error that does not cause the patent to be wholly or partly inoperative or invalid is not substantive or appropriate content for a reissue application. Such non-substantive formatting errors should be corrected using a certificate of correction, not a reissue application.

Defective Claims

A reissue application can be used to correct a defective claim if the correction requested is substantive in nature and renders the patent wholly or partially inoperative or invalid. A reissue application can also be used to correct a defective claim where the patentee claimed more than they had a right to claim. In such cases, the identified claims must be narrowed by amendment or canceled. Where the patentee claimed less than they had a right to claim, the claims may be broadened, provided that the broadening claims are presented within two years of the grant of the original patent and the broadened claims are directed to the same disclosed invention.

Correction of Inventorship

A reissue application may be used to correct inventorship as this does not enlarge the scope of the claims. The reissue oath or declaration can be signed by the assignee of the entire interest. An assignee of the entire interest can add or delete the name of an inventor by reissue without the original inventor's consent and despite the inventor's disagreement or protest.

Perfecting a Benefit Claim

A reissue application can be used to perfect a foreign, domestic, or provisional priority claim. A reissue application can be used to perfect a foreign priority claim under 35 U.S.C. §119(a)-(d). A patentee can file a reissue application to perfect a claim to foreign priority only if the patent to be reissued resulted from an application filed on or after November 29, 2000. The reissue application to perfect a first-time foreign priority claim should include the following:

- a reissue transmittal form and reissue transmittal fee;
- a claim for foreign priority under 35 U.S.C. §119(a)-(d);
- the certified copy of the priority document in the reissue application;
- a petition to accept an unintentionally delayed priority claims under §1.55(c); and
- the petition fee.

If the patent to be reissued resulted from an application filed before November 29, 2000, no petition is required.

A reissue application can also be used to perfect claiming benefit to an earlier-filed copending U.S. patent application under U.S.C. §120. Where domestic benefit is being claimed for the first time and the patent to be reissued resulted from an application filed on or after November 29, 2000, the submission should include the following:

- a reissue transmittal form and reissue transmittal fee;
- a claim for domestic priority under 35 U.S.C. §120;

- a petition to accept an unintentionally delayed priority claim under §1.78(a)(3); and
- the petition fee.

If the patent to be reissued resulted from an application filed before November 29, 2000, no petition is required.

Reissue Application Filing Requirements

The specification, including the claims and any drawings of the reissue application, is the copy of the printed patent for which reissue is requested. A copy of the printed patent should be submitted by the applicant as part of the initial reissue application filing papers. A full copy of the printed patent must be submitted in double-column format, with each page of the double-column format on one-sided paper. In addition, a reissue oath or declaration is required. If the patent has been assigned, the reissue applicant must also provide consent of the assignee to the reissue and evidence of ownership. If the patent is not assigned, the reissue applicant should affirmatively indicate that the patent was not assigned in the reissue filing papers. The initial filing of a reissue application must include the following:

- reissue patent application transmittal form;
- reissue application fee transmittal form (fees may be paid later);
- full copy of the printed patent in double-column format on one-sided paper;
- reissue oath or declaration by inventors or assignee (may be submitted later);
- consent of the assignee (if assigned including evidence of ownership, e.g., reel and frame number);
- copy of any disclaimer, certificate of correction, or reexamination certificate issued in the patent for which reissue is requested;
- identification of any prior or concurrent litigation proceedings in which the patent for reissue is or was involved, including any results of such proceedings; and
- optional: amendment, IDS, claim for priority benefit under 35 U.S.C. §119 or §120.

The basic filing, search, and examination fees are due on filing of the reissue application. The fees may be paid at a later date provided they are paid within the time period identified in the missing parts notice and include payment of a surcharge associated with last submission of fees. Any additional excess claim fees must accompany an amendment adding such claims before the amendment will be considered by the examiner.

A reissue application must notify the USPTO of any prior, pending, or concurrent proceeding in which the patent for requested reissue is or was involved. This duty of notification is continuing and exists from the time the reissue application is filed until the reissue application is abandoned or issues as a reissue patent.

AIA Impact—Reissue-Related Forms

The USPTO offers a suite of reissue-related forms that are based on the filing date of the application. For applications filed before September 16, 2012, the following reissue forms should be used:

- SB/50 Reissue Patent Application Transmittal
- SB/56 Reissue Application Fee Transmittal Form
- SB/51 Reissue Application Declaration by the Inventor
- SB/52 Reissue Application Declaration by the Assignee
- SB/53 Reissue Application: Consent of Assignee; Statement of Non-Assignment

For applications filed on or after September 16, 2012, the following reissue forms should be used:

- AIA/50 Reissue Patent Application Transmittal
- SB/56 Reissue Application Fee Transmittal Form
- AIA/05 Reissue Application Declaration by the Inventor
- AIA/06 Reissue Application Declaration by the Assignee
- AIA/07 Substitute Statement In Lieu of an Oath or Declaration For Reissue Patent Application
- AIA/53 Reissue Application: Consent of Assignee; Statement of Non-Assignment

AIA Impact—Reissue Oath or Declaration

As of September 16, 2012, the provisions of the AIA revised reissue practice as follows:

- eliminated the requirement for a reissue inventor oath or declaration to include a statement that all errors arose without any deceptive intent on the part of the applicant;
- eliminated the requirement for a supplemental inventor's oath or declaration;

- required that the inventor's oath or declaration for a reissue application to identify a claim that the application seeks to broaden if the reissue application seeks to enlarge the scope of the claims of the patent; and
- clarified that a single claim containing both a broadening and a narrowing of the claimed invention is to be treated as a broadening request.

The changes under the AIA were intended to provide more efficient processing of reissue applications and improve the quality of reissued patents. The AIA also revised the reissue practice rules to permit an assignee of the entire interest who filed an application that was patented to sign the inventor's oath or declaration in a reissue application of such a patent, even if the reissue application is a broadening reissue.

Under the AIA, a reissue oath or declaration can be signed by the inventors or the assignee. Where the reissue application does not seek to enlarge the scope of any claims of the original patent, the reissue oath or declaration may be signed by the assignee of the entire interest. If an inventor is to be added in a reissue application, a proper reissue oath or declaration including the signature of all of the inventors is required. If one or more inventors are being deleted in a reissue application, an oath or declaration signed by the remaining inventors must be filed. While the inventor being deleted need not sign the oath or declaration, if the inventor being deleted has any ownership interest in the patent (did not assign away his or her rights), the signature of the inventor must be supplied in consent to the filing of the reissue application. Where no assignee exists, the applicant should affirmatively indicate this by simply checking the "No" box of item 7 on Form SB/50. If the applicant does not affirmatively state that there is no assignee, it is assumed that an assignee does exist, and the examiner will notify the applicant of the requirement in the first office action. The reissue oath or declaration must be accompanied by a written consent of all assignees; however, it does not have to be filed with the reissue application request and specification. If the signed oath or declaration is not filed with the reissue application, the Office will accord a filing date and send applicant a Notice to File Missing Parts, requesting submission of the signed oath or declaration including payment of a surcharge. If the reissue oath or declaration is filed but the assignee consent is not included, a surcharge will still be applied until the consent is filed, as the reissue oath or declaration is considered defective. The consent of the assignee must be signed by a party authorized to act on behalf of the assignee. If the written consent of all the assignees cannot be obtained, the applicant may petition the Director for waiver of the requirement to permit the acceptance of the filing of the reissue application.

For continuation reissue applications, a copy of the consent from the parent reissue application can only be accepted by the Office if the parent reissue application is or will be abandoned. For divisional reissue applications, a copy of the consent from the parent reissue application cannot be accepted as it does not indicate that the assignee has consented to the addition of the new invention of the divisional reissue application to the original patent. However, if the divisional reissue application is filed in response to a restriction requirement made in the parent reissue application, consent is deemed to have already been provided in the parent reissue application (USPTO, Best Practice in Reissue Part II, 2010).

Amendments to Reissue Application

Amendments may be made at the time of filing of a reissue application. The amendments may be either by:

- physically incorporating the changes within the specification by cutting the column of the printed patent, inserting the added material, rejoining the remainder of the column, and then rejoining the resulting modified column to the other column of the printed patent. The columnar structure of the printed patent must be preserved; or
- providing a preliminary amendment paper directing that specified changes be made to the copy of the printed patent.

Amendment to the Claims

Any claim amendment relative to the patent being reissued must be made upon filing of the reissue application and must be shown using the following markings:

- matter to be omitted by reissue must be enclosed in brackets; and
- matter to be added by reissue must be underlined (except for amendments submitted on compact disc, which must be annotated with "<U>" preceding and "</U>" at the end).

When amending reissue claims, markings should be in comparison to the existing patent claims each time there is an amendment. Marking from the previous amendment should not be used. Any amendment paper must include the entire text of each claim being amended and each claim being added. For any claim changed by the amendment paper, a parenthetical expression "amended" or "twice amended" should follow the claim number, as shown in the following example of an amended reissue claim.

Example Reissue Claim Amendments:

1. (Original) A composition comprising acetylsalicylic acid, 95% ethanol, and distilled water.

1. (Amended) A composition [comprising] consisting essentially of acetylsalicylic acid, 95% ethanol, and distilled water.

1. (Twice Amended) A composition [comprising] consisting essentially of acetylsalicylic acid, 95% ethanol, and [distilled] water.

The text of any "new" or "new amended" claims should be presented with complete underlining (USPTO, Best Practice in Reissue Part II, 2010).

Amendment to the Specification

Any changes to the specification must be made by submission of the entire text of an added or rewritten paragraph, including markings. An entire paragraph may be deleted by a directive statement identifying and deleting the paragraph without presentation of the text of the paragraph. The precise point in the specification where any added or rewritten paragraph is located must be identified.

Amendment to the Drawings

Any changes to the drawings must be submitted as a replacement sheet of drawings attached to the amendment document. Any replacement sheet of drawings must include all of the figures appearing on the original version of the sheet, even if only one figure is amended. Amended figures must be identified as "amended" and any added figure must be identified as "new." If a figure is to be canceled, the figure must be surrounded by brackets and identified as "canceled." All changes to the drawings must be explained in the amendment to drawings section of the accompanying amendment. A marked-up copy of the amended drawing figure, including annotations indicating the changes made, may be included. The marked-up copy must be clearly labeled as "annotated marked-up drawings" and the annotations must be explained in the accompanying amendment. A marked-up copy of any amended drawing figure, including annotations indicating the changes made, must be provided when required by the examiner (USPTO, Best Practice in Reissue Part II, 2010).

Amendments in Reissue of a Reissue Application

If additional amendments are being made in subsequent reissue of a reissued patent, double underlining and double bracketing should be used to show changes. When a copy of a first reissue patent is used as the specification of a second reissue application, additions made by the first reissue will already be printed in italics and should remain in such format. The applicant should present additions to the specification or claims in the second reissue application as double-underlined text. Subject matter to be deleted from the first reissue patent should be presented in the second reissue application within double brackets (USPTO, Best Practice in Reissue Part II, 2010).

Sequence Listing Compliance

Sequence listing identification data does not transfer from the original patent to the reissue application. To comply with sequence listing requirements in a reissue application, the applicant must file a new sequence listing with a new CRF and paper copy. A statement that the CRF copy and the paper copy are the same must be included. No paper copy of the sequence listing is required if filing through EFS-Web. Compliance may also be accomplished by the less-preferred process of requesting transfer of the sequence listing from the patented file with a paper copy plus a statement accompanying the transfer request.

Proof of Ownership by Assignee

The assignee that consents to the filing of the reissue application must also establish that they are the owner of the patent. The assignee must establish their ownership by:

- filing in the reissue application documentary evidence of a chain of title from the original owner to the assignee; or
- specifying in the record of the reissue application where such evidence is recorded by indicating the reel and frame number assigned by the Assignment Division.

If an assignment document is attached with the statement under 37 C.F.R. §3.73(b), the assignment should be reviewed to ensure that the named assignee is the same for the assignment document and the statement and that the assignment document is an assignment of the patent to be reissued to the assignee. If the assignment document is not attached with the statement, but rather the reel and frame numbers where the assignment document is recorded is referenced in the statement, the assignment recorded must support the statement identifying the assignee. If there are multiple assignees, each assignee must file a statement under 37 C.F.R. §3.73(b), establishing ownership. In such cases, each assignee should indicate their percentage ownership to the title.

Broadening Reissue Applications

Broadening reissue applications are given statutory support under 35 U.S.C. §251, paragraph four. Any reissue application that has an unequivocal intent to broaden claims must be filed within two years of the issue of the parent patent. Failure to file within two years of the original patent issue date will result in a bar to obtaining a broadening reissue. In addition, broadening reissue applications are subject to recapture, new matter, and restriction-election bars. Any claim that enlarges the scope of each and every claim of the original patent is a broadening reissue claim. A reissue claim enlarges the scope of the patented claims if it is broader in at least one respect, even though it may be narrower in other respects. To determine if there is enlargement in scope, the reissue claims should be compared to the broadest patented claims. In addition, an infringement test can be applied, which stipulates that a claim is broadened if the patent owner would be able to sue any party for infringement who previously could not have been sued for infringement. As a general rule, broadening the scope of patented dependent claims is not considered broadening when a dependent claim is broadened but the independent claim on which it is based is not broadened. Of course, the reissue claims must be for the same invention as that disclosed as being the invention in the original patent; no new matter is permitted. In contrast, adding a new category of invention in a reissue application is generally deemed as broadening. For example, adding process claims as a new category of invention to be claimed in the patent, where no method claims were presented in the original patent, would generally be considered a broadening of the invention (USPTO, Broadening Reissues, 2010).

Continuing Reissue Applications

The filing of any continuing (continuation or divisional) reissue application that does not replace the parent reissue application must include an oath or declaration that identifies at least one error in the original patent that was not corrected by the parent reissue application or an earlier-filed reissue application. There must be a clear identification on filing that the application is a continuation reissue application, as opposed to a continuation of a reissue application. Filing a continuing reissue application does not permit an applicant to file broadening reissue claims if the original two-year statutory period for filing a broadening reissue application has elapsed.

Processing of Reissue Applications

Reissue applications are processed with special dispatch, meaning that they are to be taken up for examination in advance of other applications and remain special even if the applicant does not respond. All reissue applications, except those under suspension because of litigation, are taken up for action ahead of other special applications, and reissue applications involved in litigation will be taken up for action in advance of other reissue applications. Reissue applicants must notify the USPTO of any prior or concurrent proceedings in which the requested patent for reissue is or was involved, such as interferences, reissues, reexaminations, or litigations and the results of such proceedings. The duty of notification is continuing and exists from the time the reissue application is filed until the reissue application is abandoned or issues as a reissue patent.

Protest in Reissue Applications

Generally, a reissue application will not be acted on sooner than two months after announcement of the filing of the reissue has appeared in the Official Gazette. The two-month delay period is provided to allow members of the public time to review the reissue application and submit pertinent information to the USPTO before the examiner's action. The pertinent information is submitted in the form of a protest under 37 C.F.R. §1.291(a). A protest may be filed throughout the pendency of a reissue application up to the mailing date of the notice of allowance, subject to the timing constraints of the examination. Given that reissue applications are post-issuance proceedings, protest after publication of the reissue application is permitted. A protest of the reissue application should be filed within two months of the announcement of the filing of the reissue application. If the protest of the reissue application cannot be filed within the two-month period, the protest can be submitted at a later time; no petition is required unless a final rejection has been issued or prosecution on the merits has been closed for the reissue application. If the protest of the reissue application cannot be filed within the two-month delay period, the protestor can petition to request an extension of the two-month period following the announcement date and a delay in the examination until the extended period expires. A petition under 37 C.F.R. §1.182 will only be considered if it is filed before expiration of the two-month delay period and accompanied by the petition fee. The petition must explain why additional time is necessary and the nature of the protest intended. A copy of the petition must be served on the applicant for reissue. Protestors to reissue application cannot automatically assume that the two-month delay period will be available in circumstances involving related or concurrent litigation.

Recapture Rules

A patentee cannot use a reissue application to recapture subject matter that was surrendered in the original prosecution in an effort to obtain allowance of the originally filed claims. The Federal Circuit has set out a three-step process for determining whether scope has been impermissibly recaptured:

- consider whether aspects of the pending reissue claims are broader than the patented claims;
- consider whether the broader aspects relate to material that was surrendered in order to overcome a prior art rejection; and
- determine whether a substantial portion of surrendered material "has crept into the reissue claim."

The key is to look whether the reissue claims cover embodiments that were not covered by the issued claims but that were covered by the originally filed claims. The impermissible recapture rule is not strict—some small amount of recapture is allowed. The Court has ruled, for instance, that attempting to recapture a portion of previously surrendered scope is permissible if the reissue "materially narrows" the claims relative to the originally filed claims in a way that relates to the subject matter surrendered. According to the Court, a narrowed limitation may be "modified...so long as it continues to materially narrow the claim scope relative to the surrendered subject matter such that the surrendered subject matter is not entirely or substantially recaptured." However, entirely eliminating a previously added limitation will always trigger the recapture rule prohibition (Crouch, Impermissible Recapture Rule Curtails Potential for Broadening Reissue, 2011). If the examiner issues a recapture rejection, the applicant can submit a rebuttal by demonstrating that a claim rejected for recapture includes one of more claim limitations that "materially narrow" the reissue claims. A limitation is said to "materially narrow" the reissue claims if the narrowing limitation is directed to one or more "overlooked aspects" of the invention.

Limitations of Reissue Applications

A major limit on the reissue process is that "[n]o reissued patent shall be granted enlarging the scope of the claims of the original patent unless applied for within two years from the grant of the original patent." The limit on improper broadening of reissues is strict and applies when claims are "broader in any respect." A reissue application cannot be filed solely to review a patent based on new prior art; reexamination is the proper process for such review. Reissue applications cannot be used to present narrower claims where all the original patent claims were retained. The reissue statute is not a cure for all patent prosecution problems or a second chance at prosecution of the original application. A reissue application can only be used to correct an inadvertent accident or mistake. Expired patents are not eligible for reissue. A patent is reissued for the unexpired part of the term of the original patent; failure to pay maintenance fees may result in the termination of the reissued patent. Subject matter surrendered to obtain the original patent cannot be recaptured by filing a reissue. If the subject matter was surrendered in an effort to obtain allowance of the original patent claims over the prior art, a broadening reissue application cannot recapture the deliberately withdrawn subject matter. Any intention to broaden claims in a reissue application must be filed within two years of the original patent grant date. Finally, if a restriction requirement was made in the application that became the patent and the non-elected claims in the application were not pursued in a divisional application, they cannot be recovered via reissue (USPTO, Reissue Practice 2010).

Access to Reissue Applications

Reissue applications are open to inspection by the general public, and copies of associated papers may be obtained from the USPTO on payment of a fee. The electronic IFW of reissue applications are open to inspection by the general public and are accessible through PAIR. In addition, the filing of reissue applications is announced in the USPTO Official Gazette.

Reissue and Patent Term

The term of a reissued patent is limited by the unexpired term of the original patent. The maximum term of the original patent is fixed at the time the patent is granted. While the term may subsequently be shortened through the filing of a terminal disclaimer, it cannot be extended by the filing of a reissue. As a result, the deletion of benefit claims obtained earlier under 35 U.S.C. §120 in a reissue application will not result in a lengthening of the term of the patent to be reissued.

Effects of Reissue

Reissue applications are examined in the same manner as original applications but with special dispatch. Reissue applications are subject to any and all rejections that the examiner deems appropriate. A prior action in the prosecution of the patent does not prevent a rejection from being made in the reissue application. Claims in a reissue application have no "presumption of validity." Reissue applications may be merged with a reexamination proceeding. A request for continued examination (RCE) is available for a reissue application filed on or after June 8, 1995.

The USPTO views a reissued patent as if the original patent were granted in the amended form provided by the reissue. The original patent remains in effect until a reissue patent is granted. The filing of a reissue application does not alter the schedule of payment of maintenance fees on the original patent. If the maintenance fees have not been paid on the original patent and the patent has expired, no reissue patent can be granted. Maintenance fees are not required for a reissue patent if the original patent that was reissued did not require maintenance fees. If the original patent that was reissued did require maintenance fees, the schedule of payments of maintenance fees on the original patent will continue for the reissue patent. When an original patent reissues, maintenance fees are no longer due in the original patent; they are due in the reissue patent, as the original patent ceases to exist. If there are multiple reissue patents to replace a single original patent, the schedule of maintenance fee payments schedule remains that of the original patent.

If the reissue application is denied or abandoned, the original patent will still be enforceable. However, all reissue examination proceedings are of public record, which means that anybody, including competitors reviewing the prosecution record, will be able to see what happened in the reissue proceeding and if the results were unfavorable. As a result, the patent may be subject to further challenges on the grounds for filing the reissue application. Patent owners should consider reissue applications if they are aware that a competitor is possibly infringing their claims and the patent owner wants to strengthen their case before pursuing litigation. Patent owners may use reissue applications to align the patent claims with their products when the issued claims could have been broader or should be narrower.

Methods for Correcting Clerical or Typographical Errors

There two methods for correcting clerical or typographical errors in an issued patent, namely:

- a letter of correction; or
- a certificate of correction.

Letter of Correction

When errors are of a minor typographical nature or are readily apparent to one skilled in the art, a letter making the error of record can be submitted to the Office in lieu of a request for a certificate of correction. There is no fee for the submission of a letter of correction to the patent file, and it is a more informal method of correcting a minor clerical or typographical error in an issued patent.

Certificate of Correction

A certificate of correction can be used to correct a minor clerical or typographical error or other minor error in an issued patent. Certificates of correction should only be requested for errors of consequence. Certificates of correction may be requested to correct errors made by the Office or errors made by the applicant. Corrections of errors made by the applicant incur a correction fee.

Filing Requirements

An applicant request for a certificate of correction should include the following items:

- a transmittal letter or cover letter that includes bibliographic data identifying: the patent number, the application number, the inventors, the issue date, and the title of the invention;

- a certificate of correction form (SB/44) identifying the location of the error in the printed patent by column and line number or claim and line number (duplicate not required);
- a copy of any document supporting the requested corrections that are not in the Office record or file (e.g., postcard receipts, amendments, SB08 form); and
- no fee is required to correct errors made by the Office; however, if it is an applicant's error, the fee under 37 C.F.R. §1.20(a) must be included.

The transmittal letter or cover letter should be signed by the attorney of record or owner of record and should state any facts supporting the requested corrections. Applicants are urged to submit the text of the correction on a special certificate of correction form (SB/44) that can serve as the camera copy for use in direct offset printing of the certificate of correction. Applicants should not include the original letters patent with their requests for certifications of correction.

Completing the Certificate of Correction Form

The certificate of correction form, as shown in Figure R, is available as a PDF fillable form; the applicant should insert the mailing address of the sender. The completed PDF fillable form and supplemental documentation can be filed via EFS-Web. The certificate of correction form (SB/44) should be completed using the following formatting guidelines:

- Identify the exact point of error by reference to column and line number of the printed patent for changes to the specification or to claim number and line number for changes to the claims.
- Conserve space on the form by typing single space, beginning two lines down from the printed certificate of error statement.
- Start the correction to each separate column as a sentence, and use semicolons to separate corrections within the same column, where possible.
- Leave a two-inch space blank at bottom of the last sheet for the signature of the attesting officer.
- Use quotation marks to enclose the exact subject matter to be deleted or corrected.
- Use double hyphens (––) to enclose subject matter to be added, except for formulas.
- If a formula is being corrected, set out only that portion of the formula to be corrected or, if necessary, paste a photocopy onto the form.

PTO/SB/44 (09-07)
Approved for use through 08/31/2013. OMB 0651-0033
U.S. Patent and Trademark Office; U.S. DEPARTMENT OF COMMERCE
Under the Paperwork Reduction Act of 1995, no persons are required to respond to a collection of information unless it displays a valid OMB control number.
(Also Form PTO-1050)

UNITED STATES PATENT AND TRADEMARK OFFICE
CERTIFICATE OF CORRECTION

Page ____ of ____

PATENT NO. :
APPLICATION NO.:
ISSUE DATE :
INVENTOR(S) :

It is certified that an error appears or errors appear in the above-identified patent and that said Letters Patent is hereby corrected as shown below:

In the drawings, Sheet 3, Fig. 3, the reference numeral 225 should be applied to the plate element attached to the support member 207:

Column 2, line 68 and column 3, lines 3, 8 and 13, for the claim reference numeral "2", each occurrence, should read -1-.

Figure R: Certificate of Correction—PDF Fillable Form

If the certificate of correction is filed via mail, the correspondence should be addressed to:

Commissioner for Patents
Office of Data Management
Attention: Certificates of Correction Branch
P.O. Box 1450
Alexandria, VA 22313-1450

Correcting an Applicant Error

The USPTO will not issue a certificate of correction for a mistake or error made by the patentee unless the following two statutory requirements apply:

- the mistake must be clerical or typographical or a mistake of minor character; and
- the correction must not involve changes that would constitute new matter or require reexamination.

The patentee or the patentee's assignee can request a certificate of correction to correct the minor errors and must pay the non-inventorship correction fee under 37 C.F.R. §1.20(a). If the above criteria are not satisfied, then a certificate of correction for an applicant's mistake will not issue, and reissue must be employed as the vehicle to correct the patent. Generally, any mistake affecting claim scope must be corrected by reissue. A mistake is not considered to be of the minor character if the requested change would materially affect the scope or meaning of the patented invention.

Correcting a USPTO Error

When the prosecution record clearly shows an error in the patent was caused by the USPTO, the Director may issue a certificate of correction stating the fact and nature of the mistake without any associated costs to the patentee. The Director can issue a certificate of correction to correct an error discovered by the Office, in response to a request from the patentee, or when acting on information supplied by a third party. If the nature of the mistake on the part of the Office is such that a certificate of correction is deemed inappropriate in form, the Director may issue a corrected patent instead of a certificate of correction, without expense to the patentee.

Correction of Assignee Information

The patentee or the patentee's assignees can request a certificate of correction be issued to correct the name or address, or both, of the assignee on the cover page of the issued patent if the correct assignee's name and address was provided on the issue fee transmittal. In such cases, the request for correction would be considered the result of an Office error, and no petition or fee would be required.

If the error in the assignee name or address, or both, on the cover of the patent was caused by the applicant, a petition under 37 C.F.R §1.183 and payment of the associated fee must accompany the request for a certificate of correction. The submission should include the following items:

- a petition under 37 C.F.R §1.183;
- the petition fee under 37 C.F.R §1.17(f);
- a request for a certificate of correction to correct applicant's error;
- the certificate of correction fee under 37 C.F.R. §1.20(a);
- the correct name and address of the assignee; and
- the reel and frame number where the assignment is recorded or proof of the date the assignment was submitted for recordation.

Correction of Named Inventor

The Director may issue a certificate of correction to correct an error in a named inventor on an issued patent. The error of omitting inventors, or naming persons who are not inventors, will not invalidate the patent if the error was made without any deceptive intention. In such circumstances, all parties and assignees may request a certificate of correction by providing proof of the pertinent facts.

A petition under 37 C.F.R. §1.324 is the appropriate vehicle to correct inventorship in an issued patent. The submission to correct inventorship in an issued patent must include the following:

- a petition to correct inventorship under 37 C.F.R. §1.324;
- where one or more persons are being added, a statement from each person who is being added as an inventor that the inventorship error occurred without any deceptive intention on his or her part;
- a statement from the current named inventors either agreeing to the change of inventorship or stating that they have no disagreement in regard to the requested change;
- a statement from all assignees of the parties agreeing to the change of inventorship in the patent (including statement under 37 C.F.R. §3.73(b) or reference to a reel and frame number of recorded assignment); and
- the fee under C.F.R. §1.20(b).

If the inventor is not available or refuses to submit a statement, the assignee of the patent can consider filing a reissue application to correct inventorship, as an inventor's statement is not required for a non-broadening reissue application. The statutory basis for correction of inventorship in an issued patent is stricter than the requirements to correct inventorship in a pending application. Correction of inventorship in an issued patent requires petition by all of the parties and assignees, and such requirement cannot be waived. Each party must make a statement that the error occurred without deceptive intention, and all parties must be in agreement on the correction to inventorship (see Chapter 6 for more details on correction inventorship in pending applications).

Correction of Priority Benefit Claim

For applications filed before November 29, 2009, a certificate of correction can be used to correct a priority claim under 35 U.S.C. §120 and §119(e) when the patentee failed to make reference to a prior copending application or when an incorrect reference to a prior copending application was made. In general, a certificate of correction can only be used to correct a priority benefit claim if all requirements to perfect the benefit claim have been completed in the application that became the patent, and it must be clear from the record of the patent and the parent application that claim to priority benefit is entitled. If the correction requested involves a foreign priority claim, the patentee must submit with the request copies of documentation showing designation of states or any other information needed to make it clear from the record that priority benefit is entitled.

For applications filed on or after November 29, 2009, a certificate for correction cannot be used to correct an applicant's mistake by adding or correcting a priority claim under 35 U.S.C. §119(e) in the issued patent. Under certain conditions, a certificate of correction can still be used to add or correct a priority claim under 35 U.S.C. §120.

Where priority is claimed under 35 U.S.C. §120 to a national application, the following conditions must be met:

- all requirements to perfect the claim to priority must have been completed in the application that became the patent to be corrected;
- it must be clear from the record of the patent and the parent application that priority is appropriate; and
- a grantable petition to accept an unintentionally delayed claim for benefit of a prior application must be filed, including payment of a surcharge under 37 C.F.R. 1.17(t).

Where the priority is claimed under 35 U.S.C. §120 to an international application, the following conditions must be met:

- all requirements to perfect the claim to priority must have been completed in the application that became the patent to be corrected;
- it must be clear from the record of the patent and the parent application that priority is appropriate;
- the patentee must submit with the certificate of correction copies of documentation showing designation of states and any other information needed to make it clear from the record that the priority claim is appropriate; and

- a grantable petition to accept an unintentionally delayed claim for benefit of a prior application must be filed, including payment of the surcharge under 37 C.F.R. 1.17(t).

If any of the above identified conditions are not met then a certificate of correction cannot be used to correct reference to a copending application or to correct an incorrect reference to a copending application. In such situations, the only viable option to correct the priority benefit claim would be to file a reissue application.

Third-Party Information on Mistakes in Patent

Third parties can provide information to the USPTO on mistakes or errors in a patent but cannot demand the Office act on, respond to, issue, or refuse to issue a certificate of correction. The USPTO may issue a certificate of correction based on third party information in the interest of ensuring the public has correction information on a patented invention. There is no fee for submission of information supplied by a third party, but regardless of whether the third party information is acted upon, the information will not be made of record or retained in the related patent file. The Office will not correspond with third parties about information submitted and will not inform the third party if it intends to issue or deny a certificate of correction. The Office will confirm to the third-party submitter that it received the information only if the submitter includes a stamped, self-addressed return postcard.

Issuance of Certificates of Correction

Where only a part of a request can be approved, or where the USPTO discovers and includes additional corrections, the Office makes the appropriate alterations on the SB/44 form. The patentee is notified of the changes on the Notification of Approval-in-Part form PTOL-404. The certificate of correction is issued in approximately six weeks. Any interim status inquiries should be directed to the Certificates of Correction Branch.

When a certificate of correction is issued, a copy of it will be attached to each paper and digital copy of the patent and will be effectively considered as part of the original patent. Patents with attached certificates of correction have the same effect and operation in law as if they had originally issued in such a corrected form.

Electronic Publication of Certificates of Correction

Effective August 2011, the USPTO publishes on the Office website a listing by patent number of the patents for which certificates of correction are being issued. As the publication process for certificates of correction becomes more automated, certificates will publish more promptly. Electronic publication on the Office website will occur approximately three weeks prior to publication in the Official Gazette. The listing of certificates of correction in the Official Gazette will include the certificate's date of issuance. On the date on which the listing of certificates of correction is electronically published on the USPTO website, the following actions will be taken:

- the certificate of correction will be entered into the file wrapper of a paper-file patent or entered into the file history of an IFW-file patent and will be available to the public;
- a printed copy of the certificate of correction will be mailed to the patentee or the patent's assignee; and
- an image of the printed certificate of correction will be added to the digital image of the patent on the patent database.

The date on which the USPTO adds the certificate of correction to the digital IFW or paper-file history will be regarded as the date of issuance of the certificate of correction, not the date of the certificate of correction appearing in the Official Gazette.

Denial of Certificate of Correction

The USPTO has discretion to decline to issue a certificate of correction even though an Office mistake exists. If the USPTO mistakes are of such a nature that the meaning intended is obvious from the context, the Office may decline to issue a certificate and merely place the correspondence in the patented file for future reference. The USPTO can decline to issue a certificate of correction even when correction is requested by the patentee or patentee's assignee.

If the Office declines a request for a certificate of correction, the requester is notified and given a reason for the decision. A copy of the denial communication papers are retained in the physical file history or in the digital IFW.

CHAPTER-SPECIFIC REFERENCE MATERIAL

Reference Source	Correction of Patents Applicable Rules, Regulations, and Procedures
Title 35 of the U.S. Code	35 U.S.C. §251 Reissue of defective patents. §252 Effect of reissue. §253 Disclaimer. §254 Certificate of correction of Patent and Trademark Office mistake. §255 Certificate of correction of applicant's mistake. §256 Correction of named inventor.
Title 37 of the Code of Federal Regulations	37 C.F.R. Reissue §1.171 Application for reissue. §1.172 Applicants, assignees. §1.173 Reissue specification, drawings, and amendments. §1.175 Reissue oath or declaration. §1.176 Examination of reissue. §1.177 Issuance of multiple reissue patents. §1.178 Original patent; continuing duty of applicant. Correction of Errors in Patent §1.322 Certificate of correction of Office mistake. §1.323 Certificate of correction of applicant's mistake. §1.324 Correction of inventorship in patent, pursuant to 35 U.S.C. 256. §1.325 Other mistakes not corrected.
Manual of Patent Examination Procedures (MPEP, 8th Edition)	Chapter 1400 Correction of Patents

Chapter 20

Post-Issuance Citation of Prior Art and *Ex Parte* Reexamination Proceedings

AIA Impact—Post-Issuance Citation of Prior Art to a Patent File

Prior art in the form of patents or printed publications may be cited to the USPTO for placement into the patent file after issuance of a patent. Citations may be made without paying a fee and may be submitted without having to request reexamination of the issued patent. The purpose of post-issuance citation of prior art to a patent file is to inform the patent owner and the public that such patents or printed publications exist and should be considered when evaluating the validity of the patent claims. Citation of prior art to a patent file, which includes copies of the cited prior art, will also ensure consideration of the prior art during any subsequent reissue or reexamination proceeding.

Who May Cite Prior Art?

The patent owner, or any member of the public, may submit prior art citations of patent or printed publications to the USPTO at any time. A person citing prior art to a patent file may be a corporate or governmental entity as well as an individual. A person also includes patentees, licensees, reexamination requesters, real parties in interest to the patent owner or requester, persons without a real interest, and persons acting for real parties in interest without a need to identify the real party of interest. The person citing the prior art does not have to reveal their identity if they wish it to be kept confidential. In such circumstances, the person submitting the prior art should make a written request to have his or her identity excluded from the patent file and kept confidential. The USPTO will attempt to exclude any such written request from the public files, although complete assurance of exclusion during clerical processing cannot be given. As a result, the USPTO advises persons citing prior art who wish to remain confidential to not identify themselves anywhere in the papers submitted. Confidential citations should include at least an unsigned statement indication that the patent owner has been sent a copy of the citation papers. In the event that is it not possible to serve a copy on the patent owner, a duplicate copy should accompany the prior art citation when the original is filed with the USPTO.

Time for Filing Prior Art Citations

Citations of prior art may be filed at any time during the period of enforceability of a patent. The period of enforceability of a patent is the length of term of the patent plus the six years under the statute of limitations for bringing an infringement action. If litigation is instituted within the period of the statute of limitations, citations may be submitted after the statute of limitations has expired, as long as the patent is still enforceable. While the citations of prior art may be filed at any time during the period of enforceability of the patent, citations submitted after the date of any order for reexamination will not be entered into the patent file until the pending reexamination proceeding has been concluded, unless the citations are being submitted by:

- the patent owner;
- an *ex parte* reexamination requester who also submits the fee and other documents required under 37 C.F.R. §1.510;
- a pre-AIA *inter partes* reexamination requester who has submitted the fee and other documents required under 37 C.F.R. §1.915;
- an *ex parte* third-party requester's reply under 37 C.F.R. §1.535; or
- as an enterable submission under 37 C.F.R. §1.948 in a pre-AIA *inter partes* reexamination proceeding.

To ensure that prior art cited by a third party is considered without payment of another reexamination fee, it must be presented before reexamination is ordered. The purpose of this rule is to prevent harassment of the patent owner due to frequent submissions of prior art citations during reexamination proceedings.

Content of Prior Art Citations

The post-issuance prior art that may be submitted is limited to "written prior art consisting of patents or printed publications." The person submitting the prior art must provide an explanation and a broad statement of how the prior art is pertinent and applicable to the patent, as well as an explanation of why it is believed that the prior art has a bearing on the patentability of any claim of the patent. The explanation of why the prior art is believed to have a bearing on the claims could be met by a statement that the art submitted in the prior art citation was made of record in a foreign or domestic application having the same or related invention to that of the patent. The explanation of the pertinence of the prior art for a least one of the claims should include how each item cited shows or teaches at least one limitation of the claim. Citation of prior art by patent owners may include an explanation of how the claims of the patent differ from the prior art cited. It is preferred that copies of all the cited prior art patents and printed publications, and any necessary English translations, be included so that the applicability and pertinence may be readily determined by persons inspecting the patent file and by the examiner during any subsequent reissue or reexamination proceeding.

All prior art citations submitted should identify the patent in which the citation is to be placed by the patent number, issue date, and patentee. A cover sheet with an identification of the patent should be firmly attached to all the other documents relating to the citation so that the documents will not become separated during processing. Each document submitted should have a cover page identifying the patent it is being cited against.

A prior art citation submission under 37 C.F.R. §1.501 is limited to the citation of patents and printed publications and an explanation of the pertinency and applicability of the patents and publication to the issued claims. The prior art citations cannot include any issue that is not directed to patents and printed publications. A prior art citation cannot be directed to what the patent owner did or failed to do with respect to submitting or describing patents and printed publications, as these would be statements directed at the conduct of the patent owner. The citation should not contain argument or discussion of references previously treated in the prosecution of the invention that matured into the patent or references previously treated in a reexamination proceeding. If the prior art citation contains any issues not directed to patents and printed publications, it is not considered a compliant submission under 37 C.F.R. §1.501. Any submission deemed not compliant with requirements will not be entered into the patent file and will be returned to the sender.

Affidavits or Declarations

Affidavits or declarations or other written evidence relating to the submitted prior art documents may accompany the citation to explain the contents or pertinent dates in more detail. A patent owner can file an affidavit of commercial success or other evidence of non-obviousness or an affidavit that questions the enablement of the teaching of the cited prior art with post-issuance prior art citations.

Service Requirements

All prior art citations filed by persons other than the patent owner must either indicate that a copy of the citation was mailed to, or otherwise served on, the patent owner at the most recent address of the attorney or agent of record. If service on the patent owner is not possible, a duplicate copy of the citation must be filed with the USPTO along with an explanation (including proof of attempts to serve) as to why the service was not possible.

Processing of Prior Art Citations

Prior art citations received by the USPTO are forwarded to the technology center that currently examines the class and subclass of invention to which the patent pertains. It is the responsibility of the technology center to immediately determine whether a citation meets the requirements of the statute and rules and to enter it into the patent file at the appropriate time if it is a compliant submission under 37 C.F.R. §1.501.

Citations that Qualifies for Entry

If the citation is proper and limited to patents and printed publications and is filed prior to an order in a reexamination proceeding, it is immediately entered into the reexamination file. If no reexamination is pending for the patent, the citation is placed in the patent file. If the citation includes an indication of service on the patent owner, the citation is timely entered and no notice of entry is sent to any party. If the citation does not include an indication of service, the patent owner will be notified that a citation of prior art has been entered into the patent file. If a duplicate copy of the citation was filed, the duplicate copy will be sent to the patent owner with the notification. If no duplicate copy is present, no copy will be sent with the notification. The notification sent to the patent owner will indicate if the citation has been placed in the patent file or in the reexamination file. The notification will also indicate if the third-party who submitted the prior art citation was identified or if their identity is confidential.

If the prior art citation is filed after reexamination has been ordered, the citation is not entered and is stored until the conclusion of the reexamination proceeding; then the citation is entered into the patent file. The patent owner and the submitter (if known) will be notified. This notification enables the patent owner to consider submitting the prior art under 37 C.F.R. §1.555 or 37 C.F.R. §1.933 during reexamination. The notification also enables the third-party submitter to consider the desirability of filing a separate request for reexamination. If the citation does not include service on the patent owner, and a duplicate copy is submitted, the duplicate copy will be sent to the patent owner with the notification. If a duplicate copy is not present, no copy of the citation will be included with the notification to the patent owner. In such situations, the original copy held in storage will be made available for copying by the patent owner. If the citation includes service of a copy on the patent owner, the citation is placed in storage and not entered until the reexamination is concluded. The patent owner and third-party submitter (if known) will be notified of the storage action taken. If a proper citation is filed by the patent owner, it is entered into the file irrespective of whether the citation was filed prior to or after an order for reexamination has been mailed. The processing steps for post-issuance prior art citations that qualify for entry are summarized in Figure S.

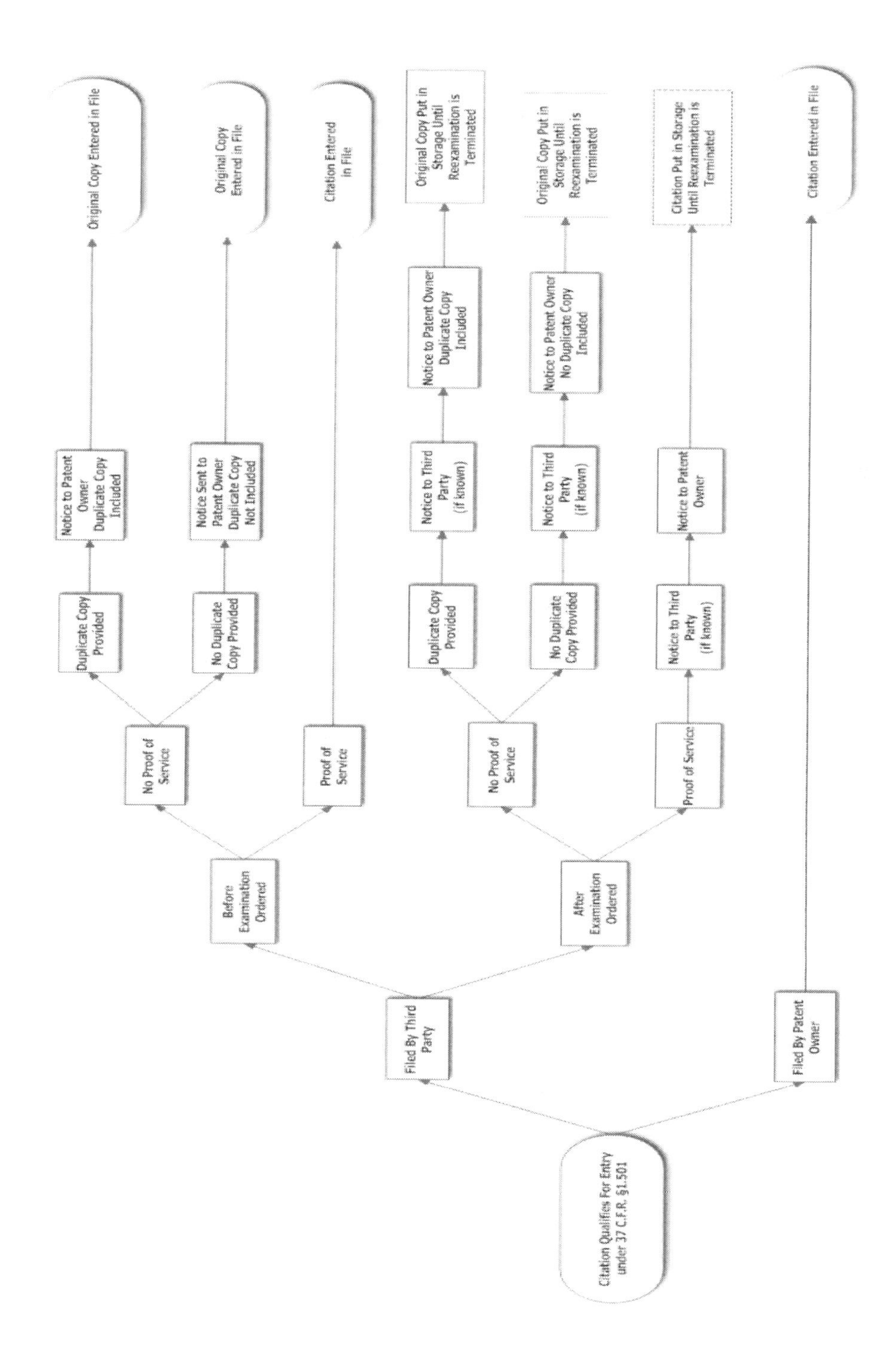

Figure S: Processing of Post-Issuance Citations that Qualify for Entry in Patent File

Citations That Do Not Qualify for Entry

If the citation is not proper (not limited to patents or printed publications or fails to include the requisite citation descriptions), it will not be entered in the patent file. The submitter (if known) and the patent owner (in all cases) will be notified that the citation is improper and that it has not been entered in the patent file. If the citation includes a service copy on the patent owner and the identity of the third party is known, the original citation paper will be returned to the third-party sender, along with the notification of non-entry. If the identity of the third party is not known, the original citation papers will be discarded. If the citation does not include an indication of service on the patent owner, the identity of the third party is known, and a duplicate copy of the citation is present, the original citation papers will be returned to the third party and the duplicate copy will be sent to the patent owner along with the notification of non-entry. If the duplicate copy is not present, the original citation papers are sent to the patent owner along with the notification of non-entry. The third-party submitter is sent a notification that the citation was not entered and that the original papers were sent to the patent owner.

If a service copy is not included and the identity of the third party is not known, and a duplicate copy of the citation is or is not present, the duplicate copy (if present) will be discarded and the original citation papers will be sent to the patent owner along with the notification of non-entry. If the patent owner files an improper prior art citation prior to an order for reexamination, the citation will not be entered in the patent file. The patent owner will be notified of non-entry, and the citation papers will be returned to the patent owner with the notification.

Entry of Court Decisions in a Patent File

The Solicitor's Office processes notices received from the clerks of the various U.S. courts and ensures they are entered in a patent file. It is desirable that the entire court decision be supplied to the USPTO for entry into the patent file. Accordingly, the USPTO will accept, at any time, from any party, submission of the following in a patent file:

- copies of notices of suit;
- copies of notices regarding other proceedings involving the patent and copies of decisions from litigations or other proceedings involving the patent; and

- other Court papers, or papers filed in a Court, from litigations or other proceedings involving the patent (including final court decisions, even if appealable, decisions to vacate, decisions to remand, and decisions as to the merits of the patent claims).

Non-merit decisions on motions will not be entered in the patent file and will be expunged from the patent file if they were entered before discovery of their nature. Paper related to a party's argument, such as a memorandum in support of summary judgment, will not be entered in a patent file and should be submitted in a reexamination proceeding. It is not required to submit copies of copending reexamination proceedings or applications; it is sufficient that submitters provide a notice identifying the application proceeding number and its status. Any submission that is not permitted to be entered in the patent file will be returned, expunged, or discarded at the discretion of the USPTO. The Office can deem the volume of papers filed from a litigation or other proceeding as being too extensive and lengthy. In such situations, the USPTO may return all or part of the submission, and the submitter may resubmit the relevant sections of the papers. Persons making such submissions must limit the submission to the notification and not include further arguments or information.

Any proper submission will be placed in the patent file by the files repository personnel unless a reexamination proceeding is pending, in which case the central reexamination unit enters the submission. Any submission of papers from a foreign jurisdiction (outside the United States) will be returned, expunged, or discarded at the discretion of the USPTO.

Post-Issuance Citation Under the America Invents Act

Effective September 16, 2012, the AIA expanded the scope of information that any party may cite in a patent file to include written statements made by a patent owner before a Federal Court or the USPTO regarding the scope of any claim of the patent, and it provides for how such information may be considered in *ex parte* reexamination, *inter partes* review, and post-grant review.

AIA Impact—Patent Owner Claim Scope Statements

The patent owner claim scope statement must have been filed in the court or Office proceeding by the patent owner. In addition, the statement may have originated outside of the court or Office proceeding in which it was filed.

Claim scope statements of the patent owner filed under 35 U.S.C. §301(a)(2) and §1.501(a)(2) must be accompanied by other documents, pleadings, or evidence from the proceeding in which the statement was filed that address the statement. The statement and accompanying information must be submitted in redacted form to exclude information subject to an applicable protective order. The party submitting a patent owner claim scope statement should provide the following information to assist the Office in identifying the proceeding:

- the forum in which the statement was made (the specific Federal court or the Office);
- the Federal court or Office proceeding designation (case citation or numerical designation);
- the status of the proceeding;
- the relationship of the proceeding to the patent in which the submission is being made;
- an identification of the specific papers of the proceeding containing the statement of the patent owner; and
- an identification of the portions of the papers relevant to the written statement being asserted to constitute a statement of the patent owner under 35 U.S.C. 301(a)(2).

Any patent owner statement regarding the scope of any claim of a particular patent made outside of a Federal court or Office proceeding is not eligible for submission even though it may be later entered into a Federal Court or USPTO proceeding by a party other than the patent owner. The submission under §1.501(b)(1) requires an explanation as to how the information in the submission is pertinent to the claims of the patent and how it is applied to each of those claims. In some instances, a combination of prior art and written statements may be cited, while in other situations only prior art or written statements may be cited. In either situation, an explanation as to how the cited information applies to those specific claims must be included with the submission of patent owner statements under 35 U.S.C. 301(a)(2). The third-party submitter can exclude their identify from the patent filing the submission anonymously. The submission must reflect that a copy has been served upon the patent owner at the correspondence address of record in the patent. If service upon the patent owner is unsuccessful, the submission must include proof of a bona fide attempt to serve. A submission will not be entered into the patent IFW if it does not include either proof of service or a bona fide attempt to serve.

Under §1.501(b)(2), a patent owner submitter is authorized to include an explanation of how the claims differ from the prior art submitted. Entry of a proper submission to the patent file that is made after the date of an order for reexamination will be delayed until the reexamination proceeding has been concluded, to prevent harassment of the patent owner by frequent submission of prior art made during a reexamination proceeding conducted with special dispatch.

The AIA provision limits the Office's use of such written statements to determining the meaning of a patent claim in *ex parte* reexamination proceedings that have already been ordered and in *inter partes* review and post-grant review proceedings that have been instituted. The AIA also provides for an estoppel that may attach to *ex parte* reexamination based on an *inter partes* review or post-grant review proceeding.

Ex Parte Reexamination

The validity of a granted patent may be challenged at any time through the filing of a request for *ex parte* reexamination. An *ex parte* reexamination proceeding is initiated by the filing of a petition, with the petitioner citing "a substantial new question" of patentability in the form of prior art patents or printed publications. Reexaminations proceedings are required by statute to be handled with "special dispatch" and are processed by the Central Reexamination Unit (CRU). The CRU gives high priority to reexaminations of patents involved in litigation. Even higher priority is afforded when trial proceedings have been stayed pending the outcome of reexamination. The highest priority is assigned to reexaminations that have been pending for at least two years. The CRU thus assigns priority based on its own statistics and research and based on patent owner notifications. Therefore, it is critical for the patent owner to keep the Office informed of the existence and status of related copending district court or litigation proceedings (Sterne, Kessler, Goldstein & Fox PLLC, 2008).

Attributes of Ex Parte Reexamination

The basic attributes of a *ex parte* reexamination are as follows:

- anyone can request reexamination at any time during the period of enforceability of the patent;

- prior art considered during reexamination is limited to prior art patents or printed publications applied under 35 U.S.C. §102 (novelty) and §103 (obviousness);
- a substantial new question of patentability must be present for reexamination to be ordered;
- if ordered, the actual reexamination proceeding is *ex parte* in nature;
- a decision on the request for reexamination must be made statutorily with three months of the request filing date, and the remainder of the proceeding is conducted with special dispatch;
- if ordered, a reexamination proceeding will normally be conducted to its conclusion, and a reexamination certificate will be issued;
- the scope of a claim cannot be enlarged by amendment;
- all reexamination files are open to the public; and
- the reexamination file is scanned into the IFW to provide an electronic copy of the file. All public access to and copying of the reexamination file must be made from the electronic copy available through PAIR. Any remaining paper files are not available to the public.

Content of the Request

Any person, at any time during the period of enforceability of a patent, may file a request for *ex parte* reexamination of any claim of the patent based on prior art patents or printed publications. Any request for reexamination must include the following parts:

- a request for *ex parte* reexamination transmittal form SB/57;
- a statement pointing out each substantial new question of patentability based on prior patents and printed publications;
- an identification of every claim for which reexamination is requested and a detailed explanation of the pertinency and manner of applying the cited prior art to every claim for which reexamination is requested. If appropriate, the party requesting reexamination may also point out how claims distinguish over cited prior art;
- a copy of every patent or printed publication relied upon or referred to, accompanied by an English translation of all the necessary and pertinent parts of any non-English language patent or printed publication;
- a copy of the entire patent, including the front face, drawings, specification, and claims, in double-column format for which reexamination is requested, and a copy

of any disclaimer, certificate of correction, or reexamination certificate issued in the patent. All copies must have each page plainly written on only one side of a sheet of paper;

- a certification that a copy of the request filed by a person other than the patent owner has been served in its entirety on the patent owner at the address of his or her attorney or agent of record. The name and address of the party served must be indicated. If service on the patent owner was not possible, a duplicate copy of the request for reexamination must be supplied to the USPTO; and
- the fee under 37 C.F.R. §1.20(c)(1).

If a reexamination request filed by the patent owner includes a proposed amendment under 37 C.F.R. §1.530, excess claims fees may apply. No attempt will be made to maintain a requester's name in confidence. After the request for reexamination is received in the Office, no abandonment, withdrawal, or striking of the request is possible, regardless of what party requests it. In some limited circumstances, such as after a final court decision where all of the claims are finally held invalid, a reexamination order may be vacated.

Fees

In order for the request to be accepted, given a filing date, and published in the Official Gazette, the request papers must satisfy all filing requirements. The entire fee required under 37 C.F.R. §1.510(c)(1) for filing a request for reexamination must be paid. If the request was filed by the patent owner and includes proposed amendments that require excess claim fees, such fees must be paid on filing the request. Fees for extension of time under 37 C.F.R. §1.550(c) and appeal brief and oral hearing fees under 37 C.F.R. §41.20(b) will also apply. There is no fee for issue of the reexamination certificate.

If the request for *ex parte* reexamination is subsequently denied or vacated, a refund will be made to the identified requester. If the request for *ex parte* reexamination is found to be incomplete and the defect is not cured, a refund will be made to the identified requester. If the entire fee for the *ex parte* reexamination is not paid or all the filing requirements are not met, the request will be considered to be incomplete. If the entire filing fee is not paid after the requester has been given an opportunity to do so, no determination on the request will be made. The request papers will be placed in the patent file as a prior art citation, if they comply with the requirements for a citation of prior art under 37 C.F.R. §1.510.

Filing Methods

All requests for *ex parte* reexamination and all subsequent *ex parte* reexamination correspondence should be addressed to:

Mail Stop *Ex Parte* Reexam
Attn: Central Reexamination Unit
Commissioner for Patents
P.O. Box 1450
Alexandria, VA 22313-1450

The mail stop information should be placed in a prominent position on the first page of each paper being filed. Certificate of mailing procedures for U.S. first-class mail and Express Mail do apply and may be used to file any *ex parte* reexamination proceeding, except for a request for reexamination and a corrected replacement request for reexamination. Requests for *ex parte* reexamination cannot be filed by facsimile. Requests for reexamination and follow-on papers can be electronically filed via EFS-Web. When a reexamination proceeding has been granted, it is assigned a reexamination control number. Any subsequently filed documents should be identified using the reexamination control number, the art unit, and the name of the examiner.

Untimely Paper Filed Prior to Order

After filing the request for *ex parte* reexamination, no papers directed to the merits of reexamination other than citations of patents and printed publications, another complete request, or notifications should be filed with the USPTO prior to the date of decision on the request.

Incomplete Request

Any failure to provide the required explanation for any document, combination, or claim will be identified in a Notice of Failure to Comply with *Ex Parte* Reexamination Request Filing Requirements. The requester has the option to respond by either:

- providing a separate explanation for each combination, document, and claim identified in the notice as lacking explanation; or
- explicitly withdrawing any document, combination, or claim for which reexamination was requested for which there is no explanation.

Irrespective of the option decided, the requester does not have to provide any further explanation for any withdrawn document, combination, or claim.

Conduct of the Proceeding

The reexamination statute and rules permit any person to file a request for an *ex parte* reexamination containing certain elements and the fee required under 37 C.F.R. §1.20(c)(1). The USPTO will intially determine if "a substantial new question of patentability" is presented. If such a new question of patentability is presented, reexamination will be ordered. The patent reexamination proceeding is very similar to regular application examination procedure, with the following notable differences:

- there are certain limitations as to the kind of rejections that may be made;
- special reexamination forms must be used;
- time periods are set to provide "special dispatch;"
- when the prosecution of a reexamination proceeding is terminated, a reexamination certificate is issued that indicates the status of all the claims following reexamination; and
- unless prosecution is reopened by the Director, the reexamination proceeding is concluded by the issuance and publication of a reexamination certificate.

Time Period for Requesting

Reexamination may be requested at any time during the period of enforceability of a patent as set by rule. The USPTO will not expend resources on deciding validity questions in patents that cannot be enforced. The period of enforceability is determined by adding six years to the date on which the patent expires. Given that the expiration date of a patent is determined by any patent term adjustment or extension, payment of all maintenance fees, and the impact of any terminal disclaimers filed, the expiration date should be carefully calculated. If litigation is instituted during the period of the statute of limitations, requests for reexamination may be filed after the statute of limitations has expired, as long as the patent is still enforceable against someone.

Persons Who May File

Any person (third party or patent owner) may file a request for reexamination of a patent. There are no persons excluded from being able to seek reexamination. Corporations and government entities are included within the scope of the term "any person." Some of the persons likely to use reexamination are patentees, licensees, potential licensees, attorneys without identification of their real client in interest, infringers, potential exporters, patent litigants, interference applicants, and International Trade Commission respondents. The name of the person who files the request will not be maintained in confidence.

The patent owner can request reexamination, which will be limited to an *ex parte* consideration of prior art patents or printed publications. If the patent owner wishes to have a wider consideration of issues, including matters such as prior public use or on sale, the patent owner may file a reissue application. Under very limited circumstances, such as a general public policy question, the Director can initiate reexamination where there is no interest by any other person.

Representative of Requester

An attorney or agent may file a request for reexamination for an identified client (the requester), acting under either a power of attorney from the client or acting in a representative capacity. While the filing of a power of attorney is desirable, reexamination proceedings will not be delayed due to its absence. In order to act in a representative capacity, an attorney or agent must include his or her name, signature and registration number. If an attorney or agent files a request for reexamination for another entity (e.g., corporation) that wishes to remain anonymous, then the attorney or agent is the third-party requester. All correspondence for a requester that is not the patent owner is addressed to the representative of the requester, unless a specific indication is made to forward correspondence to another address.

If a request is filed by a person on behalf of the patent owner, correspondence will be directed to the patent owner at the correspondence address of record, regardless of the address of the person filing the request. During a reexamination proceeding, the patent owner must be represented by a registered practitioner to permit signing of amendments and other papers filed during the reexamination proceeding on behalf of the patent owner.

Scope of Reexamination

The scope of the reexamination is limited to reexamination of the claims on the basis of patents or printed publications. Issues related to 35 U.S.C. §112 are addressed only with respect to new claims or amended subject matter in the specification, claims, or drawings. Any new or amended claims are examined to ensure that the scope of the original patent claims is not enlarged or broadened. The issue of double patenting is appropriate for consideration during reexamination if it raises a substantial new question of patentability. During reexamination, claims are given the broadest reasonable interpretation. Restriction requirements cannot be made in a reexamination proceeding. Correction of inventorship may also be made during reexamination, and the reexamination certificate that will ultimately issue will contain the appropriate change of inventorship information.

If questions of patentability based on public use, on sale or abandonment are independently discovered by the reexamination proceeding, but were not raised by the third-party requester or the patent owner, such questions will not be noted by the examiner in an office action.

For reexaminations ordered on or after November 2, 2002, reliance on previously cited or considered art as the sole basis of rejection does not necessarily preclude the existence of a substantial new question of patentability that is based exclusively on the old art. Determinations on whether a substantial new question of patentability exists will be based on a fact-specific inquiry done on a case-by-case basis. The substantial new question of patentability may be based on old art being presented or viewed in a new light or in a different way as compared with its use in the earlier examination.

For reexaminations ordered prior to November 2, 2002, old art cannot be used as the sole basis for a rejection. If prior art was previously relied upon to reject a claim in a concluded related proceeding, the USPTO will not conduct a reexamination based only on such prior art. The Office may conduct reexamination based on prior art that was cited but whose relevance to the patentability of the claims was not discussed in any prior, related Office proceeding.

Reexamination Considerations

When reexamination is ordered, any submissions properly filed and served will be considered by the examiner when preparing the first office action. The examiner will consider any proposed amendments filed by the patent owner in addition to any statement. If the third-party requester's reply to the patent owner's statement raises issues not previously presented, the issues will be treated by the examiner in the office action if they are within the scope of the reexamination. However, if an issue raised by the third-party requester in the reply is not within the scope of reexamination, it will not be considered.

When *ex parte* reexamination is ordered and the time for submitting any responses to the order have expired, no further active participation by a third-party requester is allowed. No third-party submissions will be acknowledged or considered unless they are in accordance with the scope of the reexamination. The reexamination proceeding will be *ex parte*, even if ordered based on a request by a third party. *Ex parte* proceedings preclude the introduction of arguments and issues by the third-party requester that are not within the defined scope of reexamination.

The *ex parte* reexamination proceeding is conducted with special dispatch and will result in the issuance of a reexamination certificate. The third-party requester will be sent copies of the office actions, and the patent owner must serve responses on the requester. Any citations submitted in the patent file prior to the issuance of an order for reexamination will be considered during the reexamination. The reexamination proceeding will proceed even if a copy of the order sent to the patent owner is returned undelivered. The publication of the notice of reexamination in the Official Gazette will act as constructive notice to the patent owner, and the lack of a response from the patent owner will not delay reexamination.

The reexamination will ordinarily be conducted by the same patent examiner who made the decision on whether the reexamination request should be granted. The examiner must consider the patents and printed publications cited in the reexamination request, the patent owner's statement, the requester's reply, and any prior art discovered by the examiner in searching or of record from the earlier examination of the patent, including any post-issuance citations to the patent file. The level of consideration given to the prior art patents and printed publications is normally limited by the degree to which the party filing the information citation has explained the content and relevance of the information. Submitters may provide the application or proceeding number and its status of any copending reexamination. The processing of *ex parte* reexamination proceedings prior to appeal is summarized in Figure T.

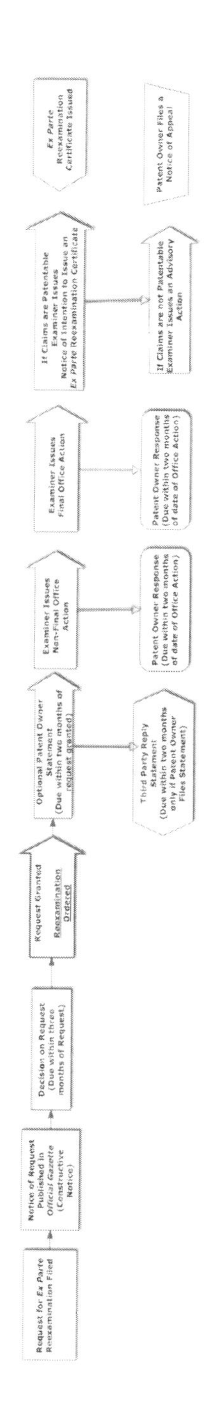

Figure T: Processing of *Ex Parte* Reexamination Proceedings Prior to Appeal

Standard of the Proceeding

The USPTO must determine if "a substantial new question of patentability" affecting any claim of the patent has been raised before ordering an *ex parte* reexamination. A request for *ex parte* reexamination must include "a statement pointing out each substantial new question of patentability based on prior patents or printed publications." If such a new question of patentability is found, an order for *ex parte* reexamination of the patent is issued. The request for *ex parte* reexamination must clearly identify in detail what the requester considers the substantial new question of patentability in view of the prior patents and printed publications. The request must point out how many questions of patentability raised are substantially different from those raised in the previous examination of the patent before the Office.

It is not sufficient that a request for reexamination merely proposes one or more rejections of a patent claim as a basis for reexamination. It must first be demonstrated that a patent or printed publication that is relied upon in a proposed rejection presents a new, non-cumulative technological teaching that was not previously considered and discussed on the record during prosecution of the application. The substantial new question of patentability may be based on art previously considered by the Office if the reference is presented in a new light or a different way that escaped review during the earlier examination.

Statement and Explanation

The request must detail the pertinency and manner of applying the cited art to every claim for which reexamination is requested. If the request is filed by the patent owner, the request for reexamination may also point out how the claims distinguish over cited prior art. Substantial new questions of patentability may be raised under 35 U.S.C. §102 (anticipation) and 35 U.S.C. §102 (obviousness) but must be limited to prior art patents or printed publications. The prior art patent or printed publication must be applied directly to the claims. The statement applying the prior art to the claims may include an assertion that the claims are only entitled to the filing date of the patent and are not supported by an earlier-filed foreign or domestic patent application for which priority benefit was claimed.

The requester must present a complete explanation of how the cited patents or printed publications are applied to all claims meriting reexamination. Ideally, the required explanation can be provided using an appropriately detailed claim chart that compares, limitation by limitation, each claim for which reexamination is requested, with the relevant teachings of each reference cited in the request. For obviousness rejections, the request must provide at least one basis for combining cited references and a statement of why the claims under reexamination would have been obvious over the proposed reference combination. The explanation must not combine the proposed rejections or proposed combinations of references.

Affidavits or Declarations, Admissions, and Other Evidence

Affidavits or declarations, or other written evidence that explains the contents of the pertinent date of the prior art patent or printed publications in more detail, may be considered during reexamination. Admissions, per se, may not be the basis for establishing a substantial new question of patentability but may be used in combination with a patent or printed publication. The admission of the patent owner of record in the file or in a Court record can reside in the patent file or may be presented during the pendency of the reexamination proceeding or in litigation. Admission by the patent owner as to any matter affecting patentability may be utilized to determine the scope and content of the prior art in conjunction with patents and printed publications in a prior art rejection. The admission must stand on its own. Any admission submitted by the patent owner is proper. A third party, however, may not submit admissions by the patent owner made outside of the record of the file or in a Court record unless such admissions were entered into a Court record.

Affidavits or declarations or other written evidence that explain the contents of the pertinent dates of prior art patents or printed publications in more detail will be considered by the examiner in the reexamination proceeding. Any resulting rejections by the examiner must be based on the patents or printed publications and not on the affidavits or declarations or other written evidence.

Copies of Prior Art

A copy of each patent or printed publication relied on or referred to in the request must accompany the filed request. If any of the documents are not in the English language, an English language translation of all necessary and pertinent parts is also required. The prior art patents and printed publications relied upon for reexamination should also be cited on a separate information disclosure statement. It is also helpful to the examiner if prior art cited during prosecution of the patent is also included to allow a comparison to be made of old and new prior art to determine if a substantial new question of patentability is present. It is not necessary to provide copies of U.S. patents and printed publications.

Copy of Printed Patent

Requesters are required to include a copy of the patent for which reexamination is requested to serve as the specification for the reexamination proceeding. A complete copy of the patent should be provided in double-column format. A copy of any disclaimer, certificate of correction, or reexamination issued for the patent should also be provided. A copy of any Federal Court decision, complaint in a pending civil action, or interference decision should also be submitted.

Certificate of Service

If the requester is a person other than the patent owner, the owner of the patent must be served with a copy of the request in its entirety. The service must be made to the correspondence address of record for the patent. The third-party requester must identify on the certificate of service the name and address of the party served, the method of service used, and the date of service. The certificate of service must be attached to the request submitted to the USPTO. The copy of the request served on the patent owner must also include a copy of the certificate of service. If the service on the patent owner was not possible, after a reasonable effort, a duplicate copy of the request papers must be supplied to the USPTO together with a cover letter providing an explanation of what effort was made to effect service and why it was not successful.

Examiner Interviews

Examiner interviews are permitted in *ex parte* reexamination proceedings. However, examiner interviews can only be held with the patent owner or the patent owner's representatives, or both. Requests by the third-party requester to participate in or attend interviews will not be granted by the examiner. Where a panel review has been conducted for an issued office action, the panel members will be present at the examiner interview. Interviews for the discussion of the patentability of claims involved in reexamination will not be held prior to the first office action unless initiated by the examiner to discuss amendments that will make the claims patentable. The examiner will not discuss the merits of the reexamination proceeding with a third-party requester. The examiner will only discuss procedural matters not directed to the merits with a third-party requester and cannot discuss any information that cannot be obtained from a reading of the IFW for the reexamination proceeding.

If the patent owner wants to initiate an examiner interview, the patent owner should contact the examiner in charge of the proceedings and indicate what issues are to be discussed. If the examiner agrees to the interview, the patent owner must file, at least three working days prior to the interview by facsimile, an informal written statement of the issues to be discussed. The duration of the interview cannot exceed one hour unless the patent owner files a petition under 37 C.F.R. §1.182 showing sufficient cause for more time. Only one interview may be requested after an office action and prior to the filing of a response to that action.

In every instance of an interview with the examiner, the patent owner's statement of the interview must be filed. The written statement must be filed within one month of the date of the interview or as a separate paper to the outstanding office action.

Duty of Disclosure

The duty of disclosure in reexamination proceedings is applied to the patent owner and their representatives and to every individual who is substantively involved on behalf of the patent owner. All such individuals have a continuing obligation to bring all patents and printed publications they are aware of, that are material to patentability, and that have not previously been made of record in the patent file to the attention of the Office. Citations of patents and printed publications should be made by filing an information disclosure statement. All such individuals who fail to comply with the ongoing duty of disclosure requirement do so at the risk of diminishing the quality and reliability of the reexamination certificate issuing from the proceeding.

Notice of Prior or Concurrent Proceedings

The USPTO must be made aware of any prior or concurrent proceedings in which the patent undergoing reexamination is or was involved, such as interferences, reissues, *inter partes* reexamination, post-grant review proceedings, and any other *ex parte* reexamination. The notification should include the results of any such prior or concurrent proceedings. The USPTO will accept at any time during the proceedings copies of decisions or papers filed in the court from litigation or other proceedings.

Such decisions include final court decisions (even if appealable), decisions to vacate, decisions to remand, and decisions as to the merits of the claims.

Amendment Included in Request by Patent Owner

A patent owner may include a proposed amendment with their request. If an amendment is submitted to add claims to the patent being reexamined, then excess claims fees must be paid. The request for examination is decided on the wording of the patent claims in effect at the time (without any proposed amendments). The decision on the request will be made on the basis of the patent claims, as the proposed amendment has not been presented. However, if the request for reexamination is granted, all subsequent reexamination prosecution and examination is based on the claims as amended.

Publication in the Official Gazette

Notice of filing of all complete *ex parte* reexamination requests will be published in the Official Gazette approximately four to five weeks after filing. The notice will include the name of any requester and act as constructive notice to the patent owner when service on the patent owner was not possible.

Decision on Request

Reexamination requests are assigned to a primary examiner, other than the original prosecution examiner, in the technology center for the subject matter. The patent claims in effect at the time of the determination will be the basis for deciding whether a substantial new question of patentability has been raised. The following amendments will not be considered or commented upon when deciding the request:

- amendments presented with the request if by the patent owner;
- amendments filed in a pending reexamination proceeding in which the certificate has not been issued; or
- amendments submitted in a reissue application on which no reissue patent has been issued.

The decision on the request for reexamination will be granted or denied. The basis for the decision is whether or not a substantial new question of patentability is found. If the decision to deny a request of reexamination is made, the requester may seek review by a petition to the Director under 37 C.F.R. §1.181.

Request Granted

To grant the request for reexamination, it is only necessary to establish that a substantial new question of patentability exists as to one of the patent claims. The request must specify the pertinency and manner of applying cited prior art to every claim for which reexamination is requested.

In the decision on the request for reexamination, the examiner should discuss all of the patent claims for which reexamination is requested. The examiner can limit the discussion of the claims as to whether a substantial new question of patentability has been raised. A prior art patent or printed publication raises a substantial question of patentability if there is a likelihood that a reasonable examiner would consider it important in deciding whether or not the claim is patentable.

The decision on the request for reexamination must be made and mailed to the requester within three months of the filing of the request. If the request for reexamination is granted, the examiner's decision will conclude that a substantial new question of patentability has been raised by:

- identifying all claims and issues;
- identifying the patents or printed publications relied on; and
- providing a brief statement of the rationale supporting each new question.

Patent Owner's Statement

If reexamination is ordered, the decision granting the order sets a two-month period within which the patent owner may file a statement and any narrowing amendments to the patent claims. An extension of time for one additional month may be granted based on good and sufficient reasons. The patent owner's statement must clearly point out why the patent claims are believed to be patentable over the cited prior art patent and printed publications alone or in any reasonable combination. A copy of the patent owner's statement must be served upon the requester unless the request for reexamination was filed by the patent owner.

If the patent owner does not wish to file a statement under 37 C.F.R. §1.530, the patent owner may expedite the reexamination proceeding by filing a paper that indicates that the patent owner waives the filing of the statement and serves the waiver on the third-party requester.

Panel Review Conference

After the examiner has determined that a reexamination order is grantable, the examiner will inform his or her central reexamination unit supervisory patent examiner of his or her intention to issue an order granting reexamination. The supervisory examiner will convene a panel review conference, and the conference members will review the matter. If the conference panel confirms the examiner's preliminary decision to grant reexamination, the reexamination will be issued and signed by the examiner with co-signatures from at least two other conference examiners.

Request Denied

If the request for reexamination is denied, the decision denying the request will indicate for each patent and printed publication cited in the request why the citation is:

- cumulative to the teaching of the art cited in the earlier concluded examination of the patent;
- not available against the claims (because of its date or because the reference is not a publication);
- not important to a reasonable examiner in deciding whether any claim of the patent for which reexamination is requested is patentable even though the citation is not cumulative and the citation is available against the claim; or
- one that was cited of record in the patent and was previously considered favorable to patentability.

The examiner will then inform his or her central reexamination supervisory patent examiner of his or her intention to issue an order denying the reexamination. The supervisory examiner will convene a panel review conference, and the conference members will review the matter. If the conference confirms the examiner's preliminary decision to deny reexamination, the examiner will issued a decision denying the request for reexamination and at least two other conferees will cosign the decision.

Petition for Review

After a request for reexamination is denied, jurisdiction over the reexamination proceeding is retained by the central reexamination unit to await the possibility of a petition seeking review of the examiner's determination. The requester must file a petition seeking review of the examiner's decision denying the request for reexamination within one month of the examiner's decision. The petition under 37 C.F.R. §1.181 is reviewed by the central examination unit Director. The Director will review the examiner's determination denying the request for reexamination. The decision by the Director of the central reexamination unit is final and non-appealable. The denial of the petition reaffirms the denial of the request for reexamination, and a partial refund of the filing fee for requesting reexamination will be made to the requester.

If the petition is granted, the decision of the Director will include a sentence setting a two-month period for the patent owner to file a statement under 37 C.F.R. §1.530. The reexamination file will be returned to the central reexamination unit supervisory patent examiner.

Amendments in *Ex Parte* Reexamination Proceedings

Amendments made in an *ex parte* reexamination proceeding must comply with the formal requirements of amendment papers that are to become a part of the permanent record in the USPTO file. If an amendment is submitted to add claims to the patent being reexamined, then excess claims fees must be paid. All amendment markings should be made in comparison to the original patent, not in comparison to any previous amendments. Where a change is made in one sentence, paragraph, or page of the patent that increases or decreases the size of the sentence, paragraph, or page, it will have no effect on the body of the reexamination specification. All insertions are made as block additions of paragraphs, which are not physically inserted within the specification papers. Each blocked paragraph is assigned a letter and number, and a caret written in the specification papers indicates where the blocked paragraph is to be incorporated. A reexamination patent owner does not need to be concerned with page formatting when presenting amendments. Any amendments submitted after final rejection will not be entered. If a patent expires during the pendency of a reexamination proceeding, all amendments to the patent claims and all claims added during the preceding are withdrawn. No amendments will be entered in an expired patent.

Amendments by the Patent Owner

The patent owner may file amendments to the patent claims on the filing of the request for reexamination. Any amendments, however, cannot enlarge the scope of the claims of the patent or introduce any new matter. The amendments do not become effective in the patent until the reexamination certificate is issued and published.

Amendments to the Specification

Amendments to the specification under 37 C.F.R. §1.530(d)(1), which include any deletions or additions, must be made by submission of the full text of any paragraph to be changed in any manner, with markings (brackets or underlining) showing the changes. An entire paragraph of specification text can be deleted from the specification by a statement deleting the paragraph without presentation of the text of the paragraph. All paragraphs that are added to the specification must be completely underlined. The precise insertion point of each amendment should be clearly indicated.

Amendments to the Claims

Amendments to the claims under 37 C.F.R. §1.530(d)(2) require that:

- for each proposed claim amended, the entire text of the claim must be presented with appropriate markings showing the changes in the claim;
- for each proposed new claim that is added, the entire text of the proposed new claim must be presented, and it must be underlined throughout;
- if a patent claim is canceled by a direction to cancel that claim, the text of the claim should not be presented; and
- a proposed new claim (previously added in the reexamination) is canceled by a direction to cancel that claim.

Each amendment submitted must identify the status of all the patent claims and all added claims as of the date of submission. The status is whether the claim is pending or canceled. Each claim amendment must be accompanied by an explanation of the support in the disclosure of the patent for the amendments. Claim amendments should be marked-up using underlining for added material and single brackets for deleted material. The original patent claims should not be renumbered. A patent claim retains its number even if it is canceled in the reexamination proceeding, and the numbering of any added claims must begin after the last original patent claim.

Amendments to the Drawings

Amendments to the original patent drawings under 37 C.F.R. §1.510(b)(3) must be in the form of a new sheet of drawings for each drawing sheet that is changed. Any amended figures must be identified as "Amended" and any added figures must be identified as "New." If a figure is canceled, the figure must be surrounded by brackets and identified as "Canceled." If the patent owner wishes to change or amend the drawings, the patent owner must submit a sketch showing the proposed amendments in red, for approval by the examiner. The submitted sketch should be presented as a separate paper and will be made of record in the file. When the examiner approves the sketch, sheets of substitute formal drawings must be submitted for each drawing sheet that is amended. The new sheets of drawings must be entered into the record in the reexamination file prior to issuance of the Notice of Intent to Issue *Ex Parte* Reexamination Certificate.

Reply by Third-Party Requester

If the patent owner files a statement in a timely manner, the third-party requester is given a period of two months from the date of service to reply. No extensions of time are available. The requester's reply does not have to be limited to the issues raised in the statement. The reply may include additional prior art patents and printed publications and may raise any issue appropriate for reexamination. If no statement is filed by the patent owner, no reply is permitted from the third party. The third-party requester must serve a copy of the reply on the patent owner. The third-party requester is not permitted to file any further papers after their reply to the patent owner's statement. Any further papers will not be considered and will be returned to the third-party requester.

Non-Final Office Action

The examiner's first *ex parte* office action on the merits should establish the issues that exist between the examiner and the patent owner. It should be signed by the examiner and two other conferees from the panel review. When the first action is issued, the patent owner has already had the opportunity to file a statement and an amendment. The third-party requester has also had an opportunity to reply. In the first action on the merits, the examiner will include a statement cautioning the patent owner that a complete response should be made to the action since the next action will be final.

The examiner's first office action on the merits must be mailed within one to two months of the filing date of the requester's reply or within one to two months of the filing date of the patent owner's statement. The first office action must be sufficiently detailed that the pertinency and manner of applying the cited prior art to the claims is clearly identified. If the examiner concludes in any office action that one or more of the claims are patentable over the cited patents or printed publications, the examiner should indicate why the claims are patentable in a manner similar to that used to indicate reasons for allowance. The first office action should also respond to the substance of each argument raised by the patent owner and requester. All actions in a third-party requester *ex parte* reexamination will be mailed to the third-party requester.

Time for Response

The examiner will set a shortened statutory period of two months for response to the office action. If the reexamination result from a Court order or litigation is stayed for the purpose of reexamination, the shortened statutory period will be set to one month.

The extension of time provisions of 37 C.F.R. §1.136(a) and (b) do not apply to *ex parte* reexamination proceedings. Any extension of time in an *ex parte* reexamination proceeding is requested under 37 C.F.R. §1.550(c) and must be filed on the day before any action by the patent owner is due and must identify sufficient cause.

Patent Owner's Response

The patent owner is required to serve a copy of any response made on the third-party requester. If the patent owner fails to file a timely and appropriate response to any office action, the prosecution of the reexamination proceeding will be terminated, and a reexamination certificate will be issued. The patent owner's response must be timely filed, must be a bona fide attempt to advance the reexamination proceeding, and must be fully responsive to the rejections, objections, or requirements in the non-final office action. If the patent owner's response to a non-final rejection contains minor inadvertent deficiencies, the examiner can identify the deficiency and the corrective action needed in the next office action. If the patent owner's response contains a serious deficiency and the time period for response has expired, the examiner will notify the patent owner of the deficiency and the corrective action required and set a one-month response period. The patent owner must address the deficiency within the period of response to avoid termination of the proceeding.

Final Office Action

A final office action can only be mailed when a clear issue has been developed between the examiner and the patent owner. The examiner will have twice provided the patent owner with the information and reference in defining the position of the Office as to the unpatentability before making the action final. The final office action will detail all outstanding grounds of rejection and will be signed by the examiner and two other conferees on the review panel. Prosecution before the examiner in a reexamination proceeding is concluded with the final office action.

Time Period for Reply

The practice of giving the patent owner a time period to supply an inadvertent omission in a bona fide response does not apply after a final office action. If a response to an examiner's final office action is filed after the final rejection but there is an inadvertent omission, the examiner will issue an advisory action explaining the omission and the action required. The two-month time period for the response to the final action continues to run and is extended by one month if the response is the first response after the final rejection.

Patent Owner's Response

Amendments after final rejection are approved for entry only if they place the proceeding in condition for issuance of a reexamination certificate or in better form for appeal. The examiner has the authority to enter the response, withdraw the final office action, issue a new office action, or issue an action closing prosecution in an otherwise allowable application.

After Final Practice

If the patent owner believes that the final rejection is improper or premature or that the amendment submitted after final rejection complies with requirements but the examiner improperly refused entry, the patent owner may file a petition under 37 C.F.R. §1.181. The petition should request that the final rejection be withdrawn and that prosecution be reopened or entry of the amendment filed. The petition must be filed within the time period for filing a notice of appeal and does not toll the time period for filing the notice of appeal.

Appeal to the Board

A patent owner who is dissatisfied with the primary examiner's decision to reject claims in an *ex parte* reexamination proceeding may appeal to the Board for review of the examiner's rejections by filing a notice of appeal within the required time. A third-party requester may not appeal and may not participate in the patent owner's appeal.

In an *ex parte* reexamination filed before November 29, 1999, the patent owner may appeal to the Board after the second rejection of the claims (either non-final or final). In an *ex parte* reexamination filed on or after November 29, 1999, the patent owner may appeal to the Board only after the final rejection of the claims.

The notice of appeal need not be signed by the patent owner or his or her attorney or agent. The fee required under 37 C.F.R. §41.20(b)(1) must accompany the filing of the notice of appeal. The period for filing the notice of appeal is the period set for response in the last office action, which is normally two months. If the patent owner does not timely file a notice of appeal or does not timely pay the appropriate fee, or both, the patent owner will be notified that the appeal is dismissed. In such circumstances, the reexamination proceeding is terminated, and the notice of intent to issue a reexamination certificate will be issued indicating the status of the claims at the time of final rejection. The processing of an *ex parte* reexamination proceeding under appeal is summarized in Figure U.

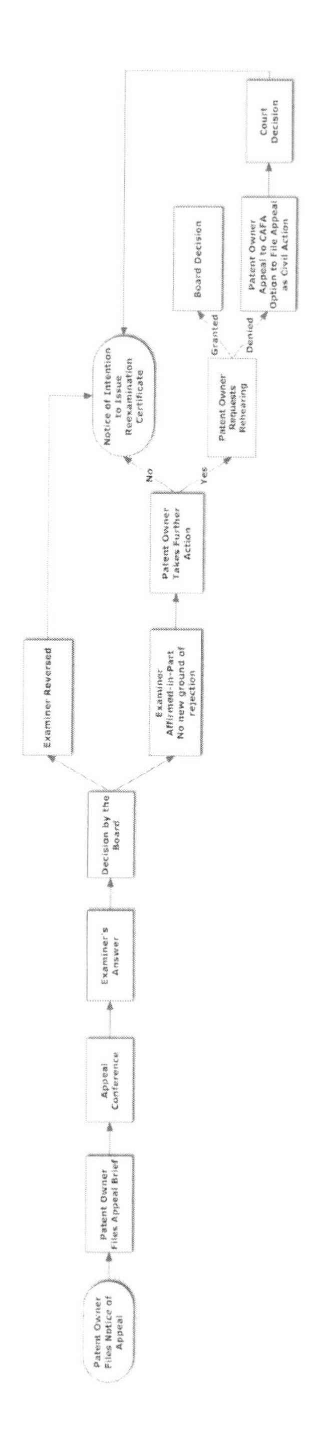

Figure U: Processing of *Ex Parte* Reexamination After Appeal

Appeal Brief

The time period for filing the appeal brief is two months from the date of appeal. An extension of time up to an additional one month is available only on petition with proof of sufficient cause. Failure to file the appeal brief and pay the associated fee within the time period will result in dismissal of the appeal. In such circumstances, the reexamination proceeding is terminated, and the notice of intent to issue a reexamination certificate will be issued indicating the status of the claims at the time of appeal.

The appellant should file a brief of the authorities and arguments on which the appellant will rely to maintain the appeal, including a summary of the claimed subject matter, which must refer to the specification by page and line number, and to the drawing, if any, by reference characters. For convenience, the copy of the claims involved should be double-spaced and should start on a new page in the brief. The copy of the claims on appeal in a reexamination proceeding must include all underlining and bracketing to reflect changes made to the original patent claims during prosecution of the reexamination. In addition, any new claims added in the reexamination should be completely underlined. The brief must be responsive to every ground of rejection stated by the examiner.

If the appeal brief filed is defective, the examiner will notify the patent owner, explain the defect and corrective action required, and set a one-month period for the patent owner to cure the defect.

Examiner's Answer

The primary examiner will provide a written answer to the appeal brief, including an explanation of the invention claimed and reference relied upon and grounds for rejection. If the examiner's answer contains a rejection designated as a new ground of rejection, the appellant must, within two months from the date of the examiner's answer, file a response to the new grounds of rejection or maintain the appeal by filing a reply brief addressing each new ground of rejection.

Appellant's Reply to Examiner's Answer

Where the appellant files a timely reply brief to an examiner's answer, the examiner must reopen prosecution to respond to the reply brief or remand the proceeding to the Board.

Oral Hearing

If the appellant desires an oral hearing, a written request for an oral hearing must be filed, accompanied by the fee under 37 C.F.R. §41.20(b)(3), within two months of the date of the examiner's answer. Oral hearings in reexamination proceedings are open to the public as observers, unless the appellant petitions the Office for a non-public oral hearing by presenting sufficient reasons and paying the associated fee.

Decision by the Board

The Board will render its final decision, which may affirm or reverse the decision of the examiner, in whole or in part, on the grounds and on the claims specified by the examiner. The affirmance of the rejection of a claim on any of the grounds specified constitutes a general affirmance of the decision of the examiner on that claim, except as to any ground specifically reversed. The Board may also remand an application to the examiner.

Appeal to the Courts

A patent owner who is not satisfied with the decision of the Board may seek judicial review. In an *ex parte* reexamination filed before November 29, 1999, the patent owner may appeal the decision of the Board to either the U.S. Court of Appeal of the Federal Circuit or to the U.S. District Court for the District of Columbia. In an *ex parte* reexamination filed on or after November 29, 1999, the patent owner may appeal the decision of the Board only to the U.S. Court of Appeal of the Federal Circuit. A third-party requester for an *ex parte* reexamination cannot seek judicial review.

Conclusion of Ex Parte Reexamination

Upon conclusion of the *ex parte* reexamination proceeding, the examiner must prepare a Notice of Intent to Issue an *Ex Parte* Reexamination Certificate (NIRC). If appropriate, an examiner's amendment will also be prepared. Where claims are found patentable, the examiner must give reasons for each patentable claim in the form of reasons for allowance. The panel review conference will confirm the examiner's decision, and an NIRC will be issued. The NIRC informs the patent owner and any third-party requester that the reexamination proceeding has been terminated. If all the claims are found patentable and an NIRC has been mailed, the examiner may change the title of the invention by an examiner's amendment to align it with the results of the reexamination proceeding.

When the NIRC has been mailed, the reexamination proceeding must proceed to publication as soon as possible. If the patent owner files a submission of patents or printed publications after the NIRC has been mailed, the submission must be accompanied by:

- a factual accounting providing sufficient explanation of why the information could not have been submitted earlier;
- an explanation of the relevance of the information submitted with respect to the claimed invention in the reexamination proceeding; and
- a petition under 37 C.F.R. §1.182 with the associated fee for withdrawal of the reexamination proceeding from the printing cycle.

Issuance of Ex Parte Reexamination Certificate

A reexamination certificate will be issued and published at the conclusion of the proceeding. The reexamination certificate will:

- cancel any patent claims determined to be unpatentable;
- confirm any patent claims determined to be patentable;
- incorporate into the patent any amended or new claims determined to be patentable;
- make any changes to the description approved during reexamination;
- include any statutory disclaimer or terminal disclaimer filed by the patent owner;
- identify the unamended claims that were held invalid by a final decision in a prior or concurrent proceeding;
- identify any claims not reexamined;
- be mailed to the patent owner with a copy to the third-party requester; and
- identify patent claims dependent on amended claims determined to be patentable.

If all of the claims of the patent are canceled, no further proceedings with respect to the canceled claims will be conducted by the Office. A notice of issuance of each reexamination certificate will be published in the Official Gazette on its date of issuance. The *ex parte* reexamination certificate is formatted in the same manner as the title page of a patent and is clearly titled. The *ex parte* reexamination certificate number is the patent number followed by a two-letter kind code suffix. The first letter of the kind code is either "B" (for reexamination published prior to January 2, 2001) or "C" (for reexamination certificates published on or after January 2, 2001). The second letter of the kind code suffix is the number of the reexamination proceeding, indicating how many times the patent has been reexamined. The reexamination certificate will indicate the following:

- the filing date and number of the request;
- the patent for which the reexamination certificate is issued;
- the prior art documents cited will only be those that were part of the reexamination file and cited on forms;
- the patent claims that were confirmed as patentable, canceled, or disclaimed, and those claims that were not reexamined. The text of the new claims will be printed in italics, and the text of any amended claims will be printed with italics and bracketing indicating the amendments; and
- any prior Court decisions will be identified as well as the citation of the Court decision.

Ex Parte Reexamination in Combination with Other Proceedings

If a request for reexamination is filed on a patent after a reissue patent has been issued, the reexamination will be denied because the patent on which the request for reexamination is based has been surrendered. If reexamination of the reissued patent is desired, a new request for reexamination based on the specification and claims of the reissued patent must be filed.

If a second or subsequent request for *ex parte* reexamination is filed while a first *ex parte* reexamination is pending, the presence of a substantial new question of patentability depends on the prior art patents and printed publications cited in the second or subsequent request. If a second or subsequently filed *ex parte* reexamination is to be granted, it must raise a complete or partial substantial new question of patentability that is different from that raised in the pending reexamination proceeding. If the second *ex parte* reexamination proceeding raises the same substantial new question of patentability as the pending *ex parte* reexamination, it will be denied. Merger of a second or subsequent request with the already pending reexamination would prolong the conclusion of the pending reexamination and be inconsistent with the requirement to process the *ex parte* reexamination with special dispatch.

Defective Submissions in *Ex Parte* Reexaminations

The USPTO identifies the following defects as the most common reasons for a defective submission in an *ex parte* reexamination:

- the paper filed does not include a proof of service;
- the paper filed is unsigned;
- the paper filed is signed by a person who is not of record;
- the amendment filed by the patent owner was not timely filed or does not comply with manner of making amendments; and
- the amendment filed by the patent owner did not include payment of excess claims fees due.

Best Practices for Filing Reexamination Proceedings

The USPTO offers the following best practices with respect to filing compliant reexamination proceedings:

- File electronically as a new utility application, selecting reexam, and designate the request as an *ex parte* reexamination.
- Use transmittal form SB/57.
- Include the correct filing fee.
- Patent owners including an amendment should include any excess claim fees that are applicable.
- Include a copy of the patent to be reexamined including any disclaimers, certificates of correction, or prior reexamination certificates.
- Provide a clear statement of a substantial new question of patentability (SNQ) for at least one patent or publication cited in each proposed rejection or application of the art, and provide a concise statement of what the new technology teaching is.

CHAPTER-SPECIFIC REFERENCE MATERIAL

Reference Source	Post-Issuance Citation of Prior Art and Reexamination Proceedings Applicable Rules, Regulations, and Procedures
Title 35 of the U.S. Code	35 U.S.C. §301 Citation of prior art. §302 Request for reexamination. §303 Determination of issue by Director. §304 Reexamination order by Director. §305 Conduct of reexamination proceedings. §306 Appeal. §307 Certificate of patentability, unpatentability, and claim cancellation.

Title 37 of the Code of Federal Regulations	37 C.F.R. §1.501 Citation of prior art in patent files. *Ex Parte* Reexamination §1.502 Processing of prior art citations during an *ex parte* reexamination proceeding. §1.510 Request for *ex parte* reexamination. §1.515 Determination of the request for *ex parte* reexamination. §1.520 *Ex parte* reexamination at the initiative of the Director. §1.525 Order for *ex parte* reexamination. §1.530 Statement by patent owner in *ex parte* reexamination; amendment by patent owner in *ex parte* or *inter partes* reexamination; inventorship change in *ex parte* or *inter partes* reexamination. §1.535 Reply by third-party requester in *ex parte* reexamination.
	§1.540 Consideration of responses in *ex parte* reexamination. §1.550 Conduct of *ex parte* reexamination proceedings. §1.552 Scope of reexamination in *ex parte* reexamination proceedings. §1.555 Information material to patentability in *ex parte* reexamination and *inter partes* reexamination proceedings. §1.560 Interviews in *ex parte* reexamination proceedings. §1.565 Concurrent office proceedings which include an *ex parte* reexamination proceeding. §1.570 Issuance of *ex parte* reexamination certificate after *ex parte* reexamination proceedings.
Manual of Patent Examination Procedures (MPEP, 8th Edition)	Chapter 2200 Citation of Prior Art and *Ex Parte* Reexamination of Patents

Chapter 21
Post-Grant Review Proceedings Under the America Invents Act

Patent Litigation

Challenging the validity of a patent in litigation can be a costly, time-consuming process that has the implied uncertainties of proceedings before a District Court judge or jury. Patent litigation can be extremely costly with endless motion practice and board discovery obligations in a process that is dependent on a jury's understanding of a technical invention. A patent litigation strategy can be driven by a number of competing interests from getting to a verdict as soon as possible, to delaying the proceeding until the patent expires, to staying litigation pending re-examination and invalidation of the patent (Janicki, 2012).

Alternatives to Patent Litigation

An alternative to litigation for challenging patent validity has historically been an *inter partes* re-examination proceeding before the examiner. Although re-examinations may be less costly than litigation, the process can last as long as litigation after all appeals are finished before the examiner. In addition, the re-examination process does not allow discovery or cross-examination of witnesses.

In an attempt to strike a balance between District Court litigation and current re-examination proceedings, the provisions of the AIA include new procedures to challenge the validity of a patent before a Board of administrative patent judges. The new post-grant review trial proceedings offer the opportunity for third parties to challenge a patent's validity in an alternative to District Court litigation. The trial proceedings have the character of a bench trial with limited discovery, motion practice, and the opportunity to cross-examine a witness. The trial is conducted before three administrative patent judges from the Patent Trial and Appeal Board (PTAB). The AIA post-grant proceedings are designed to resolve challenges to patent validity in a timely, efficient, and cost-effective manner (Janicki, 2012).

Proceedings Before the Trial Board

Under the AIA, the USPTO offers several post-grant proceedings designed to strengthen issued patents and provide third-party challengers and patent owners with a range of options to pursue. The USPTO offers two established proceedings for a third party to challenge the validity of an issued patent, namely *ex parte* reexamination and *inter partes* reexamination. The AIA, while leaving the *ex parte* reexamination process untouched, created two additional contested proceedings to replace *inter partes* reexamination, namely, post-grant review (PGR) and *inter partes* review (IPR).

Third-Party Contested Proceedings

The PGR and IPR proceedings allow a third party to actively participate in challenges to patents through discovery processes and other means. In a PGR, a third-party petitioner can challenge the validity of an issued patent and can use patents, printed publications, and other factual evidence supported by affidavits and declarations to support its challenge or question. The petitioner must file within nine months of issuance of the patent and has the burden to prove its challenge by a preponderance of evidence during the process.

When a party misses the opportunity to request the PGR, an IPR procedure may be initiated. Unlike the PGR, the petition is limited to challenges based only on patent references and printed publications. The petitioner has the burden to prove its challenges by a preponderance of evidence. The PGR and the IPR contested proceedings became available on September 16, 2012. *Inter partes* reexamination transitioned into PGR and IPR although the petitioner needs to show that there is a reasonable likelihood that it would prevail with respect to at least one claim challenged in the request. On September 16, 2011, the provisions of the AIA changed the standard for *inter partes* review from "a substantial new question of patentability" to "a reasonable likelihood to prevail on at least one claim."

Patent Owner Proceeding

The AIA created a new proceeding for patent owners only, called supplemental examination, that allows a patent owner to cure inequitable conduct or mistakes that occurred during the prosecution phase. In a supplemental examination, patent owners can submit previously undisclosed information or fix incorrect information that may affect the enforceability of a patent. If the information submitted raises a substantial new question of patentability, an *ex parte* reexamination proceeding will be ordered. If no new substantial new question of patentability is raised, such information cannot be used at a later date to show that the patent is unenforceable. However, the patent may not be protected by the supplemental examination process if it is challenged before submission or during the supplemental examination and any resulting reexamination (Warenza et al, 2011). A high-level summary of the details of the post-grant review proceedings are summarized in Table 31 and will be discussed in more detail in the remainder of this chapter.

Table 31: Post-Grant Review Proceedings

Proceeding Name	Proceeding Details
Ex Parte Reexamination	Available since 1981, unchanged by AIA. Available to patent owner or third-party challenger. Third party can remain anonymous. Third party has no participation after request is filed. Standard for ordering is "a substantial new question of patentability."
Inter Partes Reexamination	Available since 2001 to challenge patents that issue from applications filed on or after November 29, 1999. Phased out September 16, 2012. Replaced with *inter partes* review. Available to third-party challenger. Third party must be identified. Third party participates in reexamination process. Effective September 16, 2011, change in standard for ordering from "a substantial new question of patentability" to "a reasonable likelihood to prevail on at least one of the claims challenged."
Post Grant Review (PGR)	Available as of September 16, 2012. Other than for business method patents, post-grant review is available only for patents that have a priority date later than March 15, 2013. Available to third-party challenger. Petition must be filed within nine months of patent issuance. Standard for ordering is "it is more likely than not that at least one claim of the patent is unpatentable." Can be based on any grounds that are available for an invalidity defense, including patents, printed publications, and other factual evidence.

Inter Partes Review (IPR)	Available as of September 16, 2012. Available to third-party challenger. Available for all patents, regardless of priority date. The petition cannot be filed until after the later of nine months after the grant of a patent or issuance of a reissue patent or the date of termination of any post-grant review of the patent, or one year after an alleged infringer is sued for infringement. Petitioner must show that there is a reasonable likelihood that it would prevail with respect to at least one claim. Evidence limited to prior art grounds based on patents and printed publications.
Supplemental Examination	Available as of September 16, 2012. Available to patent owners only. Allows a patent owner to ask the USPTO to consider, reconsider, or correct any information the patent owner considers relevant to the patent. Can be used to correct errors during the prosecution of the issued patent that may affect enforceability. Can be used to cure issues that might otherwise make a patent subject to inequitable conduct allegations.

Source: Adapted from Warenza et al., (2011)

Terminology of Proceedings

The provisions of the AIA created four new third-party contested proceedings, namely:

- *inter partes* review (IPR);
- post grant review (PGR);
- transitional program for covered business method (CBM) patents; and
- derivation proceedings.

All four of the contested proceedings are conducted before the PTAB. Support staff will need to become familiar with the terminology and nature of these litigation-like proceedings, including the filing requirements and the dedicated PTAB filing interface. The statutory terms of the trial proceedings are as follows:

- Proceeding: used to describe both the four new review processes at the Board and the activities that occur during the review process.

- Board: refers to the Patent Trial and Appeal Board (PTAB), which consists of three administrative judges who conduct the review.
- Petition: means the request to institute a trial proceeding before the Board.
- Trial: refers to the portion of the proceeding after the Board has determined that a petition meets the threshold requirements for instituting the review.
- Motion: means the mechanism for a party to seek relief (e.g., motion to seal a document or motion to amend).

Nature of Proceedings

The USPTO released an umbrella set of rules that apply to contested trial proceedings before the Board. The Board consists of three administrative judges who conduct their review on a case-by-case basis. The duties of the Board are to review appeals by applicants requesting reversal of a decision made by the prosecution examiner, to review appeals or reexamination proceedings, to conduct interference or derivation proceedings, and to conduct *inter partes* review and post grant review.

Each proceeding begins with the filing of a petition requesting institution of a trial proceeding. The Board may institute a trial on the Director's behalf where a petition satisfies statutory thresholds. The trial is conducted on the merits; an amendment and response to the petition may be filed during the trial. The trial before the Board concludes in a final written decision unless otherwise terminated (USPTO, America Invents Act Roadshow, 2012). The petitioner must prove invalidity of a patent before a three-judge panel only by a preponderance of evidence. Patents are not presumed to be valid, and the claim terms are given their broadest reasonable interpretation, thereby potentially sweeping in more invalidating prior art.

Support Requirements

The post-grant review contested proceeding creates a challenge related to how best to staff and support these proceedings. Given that post-grant review proceedings are conducted before the PTAB, they involve a filing system more compatible with patent prosecution. However, the conduct of the proceeding after filing is more like a litigation proceeding and will often involve support by both patent prosecution and patent litigation attorneys. As these proceedings become a more viable option to litigation, patent prosecution and patent litigation support staff will have to identify how these proceedings should be supported across discrete functional support groups.

The initial information presented in this chapter is designed to give support staff a high-level understanding of the general timeline and aspects of post-grant review contested proceedings. More detailed information is then provided on the filing requirement of each individual post-grant review proceeding (IPR, PGR and CBM) to supplement the knowledge on how to complete the different types of contested proceeding filings.

Timeline of Proceeding

The USPTO has provided a representative timeline for processing of all of the contested proceedings before the PTAB, as shown in Figure V. Support staff should be familiar with the timeline for contested proceedings to enable them to follow the Scheduling Order that will be issued by the Board when a trial proceeding is instituted.

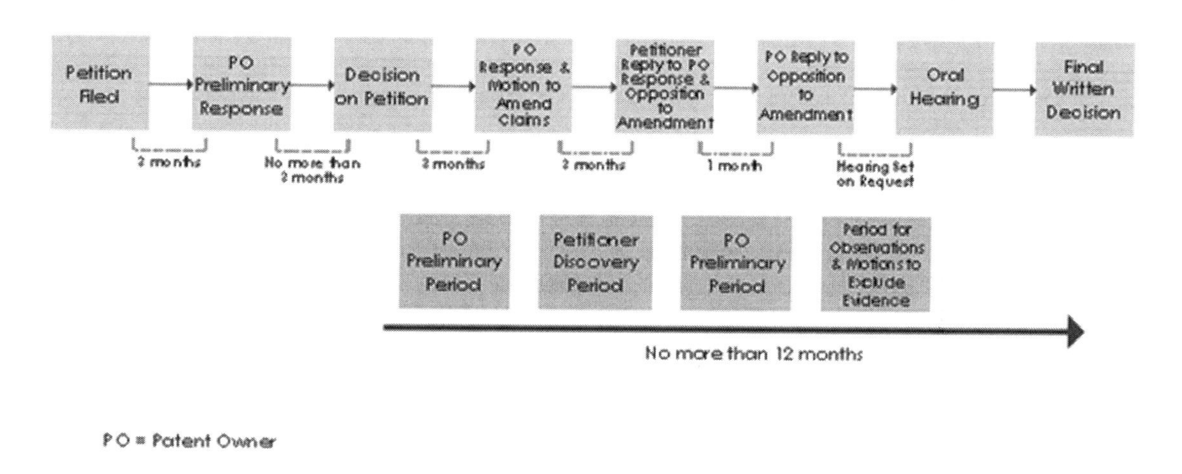

Figure V: Timeline for Proceedings before the Patent Trial and Appeal Board
Source: Stern Kessler Goldstein Fox, (2013)

Patent Owner Preliminary Response

For IPR, PGR, and CBM proceedings, a patent owner may file a preliminary response no later than three months after the grant of a petition filing date. The preliminary response may present evidence other than new testimonial evidence to demonstrate that no review should be instituted. Where a patent owner wants to expedite the proceeding, the patent owner may file an election to waive the patent owner's preliminary response. In addition, a patent owner may file a statutory disclaimer of one or more challenged claims to streamline the proceedings.

The Board will decide whether to grant the petition within three months after the date due for the patent owner's response or three months from the date the patent owner responds, whichever is later. The Board will grant the petition if there is a reasonable likelihood that at least one patent claim is unpatentable.

Decision on Petition

In determining whether to institute a trial proceeding, the Board will take into account whether the review could be timely completed. In instituting a trial, the Board will streamline the issues for final decision by authorizing the trial to proceed only on the challenged claims for which the threshold standards for the proceeding have been met. The Board will identify, on a claim-by-claim basis, the grounds on which the trial will proceed. Any claim or issue not included in the authorization for review will not be part of the trial.

If no trial is instituted, a decision to that effect will be provided. The Board expects that the decision will contain a short statement as to why the standards were not met, although this may not be necessary in all cases. A party dissatisfied with a decision whether or not to institute may file a request for rehearing before the Board, but the Board's determination on whether to institute a trial is final and not appealable.

When a trial is instituted, the Board will provide a Scheduling Order concurrent with the decision to institute the proceeding. The Scheduling Order will set due dates for taking action, accounting for the complexity of the proceeding but ensuring that the trial is completed within one year of institution. The Board expects to initiate a conference call within about one month from the date of institution of the trial to discuss the Scheduling Order and any motions that the parties anticipate filing during the trial. Generally, the Board would require a list of proposed motions to be filed no later than two business days prior to the conference call. An accurate motions list is necessary to provide the Board and the opposing parties adequate notice to prepare for the conference call and to plan for the proceeding.

Patent Owner's Response After Trial Instituted

The patent owner will normally have three months to conduct discovery and file a response to the issues raised in the petition. The patent owner's response may be supported by expert declarations and information obtained in discovery. Both the petition and the patent owner's response are subject to a sixty-page (IPR) or eighty-page limit (PGR and CBM) (Janicki, 2012).

The patent owner is permitted to file one motion to amend the patent claims and to submit a reasonable number of substitute claims. This motion has a fifteen-page limit. The Board may permit additional motions to amend upon a joint request to advance settlement. The petitioner may then take discovery, depose the patent owner's witnesses, reply to the patent owner's response, and oppose the motion to amend the claims. A hearing will be conducted before a panel of at least three administrative law judges of competent legal knowledge and scientific ability. The Board will normally issue a written decision within one year with respect to any claim challenged by the petitioner or any new claim added by amendment. The parties have sixty days from the date of the written decision by the Board to file an appeal to the Federal Circuit (Janicki, 2012). The petitioner is estopped from challenging the patent's validity in court on any ground that could have been raised before the PTAB.

Aspects of the Trial Proceeding

When a trial is instituted, the parties to the proceeding must be aware of the general rules that apply to discovery, depositions, e-discovery, expert testimony, and settlement during the proceeding.

Scheduling Order

When the Board grants a petition to institute a trial proceeding, it will issue a Scheduling Order that identifies the due dates for the petitioner and patent owner to take action in the trial. The parties may agree on different due dates for some of the dates identified, but other due dates will not be negotiable. If the parties agree to modify due dates, a notice of stipulation specifically identifying the changed dates must be promptly filed with the Board. A Scheduling Order issued by the Board will identify the following due dates:

- Due Date 1: the date by which the patent owner must file a preliminary response to the petition and a motion to amend the patent. If the patent owner elects not to file anything, the patent owner must arrange a conference call with the petitioner and the Board.

- Due Date 2: the date by which the petitioner must file any reply to the patent owner's response and opposition to the motion to amend.
- Due Date 3: the date by which the patent owner must file any reply to the petitioner's opposition to the patent owner's motion to amend.
- Due Date 4: the date by which the petitioner must file any motion for an observation on the cross-examination testimony of a reply witness. Each party must file any motion to exclude evidence and any request for oral argument by this date.
- Due Date 5: the date by which the patent owner must file any reply to a petitioner observation on cross-examination testimony. Each party must file any opposition to a motion to exclude evidence by this date.
- Due Date 6: the date by which each party must file any reply for a motion to exclude evidence.
- Due Date 7: the date by which any oral argument requested by either party must be completed.

The parties may stipulate to different dates for dues dates one through three (earlier or later but no later than due date four). The parties may not stipulate to an extension of due dates four through seven.

Cross-examination begins after any supplemental evidence is due unless the parties agree otherwise. Cross-examination ends no later than a week before the filing date of any papers in which the cross-examination testimony is expected to be used.

A motion for observation on cross-examination provides the petitioner with a mechanism to draw the Board's attention to relevant cross-examination testimony of a reply witness, since no further substantive paper is permitted after the reply. The observation must be a concise statement of the relevancy of precisely identified testimony, to a precisely identified argument or portion of an exhibit. The patent owner may respond to the observation but must also be equally concise and specific.

Discovery

The discovery rules under 37 C.F.R. §42.51-§41.65 provide for less discovery during the trial proceeding than is available in a District Court to ensure the PTAB proceeding remains cost-effective. The party requesting discovery must show that information to be discovered will be "useful." Routine discovery consists of information that is inconsistent with a position a party had taken in the review. Additional discovery consists of anything else and requires authorization from the Board. A request for additional discovery must be in the "interests of justice" and the mere possibility of finding something useful is insufficient to grant a discovery request.

The PTAB has specified five factors that control whether additional discovery will be granted (Kowalchyk et al, 2013):

- More than possibility and mere allegation: The mere possibility of finding something useful, and mere allegation that something useful will be found, are insufficient to demonstrate that the requested discovery is necessary in the interest of justice. The party requesting discovery should already be in possession of evidence tending to show beyond speculation that in fact something useful will be uncovered.
- Litigation positions and underlying basis: Asking for the other party's litigation positions and the underlying basis for those positions is not necessary in the interest of justice. The Board has established rules for the presentation of arguments and evidence. There is a proper time and place for each party to make its presentation. A party may not attempt to alter the Board's trial procedures under the pretext of discovery.
- Ability to generate equivalent information by other means: Information a party can reasonably figure out or assemble without a discovery request would not be in the interest of justice to have produced by the other party. In that connection, the Board would want to know the ability of the requesting party to generate the requested information without need of discovery.
- Easily understandable instructions: The questions should be easily understandable. For example, ten pages of complex instructions for answering questions is prima facie unclear. Such instructions are counter-productive and tend to undermine the responder's ability to answer efficiently, accurately, and confidently.
- Requests not overly burdensome to answer: The requests must not be overly burdensome to answer, given the expedited nature of the trial proceeding. The burden includes financial burden, burden on human resources, and burden on meeting the time schedule of the trial proceeding. Requests should be sensible and responsibly tailored according to a genuine need.

Depositions

Trials before the PTAB allow for limited deposition of witnesses. However, direct testimony is typically provided by a declaration, and cross-examination is limited to the scope of the direct testimony. The length of deposition testimony is seven hours for the initial testimony (direct/cross), four hours for the following phase (cross/redirect), and two hours for the last phase (redirect/recross). Video testimony may be taken, but it may not be used without permission from the PTAB. According to Rule 42.51, a party must serve relevant information that is inconsistent with a position advanced by the party during the proceeding, concurrent with the filing of documents or items that contain the inconsistency. This requirement extends to inventors, corporate officers, and persons not involved in the proceeding. This rule requires a disclosure of information from a broader range of people; however, the scope of information required is slightly narrower as it is limited to information inconsistent with a position advanced by a party (Collins, 2012).

Expert Testimony

Rule 42.65(a) includes explicit rules about the use of expert testimony. Expert testimony on U.S. patent law or patent examination practice will not be admitted. Expert testimony that does not disclose the underlying facts on which the opinion is based will not be given weight. If testing data is used, an affidavit must be provided explaining why the data is being used, how the test was performed and the data was generated, how the data is used to determine value, how the test is regarded in the relevant art, and any other information necessary for the Board to evaluate the test and data (Collins, 2012).

Settlement

There are strong public policy reasons to favor settlement between the parties to a proceeding. The Board will be available to facilitate settlement discussions and, where appropriate, may require a settlement discussion as part of the proceeding. The Board expects that a proceeding will terminate after the filing of a settlement agreement, unless the Board has already decided the merits of the proceeding.

Final Decision

For IPR, PGR, and CBM proceedings, the Board will enter a final written decision not more than one year from the date a trial is instituted, except that the time may be extended up to six months for good cause. The Board expects that a final written decision will address the issues necessary for resolving the proceeding.

A party dissatisfied with a decision of the Board may file a request for rehearing. The burden of showing that a decision should be modified lies with the party challenging the decision. The request must specifically identify all matters the party believes the Board misapprehended or overlooked and where each matter was previously addressed in a motion, an opposition, or a reply. Evidence not already of record at the time of the decision will not be admitted absent a showing of good cause. The opposing party should not file a response to a request for rehearing absent a request from the Board. The Board envisions that, absent a need for additional briefing by an opponent, requests for rehearing will be decided approximately one month after receipt of the request.

PTAB Filing Interface—Patent Review Processing System

The Patent Review Processing System (PRPS) is the electronic filing interface used to file trial proceedings before the PTAB. PRPS is also used as the case management system for trial proceedings and provides a customized docket based on the logged-on user identification. PRPS can be accessed through the PTAB portal. PRPS can be used by any member of the public to search for existing proceedings before the PTAB and to view public documents without having to register. PRPS is not the most intuitive filing interface and is different in appearance and functionality from EFS-Web. The interface moves filers through a series of tabs that have discrete functions. The document format requirements are less stringent than EFS-Web, but PRPS imposes more extensive document size limitations on the user.

User Registration

Anyone can register to use PRPS and obtain a user ID, such as a pro se patent owner or an attorney who is not registered to practice before the Office under 37 C.F.R. §11.6. When registering to use PRPS, the user must select a unique User ID and password and enter his or her name and an e-mail address. If the user is a registered practitioner, he or she should enter his or her registration number. A user must register to be able to file a petition, pay fees, or participate in a case on behalf of a petitioner or patent owner. A single User ID may be shared among a working group, including support staff. However, the PRPS docket display is based on the User ID, and the registered practitioner should ensure that sharing his or her User ID would not violate any protective order. More than one individual may review or upload documents to PRPS at the same time, even if they are sharing the same User ID.

System Limitations

All documents uploaded to PRPS must be in PDF or Motion Picture Experts Group (MPEG) format. A single uploaded file may not exceed 25 megabytes in size. There is no technical limit to the number of documents that may be uploaded per filing. There are no naming convention for documents, and file-name characters that are normally not permitted via EFS-Web (&, white space, etc.,) are permitted in PRPS, as there are no file-name and embedded-font validations through the interface. PDF-formatted documents do not have to be PTO printer-driver compatible and should not be converted as this will increase the file volume with respect to the imposed 25 megabyte size limit. However, the documents uploaded should be named using a short descriptive name (e.g., Jones Declaration), and exhibits should be numbered in order (e.g., 1001, 1002, and 1003). All documents uploaded to PRPS are public by default unless the submitting party assigns a different access level for a document. If a petitioner chooses to file a confidential document, an additional motion must be submitted with the document that will be reviewed by the Judge. The assignable access levels are parties and Board only or filing party and Board only.

PRPS Contingency Plan

If PRPS is unavailable during normal business hours, petitions (and other documents) may be submitted to the Board via e-mail: Trials@uspto.gov. Petitions submitted via e-mail must include:

- name of point of contact;
- e-mail address of point of contact;
- patent number to which the petition corresponds;
- application number of the patent;
- number of claims challenged;
- type of trial proceeding;
- power of attorney; and
- authorization to charge the petition filing fee.

In addition, a petition or document submitted via e-mail or other means must be accompanied by:

- a motion requesting acceptance of the submission, and
- a date of transmission where a party seeks a filing date other than the date of receipt at the Board.

A petition will not be accorded a filing date unless it is accompanied by a payment of the respective fees.

PRPS Practice Tips

The USPTO offers the following practice and technical tips related to PRPS:

- When registering with PRPS is completed, the user should close out of the browser completely. The user should reopen the PTAB portal in a new browser session. The user will receive an e-mail containing the verification code. On the PRPS welcoming screen, click on Login and enter the User ID and password. When the screen asks for the verification code, copy and paste the verification code from the e-mail.
- When using the Internet Explorer 8 browser, the user should click "No" on the security-warning page.
- More than one person may review documents or upload documents in a proceeding at the same time, even if they are sharing a user ID.
- Only PDF and MPEG format files may be uploaded in PRPS. Password-protected files will not be accepted.
- A single uploaded file may not exceed 25 megabytes. Users can reduce the file size by splitting a large file into multiple smaller files or converting MS Word® documents into PDF files, rather than printing documents and scanning them in as PDF files.
- Each filing screen includes a "Withdraw Petition" option; users should be careful not to accidentally select this option, as it will result in withdrawal of the entire petition and the previously entered information.

If PRPS and the Board's e-mail address are unavailable, paper filing via Express Mail (or by means at least as fast and reliable as Express Mail) is authorized. The Express Mail mailing address is:

Mail Stop PATENT BOARD

Patent Trial and Appeal Board
United States Patent and Trademark Office
P.O. Box 1450
Alexandria, Virginia 22313-1450

For hand-delivery or delivery via FEDEX or UPS overnight courier, the following address should be used:

Mail Stop PATENT BOARD
Patent Trial and Appeal Board
United States Patent and Trademark Office
Madison Building (East)
600 Dulany Street
Alexandria, Virginia 22313

Petition Filing Requirements

In general, the petition for a post-grant review proceeding should contain the following information:

- A chain-bracket format, matter-specific caption that identifies the inventor's name, title, patent number, issue date, application number, filing date, prosecution-assigned examiner, and technology center. The caption should also include identification of the petitioner, the petitioner real party in interest, and the associated attorney docket number.
- Be addressed to the PTAB address
  Mail Stop Patent Board
  Patent Trial and Appeal Board
  United States Patent and Trademark Office
  P.O. Box 1450
  Alexandria, Virginia 22313-1450

- Include a document title that is a clear indication of the type of petition being filed, including the Patent Number being challenged under the related rules.
- Indicate that the signer is acting in a representative capacity for the petitioner by identifying the real party in interest by their full legal name.
- Identify the number of claims being challenged.

- Identify the grounds under which the claims are being challenged and a showing why it is more likely than not that at least one of the claims challenged is unpatentable.
- Include a Table of Contents that includes an introduction, the petition standing, an overview of the specific grounds for filing against the challenged claims and details of relief sought, a conclusion, and an exhibit list by number.
- The introduction section should include background information on the patent, including prosecution history and assessment of the effective priority date of each claim.
- The detailed explanation section should include claim construction and a claim-by-claim identification of the grounds for filing in view of supportive references.
- The conclusion should request institution of a trial proceeding and request granting of the petition.
- A proof of service of the entire petition and exhibits on the patent owner at the correspondence address of record on the issued patent, including method and date of service.
- The signature block of the petition should include the real party in interest, the lead and backup Counsel, and their contact information.
- All required filing fees must be paid on filing the petition. Fees may be charged to a credit card or a Deposit Account or a combination of both.
- Exhibits supporting the grounds for the petition must be sequentially numbered, and each individual exhibit must be labeled and bates numbered.

Filing Component Documents

In general, when preparing to file a petition for a post-grant review trial proceeding, the following documents should be prepared as PDF-formatted documents. It is not necessary to convert the PDF documents to PTO compatible settings, as EFS-Web file format requirements do not apply to PRPS. The PTAB will not provide filing forms for the post-grant review proceedings.

The Petition

The petition has a sixty-page (IPR) or eighty-page (PGR and CBM) limit, not including table of contents, table of authorities, mandatory notice, appendices, and certificate of service. The petition should include a list of exhibits relied upon to challenge the claims. The petition should be double-spaced, portrait orientation, using fourteen-point or larger font on 8.5 x 11 sized paper with one-inch margins. If block quotes are used, they may be 1.5 spaced and indented from both sides. The petition should identify the precise relief requested for each claim challenged. The petition should identify each claim challenged, identify the specific statutory grounds on which the challenge to the claim is based and state how the challenged claim is to be construed, state how the claims are unpatentable, and identify the evidence relied upon by exhibit numbers, including specifically identifying the portion of the exhibit relied upon. The mandatory notice section of the petition must identify the real party in interest, related matters and proceedings, the lead and backup Counsel and their respective contact information, and the service information for the petitioner. If there are no related matters or proceedings, the mandatory notice should include a statement to this effect. The petitioner must also certify that the petitioner is not barred or estopped from requesting a review.

Extensive usage of claim charts in a petition is discouraged. The rules require that a petition identify how the challenged claims are to be construed and how the claims are unpatentable under the statutory grounds raised. This information is to be provided within the double-spaced sixty- or eighty-page limit requirements. The petition must specify where each element of a challenged claim is to be found in the prior art. The element-by-element showing may be provided in a claim chart, which is permitted to be single-spaced. The petitioner is not permitted to insert arguments in the claim chart to circumvent the double-spacing requirement. The Board will require correction of any petition that includes improper usage of claim charts.

Service on the Patent Owner

A complete copy of the petition and supporting documents must be served on the patent owner. Service on the patent owner should be by USPS Express Mail service to the correspondence address of record in PAIR and must be date-stamped the same day the petition was filed.

Exhibits

The exhibits relied upon as the ground for challenging the claims should be identified and sequentially numbered (e.g., Exhibit 1001, 1002, 1003, etc.). The exhibits filed with the petition should be labeled and bates numbered. An example of the exhibit label to be placed on the front page of each exhibit filed with the petition is shown below:

[Petitioner Name] Exhibit No.
Page 00001

A copy of all exhibits relied upon in the petition must be provided. The exhibits filed must match the listing of exhibits indicated in the petition. Exhibits must be sequentially numbered and labeled.

Power of Attorney

The power of attorney should be from the real party in interest appointing a lead and backup Counsel to represent their interest in the trial proceeding before the PTAB. The power of attorney should identify a lead Counsel and may appoint additional practitioners (including the backup Counsel) by Customer Number practice. The lead and backup Counsel should be registered users with PRPS.

All documents, other than drawings, must be in portrait orientation, including claim charts and arguments. The Board will require correction of any documents or portions thereof submitted in landscape orientation.

The petitioner's mandatory notices must be filed as part of the petition itself. The Board will require correction of any mandatory notices that are not filed as part of the petition.

If a petitioner files multiple petitions challenging the same patent, the petitioner should number its exhibits uniquely for both cases (e.g., 1001-1099 for Case 1, and 1101-1199 for Case 2). Similarly, the patent owner in such a situation should number its exhibits uniquely for both cases (e.g., 2001-2099 for Case 1, and 2101-2199 for Case 2). If the Board decides to consolidate the cases, the exhibits would continue to be uniquely numbered in the consolidated proceeding.

Fees

In general, when filing a petition for a post-grant review trial proceeding, all fees must be paid on initial filing. For IPR, PGR, and CBM, the filing fees due include a petition request fee and a post-institution request fee, which are dependent on the number of claims being challenged. The request and the institution fees must be paid on filing the petition. If a trial is not instituted by the Board, the post-institution request fee will be refunded.

Steps in Filing a Petition Using PRPS

To file a petition user PRPS, a logged-on registered user should take the following steps. Under "New Petitions" tab, select "Create New Petition"

- Enter Trial and Patent Information

  Select the Trial type from the drop-down menu (e.g., IPR, PGR, or CBM).
  Enter the Patent Number, and confirm patent details propagated by PRPS.
  Check box to verify that the Patent Number entered is correct.
  Select the statutory grounds for challenge (§101, §102, §103, §112).
  Enter the total number of challenged Claims (e.g., 7).
  List the Challenged claims (e.g., 1, 3, 5-10).
  Select "Submit."

- Identify Real Party In Interest

  Enter party type (e.g., Organization).
  Enter Organization name.
  Enter Organization address.
  Enter Organization e-mail, phone number, and fax number.
  Enter Additional Parties in Interest (if applicable).
  Select "Save" and "Next."

- Upload Petition and Associated Documents

  The Petition, Mandatory Notice, and related Certificate of Service should be uploaded as one complete document. The Mandatory Notice and Certificate of Service are not included in the page-count limit for the petition. The petition should be uploaded as a petition under document type.
  The exhibits should be uploaded separately and should be sequentially numbered. The exhibits should be uploaded as "exhibit under document type." A short descriptive name should also be entered to identify the content of the exhibit (e.g., Jones Declaration)
  The Power of Attorney and its related Certificate of Service should be uploaded as one document.

- Select Payment Information

  The PRPS interface will calculate the fees based on the total number of claims challenged.

  Fees can be paid using a Credit Card, Deposit Account, or Electronic Funds Transfer.

  Enter Credit Card information or Deposit Account information, or both. (Note: there is a transaction limit of $49,900 per credit card, and only one credit card can be used; the remaining fees must be authorized to a Deposit Account.)

  All fees must be paid to secure the petition filing date.

- Enter Lead Counsel and Backup Counsel Information

  Confirm if Power of Attorney includes lead and backup Counsel.

  Upload the Power of Attorney.

- Identify Any Related Court Proceedings

  Review Petition.

  Submit Petition.

PRPS has the following tab-based structure that allows users to navigate between discrete functions:

- Petition Information—Party Information and Petition Documents
- Payment Information—Deposit Account, Credit Card, Debit Card or Electronic Funds Transfer, or Make Multiple Payments
- Other Information—Counsel Information and Related Matters
- Review Petition—Review Petition Prior to Submission

Uploading documents to PRPS is a time-consuming process due to imposed file-volume limitations. Users should use "Save" options when moving between tabs to ensure that information entered or documents uploaded are saved if PRPS becomes unstable. PRPS has a series of fillable screens for entering lead Counsel, backup Counsel, and real party in interest information. The trial type, patent information, grounds challenged, parties to the matter and lead and back up Counsel can be entered in advance. Exhibits may also be pre-loaded to add efficiencies to filing through the PRPS interface. PRPS allows for interim storage of documents and trial particulars for up to thirty days. After thirty days of inactivity, the documents will be deleted from the interface.

If at any stage during the filing process, the wrong document is uploaded to PRPS, the user can delete the selected document using the trash can icon beside the document on the petition review page. Users should regularly use the save function during the filing process to allow progressive validation of the documents uploaded, especially when the filing involves a large number of exhibit documents.

Petitioner Post-Filing Validation

When the user clicks "Submit," PRPS will produce an instantaneous on-screen acknowledgment and e-mail an electronic filing receipt and confirmation of fees paid to the lead Counsel's e-mail address if the documents are acceptable. If PRPS does not produce an on-screen acknowledgment or a filing receipt, then the documents have not been uploaded properly, and the user should contact the Board. If the user requires additional validation of the submitted petition, they can review the file contents for the proceeding in PRPS to confirm all submitted documents are accounted for.

Review of Petition by the Board

When the petition is submitted, a Board paralegal will review the petition for statutory and regulatory compliance. The statutory requirements under 35 U.S.C. §312(a) and §322(a) must be complied with before a petition filing date will be accorded. More specifically, the Board paralegal will review the filing for the following:

- appropriate fee successfully paid;
- identification of the patent and the specific claims being challenged;
- identification of the real party in interest;
- copies of patents and printed publications relied upon in the petition were provided; and
- certificate of service on the patent owner is included.

If any statutory requirement is not met, the petition is incomplete. The Board paralegal will call the petitioner and explain the deficiency. The paralegal will send an electronic Notice of Incomplete Petition to the petitioner. The deficiency must be corrected within one month, and the petition will be accorded the filing date of the corrected submission. If the deficiency is not corrected within one month, the petition will be dismissed. The only exception to this rule is when the practitioner challenges more than twenty claims but does not pay the excess claim fees, the petitioner will receive a notification and can file a request to have the Board review just the first twenty challenged claims.

In addition, there are certain regulatory requirements that must be complied with to ensure the petition is not defective. The Board paralegal will review the petition for adherence to the page limit, font size, signature, and identification of lead and backup Counsel. If any of the regulatory requirements are not met, the petition is defective. The paralegal will call the petitioner and explain the defect. The paralegal will send an electronic Notice of Defective Petition to the petitioner. The defect must be corrected within one week, and the petition will be accorded the filing date of the original submission. If the defect is not corrected within one week, the petition will be forwarded to a Board Judge, who may initiate a conference call or issue an Order to Show Cause, or both, and terminate the proceeding if the petitioner fails to respond to such an Order.

If there are no statutory or regulatory errors in the petition, the Board paralegal will enter a Notice of Filing Date Accorded to the Petition. The petitioner will receive a notification via e-mail, and the patent owner will receive a copy via regular mail to the correspondence address of record for the patent.

The PAIR record for the challenged patent will show whether a petition has been filed or a decision on the petition has been granted. PAIR will have one of the following entries:

- Petition Requesting Trial;
- Request for Trial Granted;
- Request for Trial Granted in Part;
- Request for Trial Dismissed;
- Termination or Final Written Decision; or
- Review Certificate.

During the trial proceeding, the petitioner and the patent owner will be able to follow the proceeding on their respective dockets. PRPS will provide courtesy notices of filings to the parties of record. A party may directly update the real parties in interest or Counsel information using PRPS interface forms. A party may file appropriate papers such as motions, oppositions, and notices. PRPS will notify each party of record of any paper the Board enters.

Searching PRPS

The PRPS interface assigns a proceeding numbering system based on the type of proceeding filed (CBM, IPR, PGR) and the fiscal year (October 1 to September 30) in which the petition was filed. The proceeding numbering system is as follows:

[Type of Trial] [Fiscal Year]-[Number]

Example: CBM2012-00004

The PRPS function for searching by proceeding number permits wild-card searching after a string of text. A trial proceeding will only be listed in the search results only when the multistep process of submitting a petition for instituting a trial proceeding has been successfully completed. If the process of filing a petition is not yet completed or was never completed, a trial number will be provided, but it will not be listed in the search results.

Reviewing Documents in PRPS

A non-registered user may search for a proceeding and review documents related to a proceeding. However, PRPS is intended for use by the public and is not intended to be a source for bulk downloads of data. If individuals or IP addresses attempt to bulk download data from PRPS and cause a disruption of access to the public, PRPS access may be denied without notice.

Post-Trial Institution Filings

When filing post-trial institution follow-on documents, the submission should include the document caption provided by the Board in the most recent communication. Post-trial follow-on documents (e.g., motion to seal or proposed protective order) can be filed by the petitioner by logging onto PRPS using the lead Counsel's user ID. The user should select the relevant trial number under the "My Docket" tab and select the "Upload Document" tab.

The user must select what type of document is being uploaded (e.g., motion, notice, exhibit, or other). The user must enter a descriptive document name and select the level of availability, upload the document, and select "Submit." When the submission is completed, an electronic acknowledgment will be sent to the lead Counsel's e-mail address of record.

Filing Additional Exhibits

If additional exhibits are filed as part of a follow-on response, they must continue to be sequentially numbered, labeled, and bates numbered. Each time an additional exhibit is filed, an updated listing of exhibits must be provided. An example of the exhibit label to be placed on the front page of each follow-on exhibit filed is shown below.

[Petitioner Name] Exhibit Number
[Petitioner Name] vs. [Patent Owner Name]
PTAB Case No.: CBM2012-0010
Page Number 00001

Service of Follow-On Documents

Any documents filed after the institution of the trial proceeding can be electronically served on the opposing party if all parties agree to electronic service. Electronic service of documents is more efficient and reduces the time and effort related to paper service by USPS Express Mail. Follow-on documents that are to be served electronically must be electronically transmitted to the opposing party in their entirety on the day they were filed with the Board.

Patent Owner Participation

The patent owner must first register as a PRPS user and get a user ID. After logging onto PRPS using the user ID, the patent owner can select the "New Petitions" tab and select "Patent Owner Participation" to begin the process. PRPS will provide screens to search for the proceeding by patent number and enter mandatory notice information (e.g., identifying the real party in interest, lead and backup Counsel, and related matters). The Board will review the information to confirm that the user is facially authorized to act for the patent owner. When the user has been associated as the patent owner, the case proceeding will appear in the user's docket. Association as the patent owner is a prerequisite for filing an action in the proceeding. When the patent owner submits the mandatory notice information and a Board paralegal verifies the information, the patent owner will receive an e-mail notification and may then upload documents (e.g., preliminary response, motions).

If the patent owner wishes to designate a lead Counsel or a backup Counsel who is not already Counsel of record in the subject patent, a power of attorney must be filed with the designation of Counsel. The power of attorney must be signed by the assignee of the entire interest of the patent (if any) and uploaded as a PDF file. The patent owner may designate the attorney of record in the subject patent as the lead or backup Counsel. Therefore, the attorney of record in the subject patent, acting as a representative of the patent owner, may log on to PRPS and designate himself or herself as lead or backup Counsel for the proceeding.

A party may file a power of attorney using a customer number and identify a specific registered patent practitioner that is associated with the customer number as lead or backup Counsel. The party is required to identify a specific registered practitioner as lead Counsel in a proceeding. Further, the party must ensure that using a customer number in a power of attorney would not violate any protective order because all of the registered patent practitioners that are associated with the customer number may have access to the file records of the proceeding.

When the patent owner identifies its real party in interest or files a power of attorney, the Board will check the information with the assignment record (if any) to verify that the information is correct and that the paper is signed properly, if the patent has been assigned. Therefore, patent owners are encouraged to keep assignment records up-to-date.

If the patent owner's real party in interest is different than the assignee of record in the subject patent, the patent owner can submit the new assignment with the identification of the real party in interest. The patent owner should also file a copy of the new assignment with the Assignment Recordation Branch.

The patent owner can file a preliminary response within three months of the date on which the Board enters a Notice of Filing Date Accorded to the Petition. If the patent owner wishes to file a preliminary response or a statement to waive the preliminary response, the patent owner must file the preliminary response or statement within the three-month time period.

Inter Partes Review

From September 16, 2012, all existing U.S. patents will be eligible for a new high-speed *inter partes* review (IPR) system to resolve patent validity disputes. The PTAB must render its final decision within twelve months from the decision to institure a trial. IPR allows for the immediate and proactive review of newly issued patents that are of potential concern to competitors. It is a vehicle for accused infringers or corporate competitors to challenge patentability before the USPTO. IPR arguably provides for more thorough review in that it allows for depositions of witnesses submitting affidavits or declarations. IPR involves a higher standard to institute but a lower standard of proof on the challenger than in litigation. The challenger will be precluded from relitigating any defense that they raised or could have raised. IPR is a lower cost and faster alternative to civil litigation but involves significant estoppel risks (Coyne, 2011).

Differences Between Inter Partes Review and Inter Partes Reexamination

IPR has a higher institution standard from "a substantial new questions of patentability" to "a reasonable likelihood that the requester would prevail to at least one of the claims" challenged in the request. This elevated standard has been applied to *inter partes* reexamination requests filed on or after September 16, 2011. An *inter partes* reexamination can only be filed for patents filed after November 29, 1999. As of September 15, 2012, *inter partes* reexamination was replaced with IPR. An IPR cannot be filed more than one year after a patentee is sued for infringement.

An IPR is conducted by the PTAB, whereas an *inter partes* reexamination is conducted before the examiner by the central reexamination unit. IPR promotes quicker resolution, as a final determination must be made by the Board within twelve months of instituting a trial proceeding (six months extension available for good cause). An IPR decision is a final decision by the Board whereas the decision resulting from an *inter partes* reexamination is appealable to the Board. An IPR removes one layer of possible appeals, which shortens the time to resolution. Appeal of an IPR decision is filed directly with the Federal Circuit. In addition, institution of an IPR proceeding can result in a stay of corresponding litigation proceedings pending the decision by the PTAB.

Under IPR, the patent owner may file a preliminary response to a petition, identifying reasons why the Board should not institute an IPR. This option, however, is not available if the petitioner has already filed a declaratory judgment action.

In an IPR, discovery is limited to deposition of witnesses, submitting affidavits or declarations, while the grounds for invalidity are limited to §102 and §103; no challenges based on §101 or §112 are permitted. An IPR allows for much less discovery than is available in a District Court proceeding to ensure that an IPR is a cost-effective alternative to litigation.

In IPR, estoppels attach upon final written decision by the Board. In *inter partes* reexamination, estoppels attach after final decision when all appeals have been exhausted. An IPR involves differences in estoppel provisions by requiring all real parties in interest be identified and requiring the application of a "reasonably could have been raised" standard. IPR contains settlement provisions on joint written agreement of the patent owner and petitioner filed with the USPTO.

IPR Petition Filing Requirements

IPR is available for pre-AIA and AIA patents. A petitioner may request to cancel as unpatentable one or more claims of a patent based on novelty or obviousness using patents or printed publications. Any person who is not the owner of the patent and has not previously filed a civil action challenging the validity of a claim of the patent may file a request for IPR by filing the following:

- a petition to institute an *inter partes* review;
- the petition must demonstrate a reasonable likelihood that the petitioner will prevail on at least one claim challenged;
- identify all real parties in interest;
- identify all claims challenged and grounds on which the challenge to each claim is based;
- provide a claim construction, and show how the construed claim is unpatentable based on the grounds alleged;
- identify the exhibit number of the supporting evidence relied upon to support the challenge, and state the relevance of the evidence;
- provide copies of evidence relied upon;
- be accompanied by the payment of the required fee; and

- the petition cannot be filed until after the later of nine months after the grant of a patent or issuance of a reissue patent or the date of termination of any post-grant review of the patent, or one year after an alleged infringer is sued for infringement.

Processing of Inter Partes Review

An IPR will only be granted if the petitioner shows a reasonable likelihood that they would prevail with respect to one or more of the claims. The patent owner may file a preliminary response to the petition to provide reasons why no *inter partes* review should be instituted. The preliminary response is due within two months of the petition docketing date. The preliminary response may present evidence other than testimonial evidence. Testimonial evidence and discovery may be provided where necessary on a case-by-case basis. In submitting a response, the patent owner must file, through affidavits or declarations, any additional factual evidence and expert opinions on which the patent owner relies in support of the response. A patent owner may file one motion to amend a patent subject to the standards and procedures set by the Board. Amendments may cancel any challenged claim or propose a reasonable number of substitute claims, or both. Additional motions may be filed if authorized by the Board. Upon conferring with the Board, the patent owner may file a motion to amend. A motion to amend may be limited to prevent abuse and to aid in efficient administration and timely completion of the proceeding.

The IPR petition must demonstrate a reasonable likelihood that the petitioner would prevail as to at least one of the claims challenged. Where IPR standards are met, the Board will institute the trial on a claim-by-claim basis and on a ground-by-ground basis.

The USPTO must decide within three months whether or not to proceed with IPR and must render its decision within a year of deciding to proceed. IPR proceedings will be conducted before the Board rather than before an examiner. The IPR trial will be completed within one year from the institution, except the time may be extended up to six months for good cause. The Board's decision is appealable only to the Federal Circuit. Under the new IPR scheme, the USPTO has the ability to limit the number of IPR proceedings during the first four years if they exceed the number of *inter partes* reexaminations from the last fiscal year before implementation. On average, IPR would reduce the time to determination by more than 60 percent when compared to the average three-year processing time for *inter partes* reexamination. The higher turnaround time to a determination can be attributed to the review bypassing the examiner's level and starting immediately at the Board of adjudication. There is a limited scope of discovery during IPR with respect to expert declarations, with discovery limited to deposition of witnesses and submitting affidavits or declarations. Under the IPR scheme, the parties have an absolute right to settle and terminate an IPR if the Board has not decided the merits of the proceeding (Wu et al, 2011).

IPR Quick Reference Guide

A quick reference guide to the eligibility, grounds for filing, and petition filing requirements for an IPR appears in Table 32.

Table 32: *Inter Partes* Review—Quick Reference Guide

Criteria	Details
Effective Date	September 16, 2012
Eligibility	All issued and reissued patents eligible (under first-to-invent and first-to-file systems). IPR replaced *inter partes* reexamination, which was phased out on September 15, 2012.
Who Can File?	Any person who is not the patent owner and has not previously filed a civil action challenging validity of the patent
Grounds for Filing	A petitioner for IPR may request to cancel as unpatentable one or more claims of a patent on a ground that could be raised under §102 or §103 and only on the basis of prior art consisting of patents or printed publications. Petitioner must demonstrate reasonable likelihood that they would prevail as to at least one of the claims challenged.
Timing Considerations	Petition cannot be filed until the later of: ▪ Nine months after grant of patent or issuance of reissue patent; or ▪ The date of termination of any post-grant review of the patent.
Standard to Institute	To institute an IPR, a party must file a petition establishing certain statutory requirements. The PTAB will decide petitions for IPR and conduct any ensuing reviews. In instituting a review, the Board may take into account whether, and reject the petition or request because, the same or substantially same prior art or arguments previously were presented to the Office. A party is statutorily precluded from appealing the Board's decision whether to institute an IPR.

Filing Requirements	An IPR petition must: ▪ Adhere to the sixty-page limit, not including table of contents, table of authorities, mandatory notice, and certificate of service; ▪ identify the real parties of interest; ▪ identify all claims challenged and the grounds (under §102 or §103 only) on which the challenge to each claim is based; ▪ provide a claim construction, and show how the constructed claim is unpatentable based on the grounds alleged; ▪ provide copies of evidence relied upon; ▪ identify the exhibit number of the supporting evidence, and state the relevance of the evidence; ▪ demonstrate a reasonable likelihood of prevailing with respect to at least one claim challenged; ▪ include a power of attorney; and ▪ include authorization to charge petition fees.
Filing Fees	The filing fees for an IPR are dependent on the number of claims being challenged as indicated below: ▪ IPR request fee under 37 C.F.R. §42.15(a)(1) for up to twenty claims challenged. ▪ IPR post-institution fee under 37 C.F.R. §42.15(a)(2) for up to fifteen claims challenged. ▪ IPR request fee under 37 C.F.R. §42.15(a)(3) for each claim in excess of twenty claims. ▪ IPR post-institution request fee under 37 C.F.R. §42.15(a)(4) for each claim in excess of fifteen claims. A request fee and a post-institution fee depending on the number of claims challenged must be paid on filing the petition. Small entity and micro-entity discounts do not apply.
Patent Owner's Response	The patent owner will be given an opportunity to file a preliminary response within two months of petition docketed date. In the preliminary response to the petition, the patent owner must give reasons why no IPR should be granted. The patent owner's response may include affidavits, declarations, or any additional factual evidence and expert opinion in support of the response. During the review, the patent owner may file one motion to amend the challenged patent claims. Amendments may cancel any challenged patent claim or propose a reasonable number of substitute claims, or both.

Nature of the Proceeding	If IPR standards are met, the Board will institute a trial on a claim-by-claim basis. A petitioner may supplement information provided in the petition for *inter partes* review by filing a motion within one month of the date the trial is instituted. The file of an IPR is open to the public, except that a party may seek to have a document sealed by filing a motion to seal. There are also provisions for protective orders to govern the exchange and submission of confidential information. Discovery is limited to the depositions of witnesses submitting affidavits or declarations and what is otherwise necessary in the interest of justice A party may request relief during an IPR by filing a motion. Either party to an IPR may request an oral hearing. The Board will issue a final written decision. The decision will address the patentability of any challenged patent claim and any new claim added via amendment during the IPR. A party dissatisfied with the final written decision in an IPR may appeal to the Federal Circuit.
Duration	An IPR is statutorily required to be completed within one year of institution, except that the time may be extended up to six months for good cause.
Settlement	A settlement terminates the proceeding with respect to the petitioner, and the Board may terminate the proceeding or issue a final written decision.
Estoppels	A petitioner in an IPR may not request or maintain a subsequent proceeding before the Office with respect to any challenged patent claim on any ground that was raised or reasonably could have been raised in the IPR. A petitioner in an IPR may not assert in a subsequent District Court or the International Trade Commission (ITC) action that a claim is invalid on any ground that the petitioner raised or reasonably could have been raised in the IPR.
Limitations	Cannot be instituted after petitioner or real party in interest has filed civil action challenging validity. Must be filed within one year after service of complaint. Estoppels attach upon final written decision of the Board. Estoppels apply to both District Court and ITC proceedings.

Advantages of Inter Partes Review

Inter partes review proceedings offer the following advantages (Lagatta et al, 2013):

- IPR is a more effective, efficient, and lower-cost option than District Court litigation to challenge the validity of a patent.
- The challenging party has the opportunity to participate in the review.
- IPRs are not subject to the backlog in the reexamination unit, as they are filed with the PTAB.
- IPR favors the challenger, not the patentee. The likelihood of the patent emerging unscathed is very low, as the statutory presumption of validity and burden on the challenger to prove invalidity do not apply.
- Initial rulings on petitions for IPR indicate that while technical and formal requirements are stringent, the grant of petitions showed the standards for initiating the proceeding was reasonable and consistent.
- Most of the procedural issues are initiated by and resolved by a conference call with the Board.
- The PTAB will issue a final determination of validity within the twelve- to eighteen-month time period from the date the IPR is instituted. This time frame is substantially shorter than District Court litigation or prior *inter partes* reexamination proceedings. Short time frames are set for responses by the patent owner, which places the patent owner on the defensive for the entire proceeding.
- An IPR decision is considered a final decision by the Board, which further shortens the anticipated time to a final decision.
- Limited discovery in an IPR contains related costs and ensures that additional discovery is only granted in the interests of justice.
- An IPR limits the scope of the issues considered to the question of if the references cited invalidate the claims in the patent. The scope of issues to argue is relatively contained.
- In the majority of proceedings to date, institution of an IPR proceeding has resulted in stay of the corresponding litigation. This delays the cost of defending an infringement and any other claims until the patent clears the invalidity challenge. This helps contain costs to defending both invalidity and infringement of the claims at the same time.
- The PTAB applies the broadest reasonable construction of the claims, which is a standard more favorable to the party trying to invalidate the claims. In addition, in an IPR there is no presumption of patent validity that must be overcome.

- The guidance provided in the claim construction used by the PTAB will provide insight into how the parties see the merits of the infringement case.
- In an IPR, the PTAB gives considerable weight to expert declarations to support facts or to present technical information.
- Regardless of the outcome of an IPR proceeding, it creates prosecution history estoppel on issues directly relevant to the patent claims and the cited prior art. Even if the IPR is not instituted, the patent owner has an opportunity to respond prior to the Board's decision to institute. The patent owner's response can include statements regarding the scope of the claims of the challenged patent.
- An IPR can be used to place a patent owner on the defensive. It can also be used to isolate invalidity matters from issues in litigation, deferring or avoiding litigation costs, while quickly obtaining invalidity decisions.

Post Grant Review

Most aspects of the post grant review (PGR) and IPR are effectively the same. PGR proceedings are conducted by the Board to reconsider already issued patents and can lead to the confirmation, cancellation, withdrawal, or modification of patent claims. Only patents in the first-to-file system will be eligible for PGR. A PGR allows a third party to challenge a patent to a greater degree than possible with prior administrative procedures. PGR can be sought by any third-party challenger and is similar to the European Patent Office (EPO) opposition practice. Under PGR procedures, a challenger has nine months from patent grant or broadening reissue to initiate such a proceeding. Anyone other than the patent owner may file a petition to institute a PGR as long as they have not challenged the validity of the patent in a civil action (Tridico et al, 2011). The petition must demonstrate that it is more likely than not that at least one of the claims challenged in the petition is unpatentable (higher threshold than IPR).

Unlike existing reexamination and reissue proceedings, which are limited to patents and printed publications, PGR challenges can be based on any grounds for invalidity of a patent, including prior art, lack of utility, improper subject matter, as well as lack of written description, enablement, and indefiniteness. A PGR challenge cannot be based on best mode or inventorship. The claims are given their broadest reasonable interpretation, and the challenger needs to establish invalidity only by a mere preponderance of the evidence.

The USPTO must make a decision on the request for PGR within three months of the petition filing. If a trial proceeding is instituted, the PTAB must render a decision within a year of deciding to review the patent (Coyne, 2011).

PGR Petition Filing Requirements

From a procedural perspective, the PTAB has provided the following guidance for filing of a post grant review:

- must be filed by a person who is not the owner of the patent and has not previously filed a civil action;
- must identify the real parties in interest;
- must be accompanied by payment of the required filing fees;
- must include a petition to institute a post grant review of the patent;
- the petition must demonstrate that it is more likely than not that the petitioner will prevail on at least one claim challenged or raises a novel question that is important to other patents or publications; and
- must be filed only within nine months after the grant of a patent or issuance of a reissue patent.

Processing of Post Grant Review

As specified in the AIA, the Director can determine the manner in which post grant review or other proceedings may proceed, including providing for stay, transfer, consolidation, or termination of any such matter or proceeding. The Director can reject the petition or request on the basis that the same or substantially the same prior art or arguments were previously presented to the USPTO.

If the PGR proceeding is granted, the patentee may respond and the Board will issue a preliminary response within three months of the patentee's statement or lapse of the patentee's response window. In addition, discovery is allowable, and the patentee may comment or amend the claims, or both. The AIA provides for settlement of PGR proceedings or for arbitration of any issue. A PGR can be terminated with respect to any petitioner on the joint request of the petitioner and the patent owner unless the Board has rendered a decision on the merits before the request for termination was filed. If no petitioner remains in the PGR, the Board may terminate the PGR or proceed to a final written decision.

If a PGR is instituted and not dismissed prior to a written decision, the decision will include a determination of the patentability of any claim challenged by the petitioner and any new claim added. Final written decisions will estop any remaining petitioner from raising any defense that was raised or could have reasonably been raised in subsequent proceedings before the USPTO, any District Court or the International Trade Commission. The AIA provides for appellate relief to those dissatisfied with the Board's decision, but only by way of appeal to the Federal Circuit; no appeal to the District Court is authorized (Tridico et al, 2011).

PGR Quick Reference Guide

A quick reference guide to the eligibility, grounds for filing, and petition filing requirements for a PGR are summarized in Table 33.

Table 33: Post Grant Review—Quick Reference Guide

Criteria	Details
Effective Date	September 16, 2012
Eligibility	Available for patents issuing from applications filed after March 16, 2013, under the first-to-file provisions of the AIA.
Who Can File?	Any person who is not the patent owner and has not previously filed a civil action challenging validity of the patent.
Grounds for Filing	A petitioner for PGR may request to cancel as unpatentable one or more claims of a patent on any ground that could be raised relating to invalidity (i.e., novelty, obviousness, written description, enablement, indefiniteness, but not best mode).
Timing Considerations	A PGR can be requested on or prior to the date that is nine months after the grant of a patent or issuance of a reissue patent.
Standard to Institute	Petitioner must demonstrate that it is more likely than not that at least one of the claims challenged in the petition is unpatentable to trigger a PGR. Alternatively, the petitioner may show that the petition raises a novel or unsettled legal question that is important to other patents or patent applications. The PTAB will decide petitions for PGR and conduct any ensuing reviews. In instituting a review, the Board may take into account whether, and reject the petition or request because, the same or substantially same prior art or arguments previously were presented to the Office.

Filing Requirements	A PGR petition must: ▪ identify all real parties in interest; ▪ identify all claims challenged and all grounds on which the challenge to each claim is based; ▪ provide copies of evidence relied upon; ▪ include a power of attorney; ▪ include authorization to charge petition fees.
Filing Fees	The fees for PGR depend on the number of claims being challenged as indicated below: ▪ PGR request fee under 37 C.F.R. §42.15(b)(1) for up to twenty claims challenged. ▪ PGR post-institution fee under 37 C.F.R. §42.15(b)(2) for up to fifteen claims challenged. ▪ PGR request fee under 37 C.F.R. §42.15(b)(3) for each claim in excess of twenty challenged. ▪ PGR post-institution fee under 37 C.F.R. §42.15(b)(4) for each claim in excess of fifteen challenged. A request fee and a post-institution fee depending on the number of claims challenged must be paid on filing the petition. Small entity and micro entity discounts do not apply.
Patent Owner's Response	The patent owner will be given an opportunity to file a preliminary response within two months of petition docketed date. In the preliminary response to the petition, the patent owner must give reasons why no PGR should be granted. During the PGR proceeding, the patent owner may file one motion to amend the challenged patent claims. Amendments may cancel any challenged patent claim or propose a reasonable number of substitute claims, or both. The patent owner bears the burden of distinguishing any amended claims from the prior art.

Nature of the Proceeding	A petitioner may supplement information provided in the petition for PGR by a motion within one month of the date the trial is instituted. The file of a PGR is open to the public, except that a party may seek to have a document sealed by filing a motion to seal. There are also provisions for protective orders to govern the exchange and submission of confidential information. Discovery is limited to evidence directly related to factual assertions advanced by either party in the proceeding. A party may request relief during a PGR by filing a motion. Either party to a PGR may request an oral hearing. Where a PGR is instituted, the Board will issue a final written decision. The decision will address the patentability of any challenged patent claim and any new claim added via amendment during the PGR. A party is statutorily precluded from appealing the Board's decision whether to institute a PGR. A party dissatisfied with the final written decision in a PGR may appeal to the Federal Circuit.
Duration	A PGR is statutorily required to be completed within one year of institution, except that the time may be extended up to six months for good cause.
Settlement	A settlement terminates the proceeding with respect to the petitioner, and the Board may terminate the proceeding or issue a final written decision.
Estoppels	A petitioner in a PGR may not request or maintain a subsequent proceeding before the Office with respect to any challenged patent claim on any ground that was raised or reasonably could have been raised in the PGR. Similarly, a petitioner in a PGR may not assert in a subsequent District Court or the ITC action that a claim is invalid on any ground that the petitioner raised or reasonably could have been raised in the PGR.
Limitations	Only available for first-to-file patents filed after March 16, 2013. Cannot be instituted after petitioner or real party in interest or its privies have filed a civil action challenging validity. Estoppels attach upon final written decision of the Board. Estoppels apply to both District Court and ITC proceedings.

Covered Business Methods Review

Covered business method review is a subset of post grant review for business method patents. To be eligible for a covered business methods (CBM) review, the patent must be a business method patent as defined in statute as "a method or corresponding apparatus for performing data processing or other operations for a financial product or service." The business method patent definition excludes patents for technological inventions. Both first-to-invent and first-to-file patents are eligible for CBM review, although prior art is limited when challenging a first-to-invent patent.

The differences between a CBM review and a PGR are dictated by the circumstances. A CBM petition cannot be filed during the time a PGR could be filed (i.e., nine months after issuance of a patent). To file a CBM review, the petitioner must be sued or charged with infringement. The petitioner has the burden of establishing that the patent is eligible for CBM review and must certify that it is not estopped from proceeding (USPTO, America Invents Act Roadshow, 2012).

CBM Petition Filing Requirements

To file a CBM petition, the challenged patent must be within its period of enforceability, which includes six years after expiration. The CBM petition must be filed against a first-to-file patent and cannot be filed during the period in which a PGR is available. The petitioner must have been sued or charged with infringement. The petitioner, the real party in interest, and their privies cannot be estopped from challenging the claims on the grounds identified in the petition. The challenged patent must be a covered business method patent as defined in the statute. The petitioner must demonstrate that it is more likely than not that at least one of the challenged claims is unpatentable.

CBM Quick Reference Guide

A quick reference guide to the eligibility, grounds for filing, and petition filing requirements for CBM review are summarized in Table 34.

Table 34: Covered Buisness Method Review—Quick Reference Guide

Criteria	Details
Effective Date	September 16, 2012
Eligibility	Patent must be for a method or corresponding apparatus for performing data processing or other operations for a financial product or service. The ability to file a petition for a CBM review sunsets after eight years. The PTAB will not accept a petition for a CBM review filed on or after September 16, 2020.

Who Can File?	Only a person who is sued or charged with infringement may file a CBM.
Grounds for Filing	A petitioner for CBM review must show that it is more likely than not that at least one challenged claim is unpatentable.
Timing Considerations	A petition for CBM review can be filed against patents under the first-to-invent and first-to-file system. ▪ If the patent challenged was filed on or after September 16, 2012, a petition for CBM review cannot be filed within nine months of the grant of the patent. The petitioner must wait nine months after the grant of the patent, or file a PGR. ▪ If the patent challenged was filed before September 16, 2012, a petition for CBM review can be filed even within the first nine months of the patent grant, although there must be a current litigation proceeding.
Standard to Institute	The petitioner must demonstrate that it is more likely than not that at least one of the claims challenged is unpatentable. The PTAB will decide petitions for CBM review and conduct any ensuing reviews. In instituting a review, the Board may take into account whether, and reject the petition or request because, the same or substantially same prior art or arguments previously were presented to the Office.
Filing Requirements	A CBM petition must: ▪ adhere to the eighty-page limit, not including table of contents, table of authorities, mandatory notice, and certificate of service; ▪ identify the real parties of interest; ▪ identify all claims challenged and the grounds (under §101, §102, §103 or §112) on which the challenge to each claim is based; ▪ provide a claim construction, and show how the constructed claim is unpatentable based on the grounds alleged; ▪ provide copies of evidence relied upon; ▪ identify the exhibit number of the supporting evidence, and state the relevance of the evidence; ▪ demonstrate that it is more likely than not that at least one of the claims challenged is unpatentable; ▪ include a power of attorney; and ▪ include authorization to charge petition fees.

Filing Fees	CBM fees depend on the number of claims being challenged as follows: ▪ A covered business method review request fee under 37 C.F.R. §42.15(b)(1) for up to twenty claims challenged. ▪ A covered business method review post-institution fee under 37 C.F.R. §42.15(b)(2) for up to fifteen claims challenged. ▪ A covered business method review request fee under 37 C.F.R. §42.15(b)(3) for each claim in excess of twenty challenged. ▪ A covered business method review post-institution fee under 37 C.F.R. §42.15(b)(4) for each claim in excess of fifteen challenged. A request fee and a post-institution fee depending on the number of claims challenged must be paid on filing the petition. Small entity and micro entity discounts do not apply.
Patent Owner's Response	The patent owner will be given an opportunity to file a preliminary response within two months of the petition docketed date. In the preliminary response to the petition, the patent owner must give reasons why no CBM review should be granted. During the CBM proceeding, the patent owner may file one motion to amend the challenged patent claims, subject to the standards and procedures set by the Office. Amendments may cancel any challenged patent claim or propose a reasonable number of substitute claims, or both.
Nature of the Proceeding	A petitioner may supplement information provided in the petition for CBM review by a motion within one month of the date trial is instituted. The file of a CBM review is open to the public, except that a party may seek to have a document sealed by filing a motion to seal. There are also provisions for protective orders to govern the exchange and submission of confidential information. Discovery is limited to evidence directly related to factual assertions advanced by either party in the proceeding. A party may request relief during a CBM review by filing a motion. Either party to a CBM review may request an oral hearing. Where a CBM review is instituted, the Board will issue a final written decision. The decision will address the patentability of any challenged patent claim and any new claim added via amendment during the CBM review. A party is statutorily precluded from appealing the Board's decision whether to institute a CBM review. A party dissatisfied with the final written decision in a CBM may appeal to the Federal Circuit.

Duration	A CBM is statutorily required to be completed within one year of institution, except that the time may be extended up to six months for good cause.
Settlement	A settlement terminates the proceeding with respect to the petitioner, and the Board may terminate the proceeding or issue a final written decision.
Estoppels	A petitioner in a CBM review may not request or maintain a subsequent proceeding before the Office with respect to any challenged patent claim on any ground that was raised or reasonably could have been raised in the CBM review. Similarly, a petitioner in a CBM review may not assert in a subsequent District Court or the ITC action that a claim is invalid on any ground that the petitioner raised or reasonably could have been raised in the CBM review.
Limitations	Claims must be direct to practice, administration, or management of financial services or products. Does not include technological inventions. Petitioner or real party in interest or privies must have been sued for infringement or charged with infringement. Estoppels attach upon final written decision of the Board. Estoppels apply to both District Court and ITC proceedings. Estoppels limited to what petitioner raised during the CBM proceeding.

Derivation Proceeding

Under the AIA, derivation proceedings will replace interference proceedings effective March 16, 2013. Only an applicant for patent may file a petition to institute a derivation proceeding. The petition for a derivation proceeding must identify with particularity the basis for finding that an inventor named in an earlier application derived the claimed invention from the petitioner. The petition must be made under oath and supported by substantial evidence. The petition must be filed within one year of the date of the first publication of a claim to an invention that is the same or substantially the same as the earlier application's claim to the invention (USPTO, America Invents Act Roadshow, 2012).

Petition Filing Requirements

In a petition for a derivation proceeding, the petitioner must:

- identify which application or patent is disputed; and

- provide at least one affidavit addressing communication of the derived invention and the lack of authorization for filing the earlier application.

A derivation petition must include the following:

- an identification of the application for patent for which the derivation proceeding is sought;
- a certification that the petition was filed within the one-year time period set by statute;
- a demonstration that the petitioner has a pending application;
- a showing that the petitioner has at least one claim that is the same or substantially the same as the respondent's claimed invention.

Processing of Derivation Proceedings

A derivation is not likely to be instituted, even where the Director thinks the standard for instituting a derivation proceeding is met, until a patent with the claimed invention issues. The parties to a derivation proceeding may resort to binding arbitration, but the Office is not bound by, and may independently determine, any question of patentability.

If a derivation proceeding is instituted and not dismissed, the Board will issue a written decision that states whether an inventor named in an earlier application derived the claimed invention from an inventor named in the petitioner's application without authorization. A party dissatisfied with a final decision in a derivation proceeding may appeal to District Court or the Federal Circuit. In lieu of a derivation proceeding, parties to a derivation proceeding may resort to binding arbitration to determine inventorship. A settlement in a derivation proceeding will be accepted by the Board unless inconsistent with the evidence of record.

Supplemental Examination—Patent Owner Proceeding

The AIA created a supplemental examination procedure that allows a patent owner to cure inequitable conduct or mistakes that occurred during the prosecution of an issued patent. Supplemental examination procedures became available on September 16, 2012, and apply to any patent issued before, on, or after the effective date (retrospective effect). A request for supplemental examination must be filed by the patent owner—it is not available to third-party challengers—and must request that the Office "consider, reconsider, or correct information believed to be relevant to the patent, in accordance with such requirements as the Director may establish." The information that forms the basis of the request is not limited to patents and printed publications and may include other issues, such as those issues specified under 35 U.S.C. §112. The standard for granting the request is whether one or more items of information raises a substantial new question of patentability, which requires a showing that a reasonable examiner would consider the item of information important in determining the patentability of the claims. Patent owners can submit previously undisclosed information or fix incorrect information that may affect the enforceability of a patent. If the submitted information raises a substantial new question of patentability, an *ex parte* reexamination procedure will begin. If no new substantial question is raised, such information cannot be used at a later date to show that the patent is unenforceable. However, the patent may not be protected by this process if the patent is challenged before the submission or, in some cases, during the supplemental examination and resulting reexamination (Warenzak et al, 2011).

Supplemental Examination Filing Requirements

Only a patent owner may file a request for supplemental examination. The Board is not authorized to permit a party who is not a patent owner or a party who merely states that it is, for example, an exclusive licensee or a person with sufficient proprietary interest under 35 U.S.C. §118, to file a request for supplemental examination. All parties having an ownership interest in the patent must act together as a composite entity in a supplemental proceedings before the Office. Under rare circumstances, such as in the case of a deceased or legally incapacitated joint owner, the Office may permit less than all of the joint owners to file a request if a grantable petition under 37 C.F.R. §1.183 requesting waiver of the provisions of 37 C.F.R. §3.71 and §3.73(c) is filed. If the owner of all or a portion of the entire right, title, and interest in the patent is an organization that is dissolved, the Office may require that a determination of the ownership of the patent be obtained from a Court of competent jurisdiction.

There are no page limits to a request for supplemental examination. However, if any document other than the request is over fifty pages in length, the patent owner must provide a summary of the relevant portions of the document with citations to the particular pages. In addition, any non-patent document over twenty pages in length that is submitted as part of the request is subject to document size fees.

A request for supplemental examination may include up to twelve items of information. If the discussion within the body of the request is based, at least in part, on a supporting document, then the supporting document—not the discussion within the request—will be considered as the item of information. If a request for supplemental examination is filed to correct a declaration or affidavit in the prior examination, the corrected declaration would be counted as one item of information, and the marked-up copy of the previously filed declaration would be counted as a second item of information. In such situations, the Office holds that the request include two separate documents for the examiner to consider, reconsider, or correct.

Processing of a Request for Supplemental Examination

A request for supplemental examination that fails to satisfy the filing requirements of 37 C.F.R. §1.605, §1.610, and §1.615 will not be granted a filing date. The Office will not make a request for supplemental examination public until the request is granted a filing date. The Office has a procedure in which the request, and any other papers or information submitted as part of or accompanying the request, is not viewable in public PAIR until a filing date is granted.

The patent owner identified as requesting supplemental examination will be notified of the defects and will be given an opportunity to complete the requirements of the request within a specified time. A Notice of Non-Compliant Supplemental Examination Request under 37 C.F.R. §1.610(d), will be used to provide the notification for supplemental examination. If further explanation is needed as to a non-compliance item, the box at the bottom of the form will be checked. An attachment will then be completed to specifically explain why the request does not comply. If the patent owner timely files a corrected request in response to the notice that properly addresses all of the defects identified in the notice and that otherwise complies with all of the filing requirements, the filing date of the supplemental examination request will be the receipt date of the corrected request. If the patent owner does not timely file a corrected, compliant request in response to the Office's notice, the request for supplemental examination will not be granted a filing date, and the fee for reexamination under 37 C.F.R. §1.20(k)(2) will be refunded. The supplemental examination proceeding also will be terminated.

The most common reasons for a request for supplemental examination not being accorded a filing date include the following (Coller et al, 2013):

- failure to provide a list of the "items of information" to be considered;
- failure to identify each claim of the patent for which supplemental examination is requested;
- failure to provide a separate, detailed explanation of the relevance and manner of applying each item of information to each claim of the patent for which supplemental examination is requested;
- failure to provide a copy of the patent for which supplemental examination is requested (including any disclaimer or certificate issued for the patent);
- failure to provide a legible copy of each item of information (other than U.S. patent documents) and/or an accompanying English language translation (if necessary); and
- failure to provide a summary of the relevant portions of any submitted document, other than the request itself, that is over 50 pages in length.

The Office will conclude a supplemental examination by issuing a certificate of supplemental examination. The certificate will indicate the results of the Office's determination as to whether any item of information filed by the patent owner in the request raised a substantial new question of patentability.

The Office will mail the following two documents to the patent owner at the conclusion of the supplemental examination:

- the Supplemental Examination Certificate; and
- the Reasons for Substantial New Question of Patentability Determination.

The certificate will state whether a substantial new question of patentability was or was not raised by the request for supplemental examination. The certificate also will list the items of information considered. The reasons for the substantial new question of patentability determination will be identified in the examiner's determination as to whether each item of information reached the standard.

At the conclusion of a supplemental examination, the Office will issue an electronic supplemental examination certificate as part of the public record for the patent. If the certificate states that a substantial new question of patentability is raised by one or more items of information in the request, *ex parte* reexamination of the patent will be ordered under 35 U.S.C. §257 by a subsequent communication. Upon the conclusion of the *ex parte* reexamination proceeding, an *ex parte* reexamination certificate, which will include a statement specifying that *ex parte* reexamination was ordered under 35 U.S.C. §257, will be published as an attachment to the patent. If the supplemental examination certificate indicates that no substantial new question of patentability was raised by any of the items of information in the request, *ex parte* reexamination will not be ordered, and the fee for reexamination ordered as a result of supplemental examination under 37 C.F.R. §1.20(k)(2) will be refunded in accordance with 37 C.F.R. §1.610(d). In this case, the electronically issued supplemental examination certificate will be published in due course as an attachment to the patent. Supplemental examination cannot be used to correct fraud on the Office and cannot be used as a shield against a finding of unenforceability if the culpable conduct was previously alleged with particularity in a civil action.

The AIA specifically provides that a patent cannot be held unenforceable based on information that was not considered or was not adequately considered in a prior examination if the information is considered, reconsidered, or corrected during a supplemental examination. The process, however, is not free from risk; if the patentee submits information on supplemental examination that the USPTO determines to be material to patentability, a potential infringement target may be able to use that evidence against the patentee in a declaratory judgment or other action (Coyne, 2011). The supplemental examination provision is intended to boost the value of issued patents by driving down claims of inequitable conduct. When the patentee submits the relevant information for consideration by the USPTO and no new substantial question of patentability is raised, such information cannot be later used as ammunition for an equitable conduct claim by an accused infringer. Supplemental examination procedures allow patent owners to conduct a pre-litigation analysis to determine if they need to take advantage of the procedures before bringing an action. In most cases, it may be easier to address the concerns before the USPTO than in litigation against a hostile alleged infringer. Under the supplemental examination procedures, patent owners may amend claims and still inoculate the patent against an inequitable conduct claim (Coe, 2011).

Supplemental Examination Quick Reference Guide

A quick reference guide to the eligibility, grounds for filing, and filing requirements for supplemental examination are summarized in Table 35.

Table 35: Supplemental Examination—Quick Reference Guide	
Criteria	Details
Effective Date	September 16, 2012.
Eligibility	Available for all issued and reissued patents.
Benefit to Patent Owner	The patent owner can immunize the patent against allegations of inequitable conduct by completing a SE. Specifically, information considered, reconsidered, or corrected during a SE cannot be the basis for rendering a patent unenforceable for inequitable conduct, so long as the SE and any resulting *ex parte* reexamination are completed before the civil action is brought. The patent owner, however, cannot secure inequitable conduct immunization for information raised in a civil action brought before a SE. Provides patentees with an alternative to litigation to cleanse their patents of allegations of inequitable conduct. Provides an alternative route to reexamination.
Who Can File?	The patent owner may file a SE; a third party is not permitted to seek a supplemental examination.
Grounds for Filing	The patent owner may request a SE for a patent so that the Office can consider, reconsider, or correct information believed to be relevant to the patent. The patent owner may present any information believed to be relevant to the patent. The information is not limited to patents or printed publications but instead may include information concerning any ground of patentability, i.e., patent-eligible subject matter, anticipation, obviousness, written description, enablement, best mode, and indefiniteness.
Timing Considerations	Must be filed before allegations against the patent owner were served; otherwise no additional time limit.
Standard to Initiate	In a SE, the Office will determine whether any item of information presented in the request raises a substantial new question of patentability. The substantial new question of patentability standard is triggered when there is a substantial likelihood that a reasonable examiner would consider an item of information important in determining the patentability of the claimed invention.

Filing Requirements	The request for SE must: ▪ identify each aspect of the patent for which SE is sought; ▪ identify each item of information being submitted and whether the item was not considered, not adequately considered, or incorrect during the original prosecution; ▪ adhere to the restriction of no more than twelve items of information per request for SE; ▪ identify why consideration is being sought, and provide a detailed explanation of relevancy; ▪ include a list of each item of information being submitted and its publication date if applicable; ▪ include copies of each item of information being submitted (except for U.S. patent and published applications), and include English translation where necessary; ▪ provide a summary of the relevant portions of any submitted document that is over fifty pages in length; and ▪ include authorization to charge associated fees.
Filing Fees	A request for SE must include the following fees: ▪ Request for supplemental examination under 37 C.F.R. §1.20(k)(1); ▪ Reexamination fee ordered as result of request for supplemental examination fee under 37 C.F.R. §1.20(k)(2); ▪ Supplemental Examination Document Size Fee for non-patent document having between twenty-one and fifty sheets under 37 C.F.R. §1.20(k)(3)(i); and ▪ Supplemental Examination Document Size Fee for each additional fifty sheets or a fraction thereof in a non-patent document under 37 C.F.R. §1.20(k)(3)(ii). Request for SE request fee and reexamination fee must be paid on filing. Document size fees may also apply for non-patent documents over twenty sheets in length. If a reexamination is not ordered by the Office, the reexamination filing fee will be refunded.

Nature of the Proceeding	Within three months of the filing date of a request for SE from a patent owner, the Office will determine whether any of the items of information filed with the request raises a substantial new question of patentability. If a substantial new question of patentability is found for any item of information, then the Office will order an *ex parte* reexamination of the patent. The *ex parte* reexamination will be conducted in accordance with the existing rules governing *ex parte* reexamination, except that: the patent owner will not have the right to file a patent owner statement; and the Office will address each substantial new question of patentability without regard to whether it is raised by a patent or printed publication. If an *ex parte* reexamination is ordered, the patent owner may file an amendment after the issuance of the initial office action in the *ex parte* reexamination proceeding.
Duration	Process to be completed within the three-month statutory period.
Conclusion	The Office will conclude a SE by issuing a certificate of supplemental examination. The certificate will indicate the results of the Office's determination as to whether any item of information filed by the patent owner in the request raised a substantial new question of patentability.

Differences Between Post-Grant Review Proceedings

The AIA contains provisions for three new post-grant review proceedings that can be filed by third-party challengers or patent owners. Portfolio strategic planning will inform which option is the best to pursue with respect to time, costs, and potential outcomes. The attributes of the post-grant review proceeding options are compared and contrasted in Table 36. Potential patent challengers will have to weigh the potential benefits of the new PGR and IPR options before the PTAB against the costs of District Court litigation and the potential estoppels. The strict time frames for resolving PGR and IPR may be especially attractive for parties accused of infringement or a party under a license request, but the attached estoppel will require careful consideration. The statutory time lines and the new role of the PTAB are expected to dramatically shorten the length of trial proceedings compared to current reexamination proceedings. This may lead to more final decisions issuing with estoppel effects. The higher threshold for initiation of PGR and IPR may play a significant role in determining the degree to which requesters make use of these new proceedings.

Defendants in concurrent litigation will need to consider the impact of any ongoing reexaminations filed on litigation stay strategy. Defendants in concurrent litigation will need to develop defensive strategies as soon as they have notice of the suit to keep their options open and avoid being precluded from filing a PGR or IPR. The wider scope of PGR to allow review of patentability on §112 grounds, e.g., for lack of enablement, may be especially attractive to defendants facing patents asserted in technologies such as biotechnology or the chemical arts, where §112 has created greater patentability and validity hurdles for patentees.

On the other side, patent owners may wish to take advantage of the new supplemental examination as part of their strategy prior to bringing a patent infringement suit. Patent owners also may adjust their own licensing or enforcement strategies to account for when the window for PGR closes. Significant resources and work will be required to benefit from the array of post-grant review proceedings available (Messinger et al, 2011).

Table 36: Comparison of Post-Grant Review Proceedings Under the America Invents Act			
	Post Grant Review (PGR)	*Inter Partes* Review (IPR)	Supplemental Examination (SE)
Who Can File?	Only third parties; not available to patent owners.	Only third parties; not available to patent owners.	Only patent owner; not available to third parties.
When to File?	Within first nine months of issuance of the patent or issuance of a broadening reissue patent.	Nine months after patent issue date or completion of any previously initiated post-grant review proceeding.	Any time after issuance.
Grounds for Filing	Petition may be based on any grounds for invalidity of the patent (such grounds exclude failure to comply with the best mode requirement).	Petition may be based only on revised §102 and §103, and only on the basis of prior art patents and printed publications.	Petition may be based on any information believed to be relevant, including prior art patents or publications to inventorship issues. Serves as a vehicle for patent owners to clear up or correct any inadvertent or even negligent errors in prior prosecution that could have previously led to allegations of inequitable conduct. Allows the patent holders a chance to correct mistakes they failed to catch during prosecution. USPTO will order a reexamination if the information raises a substantial new question of patentability.

Filing Requirements	Petition, authorize associated fees, identify real party in interest, grounds and supporting evidence, proof of service, and power of attorney.	Petition, authorize associated fees, identify real party in interest, grounds and supporting evidence, proof of service, and power of attorney.	Request, authorize associated fees, present information relevant to patentability.
Filing Fee	A petition request fee and post-institution fee dependent on the number of claims challenged must be paid on filing.	A petition request fee and post-institution fee dependent on the number of claims challenged must be paid on filing.	A supplemental request fee and reexamination fee and any examination document size fees applicable must be paid on filing.
Patent Owner's Response	Patent owner has a right to file a preliminary response identifying reasons and supporting evidence why no PGR should be initiated. Petitioner gets at least one opportunity to comment.	Patent owner has a right to file a preliminary response identifying reasons and supporting evidence why no IPR should be initiated. Petitioner gets at least one opportunity to comment.	Not applicable. Filed by the patent owner.
Deadline for Order of Proceeding	The PTAB has three months from patent owner response deadline to determine whether PGR proceeding should be granted.	The PTAB has three months from patent owner response deadline to determine whether IPR proceeding should be granted.	Director has three months to determine whether an *ex parte* reexamination should be ordered.

Standard to Institute	After reviewing the petition and any response, the PTAB must determine whether the information presented in petition, if not rebutted, would demonstrate that it is more likely than not that at least one of the claims challenged in the petition is unpatentable or that the petition raises a novel or unsettled legal question that is important to other patents or patent applications.	After reviewing the petition and any response, the PTAB must determine whether there is a reasonable likelihood that the petitioner would prevail with respect to at least one of the claims challenged in the petition.	After reviewing the request, the Director must determine if a substantial new question of patentability has been raised.
Effect of Director Decision	Director's decision to order PGR is final and not appealable.	Director's decision to order IPR is final and not appealable.	Decision to grant a supplemental examination and order an *ex parte* reexamination is final and not appealable.

Impact of Other Proceedings	PGR cannot be instituted if petitioner or real party in interest already filed a declaratory judgment action for patent invalidity. Any declaratory judgment action for patent invalidity is automatically stayed in favor of a PGR until: ▪ patent moves to lift stay; ▪ patent owner files a civil action or counterclaim for infringement; or ▪ petitioner moves court to dismiss the civil action.	IPR cannot be instituted if petitioner or real party in interest already filed a declaratory judgment action for patent invalidity. Any declaratory judgment action for patent invalidity is automatically stayed in favor of a IPR until: ▪ patent moves to lift stay; ▪ patent owner files a civil action or counterclaim for infringement; or ▪ petitioner moves court to dismiss the civil action. Additionally, a third party may not petition for IPR on a patent more than one year after being served with a complaint for infringement of that patent.	Can be used to reduce or eliminate known weaknesses in a patent prior to litigation.

Estoppels	Estoppels only apply after a final written decision on the merits. Petitioner is estopped from further challenging the patentability in the PTO of any previously reviewed claim on any ground raised or that reasonably could have been raised in the prior PGR proceeding. Petitioner is also estopped from further challenging validity in a District Court or in the ITC on any ground raised or that reasonably could have been raised in the PGR proceeding. Estoppel may be avoided by settlement.	Estoppels only apply after a final written decision on the merits. Petitioner is estopped from further challenging the patentability in the PTO of any previously reviewed claim on any ground raised or that reasonably could have been raised in the prior IPR proceeding. Petitioner is also estopped from further challenging validity in a District Court or in the ITC on any ground raised or that reasonably could have been raised in the IPR proceeding. Estoppel may be avoided by settlement.	Information considered in the procedure may not be used to hold the patent unenforceable in subsequent litigations and gives the patent owner an opportunity to cure potential allegations of inequitable conduct.

Review Process	Review conducted by the PTAB. Multiple parties may join a single PGR. A protective order will govern disclosure of confidential information. Patent owner may file a motion to cancel claims or propose a reasonable number of substitute claims, but no enlargement of claim scope permitted. Both parties have a right to an oral hearing. PTO may impose sanction for abuse of discovery, abuse of process, harassment, delay, or unnecessary increase in cost.	Review conducted by the PTAB. Multiple parties may join a single IPR. A protective order will govern disclosure of confidential information. Patent owner may file a motion to cancel claims or propose a reasonable number of substitute claims, but no enlargement of claim scope is permitted. Both parties have a right to an oral hearing. PTO may impose sanctions for abuse of discovery, abuse of process, harassment, delay, or unnecessary increase in cost. IPR also includes additional limited discovery, such as depositions of any witness submitting an affidavit or declaration.	If request for supplemental examination is granted and *ex parte* reexamination is ordered and conducted by the reexamination unit.
Settlement	PGR terminated upon a joint request of the petitioner and patent owner. Settlement must be in writing and a copy filed with the Office.	IPR terminated upon a joint request of the petitioner and patent owner. Settlement must be in writing and a copy filed with the Office.	Not applicable; no adverse party.

Appeal of Decision	Either party may appeal an adverse decision only to the U.S. Court of Appeals for the Federal Circuit. There are no provisions for review by a District Court.	Either party may appeal an adverse decision only to the U.S. Court of Appeals for the Federal Circuit. There are no provisions for review by a District Court.	Not applicable; no adverse party.
Quota Limit	Director may impose a limit on the number of PGRs that may be instituted during each of the first four one-year periods in which the law is in effect.	Director may impose a limit on the number of IPRs that may be instituted during each of the first four one-year periods in which the law is in effect, if such number in each year exceeds the number of *inter partes* reexaminations that are ordered in the last fiscal year ending before the effective date of the law.	Not applicable.

Source: Messinger et al., (2011)

Observations on Trial Proceedings before the PTAB

The first year of contested proceedings before the PTAB has been used to compile the following practice observations on trial proceedings before the Board (Sterne, Kessler, Goldstein & Fox PLLC, 2013):

- Prior to filing a petition, the lead and backup Counsel must be registered in PRPS; each must have a User ID and password.
- The petition filed must identify the issues to be raised and support for the argument; it is the one change to present challenges to the validity of the patent. The petition must contain detailed analysis of where in the reference the claimed subject matter can be found. The petition must meet procedural requirements under 35 U.S.C. §312(a) and substantive threshold requirements under 35 U.S.C. §314(a).
- The page limits are strictly enforced, and the petitioner has to file a motion for cause for an exception.
- The PTAB strongly encourages petitioners to choose the best rejections and explain them fully, rather than adding numerous poorly supported cumulative rejections to the petition. The PTAB will not fill in missing information for the petitioner. The petition must be substantively complete for the trial to be instituted.
- IPR and CBM reviews have different standards for instituting a trial. In an IPR, there must be "a reasonable likelihood" that at least one of the claims challenged is unpatentable. A CBM review must show that the claim is "more likely than not" to be unpatentable.
- Expert declarations are critical to the trial proceedings; experts used in a trial proceeding do not have to be the same experts used in prosecution, but their previous declarations should not be inconsistent with the position being advanced. All declarants are subject to cross-examination.
- Every trial decision is accompanied by a scheduling order that sets the due dates for the trial phase. The scheduling order will indicate which dates may be extended by agreement and which may not be extended.
- The PTAB has a mandate for completion of the trial proceeding within one year of institution. The Board can set deadlines shorter than three months for patent owner and petitioner discovery.
- The PTAB will not consider a motion to amend unless the patent owner is unsuccessful in defending the original claim or chooses not to defend an original claim.

A patent owner may file one motion to amend a patent but only after conferring with the Board. The amendment may cancel or propose a reasonable number of substitute claims but must identify the support in the original disclosure for each claim that is amended. A proper substitute claim may only narrow the scope of the challenged claim it replaces. The patent owner must identify the features added to each substitute claim and persuade the Board that the proposed substitute claim is patentable over the prior art of record and over the prior art not of record but known to the patent owner.

- Parties should not file any documents unless they have a specific authorization to do so by rule or order. Parties seeking relief must file a motion; failure to do so can result in expungement of documents.
- Oral hearings are limited in time (typically twenty to thirty minutes for each side). The administrative patent judges will have certain points they want to discuss. PowerPoint presentations should not be used; parties should prepare key points and supportive arguments. Parties need to be cooperative with the administrative patent judges and answer their questions.
- An exhibit relied upon should be submitted to the Board even if it is already part of the prosecution file or considered well known.
- The statute and rules provide for the submission of confidential information subject to a protective order. Any submission of confidential material must be accompanied by a motion to seal, a discussion of the confidential information, a redacted version, and an explanation of the need for confidentiality. The Board has a statutory mandate to ensure the proceedings are made public. If the motion is not granted, there are provisions for expungement. Papers will be made public forty-five days after termination of the trial unless there is a motion to expunge.
- Discovery is limited in scope to "in interests of justice" (IPR and derivation) or "good cause" (PGR and CBM). Parties may agree to additional discovery between themselves. Where the parties fail to agree, a party may move for additional discovery. The Board may also specify conditions for additional discovery. Additional discovery under the Federal Rules of Civil Procedure do not apply to trial proceedings.
- The parties may agree to settle any issue in a proceeding, but the Board is not a party to the settlement and may independently determine any question of jurisdiction, patentability, or practice. The earlier the settlement is reached, the more likely the case will be terminated before the Board. A party to a settlement may request that

the settlement be treated as business confidential information and be kept separate from the files of an involved patent or application.

As the provisions of the AIA continue to evolve, it is likely that the patent rules related to contested proceedings will be further defined.

CHAPTER-SPECIFIC REFERENCE MATERIAL

Reference Source	Post-Grant Review Proceeding Under the America Invents Act Applicable Rules and Practice Guide
Patent Trial and Appeal Board (PTAB)	PTAB Homepage http://www.uspto.gov/ip/boards/bpai/index.jsp
PTAB Rules and Practices	Board Trial Rules and Practice Guide http://www.uspto.gov/ip/boards/bpai/board_trial_rules_and_practice_guide.jsp
PTAB Representative Orders and Opinions	PTAB Representative Orders, Decision and Notices http://www.uspto.gov/ip/boards/bpai/representative_orders_and_opinions.jsp
Filing Interface (PRPS)	Patent Review Processing System http://www.uspto.gov/ip/boards/bpai/prps.jsp
AIA Microsite	AIA Implementation—FAQ http://www.uspto.gov/aia_implementation/

Contested Proceedings Guides	*Inter Partes* Review http://www.uspto.gov/aia_implementation/bpai.jsp#heading-1 Post Grant Review http://www.uspto.gov/aia_implementation/bpai.jsp#heading-2 Transitional Program for Covered Business Method Patents http://www.uspto.gov/aia_implementation/bpai.jsp#heading-3 Derivation Proceedings http://www.uspto.gov/aia_implementation/faq.jsp
Supplemental Examination Final Rules	http://www.uspto.gov/aia_implementation/Supp_Exam_Rules.pdf

References

Armstrong Teasdale LLP. (2014, January 21). Patent Term Adjustment Update—Novartis v. Lee. Retrieved from www.lexology.com.

Ashbrook et al. (2010, January 28). Patent Term Adjustment After Wyeth V. Kappos. Retrieved from www.law360.com. Reproduced with permission from Portfolio Media, Inc.

Bellis, M. (2012). Patent Term Extension and Adjustment. Retrieved from About.com Inventors.

Chisum. (1993). Historical Development of Patent Law. In Chisum on Patents (pp. OV1-15). Matthew Bender & Co., Inc.

Coe, E. (2011, September 23). Patent Reform Law to Curb Inequitable Conduct Claims. Retrieved from www.law360.com. Reproduced with permission from Portfolio Media, Inc.

Colice et al. (2013, February 20). Beware Risks When Expediting USPTO Examination. Retrieved from www.law360.com. Reproduced with permission from Portfolio Media, Inc.

Coller et al. (2013, December 16). Lessons from the 1st Year of Supplemental Examination. Retrieved from www.law360.com.

Colice et al. (2013, June 4). PPH 2.0 Offers Ways To Reduce Prosecution Time and Costs. Retrieved from www.law360.com. Reproduced with permission from Portfolio Media, Inc.

Collins, B. (2012, September 5). USPTO Trials: Understanding The Discovery Rules. Retrieved from www.law360.com. Reproduced with permission from Portfolio Media, Inc.

Covington & Burling. (2001, May 23). American Inventors Protection Act. Retrieved from www.cov.com.

Coyne, P. J. (2011, October 28). The America Invents Act: How Does it Strengthen the Patent System? BNA's Patent, Trademark & Copyright Journal, 1-7. Reproduced with permission from BNA's Patent, Trademark & Copyright Journal, 82 PTCJ 901 (Oct. 28, 2011). Copyright 2011 by The Bureau of National Affairs, Inc. (800-372-1033) http://www.bna.com.

Crouch, D. (2004, November 10). USPTO Releases Notes on Restriction Practice. Retrieved from Patently-O.

Crouch, D. (2009, August 23). Reissue Applications Over Time. Retrieved from Patently-O.

Crouch, D. (2010, June 5). Calculating Patent Term. Retrieved from Patently-O.

Crouch, D. (2010, March 3). Rise in Restriction Requirement: A Response from USPTO. Retrieved from Patently-O.

Crouch, D. (2011, May 04). Impermissible Recapture Rule Curtails Potential for Broadening Reissue. Retrieved from Patently-O.

Crouch, D. (2011, November 22). New BPAI Final Rules. Retrieved from Patently-O.

Crouch, D. (2012, August 14). AIA Shifts USPTO Focus from Inventors to Patent Owners. Retrieved from Patently-O.

Crouch, D. (2013, September 20). AIA Changeover: Claiming Subject Matter Not Found in the Provisional Application. Retrieved from Patently-O.

Crouch, D. (2013, January 15). AIA Technical Amendment Becomes Law. Retrieved from Patently-O.

Davis, R. (2013, April 2). USPTO Patent Term Adjustment Rules Praised by IP Attorneys. Retrieved from www.law360.com. Reproduced with permission from Portfolio Media, Inc.

Durta, T. (2014, January 28). PTO Publishes Proposed Rules for Periodic Reporting of Application, Patent Ownership. Retrieved from www.bna.com.

Durta, T. (2012, June 1). PTO Proposes Rules for Patent Applicants Meeting AIA-Mandated Micro Entity Status. Retrieved from www.bna.com: Reproduced with permission from BNA's Patent, Trademark & Copyright Journal, 84 PTCJ 176 (Jun. 1, 2012). Copyright 2012 by The Bureau of National Affairs, Inc. (800-372-1033) http://www.bna.com.

Gallagher, D. (2003, November). Final Rejection of a Patent Application—What to Do? Retrieved from www.invention-protection.com.

Gaudry, K. (2013, September 6). Track 1 Stats: Higher Allowance Rate, Speedy Prosecution. Retrieved from www.law360.com. Reproduced with permission from Portfolio Media, Inc.

Gomez, B. (2012, January 17). New Track I Prioritzed Examination for RCE Applications. Retrieved from www.patentlyo.com.

Halstead, D. (2011, October). U.S. Patent Reform: Path to Harmonization. Retrieved from Managing Intellectual Property.

Horton, K. (2010, August 20). 9 Tips for 3rd-Party Prior Art Submission. Retrieved from www.law360.com. Reproduced with permission from Portfolio Media, Inc.

Janicki, W. (2012, September 17). Implementing The Rules For Administrative Patent Trials. Retrieved from www.law360.com. Reproduced with permission from Portfolio Media, Inc.

Jester, M. H. (1964). Patents and Trademarks—Plain & Simple. Career Press.

Jewik, P. (2010, August 24). How to Fast-Track Your Patent Application. Retrieved from www.law360.com. Reproduced with permission from Portfolio Media, Inc.

Johnson et al. (2013, November 15). How Patent Procedures Will Change Under the Patent Law Treaty. Retrieved from www.law360.com.

Kamholz, S. E. (2009, October 17). Patent Term Adjustment for Fun and Profit. Retrieved from www.patentlyo.com.

Karny, G. M. (2005). How to Set a Patent Strategy. Legal Times, pp. 40-41.

Kilpatrick Townsend & Stockton LLP. (2012, November 2012). New PTA Calculation to Extend PTA Length For Many New Applications. Retrieved from www.lexology.com.

Kowalchyk et al. (2013, August 19). Post-Grant Patent Proceedings: The Limited Scope of Additional Discovery. Retrieved from www.iplaw.bna.com: Reproduced with permission from BNA's Patent, Trademark & Copyright Journal, 86 PTCJ 824 (Aug. 16, 2013). Copyright 2013 by The Bureau of National Affairs, Inc. (800-372-1033) http://www.bna.com.

Ladas & Parry LLP. (2009, July 17). A Brief History of Patent Law of the United States. Retrieved from www.ladas.com.

Lagatta et al. (2013, August 16). How *Inter Partes* Review Became a Valuable Tool So Quickly. Retrieved from www.law360.com. Reproduced with permission from Portfolio Media, Inc.

Messinger et al. (2011, September 16). Patent Litigation at the PTO Under The America Invents Act of 2011. BNA's Patent, Trademark & Copyright Journal.

Migliorini, R. D. (2007). Twelve Years Later: Provisional Patent Application Filing Revisited. Journal of the Patent and Trademark Office Society, 89, 437-455.

Mollaaghababa, R. (2013, February 22). 10 Reasons To File Patent Applications Before March 16. Retrieved from www.law360.com. Reproduced with permission from Portfolio Media, Inc.

Nutter McClennen & Fish LLP. (2014, January 15). USPTO Gives Applicants Two Months to Reply to Restriction Requirement and Other Actions Without Having to Pay a Fee. Retrieved from www.lexology.com.

Oppedahl, C. (2012, August 30). What Will Change About the Oath or Declaration On September 16, 2012. Retrieved from www.oppedhal.com.

Patent Lens. (n.d.). What is a Continuing Application? Retrieved from www.patentlens.net.

Patent Resources Institute, Inc. (2004). Patent Practice. Eighth Edition. Patent Resources Institute, Inc.

Pelletier, D. (2011, October 12). Top 10 Provisions of the America Invents Act. Retrieved from www.law360.com. Reproduced with permission from Portfolio Media, Inc.

Ramage et al. (2011, September 19). Patent Reform's 'Brave New World'. Retrieved from www.bio-itworld.com.

Silverman, R. (2005). Patent Filing Strategies for Pharmaceutical Products. AIPLA Quarterly Journal, 153-187.

Sterne, Kessler, Goldstein & Fox PLLC. (2008). Reexamination Timeline. Retrieved from www.reexamcenter.com.

Sterne, Kessler, Goldstein & Fox PLLC. (2013, January 15). AIA Technical Corrections Bill Signed into Law. Retrieved from www.jdsupra.com.

Sterne, Kessler, Goldstein & Fox PLLC. (2013, September 16). One Year Later: Observations from the First Year of Contested Proceedings at the USPTO. Retrieved from www.lexology.com.

Sunstein, B. (2011, September 28). America Invents Act: Highlights of First-to-File. BPLA Meeting Slides. Boston Patent Law Association (BPLA).

Tietz, P. (2013, February 19). Patent Term Adjustment Is Hiding in AIA Corrections Law. Retrieved from www.law360.com. Reproduced with permission from Portfolio Media, Inc.

Tridico et al. (2011, October 20). Post Grant Review vs. EPO Oppositions. Retrieved from www.law360.com. Reproduced with permission from Portfolio Media, Inc.

Tu et al. (2013, September 5). USPTO's Final Rejection of a Patent Isn't So Final. Retrieved from www.law360.com. Reproduced with permission from Portfolio Media, Inc.

USPTO. (2006, November 2). Revised Accelerated Examination Program and Petition to Make Special Procedures. Retrieved from www.uspto.gov.

USPTO. (2009, March 2). Expedited Examination. Retrieved from www.cabic.com/bcp/.

USPTO. (2009, June 4). Patent Term Guarantee. Retrieved from www.uspto.gov.

USPTO. (2010). A Guide to Filing a Utility Patent Application. Retrieved from www.uspto.gov.

USPTO. (2010, March 2). Best Practice in Reissue Part II. Retrieved from www.cabic.com/bcp/.

USPTO. (2010, September 8). Broadening Reissues. Retrieved from www.cabic.com/bcp/.

USPTO. (2010, June 1). Information Disclosure Statements. Retrieved from www.cabic.com/bcp/.

USPTO. (2010, May 25). Overview of the Patent Prosecution Highway (Video). Retrieved from www.uspto.gov.

USPTO. (2010). Patent Practice Tips. Retrieved from www.cabic.com/bcp/.

USPTO. (2010, April). Reissue Practice. Retrieved from www.cabic.com/bcp/.

USPTO. (2012, February 12). America Invents Act Roadshow. Retrieved from www.uspto.gov.

USPTO. (2012, Febuary 3). Rules of Practice Before the BPAI in *Ex Parte* Appeals. Retrieved from www.uspto.gov.

Venable LLP. (2013, January 11). The U.S. First-To-File Patent System Takes Effect March 16, 2013. Retrieved from www.lexology.com.

Warenza et al. (2011, September 27). America Invents Act Provisions and Its Implications on U.S. Patent Law. Retrieved from www.lexology.com.

Witchey et al. (2011, October 2). Guest Post: Accelerated Examination and Prioritized Examination. Retrieved from www.patentlyo.com.

Wu et al. (2011, November 15). Examining AIA's High Speed *Inter Partes* Review System. Retrieved from www.law360.com. Reproduced with permission from Portfolio Media, Inc.

Yarbrough, R. J. (2008, July). Appeal of Patent Claim Rejections. Retrieved from www.yarbroughlaw.com

Index

A

B

C

D

E

F

G

H

I

L

M

N

O

P

Made in the USA
San Bernardino, CA
10 April 2015